TRACES:
a multilingual journal of cultural theory and translation

SPECTERS OF THE WEST AND THE POLITICS OF TRANSLATION

Naoki SAKAI and Yukiko HANAWA, Editors

TABLE OF CONTENTS

    v   Introduction

I. The West and its Vicissitudes

UKAI Satoshi	3	The future of an affect: the historicity of shame *tr. Sabu Kohso*
Pheng CHEAH	37	Universal areas: Asian Studies in a world in motion
Naoki SAKAI	71	The dislocation of the West
John KRANIAUSKAS	95	Translation and the work of transculturation

Interludes

Jean-Luc NANCY	110	Traces *tr. Jon Solomon*
MORINAKA Takaaki	113	Fragments for Restance *tr. Naoki Sakai*
YU Chi-chung	115	Mulitplicity
Brett DE BARY	116	Contribution to the inaugural issue of *Traces*
CHE Qianzi	118	Sign: inspired by a letter *tr. Yunte Huang*

II. Theory and The Politics of Locale

KANG Nae-hui	123	Mimicry and difference: a spectralogy for the neo-colonial intellectuals *tr. Kang Nae-hui*
Dipesh CHAKRABARTY	159	Europe as a problem of Indian History
Ulrich Johannes SCHNEIDER	183	Intellectual appropriation No piracy *tr. Ulrich Johannes Schneider*
Tani BARLOW	195	Spheres of debt and feminist ghosts in area studies of women of China

		Interludes
Jacques DERRIDA	228	A letter to *Traces* tr. Thomas Lamarre
Christopher FYNSK	231	There are no encounters in theory
KANG Sangjung	233	Communication
Kojin KARATANI	235	Toward the "Dictatorship of the Proletariat" tr. Sabu Kohso

III. Translation and Modernity

LAU Kin-chi, HUI Po-keung, and CHAN Shun-hing	241	The politics of translation and accountability: A Hong Kong Story
WANG Xiaoming	269	The politics of translation tr. Kenneth Dean
KIM Soyoung	301	Modernity in suspense: the logic of fetishism in Korean cinema
Peter OSBORNE	319	Modernism as translation

		Interludes
Gayatri Chakravorty SPIVAK	331	Echo multinome tr. Siddhartha Deb
SAKIYAMA Masaki	337	Toward a translation that resists "Technologies of Individuation" tr. J. Victor Koschmann
CHUA Beng Huat	339	Multiplicity
J. Victor KOSCHMANN	341	Translation
Harry D. HAROOTUNIAN	343	Modularity

IV. Internationalism and Traces

LAU Kin-chi, Peter OSBORNE, WANG Hui, and Naoki SAKAI	347	Zadankai in Beijing

		Interludes
Éric ALLIEZ	376	Traces of a b c d. . . tr. Naoki Sakai
CHE Qianzi	378	The night in the end tr. Yunte Huang

INTRODUCTION[1]

Until recently the global circulation of academic and intellectual information has customarily been imagined to follow cartographic visions which map two distinct flows. The first is a centripetal flow of "raw" and particularistic factual data from peripheral sites to various metropolitan centers "in the West." The second is a centrifugal flow of information about how to classify domains of knowledge, how to evaluate given empirical data, how to negotiate with the variety and incommensurability which is inherent in the body of empirical data from the peripheries, and how to render intelligible the details and trivia coming from particular peripheral sites to "a Western audience." Academic information of this second kind is generally called "theory" and, in contrast to the particularistic nature of the first kind, it is believed to be universalistic and hostile to the presumption that only those who are involved in the locale can tell what it is that they are concerned with. This is to say, the second kind of knowledge, "theory," does not seek its authorization in the assumption of the immediate comprehensibility of the raw datum in the original context at a particular locus. Instead, it claims to mediate the datum with general forms in such a way that it can be comprehensible to those who are outside the locus.

The production of such knowledge has largely occurred according to a historically specific division of intellectual labor in which "theory" is associated with that historical construct, "the West," and moves from there to the Rest of the world. It goes without saying that such a vision of the global circulation of academic information is a matter of imagination, but it is a powerful and effectual social imaginary on a global scale and prescribes, as a sort of regulative machinery, what the modern world must look like.

Against the background of such a cartographic imaginary of the globe, the essentially colonialist distinction between the West and the Rest of the world has been established and maintained for some time, albeit with constant vicissitudes. As Takeuchi Yoshimi, a sinologist specializing in modern Chinese literature, observed more than half a century ago, the East, which Takeuchi more or less took to be the representative of the Rest, arrived at its self-consciousness as a consequence of its defeat by the West or Europe.[2] Negativity, without which reflectivity essential for self-consciousness cannot be reached, never originated in the East, and the absence of reflectivity was certainly implied in Takeuchi's word "defeat (*haiboku*)." The East could never be conscious of itself, he claimed, before it was invaded by Europe. Only through the acknowledgment of its lost autonomy, of its dependence upon the West—or only in the mirror of the West, so to say[3]—could the Rest reflectively acquire its civilizational, cultural, ethnic, and national identities.

Because of his uncompromising faith in the Enlightenment values of modernity which, he believed, could only be concretized in the institutions of the nation-state, however, Takeuchi could not envision the future of Asia—and by implication, the future of the Rest—along historical trajectories other than that of historicism. Like many intellectuals of Asia and Europe who passed their formative years in the 1930s, Takeuchi had internalized modern historicism to such an extent that, for him, an effective struggle against the colonizing forces of the West could not bypass the creation of national subjectivity. His furtive loyalty to Hegel prevented him from conceiving of other historical trajectories than the historicist one in which the actualization and appropriation of modern values must first require a radical negation of external forces as well as of its internal heritage of a feudal past. To be modern for the East, therefore, meant appropriating the essence of Western modernity by resisting the West without and overcoming the reactionary heritage within. In other words, the East modernizes itself by negating the West and its own past. Where there was no resistance to, or negation of, the West, there was no prospect of modernity for the Rest. Where else, he would ask, if not in the midst of a struggle against colonial powers and the oppressive remnants of the past, could one possibly actualize the concrete and practical senses of liberty, equality, and fraternity?

One would not be able to apprehend Takeuchi's commitment to modernity without perceiving his profound shame over the Japanese imperialist maneuvers in Asia in the 1930s and early '40s, and his rage against the American imperialism which was about to

Introduction

take over the Greater East Asian Co-prosperity Sphere in the late 1940s. Hence, he diagnosed Japan's modern history as a case where genuine negativity was absent. This perhaps explains his excessive idealization of China which, he thought, unlike Japan which had imitated the West to the extent of reproducing its imperialism, would actualize a truly authentic modernity by negating the West's intervention as well as the remnants of the past. Yet the historical dialectic which he anticipated could not have made sense unless the externality of what the East should resist had been postulated. For peoples in the Rest, then, modernity was considered a sort of historical movement which consolidated the unity and substantiality of a political grouping called "the nation" spatially, by negating external forces, while at the same time temporally constituting itself as a subject, as an agent of self-determination, by continually overcoming its own past.

In a schematization such as was operating in his discussion of modernity, the unity of the nation depended upon the externality of what had to be resisted, which was more often than not mapped onto the cartographic plane. Just as with the Japanese invasion of China, that which must be resisted must come from the "outside" of the presumed integrity of the nation. A nation of the East, such as China, was located within the reach of the West, but the West itself was external to it. The externality of what had to be resisted was thus comprehended in terms of the geographic distance between Western Europe and Asia. The possibility that the West could be inherent in the Rest was deliberately precluded. Although Takeuchi was unambiguously critical of the modernization theory, he could not avoid the cartographic imaginary of the globe upon which the modernization theory invariably depends. A critique of Takeuchi's historical consciousness, of an inherently historicist consciousness, therefore, should serve as our starting point for a new conception of modernity.

According to the conventional narrative of modernity, the massive social transformation in Western Europe which was accompanied by industrialization is thought to mark the beginning of modern society. One may trace the modernity of modern society back to a number of historical precedents: the signs of industrialization in England in the eighteenth century, the formation of bourgeois culture and the new sense of public and private, a series of political events which led to the establishment of polities legitimizing themselves in the name of the sovereignty—Subject as "the nation-state" which produces itself by representing itself to itself—and so forth. And all these precedents and the subsequent realization of modern societies are ascribed to an imagined cartographic area called "the West." Thereupon, it is claimed, more often than not, that these events which symbolize modernity all happened to have taken place within the West. Furthermore, the consequences, influences, and effects of this unitary process of social transformation, which are supposed to have occurred strictly within "the West," are said to be detected and observed in remote areas such as Africa, Latin America, Oceania, and of course in Asia.

What is overlooked in this narrative is not only the undeniable economic, social, cultural, ethnic, and religious heterogeneity which has continued to exist up to the present in the geographic areas imagined to constitute the West—mainly Western Europe in the nineteenth century, with North America being added later in the twentieth century. But also overlooked is the fact that the contour of the West itself is drawn by this historicist narrative of modernization.

Whereas the West was referred to as a unitary geographic site far away from the East, it was also supposed to expand and radiate towards the peripheries of the world. Consequently, modernity as a historical movement was represented as an emanative flow, just like the information of "theory" in the cartographic imaginary of the globe. Underlying the historicist apprehension of modernization was a certain vision of emanation without which the centeredness of Eurocentricity could never be retained. Undoubtedly, there is no room for a multiplicity of modernities in such a representation. What we have customarily comprehended in terms of modernity and "the West" must be called into question precisely because the historicist schema of the world collapses and reduces the multiple emergence of modernities to the single overarching process of homogenization, of modernization that is immediately taken to be Westernization. "The West" is given rise to precisely because modernity has never managed to escape from its imprisonment, its seizure by the emanation model.

I maintain that the coming of modernity can be attributed to no single cause, process, or territory. The time of modernity is never unitary; it is always in multiplicity. Modernity always appears in multiple histories. Yet the multiplicity of modernity must not be understood to mean its plural origins which exist side by side in a homogeneous geographic space of the globe.

Although we are aware that modernization theory—a post-World War II appropriation of historicism serving the interests (economic, political, and even sexual in the psychoanalytic sense of national identity formation) of the United States—is hardly sustainable today, we are not entirely free of the binary structuring schemata which are constantly utilized by modernization theory within contemporary discussions of modernity. Because it reduces modernity to modernization, and equates modernization to Westernization, the representation of the world such schemata prescribe is hierarchically organized into the West and the Rest, the modern and its Others, the white and the colored. Worse still, these binaries are supposed to overlap! This being so, I must adhere to the imperative to find other ways to discuss global modernities.

The emanation model of modernity, which underlies any modernization theory, stems from a fundamental misconception of the basic element of modernity. Modernity is

Introduction

inconceivable unless there are occasions where many regions, people, industries, and polities are in contact with one another *despite* geographic, cultural, and social distances. Modernity, therefore, cannot be considered unless in reference to translation. In this respect, modernity is first of all a form whereby people transcend distances of many kinds in order to be in contact with one another. One would fail to understand the nature of modernity in misconceiving the fact of being in contact with others. Contact can never be construed as a one-way process of transmitting a doctrine or value from one party to another. Unless contact is a social relation, that is, unless it involves more than one party in some transaction affecting people involved in it, even the transmission of a doctrine or commodity exchange cannot take place. Thus contact is capable of transforming both parties involved in the transaction. If a social process of transforming, distorting, or destroying the way people are is called violence, contact is indubitably a violent event whose violence is from the outset a danger for both parties. Yet, in the emanation model of modernity, an economy prevails according to which the West is assumed active in affecting social transformation, while the Rest always remains passive. Accordingly, what may be regarded as the content of modernity, such as ideas, institutions, and the ways of life particular to the modern social formation, cannot be circulated other than in the one-way process of indoctrination. It is a vision of the civilizing mission which follows culturalism and covertly posits the unity of the West as a transhistorical entity like the essentialized national culture. The representation of a contact according to the emanation model is, rather, a political and colonialist intervention before it is a description.

The global emergence of modernities has no doubt been accompanied by a drastically increased frequency of social encounters and commodity exchanges all over the world, but nonetheless it cannot be described one-sidedly as a process of homogenization. For while social encounter and commodity exchange respectively give rise to demands for transparency in communication and equivalence in value, they inevitably evoke the incommensurable in our sociality, and the excessive in equation. Yet the incommensurable and the excessive cannot be apprehended outside the contexts of contact. It is for this reason that we must not lose sight of the fact that the particularistic insistence upon the immutable ethnic and national cultures and traditions goes hand in hand with the universalism of historicism. The culturalist insistence upon the integrity of an ethnic and national culture in the Rest is always matched by the covert obsession with the culturalist uniformity of the putative unity of the West. The rhetoric of Asian values, for example, is the simple reversal of the Eurocentric culturalism.

Today, it is increasingly difficult to overlook the fact that the historicist disposition of "theory" and "culture" is both politically dubious and intellectually inadequate. This prevailing view of global academic exchange is no longer acceptable, not only because its material conditions are in the process of being undermined, but also because we ought to refuse to view the relationships among many locations in the world according to the cartographic imaginary of historicism. Its definition of theory is obviously grossly inadequate in view of the academic conversation happening between various locations in the world.

Global modernity has accelerated cultural, economic, and political interchange between different regions and brought different forms of power-knowledge into more intense interaction. These forms of "theory," which are no longer merely "indigenous," make up the power-knowledge in everyday life, not only in the Euro-American world, but also in many parts of the world, including East and South East Asia. What once appeared exclusively European no longer belongs to the Euro-American world, and there are an increasing number of instances in which non-Euro-American loci are more "Western" than some aspects of North American and European life. This diversification of the West allows us to discover something fundamentally "Asian" and "African" in those people who fashion themselves as "Westerners," and to conceive of relations among people in many locations of the world in an order other than the racialized hierarchy of the Eurocentric world. After all, is not the West one of the most effective and affective culturalist imaginaries today? Racism being the institutionalized form of desire to naturalize and dehistoricize social relations and identities, the notion of the West cannot be cleansed of its racist implications as long as culturalism is a most prevalent means of naturalizing and essentializing a person's social status and a social group's identity.

Can we continue to presume that the West is essentially a cartographic category? Can we continue to overlook the fact that the distinction between the West and the Rest is increasingly independent of geography, race, ethnic culture, or nationality but is, in fact, a matter of cultural capital shaping the individual's socio-economic status? Can we continue to ignore the economic and social conditions that allow some people to *afford* to be "Western" while others cannot?

The globality of theory calls for a genuinely comparative cultural theory. I believe that the journal *Traces* is a response to this demand. What is meant by "comparative cultural theory" is a form of theorizing which is attentive to the transnational connectedness and global traces within knowledge produced in geopolitically-specific locations, and which explores how theories are themselves transformed in their practical effects when they are performed in other sites. The idea of theorizing, which is advocated here, would never neglect the form of the act which gives rise out of differences to that which is commensurate and thereby brings heterogeneous items onto the plane of comparison. This act, which precedes comparison and makes comparison possible, is translation: therefore, our enterprise is indispensably organized around

Introduction

translation. This comparative enterprise is also political insofar as it seeks to examine the theoretical bases and conflicting desires at the heart of contemporary politics and forms of violence.

To demonstrate the scope of this enterprise in regard to the topoi—in the sense both of topic and place—of the West and translation is the guiding motive of this first and inaugural issue of *Traces*. The form of cultural and political criticism envisaged in the project of *Traces* is already being produced by many intellectuals and cultural workers firmly located in the South—Asia, Africa, and Latin America—as well as those from the North Atlantic who are concerned with the transformative dissemination and living-on of Euro-American ideas in non-Euro-American sites, as well as with the legacies and political futures of non-European theories in Northern locations. It is a form of criticism based on the acknowledgment of the traces of the other in a specifically local text.

The journal *Traces* aims to initiate a different circulation of academic conversation and debate, a different geopolitical economy of theory and empirical data, and a different representation of the global circulation of academic information. The current inaugural issue, entitled "Specters of the West and the Politics of Translation," addresses the vexed questions of how knowledge production in the Humanities is still haunted by the West/Rest distinction, and how translation serves to create the senses of modernity. The second issue, "Race Panic and the Memory of Migration," will explore racial memory and the global politics of immigration. Subsequent issues may address topics such as the impacts of modernity in many sites of the world in the late nineteenth and early twentieth centuries; Romantic aesthetics and the legacies of colonial injury in South and East Asia; the fate of modernist aesthetics and avant-garde arts today; and so on.

The distinctive orientation of our journal is in our eagerly seeking theory produced in other sites, sometimes in a curious hybrid reaction to North American or West European "theory," as a result of the colonialism and quasi-colonialism of the last few centuries. The study of European philosophy by scholars in East and South Asia and Africa, for instance, will be welcomed positively. *Traces* will create and sustain an international space of theoretical exchange in a multilingual medium by regularly publishing issues in multiple language versions.

Every essay to be included in *Traces* will be available in all of the languages of this journal.[4] Therefore, to write for *Traces* is always to address oneself to readers in different languages. When one writes in one of the languages of the journal, one is simultaneously read in Korean, English, German, Japanese, one of the languages of China, and still others. Every contributor to this journal is expected to be fully aware that she or he is writing for and addressing a heterogeneous and multilingual audience: just like a local intellectual under a colonial regime, every contributor is, in a manner of speaking, expected to speak in a forked tongue. This social space in which we argue and converse has very little in common with the space of national language, the national space of a homogeneous language medium. In this respect, *Traces* is an international journal. Yet, the international space which it generates and sustains, and to which contributors as well as readers are invited, is fundamentally different from that of an internationalism based on one major language's subjugation of other minor languages. Recognizing how difficult and even impossible it is to evade the subjugation of a minor language by a dominant language, since almost every language could be a major one in relation to a less dominant one, we are committed to establishing a social space where such an imperative is seriously implemented in terms of translation. This is a social space maintained by translation, and constituted in the conjunction of plural translational moves from one language to another.

It is impossible to conceive of translation as an operation by which to establish equivalence in signification of the same text between two versions in two languages. In other words, translation is not conceptualized according to the model of communication upon which the emanation model of modernity, for instance, is based. Instead, we understand translation as an operation which opens up possibilities for questioning and counter-questioning among people, and for doing so about the same text. Translation facilitates conversation between people in different geographical and social loci who would otherwise never converse with one another; but it also provides them with a space where the appropriateness and validity of translation is constantly discussed and disputed. In this space, we acknowledge that we misunderstand and mistranslate one another; but we also recognize the urgent need to strive to understand and translate one another so that we can discover how we misunderstand and mistranslate. So translation itself always holds in dispute the very sameness of what is supposedly conveyed in translation. The international space for *Traces* is formed around this dispute enabled by translating the sameness of the message. To participate in the international space of *Traces* implies a commitment to the continuation of this dispute by translating others' words, and by questioning what has been taken for granted in academic and non-academic knowledge.

Those of us who have gathered together around this project will also sustain the possibility of our electronic conversation in multiple languages through the global networking of the Internet, and will secure access for our readership to the editorial collective by creating a World Wide Web site for our journal, while at the same time publishing *Traces* in the print medium. This is because we believe that genuine international collaboration is absolutely essential for the existence of *Traces*.

Introduction

Endnotes

1—This article grew out of the prospectus for *Traces* which Thomas Lamarre, Pheng Cheah, and I co-authored. I would like to express my thanks to the co-authors. As goes without saying, however, responsibility for the content of this article rests with me.

2—Takeuchi Yoshimi, "*Chûgoku no kindai to nihon no kindai* (Chinese modernity and Japanese modernity)" (originally in 1947) in *Nihon to Ajia* (Tokyo: Chikuma Shobô, 1993): 11–57 (also published with a different title "*Kindai towa nanika* [What is modernity?]" in 1948). For a discussion of universalism and particularism in modernity, see; Sakai, "Critique of Modernity: the Problem of Universalism and Particularism" in *South Atlantic Quarterly,* 87.3 (Summer 1988), or its Japanese translation in *Gendai Shiso,* 15.15 (December 1987).

3—Takeuchi Yoshimi, "*Chûgoku no kindai*" 15-9.

4—In principle the editorial collective of *Traces* will abide by this rule. However, this rule does not apply where copyright arrangements do not allow for the translation and publication of an article at issue in different languages and markets. Neither does it apply in the cases of censorship imposed, beyond the control of *Traces* collectives, by the government of the country where a version of *Traces* is published.

I

THE WEST AND ITS VICISSITUDES

THE FUTURE OF AN AFFECT: THE HISTORICITY OF SHAME

UKAI Satoshi

translated by Sabu KOHSO

All of the words written for *Traces* are, from the outset, destined to be translated immediately. This possibility must ultimately be shared by all other words. Yet, inasmuch as the words for *Traces* cannot be indifferent to their destiny, they might be more anxious and tense—more standing on their guard—than others. These words expect and fear their fate of being translated. Though "being translated" might be an honor for their author, the words themselves are not necessarily giddy with joy as they await their transposition into other languages. The words that are aware of being translated are not trembling for joy, but for *an affect*.

In order to approach the affect, speak of it, make it speak, or more precisely, let it speak, it seems that we can invoke the following two figures at least. One is to liken translation to a dual event: arriving before the words, depriving them of their lives, and giving them another life—what Walter Benjamin called an "afterlife" [*das Fortleben*]. Then the words appear in the figure of a life form, that of an animal which exposes its finiteness to a deadly accident. This is one of the reasons why Jacques Derrida calls for the figure of the "*hérisson* [hedgehog]" in his "Che cos'è la poesia?".[1] Leaping out onto a highway, the hedgehog rolls itself up in its armor to protect itself from the anticipated danger. But, precisely by this act, it blinds itself and ends up being exposed to an even larger danger.

Here, the allusion to translation is the movement of a car, approaching at full speed, as the hedgehog, which is trembling with the expectation of disaster, sends us from the lowest beastly place with the lowest voice an imminent cry, "remember!" The car bears down, crushing the hedgehog, and driving away. By way of the idiomatic French expression, "*apprendre par coeur* [learn this by heart]," an expression that is already a piece of a *poéme* to him, Derrida connects the questions of rhythm, memory, poetry, and animal. It is rare that finiteness—finiteness 'in general', but the finiteness of words, more than anything else—is spoken of so secretly and so densely. The affect of words that are destined to be translated barely lets itself speak, that is, within the question that swells out the human definition of finiteness, or more precisely, with the experience of finiteness that is almost like a prayer before all questionings.

There is another figure that is perhaps, on the basic level, related to the one of the animal, and it is also inexorably invoked vis-à-vis the words being translated. That is, proper language, the "original," hides the fruit of its meaning in its skin of expression. As if it were embarrassed to expose its bare meaning, it resists translation. When we follow this figure, translation is represented as a double operation of exposing the meaning of the original and immediately—simultaneously—covering it with another "robe" to employ Benjamin's figure. Or rather that it is in the shift from the series of natural metaphors related to plant life (skin and fruit) to anthropomorphic ones (clothes and the naked body) where the layered grasping of the act of translation is at stake—though, whether or not shame is an affect proper to humans should be questioned separately.

> While content and language form a certain unity in the original, like a fruit and its skin, the language of the translation envelops its content like a royal robe with ample folds. For, it signifies a more exalted language than its own and thus remains unsuited to its content, overpowering and alien.[2]

Reading into this passage the narrative of the original sin—the forbidden fruit, the origin of shame, and the need for the fig leaf—would be a rather violent spur-of-the moment idea without the prerequisite arguments. Nonetheless, at the very least it seems evident that Benjamin's famous text consists of a number of insights that could not have been achieved if not for his deep perception of the translator's desire and the affect of the words being translated, though it does not touch upon them thematically. To say it conversely, it is possible that Benjamin sublimated the desire and the affect to a "task" via the messianic teleology, "pure language." In any event, what is crucial for us at this moment is the fact that the figures appear to speak—though, without speaking—of the essential "affectness" of language as what can be called the *shame of language* facing translation.

The anxiety of death and the anxiety of shame. These original affects, without which language can no longer speak, are also a dynamic expression of the relative opacity of a proper culture *apropos* a proper language. In this sense, the concept of "shame cultures" somewhat contains an echo of redundancy. That is to say, is there any one entity of those which are called culture or call themselves culture that does not tremble when facing the anxiety of shame vis-à-vis other cultures and the anxiety of death? —for these are the experiences of the finiteness of culture or the experiences of the cultural boundary. Furthermore, it is here where the power relation between cultures in a particular historical context is most cruelly exposed. It is not that a certain culture feels equally ashamed in front of any other culture; while it sensitively recognizes and responds to the gaze of certain cultures, to the gaze of other cultures it can pretend that it does not notice and refuse to respond, or more pointedly, feel ashamed of being ashamed, and immediately deny the work of the affect.

Doesn't the challenge of *Traces* exist, at least in part, in making visible, sensible, and thinkable the translation, the liminal inter-lingual and inter-cultural experiences, that include the shift of affect from the anxiety of death to that of shame? Or in inventing a technique to let the affect's work speak for itself? In discovering a technique to *affirm* shame, instead of feeling ashamed of the shame directly?

Perhaps the space of post-1945 Japanese thought has had a peculiar experience concerning this problematic in general, that could not have occurred in any other regional or historical context. That is, the concept of "shame cultures," as proposed as an expression of the essence of this culture by Ruth Benedict, a female scholar of the victor nation (being female is not completely irrelevant to the core of the matter). The influence of *The Chrysanthemum and the Sword* over the Japanese intellectual scene cannot be measured merely by the innumerable commentaries and critiques of the book. The fact that the range extends far beyond the academic world is evidenced by the still-increasing sales of the Japanese version (in its 98th edition, with 1,400,000 copies sold in 1994). Beginning from the temporally and spatially limited experience, this essay is a preliminary attempt to trace the process through which various thoughts and expressions concerning "shame," seen in the political, philosophical, and scholastic events that occurred in different cultural and historical contexts of the contemporary world, have gradually been becoming a "universal" question. Of course, we cannot know if an experience of shame can be translated to another one *ex ante facto*; therefore, within this adjective "universal," the anticipated time of translation is condensed to the extent that it cannot be seen in any other place.

1

True shame cultures rely on external sanctions for good behavior, not, as true guilt cultures do, on an internalized conviction of sin. Shame is a reaction to other people's criticism. A man is shamed either by being openly ridiculed and rejected or by fantasizing to himself that he has been made ridiculous. In either case it is a potent sanction. But it requires an audience or at least a man's fantasy of an audience. Guilt does not. In a nation where honor means living up to one's own picture of oneself, a man may suffer from guilt though no man knows of his misdeed and a man's feeling of guilt may actually be relieved by confessing his sin.

> . . . .The primacy of shame in Japanese life means, as it does in any tribe and nation where shame is deeply felt, that any man watches the judgment of the public upon his deeds. He need only fantasy what their verdict will be, but he orients himself toward the verdict of others. When everybody is playing the game by the same rules and mutually supporting each other, the Japanese can be lighthearted and easy. They can play the game with fanaticism when they feel it is one which carries out the "mission" of Japan. They are most vulnerable when they attempt to export their virtues into foreign lands where their own formal signposts of good behavior do not hold. They failed in their "good will" mission to Greater East Asia, and the resentment many of them felt at the attitudes of Chinese and Filipinos toward them was genuine enough.[3]

"Guilt cultures" and "shame cultures"—today, a full half century after the publication of the book, the paired concepts are understood mostly in a highly schematized manner: that "guilt cultures" represent Western Christian cultures, while "shame cultures" represent the whole of non-Western cultures. The plural form—"cultures"—might suggest that this interpretation is not necessarily wrong. Meanwhile, what is surprising is the fact that in Japan many think that the "culture of shame" is found in Japan and in Japan alone. And what further induced this prejudice was not only the national shame of defeat, but also something that exists in the book itself.

First of all, it should be stressed that Ruth Benedict's research had the strategic purpose of designing a policy for America's occupation of Japan. Thus Benedict had to present the proper nature of the culture of a nation (that fought a war in a way previously unimaginable to Americans) in comparison not only to America but also to the neighboring nations that were invaded and occupied by the Japanese Empire—China and Korea. As a consequence, the text came to be tacitly structured by a scheme of triadic comparison: 1) Japan vs. the rest of the world (including America); 2) America vs. the rest of the world (including Japan); 3) America vs. Japan.

Counter to the understanding that was schematized later as the pair concepts of "guilt cultures" vs. "shame cultures," surprisingly, in the text itself, neither comparison, between the West vs. non-West nor even that of the West vs. Japan, is dominant. This was because to Benedict's eye, American culture was still reflected as a "marked" existence to European cultures, and thus she persisted in assuming the stance of a cultural relativist. 1) In order to fully define Japanese culture, she sought to explain the reason why the Confucianist morals of loyalty [*chû*] and filial piety [*kô*] were transformed into the Tennoist ideology of loyalty and piety to *the one and only* [*chûkô ichinyo*], a transmutation from Chinese culture.[4] 2) Yet, in order to understand the culture of a nation engaged in conflict, American national centrism had to be relativized; it is imperative to recall how the egalitarianist principle—which is quite natural to Americans—was a shock not only to Japanese but also to Europeans (i.e., Alexis de Tocqueville in the 1830s).[5] 3) Benedict does not always identify "guilt cultures" with America and "shame cultures" with Japan, nevertheless she depicts America as a society of *high* "guilt culture" and Japan as a society of *high* "shame culture." In this sense, the comparison between America and Japan tends to be described less as a contrast between marked and unmarked cultures than between two marked cultures. This structure is consistently inscribed in her own career as a thinker, as we shall see in more detail later.

Recently, there have been signs of reappreciation of *The Chrysanthemum and the Sword* among conservative Japanese thinkers. This is perhaps because of the rumor that Benedict's report to the military intelligence bureau—the basis for the book—influenced the American occupation policy toward its acquittal of Tennô's war criminality and the protection of the Tennô system; and because the idea was favorable to a "redefinition" of the US-Japan Security Treaty, a cultural and political interpretation that corresponded to the new idea of "partnership."[6] But, as is easily imagined, the response of Japanese conservative historians, philosophers, and ethnologists to the book was more or less negative immediately following its publication. There were roughly two types of critical response. Let us scrutinize the basic difference between the two by taking as examples essays by Watsuji Tetsurô and Yanagida Kunio. Watsuji's essay, "Doubting Scientific Value [*Kagakuteki kachi ni-taisuru gimon*]" appeared in the journal, *Ethnological Research* [*Minzokugaku kenkyû*] (Vol. 14, No. 4, May 1950) right after the Japanese publication of *The Chrysanthemum and the Sword*. In the style of a letter responding to the ethnologist Ishida Eiichiro, Watsuji posed a stance that wholeheartedly denied Benedict's work in terms of one point, its "scholastic value." This was based upon the observation—which is agreeable in itself—that Benedict overgeneralized based upon limited data, neglecting to seek out conflicting data. However, the concrete facts Watsuji exemplified, and his commentary on them, can only give contemporary readers a sense of tragi-comical disappointment.

In the beginning of the book, she writes: "Conventions of war which Western nations had come to accept as facts of human nature obviously did not exist for the Japanese." This point is fully developed in the second chapter, where it is clearly said that this fact was materially important for understanding the Japanese view of life and their belief concerning the whole of human duty. If "Japanese" were replaced with "a small group of servicemen," it would be fine. Then, this book would be about a "type of Japanese serviceman," instead of a "type of Japanese culture." Or rather, even a "type of Japanese serviceman" is too general, and should be limited to a "type of ultranationalistic serviceman." The majority of Japanese people did not commit [war crimes]. Nor did they know clearly that violations were committed by their fellow countrymen. Although rumors of the atrocities were heard, Japanese thought they were committed by small groups of rogue servicemen. They never dreamt that these were official acts of the Japanese army. For that matter, the Japanese army also attempted to hide from its people the facts of the Nanjing Massacre and its mistreatment of war-prisoners. Should the Japanese have committed such violations with the *sang-froid* Benedict claims, why on earth should the facts have had to be veiled in the country? (p. 286)

Nonetheless, the Japanese government has sought to de-emphasize these facts as much as it can in its oversight of public education and through the institution of "textbook certification," even after 1950. Can this attitude be explained by Watsuji's point that, because the general Japanese public would get angry should they learn the facts, the Ministry of Education has had to hide them? This reasoning is wrong. Furthermore, those who persist in making all-out efforts to deny or underestimate the facts, though knowing them, will never vanish, be they bureaucrats, politicians, intellectuals, or the general public, as evidenced by the "Nanjing Massacre Fiction Debate" of the 1970s to the recent activities of the Committee to Make New Textbooks. And these discourses have not necessarily drawn strong criticism from the public. It is true that there still exists a strong sense of resistance among Japanese to the universalist ideas of human rights and international law; in this respect, Benedict's view seems to sustain a certain pertinence. From the beginning, hiding inconvenient facts and denying or underestimating their negativity when they are revealed ("it was inevitable in war," "every country does it," "it didn't happen often," etc.) are *not* as incompatible as Watsuji tacitly takes for granted here. Those who know a little about human societies can recognize this fact, but Watsuji can not. Is it too much to see a blindness in Watsuji, perhaps caused by a spasm of shame? Or to see that, by this spasm, Watsuji ended up performatively confirming Benedict's thesis?[7]

In contrast, Yanagida Kunio's critique of Benedict was far more distanced and logical, to the extent that even an intellectual margin is felt. In his "Guilt Cultures and Shame Cultures [*Tsumi-no-bunka to haji-no-bunka*]" published in the same issue of *Ethnological Research*, Yanagida first casts doubt on Benedict's central thesis. He insists that guilt cultures exist in Japan, too. His primary reasoning is that in the Japanese language there are more colloquial expressions containing the terms for guilt—such as "sin-causing" (sinful) being [*tsumi tsukurina hito*], or a "guiltless" (innocent) smile [*tsumi-no-nai Egao*]—than in other languages. His point is concerned further with Benedict's understanding of Japanese Buddhism. According to Benedict, the idea of the transmigration of the soul based upon the Buddhist view of sin, never took root in Japan. (This is one of the important points that distinguishes Japan from other East Asian Buddhist cultural spheres in her first scheme of comparison.) Which, to Yanagida, is totally counter-factual. The doctrine of retribution deeply permeated the masses, syncretized as it was with the Shinto doctrine, especially the prejudice that considers women as sinful beings that was brought in specifically by Buddhism.

> First of all, while the power of Buddhist practice was only partially influential, its view of sin thoroughly permeated the Japanese mind. Many proverbs stressing the sins of a previous life— "glaring at one's parents turns one into a flounder" or "lying down immediately after eating turns one into a cow"— were admonitions against crimes in this life for the sake of the afterlife. . . . If we think about it, it is sad that in Japan the term *ingua* [fatal result] always signifies misfortune for which the causes are never known. The Japanese nature to be easily resigned to fate was an attempt to be prudent in this world, attributing troubles and pains to the sins their spirits committed in previous lives. While sins in Shintoism could be cleansed by exorcism and atonement in this world, in Buddhism they were considered to transmigrate from one life to many lives. Thus the term *ingua* became another name for incomprehensible hardship. One thing I would want to tell Professor Benedict if she were alive would be the fact that until recently in Japan, the preaching that all women were sinful was persistently believed. Being born a woman was already determined by sinful deeds of previous lives, and being a woman was deemed to signify a propensity to commit sins. Such logic was believed. Without questioning or doubting, religious women sought to compensate for their double sins by exercising extra patience in their daily lives . . . [8]

Yet Yanagida does not attribute responsibility for this mistake to Benedict alone. The cause of Benedict's misunderstanding, Yanagida insists, rather exists in the way Japanese have introduced their culture abroad. A typical example would be Nitobe Inazô's *Bushidô*

[*The way of the samurai*]; the main tendency has been to explain the whole of Japanese culture by exemplifying only one class, the *samurai* class. Thus Benedict's analysis—in paying too much attention to *Chûshingura* [*Forty-seven Ronin's Vengeance for Loyalty*]—is not free from this inclination. To Yanagida, extreme sensitivity to being laughed at by others—what Benedict points out as a typical example of Japanese shame—originated in the culture of the *samurai* class. This has, however, nothing to do with the basic culture of the majority of Japanese—Yanagida's *jômin* [populace]—centered on rice farmers. Now and then, Yanagida stresses his respect and thanks to the enlightenment and stimulation of *The Chrysanthemum and the Sword,* to the extent of appearing to be offensively obsequious. This is in striking contrast to Watsuji's almost irrational response. Our objective here is not to inspect the correctness or incorrectness of Benedict's accounts or those of her critics, concerning the essence of Japanese culture. Our concern is in observing the subtle workings of the affect that exist in the way these texts distance themselves from each other. For what radically defines these texts not only on the level of rational logic but also on the level of the affect (that is inseparable, yet requires individual analysis) is how their authors experienced World War II and how they acknowledged that they either belonged to the victorious country or the one that was defeated.

2

When the translation of *The Chrysanthemum and the Sword* was published, Watsuji and Yanagida had already long established their unshakable positions in academia as philosopher and ethnologist respectively. Their judgments of Benedict's work were based upon their own understandings of Japanese culture. In this sense, "guilt cultures" and "shame cultures" never affected them to the bone. But to those who encountered *Chrysanthemum* in the process of self-formation—after having experienced pre-war Japan, the war, and the defeat—things were not the same. Sakuta Keiichi's "Reconsideration of Shame Cultures [*Haji no bunka saikô*]" (1964) is one of the best responses to the book by an intellectual who could not avoid the serious influence.

What both Watsuji and Yanagida problematized was Benedict's stance to explain the whole of the reality of a culture that is historically, socially, and regionally diverse by observing only one part. Using a more up-to-date expression, Benedict's view could be described as "essentialist." Acknowledging the adequacy of that critique, Sakuta yet defends Benedict: "the gestalt grasped by intuition seems to be still effective in presenting the national characteristic in relief." He goes on to point out that the gestalt, however, "covers only half of the shame cultures."

Ukai Satoshi

According to Sakuta, Benedict noticed only the "public shame" within the whole category of shame. He asks if we aren't "embarrassed (ashamed)" before others even when we are being praised? This is because what causes a sense of embarrassment (shame) is not the gaze of others in general but "a particular kind of scrutiny." In reference to Max Scheler's *Über Sham und Shamgefühl* (1913), Sakuta explains the "scrutiny" as a discrepancy between others' intention toward self and self's intention toward self. Models do not feel embarrassed (ashamed) in front of a painter; patients do not feel embarrassed (ashamed) in front of a doctor, because in these cases, both others and self see the self as a general being. When the intention of others is to see the self as a singular being, the feeling of embarrassment (shame) arises. When the private experience of a love affair is observed as an example of universal phenomena, there is an inconsistency of intentions (in reverse) and embarrassment (shame) appears.

But the feeling of shame involves not only an inconsistency of intention but also an idea of superiority and inferiority of ego. Sakuta's observation is obviously based upon the position of psychoanalysis, beginning with Freud, that explains guilt in terms of the conflict between super-ego and ego, and shame in terms of the inconsistency between ego ideal and ego reality. I shall detail this later. But what Sakuta draws from it is also important to us.

The scrutiny of others makes us feel embarrassed, because we are afraid of the exposure of our inferior parts which we wish to keep private. What Benedict emphasized was a situation in which the exposed is the part of our ego we believe to be inferior according to public standards of superior/inferior. Nevertheless, the standards upon which superior and inferior diverge are not always those that belong to our own group. There are also standards of superior/inferior that belong to larger groups (such as class or the human race); when the standard is different from that of the group one belongs to, the former is often recognized as a private standard. If this standard is fully interiorized, one privately suffers from the feeling of shame for acts that would not be disdained according to the standard of one's own group . . . . This aspect, that can be called "private shame" as opposed to "public shame," inexorably tends to involve an *inconsistency of intentions* because of its formation, wherein self and others are in different positions from the beginning. Because the *inconsistency of intentions* was precisely the aspect that Benedict neglected, "private shame" was dropped from her analysis.[9]

It is hard to imagine that the modern West—a society based on the competition between superiority and inferiority—would be drastically different from Japan with respect to the level of "public shame." Therefore, in order to define Japanese culture as a "shame culture," Sakuta argues, Benedict should have also paid attention to the aspect of "private shame." He thinks that in Japanese society, "private shame" tends to be dominant because "the independence of groups that are placed between society and individuals is weak." "When I see an Italian movie in which a church shelters a resistance fighter, I cannot help but see an image of a society far far removed from ours." In so saying, Sakuta, a sociologist who conducted outstanding research into the wretched reality of Japanese soldiers' war-crimes, must have felt a bitter disheartening toward a Japanese society that could muster almost no resistance to the state's war policy. However, while many modernist intellectuals of Sakuta's generation, i.e. who learned from the same war experience, came to deem the "shame culture" a pre-modern, feudal ethos, and thus fetters from which to break in order for Japan to become a modern society consisting of autonomous individuals, Sakuta believed that it is precisely in the society where the individual record of competition assumes the only standard by which to judge people, namely, in "a highly industrialized mass society," that shame could and would eventually present its positive sense. Thus our attempt in today's conjuncture of the post-cold-war world, where the principle of market-economy persists in all fronts, should be to draw as much as possible an immanent potential of the conceptualization of the Japanese intellectual who faced *The Chrysanthemum and the Sword* most directly, by way of some other theoretical prospects. In concluding his reflections, Sakuta writes: "The unification of those men who have lost the ground on which to insist on their egos-as-being, whose internal inferiority is transparently seen from all corners, and whose protective shells of group membership are all deprived, is *the* unification beyond the fortress of groups." Now our concern is if the "community of shame"—that which, in this work, is still identified as Japanese 'tradition'—can go beyond the 'fortress' of the group called nation.

3

So far, we have dealt with *The Chrysanthemum and the Sword* from the side of those who are the objects of its analysis. The objective has been to depict the contour of the events caused by the book, rather than the individual responses themselves, in order to scrutinize it later from a universal prospect. How can one respond to a victor who determines that your culture is a "shame culture"? Behavior like Yanagida's could not be if not for a tremendous confidence in one's own intelligence. It is rather an exception. And isn't a response like Watsuji's—performing the other's proposition itself by denial and simultaneously internalizing it—more common? Something like this has been repeated not only in the US-Japan relationship but throughout history. Sakuta, in contrast, carefully avoided the simple denial and thus the internalization of others' propositions, thereby discovering another way out of the confrontation—by a meticulous scrutiny of the "shame culture."

Then the advent of another event in this series of events—an intervention that is really worth such a description—came from America. This was truly serendipitous for the space of postwar Japanese thought. C. Douglas Lummis came to Okinawa in 1960 as a US Marine. Later, he participated in the anti-Vietnam War movement, and now lives in Japan teaching in a university. His book on Benedict, *A New Look at* The Chrysanthemum and the Sword (1981) is an attempt to liberate himself from the work of an anthropologist that radically influenced his own view of Japan.

The salient characteristic of Lummis' approach lies in his attempt to decode the book in relation to the author named Ruth Benedict, as much as or more than in relation to the historical phenomenon called Japan. Lummis first touches upon the formation of American anthropology, which nurtured Benedict as an anthropologist. Among others, he makes a simple yet important suggestion on the work of Franz Boas, who was Benedict's teacher. Born in Germany, Boas went to America in the 1880s; contrary to the evolutionism that was then dominant in America, he conducted research into the structure of meanings immanent in cultures. To Boas, the primary concern of anthropology must be to "understand the characteristics of individual cultures" without ignoring the inquiry into the objective sides of cultures, yet at the same time, "to understand what kind of meanings those things contain to the people."

Lummis draws two problematic points from this. One is that the theoretical premises of Benedict can be found in the cultural-relativist stance of her teacher, Boas. Another is that Boas' method of analyzing individual cultures as works of art, spoke to Benedict, who was also a poet and had once been a scholar of literature before becoming an anthropologist. Lummis is also interested in Benedict's non-anthropological writings, her poetry, for which she used the *nom de plume* Anne Singleton. What he read therein was her longing for her father, who had died when she was twenty-one months old, and about whom her mother spoke constantly, and her aspiration to find the serenity and beauty of the world of death where he went. How, then, did Hades' charm motivate her transformation into an anthropologist? Lummis has a suggestion:

> Why would *this* poet turn to anthropology? Again, we can only speculate, but Margaret Mead, who decided to take up anthropology under Benedict's influence, has stated her own reason quite clearly. She says that in those years the principal task of American anthropology was "collecting masses of vanishing materials from the members of dying American

Indian cultures, and it was in terms of the urgency of this salvage task that I became an anthropologist."

Dying cultures! It is not difficult to imagine how Anne Singleton might see beauty in this enterprise. Is it not precisely in anthropology that she could make a career of quietly exploring "the country over the hill," and contemplating the beauty of the dead? And can it be a coincidence that the man who provided her access to this country—"the world of my father"—was the man she came to call "Papa Franz"?[10]

Thus it becomes clear that what Benedict calls "cultural type" is less something that is presently functioning as an existing cultural norm than something that is constructed by the poet/anthropologist from the fragments of dead cultures. "[I]ts death is precisely what enables the anthropologist to write about it with beauty, honor, and respect."[11] In other words, no one can live in the "cultural type" that Benedict describes. In fact, it is easy today to point out the ahistorical nature of the "cultural type" concept and reject it as an essentialist misdeed. But, Lummis gives attention further to the fact that the concept is supported by an almost necrophiliac desire. He even suggests that part of the charm of the book derives from it.

Another important aspect of Lummis' intervention was that it intricately traced Benedict's political stance—the transformation of her position toward war. As I mentioned, Boas belonged to a school of anthropology later called cultural relativism, which criticized Western ethnocentrism and stressed the individuality and difference of other cultures. When Hitler gained power in Germany, Benedict, along with Boas, participated in the distribution of anti-racist and anti-fascist propaganda. Quoting Benedict's short essay, "The Uses of Cannibalism" (1925), Lummis shows how Benedict's relativism was some of the most radical thinking of the time, rather than the moderate, sensible stance we might imagine from the word today. In the post-World War I climate, Benedict compared a culture wherein people satisfy their "craving for violence" by eating "one useless body per year" with the destructive total war of self-claimed civilized men. What echoes throughout is a tone of impeachment against civilization with "her fit of almost nihilistic bitterness" far beyond the exhortation of tolerance. In other words, at least before World War II, Benedict never believed in the claims of legitimacy made by the perpetrators of the wars of Western nation-states. Her cultural relativism was perhaps linked to the most radical anti-war stance of the time. Then, she came to embrace America's war policy and wrote a book—*The Chrysanthemum and the Sword*.

Lummis does not go into the cause of the transformation very much. He just suggests, "[p]erhaps it was her horror of fascism that convinced her, as it convinced so many others, to cooperate with the American war machine." In the climate of 1981, this might have been adequate. But, for us who are living after the end of the Cold War, us who have been observing a new type of war, from the Gulf War to the Kosovo conflict, that is conducted under the name of "humanitarian intervention" with the objective of securing a new world order, the path of pacifist Benedict, who had gradually inclined toward collaboration by taking for granted the dual scheme of democracy vs. fascism, appears to be the prototype for many leftist intellectuals who somehow came to affirm the recent interventions of the allies, the UN and NATO forces. This repetition also reminds us Japanese of the time when we were in the place of today's Iraqis and Yugoslavians, and at the same time, charges us with the responsibility to *think how to recall past events today*. As Lummis points out, "in a strange way" this book "achieved the position of a classic," and never stops re-achieving it in new contexts.

It is hard to believe that Ruth Benedict's reconciliation with American society and American power could have failed to be accompanied by profound changes in the structure of her thought. Alienation from that society had been at the foundation of her personality from her childhood. Alienation had set the little girl dreaming about a "country over the hill"; alienation had given the mature woman two personalities, one promoting cultural relativity (which, taken to the extreme, is alienation from all cultures), the other writing poetic manifestoes of rebellion against the restrictions of the human condition itself. What would be the effect on Benedict of an end to this alienation? There is evidence that she may have undergone important changes—for example in 1933 she published her last poem, which seems to renounce the spirit of Anne Singleton (it is called "Ways Not Wind's Ways") and is signed "Ruth Benedict." . . .

And there is the testimony of Mead, cited earlier, that *The Chrysanthemum and the Sword* is the first work which she wrote her whole self—in which the voices of Anne Singleton and Ruth Benedict become one. That may be true, but what is more important for our purposes—and also easier to demonstrate—is the fact that in *The Chrysanthemum and the Sword* the self-critical spirit of cultural relativity disappears altogether, and is replaced by the attitude of the confidant conqueror: tolerance."[12]

In the concept of tolerance, too, there is a long history going back to the religious wars in Europe. It is self-evident, however, that the concept of tolerance operating within the text of *The Chrysanthemum and the Sword*—and which the text is asking Americans to adopt—is consistent with a certain ethnocentrism. It is also self-evident at this point that the paired concepts, "guilt cultures" and "shame cultures" were formed and proposed in conformity with an almost officially sanctioned hierarchy, which was totally counter to relativism. Benedict's proposal to the Occupation Army was to "use that amount of hardness, no more no less, which will break up old and dangerous patterns of aggressiveness and set new goals"; the concept of "shame cultures" was required precisely to establish the measure of the "hardness."

Nonetheless, the fact that the book was written at the end of the long and meandering career of the peculiar individual, Benedict, and that the paired concepts, "guilt cultures" and "shame cultures," were proposed therein, signifies that the text is, at the same time, claiming another reading beyond the direct context of its language act. When Lummis warns Japanese readers that "there is nothing in Benedict's aesthetic pleasure in the beauty of the pattern of Japanese culture that would lead her to conclude that it should be allowed to continue," his intention is just in terms of revealing the overtly political nature of the book, which had been read mostly in the context of Japanology or the study of Japanese culture. But how Benedict understood the experience of shame in general when she approached the "shame culture," or the society based upon it, is something we should ask of the text on another level. In recent years, it has often been mentioned that Benedict was gay, aside from being hearing-impaired.[13] "Shame" is an experience determined by body conditions—gender and sexuality—as deep as, but separate from "guilt." Isn't it finally impossible to ignore that it was a woman who proposed the pair concepts? What is required here is an alternative reading that lets *The Chrysanthemum and the Sword* speak about how the author confronted her own shame, struggled with it, "overcame" it, and simultaneously denied it, after she began to walk the path of war collaborator, until she identified the "guilt cultures" with humane "liberty" or "natural expression."

4

When we chose this theme for *Traces*, our thinking was this. There were two things that we should do. One was to present the political and intellectual events that occurred in individual cultural/lingual spheres without (as much as possible) threatening their singular characteristics. Another was to transform the events into "universal" questions in some way, and create a new topos for discussions between people who live and think in the six languages represented (Chinese, Korean, Japanese, English, German, and French). The development from the first task to the second cannot be done simply by applying pre-existing conceptual devices. It must already be nothing other than a labor of translation. That is to say, in the "original," "translation" must be already ongoing.

In what way, via what process, can the response of those who belong to the defeated nation—to the definition of "shame culture" by the other who belongs to the victorious nation—be a translatable, sharable experience? If, as we saw in the beginning, the experience of translation itself is already affected by the anxiety of death and/or shame, a certain "anxiety" that is beyond the psychological dimension, this situation is no longer as simple as it seems. The experience of shame *in its nature* insists on its one-and-only-ness. If it learns that it can be observed, decoded, and translated by the external gaze, the experience will cause it to solidify its body like the hedgehog. Then, what needs to be done is not to loosen the hedgehog's armor, but to present the "necessity" that its "stiffening" will never assume a "totalizing individuality" but rather that, as it stiffens more, it will be more vulnerable to the "accident" called translation or the "contingency" itself. But, there is no method *in definition* to present the "necessity." Paying attention to the available signs, it has no other choice but to grope its way along.

The stance of juxtaposing the comparative scheme of "guilt cultures" and "shame cultures" over the giant oppositional scheme of West and non-West, beyond the America and Japan comparison—appears to have developed autonomously in the post World War II world. But it could not have happened that way. As H.D. Harootunian pointedly criticized, *The Chrysanthemum and the Sword* and this very manner of thinking that opposes shame to guilt came to grasp a certain hegemony (that is, only as a theoretical excuse to justify modernist development) in the age of the cold war.[14] At the end of *Orientalism*, Edward Said criticized the conservatives in the Arabic world, saying that the serious problem today is that the people or the ruling class of the people who are represented by Orientalism themselves deepen their complicity with Orientalism, equally or more so than the "representation" or "creation" of the Orient by the West.[15] This situation is consistent with post-war Japan. In this precise manner, it might be said, the American side achieved the partial agreement of the other and reaffirmed its representation *qua* "guilt culture," at the same time as enlarging the applicable domain of "shame culture" to the whole of the non-Western world.

What is the status quo? As the "guilt culture" questions its representation less, it becomes more insensitive to the others' gaze and more shameless in imposing the universality of human rights and modern technology. Nothing speaks of the situation more eloquently than the president who ordered a missile attack on Afghanistan, with the excuse of abolishing terrorism, in order to drown out news coverage of his own sex scandal. Meanwhile, the side of "shame culture" is standing at the crossroads by internalizing the representation of "shame culture": (1) either it becomes shameless before the gaze not only of "guilt cultures" but of all others, by fundamentalistically standardizing the given self-image and internalizing the shame; (2) or it feels ashamed of being the "shame culture" and deepens its shame in the effort of assimilating the "guilt culture." This vicious circle that can be observed over and over in the drama of world politics must be severed somewhere somehow, and for this purpose, a reconsideration of the hegemony of cultural representations constructed according to the dichotomy takes on an urgency.

Within the evident and latent struggles between America and China, the conflict between "guilt cultures and shame cultures" is repeated. And this conflict is, if I may dare to say so, becoming synonymous for the Western world to the standard of who can own nuclear weapons. The fact that China, a giant that belongs to the "shame cultures," is a permanent member of the UN Security Council and owns nuclear weapons is the most dreadful heritage of the Cold War. How can the human race, or especially we Asians, escape the bottleneck—it is impossible to find a way without radically questioning the dichotomy of "guilt cultures/shame cultures."

5

In this very sense, one cannot stress enough the importance of the fact that in the late 20th century, in the Europe of the post-Shoah period, various developments of accounts concerning "shame" in both politics and thought have been observed. This genealogy can be traced back beyond Max Scheler in the pre-World War II period to Nietzsche. Today, when the security of the new world order based upon panoptic satellite surveillance is about to be imposed as the "universal" responsibility of humanity, we have to begin by recalling Nietzsche's words of 1886: "'Is it true that God is present everywhere?' a little girl asked her mother; 'I think that's indecent'—a hint for philosophers! One should have more respect for the bashfulness [die Sham] with which nature has hidden behind riddles and iridescent uncertainties."[16]

After World War II, it was Sartre who first and most vividly posed the theme of shame. In *Being and Nothingness*, there is a phenomenological analysis of shame [*honte*]. In the beginning of part three, "Being-for-Others," shame is described as the major example that proves the structural necessity of the being of others in order for me to recognize me.

> Consider for example shame. . . It is a non-positional self-consciousness, conscious (of) itself as shame; as such, it is an example of what the Germans call *Erlebnis*, and it is accessible to reflection. In addition, its structure is intentional; it is a shameful apprehension *of* something and this something is *me*. I am ashamed of what I *am* . . . Yet although certain complex forms derived from shame can appear on the reflective plane, shame is not originally a phenomenon of reflection. . . . [I]t is in its primary structure shame *before somebody* . . . [T]he Other is the indispensable mediator between

myself and me. I am ashamed of myself *as I appear* to the Other.

By the mere appearance of the Other, I am put in the position of passing judgment on myself as on an object, for it is as an object that I appear to the Other. . . Thus shame is shame *of oneself before the Other*; these two structures are inseparable.[17]

Sartre exemplifies such a situation as being caught while peeping into a room through a keyhole. Recognizing the gaze of others is not the same as perceiving the phenomenon of gaze within the world, but becoming conscious of being gazed at, that is, acknowledging one's being as the object of the other's gaze. What drove post-war Sartre was definitely related to his experience of shame as such during the war. But what is suggestive to us now is the fact that this philosopher, who was most influential politically and intellectually in that period, could not finally complete the ethics of which he had given notice in *Being and Nothingness*. From this fact, we might already be able to anticipate a range in the *affect* (though this was not Sartre's term) of shame that fits neither into the phenomenological task of proving "being-for-others" nor the project of ethics.

Being and Nothingness was written after the "strange defeat" of June 1940, around the time Sartre returned home from captivity. According to a recent discovery, it is possible to discern, to a large degree, the part that was finished before mobilization from the part colored by his war experience. It is quite important to decide whether the phenomenology of shame was written before or after the camp experience. For, just as Sartre was very interested in the case of individual shame earlier in his novel *Nausea* (1938), the shame experience came to be treated also at a collective, even national, level in his writing during the period of the German Occupation and Resistance, when *Being and Nothingness* was written.

. . . we had a bad conscience. This secret shame that tormented us—I experienced this first in captivity. Prisoners were unhappy but they had not reached the point of self-pity. . . They felt shame before France. But France felt shame before the world. It is sweet to mourn for oneself a little. But how could we feel pity for ourselves when we were surrounded by the contempt of others.[18]

Soldiers were ashamed before the gaze of France; France was ashamed before the gaze of the world. Herein was situation that could not possibly have occurred after World War I. The situation Sartre depicted can no longer be reduced to the thinking style commonly identified as Sartre's own—the obsession with the gaze. The experience of shame thus became an indispensable element in thinking about war, motivated as it was by World War II, in both Europe and Asia.

6

But was it an accident that the sense of shame burned most intensely in the time and place where the most painstaking attempt was made to deny the unification of the human race? The horrifying reality of the Nazi's planned erasure of Jews, Sinti, Rom, the mentally impaired, homosexuals, communists, and resistance fighters, as well as the concentration and extermination camps, etched on the minds of the few survivors an enigmatic trace of shame which humans had never experienced before. What tackled this problem head-on was perhaps Primo Levi's work. Tzvetan Todorov categorizes three elements in Levi's shame.[19]

The first element is the "shame of remembering." In order to survive the death camps, one has to obey guards' orders against one's will. Those who experienced a collapse of will by pressure of punishment, warning of execution, and torture, continue to feel that they are inhumane even more than the assailants. "It is man who kills. . . it is no longer man who, having lost all restraint, shared his bed with a corpse." (*If This Is a Man*, 155-56)

The second element is what is called "survivor's guilt." The survivors cannot help feeling that they are living in the place of those who died. That I get some of the scarce water and food means that someone else is denied those things. A third person may easily suggest that the survivors do not have to feel guilty, but for the survivors, the third person does not have a right to intervene. "It is the impression that the others died in your place, that you're alive gratis, thanks to a privilege you haven't earned, a trick you've played on the dead. Being alive isn't a crime, but we feel it like a crime." (*If Not Now, When?* 295)

The third element is the "shame of being a human being." Although the survivors are victims, they feel ashamed of belonging to the same species of humans as the assailants. Auschwitz was, after all, what humans created, and we could not stop it: "[T]he shame. . . that the just man experiences at another man's crime; the feeling of guilt that such a crime should exist, that it should have been introduced irrevocably into the world of things." (*The Periodic Table*, 151)

Todorov compared the last "very abstract shame" with the concept of "metaphysical guilt," that Karl Jaspers proposed in his *Question of German Guilt*.[20] In contrast to "criminal guilt"—what criminals are charged with before the law—"political guilt"—what those belonging to the same community as the criminals are charged with before victorious countries—and "moral guilt"—what criminals are charged with before their own conscience, whether they are guilty or not guilty in court, "metaphysical guilt" is a "rapport" that we have with all human crimes, or especially with the crimes that were committed where we happened to be; and the "judgment" of this, according to Jaspers, belongs only to God. But Todorov quickly stresses that the "shame of being a human being" is felt even by those who have nothing to do with metaphysics. In other words, this "shame" is by no means an idea, but an emotion or more precisely, an affect. And Todorov, who, in the first chapter of the book, employed the expression, survivors' "shame or guilt," in this chapter directs our attention to the dimension of "shame" that overflows all domains covered by the concept of "guilt."

Yet it must be noted first that for survivors of Auschwitz, feelings of "guilt" and "shame" are far from conflicting; rather they mingle deeply. This acknowledgment shifts the scope of our problematic concerns. We, who have been familiar with the works of such authors as Levi, cannot believe the dichotomy of the cultural types "guilt cultures/shame cultures" in this context: i.e., that the survivors of Nazi camps, who mostly belong to Judeo-Christian cultures, have more sense of guilt and less sense of shame than the survivors of atrocities in the non-Western world. Sartre's "shame" that appears on the point of contact between his philosophical work and situational statements and the "shame" that repeatedly returns in the almost impossible attempts to represent the camp experience—they are, more than anything else, traces of the same war that produced *The Chrysanthemum and the Sword*. Isn't the fact that at this moment of history the ultimate expression, "shame of being human," has appeared—isn't it a sign that a demarcated historicity of shame is calling for an unprecedented thinking by involving many differences that resist translation and traversing individual cultures and geopolitical conditions?

7

In what aspect is the expression "shame *of* being human" shocking? It becomes clear by comparing it with another expression that seems similar but is perhaps the polar opposite: "shame *as* human." "Shameful as human" is an enunciation of humanism, and it points to a situation in which either self or the other—inasmuch as being the object of shame—is questioned about his/her belonging to humanity. Yet as for the enunciating subject him/herself, the belonging to humanity is secure without being questioned. By "being ashamed," by telling someone that "I am ashamed," his/her belonging is reaffirmed and even enforced. Even if the shame is of the self, the one who becomes the object of shame and whose "status" of being human is questioned, is, if the subject of statement, not the enunciating subject. Therefore, even though there are occasions in which making the enunciation is very difficult, the difficulty is, in principle, not of the kind that can never be overcome.

On the other hand, "shame of being human" is the enunciation of the *limit* of humanism. This is the enunciating act that can be executed only at the limit of "being human." It expresses the sense of wrongness and resistance toward belonging to "humanity" itself; it unequivocally problematizes the belonging. In this case, the subject of statement and the enunciating subject cannot be squarely separated as in the case of "shameful as human." Using the Japanese idiom, this is a situation where "one cannot put oneself on a shelf." Contained in this expression "shame of being human" is the drive to escape from being human in order to escape from the shame. But, then, before whose gaze is one ashamed? To whom does one speak?

This implication would become clearer if compared with belonging to a lower group than "humanity," i.e., a "nation." For instance, what is each of these expressions—"shameful as Japanese" and "shameful of being Japanese"— trying to say? The former is said of those (either the self or others) who lack the virtues that all Japanese are supposed to have. And the enunciating subject, even in the case of being ashamed of oneself, *in fact* denies his commitment obliquely and affirms his belonging to Japan. The latter expression addresses that Japanese as a whole are shameful, therefore, the enunciating subject cannot affirm his belonging to "Japanese," and has to get out of the belonging in order to deny his commitment. Herein belonging is problematized and identification is left incomplete.

But in the case of "national" belonging, even in the latter statement, "shameful of being Japanese," it is not that the enunciation is always difficult. One can express his/her resistance to the belonging to Japan to non-Japanese (foreigners), and to those Japanese who seem to share the resistance. Or, though it is harder, it is possible to express this to those who do not doubt their belonging to Japan. It is even possible to say that it is rather only in this case that the statement can achieve full significance as an enunciation. Because the exteriority of Japaneseness exists within the human as species-being, and because everyone knows it. At the same time this fact prompts the situation where "shame as" and "shame of" are not necessarily inconsistent with respect to "nation," and various combinations of them can occur. 'Shame of being Japanese' implies the acknowledgment that all Japanese lack the virtues that all humans are supposed to have; however, the virtues that Japanese are thought to have—the premise of "shame as Japanese"—for the most part overlap with those that humans in general are supposed to have, when carefully observed. Imagine how Japanese conservative thinkers pervertedly applaud *The Chrysanthemum and the Sword*, and internalize Benedict's proposition that "Japanese culture is a shame culture." All of their discourses must contain the logic or nuance that "shame culture" is more humane than "guilt culture" and appropriate for the essence of a human, who wears clothing, unlike animals; meanwhile, Westerners are shameless and less humane. Rather, it is very difficult to define the characteristics that are thought to be proper to a national community in a way untranslatable to humanist discourses. Because of this structural cause, nationalism is always humanism; nationalism can always come to terms with globalism.

Ukai Satoshi

8

When he spoke of the "shame of being human," Primo Levi was no longer a resident of the nationalist/humanist space. The "shame of being human" does not have an exteriority that the "shame of belonging to a nation" can easily assume. Seen from a theological stance, the "shame of being human" would be interpreted as the "shame" one feels in front of God. But, when such a return—to fundamentalism—is no longer possible, what kind of affect can the "shame of being human" be?

When Levi's reflection is pushed to the limit of the orientation where "shame" is totally dissociated with "guilt," we encounter an inconspicuous yet important aspect of Gilles Deleuze's thinking. It might appear to many that Deleuze and "shame" are totally incompatible, but this is not the case. As far as we know, it was in his dialogue with Antonio Negri, "Control and Becoming," that Deleuze touched upon this theme for the first time. In response to Negri's comment on the "tragic tone" that once in a while mingles with the affirmative tone of *A Thousand Plateaus*, he says:

> You say there's a certain tragic or melancholic tone in all this. I think I can see why. I was very struck by all the passages in Primo Levi where he explains that Nazi camps have given us "a shame at being human." Not, he says, that we're all responsible for Nazism, as some would have us believe, but that we've all been tainted by it: even the survivors of the camps had to make compromises with it, if only to survive. There's the shame of there being men who became Nazis; the shame of being unable, not seeing how, to stop it; the shame of having compromised with it; there's the whole of what Primo Levi calls this "gray area." And we can feel shame at being human in utterly trivial situations, too, . . . This is one of the most powerful incentives toward philosophy, and it's what makes all philosophy political.[21]

The authors of *Anti-Oedipus* later returned to this point in *What is Philosophy?* and clearly distinguish "the shame at being human" from "an unwholesome culpability [*une culpabilité malsaine*]." Thus notified is the fact that for them shame was a theme Nietzschean *par excellence*. They write: "We are not responsible for the victims, but responsible before them." [*Nous ne sommes pas responsables des victimes, mais devant les victimes.*] The use of the preposition "before [*devant*]" is obscure. But this delicate word is so important to the extent that the way Deleuze & Guattari's thought and their politico-historical struggle are linked is at stake. Two pages later, they quote Antonin Artaud: "[T]o write *for* the illiterate—to speak for the aphasic, to think for the acephalous," and state that this "for [*pour*]" is neither "for their benefit [*à l'intention de*]" nor "in their place [*à la place de*]," but "before [*devant*]" and as such "a question of becoming." This is a double becoming in which thinkers become something else by becoming the "illiterate," "aphasic," and "acephalous." In this sense, we write *for* animals, and even think *for* them. Only this kind of becoming is the "resistance to the present," and "constitutes the people to come and the new earth." What Deleuze (and Guattari) sought to see in the "shame of being human" qua the limit of humanism was nothing but the motive drive for the becoming that has no longer to do with resentment.[22]

9

It goes without saying that shame, to Deleuze, is not a simple affirmative affect. He even speaks of resistance against shame as well as escape from shame. But, in any event, it is certain that his thought suggests an alternative work of the affect called shame, or an alternative way of dealing with the affect. What should we think from the almost geometric contrast between Benedict and Deleuze? With respect to their manner of grasping "shame" and "guilt" in an incompatible, discontinuous aspect, they might be on the same side vis-à-vis those who grasp them as one continuous aspect. But, while Benedict's scheme insists on the superiority of "guilt cultures" based upon modernism and Eurocentrism, like a flattened version of such theories as Max Weber's *The Protestant Ethic and the Spirit of Capitalism* and the Oedipus complex of psychoanalysis, Deleuze overturns the scheme in reference to Auschwitz, the main focus of the discourses concerning the guilt of World War II. Nonetheless, when he says that the affect of shame rather than the sentiment of guilt ignites becoming, it is not that he is praising certain shame cultures. The "shame of being human" cannot be, in definition, an attribute of any particular culture. It is nothing but something "universal," or more to the point, something that is beyond universality. This something must mean trouble for both those who praise "guilt cultures" and those who barricade themselves in "shame cultures." To this extent precisely, this affect belongs to the future.

We have been using the term "affect." But, in the phenomenological approaches of both Scheler and Sartre, shame is not analyzed within the category of affect. What Deleuze recognizes as the "shame of being human" is perhaps something that cannot be induced from the experience of shame in general, which is phenomenologically described in relativity to humane others. Herein exists the necessity to think shame as an affect. In Deleuze's philosophy, it is well-known that the concept of affect derived from Spinoza. In Spinoza, affects [*affectus*], as distinct from affections [*affectio*], do not contain the substance of the external body that causes affections, but have to do mainly with the increase or diminishment of the acting power of body or mind by affections.[23] In *What is Philosophy?* affect as a faculty is redefined even more sharply as "man's nonhuman becoming [*devenir non humain de l'homme*]" instead of the passage from one lived state to another, between two quantities.[24] To Deleuze, shame or the "shame of being human" in particular is evidently one of the affects. Or it is perhaps more than just one of many affects—an affect of special status that has to do with the essence of affects in general. If the affects, interpreted in this manner, tend toward the vector of inevitably escaping the world of signification of the human community, did Deleuze see the lineage of inventors of shame or some similar affect in "great novelists" or "inventors of unknown and unrecognized affects": Kafka, Proust, Melville, T.E. Lawrence, and Francis Bacon?[25]

We also choose the stance from which to think shame as an affect. This is because this concept is a *sine qua non* to analyzing nationalism, one of our main focuses, and the series of affects, such as shame, disgrace, and humiliation, is the main ingredient of what might be called *national affect*. Another reason is that it is imperative today for the "other side [*Jenseits*]" of nationalism to be searched, called for, and thought, not only on the level of theory, but also on the level of affect. It is the time when even "the shame of being human" has been discovered, and only in such a moment in history, for the first time, does the possibility that the affects drift out of "nation" and "humanity" begins to be glimpsed or sensed, doesn't it?

10

Now, when we seek to deal with psychoanalysis as our third theoretical prospect, it can again be acknowledged that it has been only several years since the position to treat shame as an affect has achieved citizenship. Before thinking of the "immanent" cause, however, it is necessary here again to refer to the overdetermination by the historical context. Serge Tisseron begins his *La honte—Psychanalise d'un lien social* (1992) in the following manner:

> Confronting the necessity of finding an illustration for the present volume, I discovered that while there are abundant iconographic representations of love, anger, envy, or repentance, there are very few of shame. This is because shame does not say, show, and represent itself. Besides, few works are dedicated to it. As for psychoanalysts, neither is their position exempted from this ambiguity. The psychoanalysts Bettelheim and Rappaport verified it with their own lives. Both concentration camp survivors, they sought to make their colleagues understand their experiences, and particularly the humiliation and shame they lived through. But, for the psychoanalysts of the period, the violent effect of trauma was consistently tied to the way in which an individual does not sufficiently solve his/her primary psychic conflict, namely, what is, since Freud, called the "nuclear

complex of infantile neurosis." It was totally impossible for Bettelheim's and Rappaport's colleagues to understand the shame experienced by the victims in relation to both the physical and psychic violence that they suffered in the camps, and the graveness of the humiliation to which they were exposed.

Today, almost half a century later, psychoanalysts still seem to be unprepared to tackle the situation of shame. This is clear by the fact that they finally began to deal with the shameful situation that marked their own group during the last war only at the moment when the debate on the [Nazi] collaboration was taken public, or the fact that they are still reticent in questioning, at least as a group, their attitude during the Algerian War.[26]

According to Tisseron, there are three causes for the strange 'lack.' First, the fact that, as implied in the above quotation, in analyzing cases in which an adult is humiliated, psychoanalysis has, since Freud, always identified the one who humiliated the person with the *imago* of his parents formed in his/her infancy. Nevertheless, the situations of shame are varied, and not necessarily the repetition of family circumstances. This family-centered tendency has allowed psychoanalysis a theoretical idleness that has reduced violence suffered in the camps to trauma suffered in infancy. Second, the fact that shame is, more than anything, a feeling, and one that is hard to name, therefore, analysts need a special sensitivity to be able to perceive the shame of analysands and make it known to them. The attempt to develop sensitivity to this during the analysts' educational process has been incompatible with the tendency of psychoanalysis after the "linguistic turn," which has focused too much on discursive analyses while declining to give a theoretical position to affect and thereby neglecting the emotional outbursts of analysands.[27] Third, the fact that, far from opposing shame with guilt, like Benedict, psychoanalysis has not even clearly distinguished the feeling of shame from that of guilt. This tendency has been responsible for the delay of the analysis of the structure proper to shame. Recently, however, many analysts have gradually come to acknowledge that shame can be a far more dreadful cause for character disorder than infant trauma.

Freud consistently sought to explain the rise of shame as an effect of repression. What was in the beginning an object of pleasure turns into an object of humiliation, hatred and shame by being repressed. An infant in the anal-sadistic stage has to learn to hide his excrement that he used to enjoy showing off to his parents; this becomes the origin of shame, and the shame extends to his genitalia because of the adjacency. (A Letter to William Fliess, January 1st, 1896) In the first experience of excrement and genitalia, visual perception plays an important role, whereupon shame and gaze enter into a privileged relationship. The primary shame thus begins with hiding the body and its desire from the gaze of the intruder. The parents' prohibition of making the genitalia an object of pleasure is introjected over the course of time, and forms the psychical instance called super-ego in Freud's second theory of the psychical apparatus (or part object). Freud acknowledged three functions of the super-ego: conscience, self-observation, and the formation of ideas. That is, he included the ego ideal in the super-ego. (*The Ego and the Id*, 1923) This stance of the founding father was a distant cause for psychoanalysis not to distinguish shame from guilt. But what is dominant today is the stance that considers the ego ideal as independent from the super-ego, and explains guilt as resulting from the struggle between ego and super-ego and shame from the inconsistency between ego and ego ideal. For this viewpoint, guilt has to do with the standard of good and evil, while shame has to do with the standard of superior and inferior. That is to say, shame came to be defined in correspondence with narcissism. Benedict associated guilt with the fear of the "internal eye" called super-ego, and shame with that of the "external eye" of others; this stance can not coexist with the status quo of psychoanalytic theory that defines both in rapport with different instances in the psychical apparatus.

On a tangent to this major line are two psychoanalysts who contributed a great deal toward overcoming the three causes for the neglect of shame—Sandor Ferenczi and Imre Hermann. Ferenczi maintained that (1) the trauma that causes shame is not always sexual, as Freud thought, but could be of another kind, such as violence or illness; (2) humans sense not only their own shame, but also others'. ("Confusion de langue entre les adultes et l'enfant.") Hermann sought to decode the social characteristic of shame using his own concept, the "clutching instinct [*l'instinct de cramponnement*]." According to him, humans are distinguished from anthropoids by the loss of body hair. This signifies the loss of a handhold for neonates to cling to their mothers, and the social rapport that humans form are all proxies for that lost tie. Lurking behind the formation of social rapport is the intense anxiety of neonates who cannot realize their "clutching instinct," and this expresses itself in the form of jealousy, shame, and remorse. Shame is "a state of dominated submission, causing the phenomena of immobilization that prevents the search for protection by clutching. This is also a social anxiety—the fear of being excluded from community."[28] The relationality between shame and belonging that we dealt with earlier is explained by Hermann as an original "social anxiety" immanent to the affect. The sense of belonging to family, nation, or class is, if seen from the flip side, an anxiety of being excluded from and unable to cling to the group. Ferenzci's point (2): humans sense not only their own but also others' shame is also structurally rooted here. And Tisseron defines the experience of the camps where victims sense their assailants' shame, or Primo Levi's "shame of being human," as extremity of social anxiety.[29]

11

Thus psychoanalysis finally began to grasp shame *qua* "social affect" at the center of its practico-theoretical task. Tisseron points out five elements that psychoanalysts must take into consideration in approaching shame correctly: (1) affect—except that there are cases in which shame is veiled under the mask of anger, and in which the mask of shame veils anger; (2) analysands' present perception, mental picture, and memory traces, of the shame; (3) linguistic representation of the shame that analysands impose on themselves and are sometimes able to voice; (4) action provoked by the shame, or the possibility of action to take in order to get out of the shame; (5) "the psychoanalytic symbol" that synthesizes the four elements.[30]

The last concept derived from Nicolas Abraham, who was, like both Ferenczi and Hermann, a Hungarian Jew and survivor of the camps. In collaboration with Maria Torok, he proposed a structure, called "crypt," which is quite suggestive. The shame to which one responds is neither necessarily his own nor his contemporaries', it can be ancestor's shame. The shame can be gifted beyond generations, sometimes bypassing verbal communication. Such shame is "buried alive" in one's ego, and one can be shameless in attempting to hide it.

René Major analyzed the three destructive ideologies of the 20th century: Nazism, Stalinism, and American Imperialism, in terms of the leaders' chosen illusion and the peoples' sharing of it. He happened to refer to the theme of shame and the work of Abraham and Torok. For instance, let us look at the structure of war memory in post-war Germany. On the 21st of April, 1985, the prime minister of West Germany, Helmut Kohl, stood at Bergen-Belsen, the former concentration camp, and officially acknowledged Germany's historical responsibility, and mentioned *"the unending shame"* Germans feel before the world. How could such a confession of shame be uttered by a leader of state? Now we can understand why: it is because the shame is of his other, namely, his ancestor, if not his own. The aim of his talk was to break off from the residue of national identification with the former ego ideal (Hitler) by stating that he is ashamed of this individual's deed.

So far we have been surveying the situation that clearly indicates that in the West, too, after World War II, the major trends of thought have developed along the axis of shame rather than guilt. Major's work points to the tendency of seeking to synthesize shame as a positive moment in political discourse in the narrow sense, even in a conservative discourse like Kohl's. In this shift, which can even be figured as a demarcation of history, Benedict's dichotomy can no longer work as a theoretical device. Now what concerns us deeply is the fact that there has not been a single public discourse like Kohl's in the shame culture Japan up until today, in the year 2000. Or worse still, what is still prevalent are discourses of denial—that which we can only call "shameless"—in response to Asian nations' questionings of war responsibility, including the "comfort women" issue. Why can we fall into such "shamelessness"? How is "shame" functioning behind the phenomenon? Major's argument offers us some useful prospects for our future work.

> If there is confessed shame—of which one is proud—and unconfessed shame—which ambition devours—there is also unconfessable shame: the shame of impurity that makes all rituals happen, and the shame of envy that can go so far as to transform impotent anger into a barbaric blind explosion.
>
> There is shame of having shame, and shame of not having shame. A son can only be ashamed of the sentiment that he has before his humiliated father. We can only be ashamed of not having recognized the blindness of passion that prevents us from having shame; then, when our ideal leaves the field of alienation, this shame becomes imposing. Communists are ashamed of not having been ashamed of Stalin; Heideggerians are ashamed that Heidegger was not ashamed of Hitler; psychoanalysts are ashamed of the fact that German psychoanalysts were not ashamed of being implicated in the National Socialist regime. In each of these cases, what is at stake is evidently not guilt but a rupture of the uniting tie in a community of thinking, a rupture of the identification of members on the level of collective Ego ideal, in the name of the Name that unites them [au nom du Nom qui les réunite].[31]

Individuals who are entrapped in the illusion of being chosen, messiahs—be it Woodrow Wilson, Stalin, or Hitler—can no longer see the fact that they are seen by others. And most of them die with their illusion intact. Therefore, their shamers are inevitably their families, advisors, contemporaries who admired them, and descendants. But it is historical conditions that determine when and how the shame appears, or if it continues to function in the unconscious. Up until a half century ago, Japan was dominated by the "God-nation" ideology, the ideology of being chosen. On the surface, this ideology was denied by the defeat and the post-war constitution. Yet the shame of belonging to this community, if it often became a strong motive drive for the formation of individual thinking, has never been acknowledged publicly and socialized. One of the main causes that have prevented this from happening was the survival of Tennô Hirohito as the national symbol up until 1989, almost to the end of the Cold War. Although he was the commander-in-chief of the Asia/Pacific War, and it was under his name that the War was conducted, his Tenno-ship survived with an alteration of his constitutional position and a willingness to deny his previous status as "a living God [arahito gami]." It is so that in Japan, the ritual of mourning did not start "normally," despite the defeat. In contradistinction to the post-monarchical situations that Major analyzed, in Japan under the Tennô system that was succeeded to the next generation without a public denial of the mythology of Tennô's unbroken line [*bansei ikkei*], even the death of a Tennô did not mean that "our ideal leaves the field of alienation."

It was under such historical conditions that the shame of the Japanese people appeared, first at the time of defeat, as shame before Tennô that they had not done well enough to be "worthy" of being Japanese, and then secondly as the shame (like the so-called "penitence of a hundred million" [*ichioku sôu zange*]) for having believed in the irrational war ideology. The second shame was essentially the one set before the gaze of the Western victors, of America especially. And it was amidst this affect that *The Chrysanthemum and the Sword* was received in Japan. But, after all, Japanese have never been publicly ashamed of their Tennô. It is said that the Tennô himself was ashamed before his ancestors of having damaged the domain he inherited, but it does not seem that he has ever felt ashamed of himself before the Japanese people, or especially before the foreign victims. Thus, feeling, thinking, and discussing the private shame of the Tennô continued to remain outside the Japanese social/historical imagination; it continued to remain private.[32] This was "unconfessable shame." People could make fun of Tennô, ignore the Tennô system, or be disinterested in it—which was nevertheless nothing but a denial of shame. But in the beginning of the 1990s, with the death of Hirohito, the end of the Cold War, and the democratization of Asian nations, things changed. When the demand for an apology and compensation from the victims of the Asia Pacific War came to be forwarded directly to the Japanese government, the Japanese could no longer ignore the fact that they were the object of scrutiny. A new experience of shame began before the gaze of Asian others. Presently, this shame became a motive drive for various new movements to question war responsibility on the one hand, and on the other hand, it fueled right wing discourses that seek to modify history by being shifted to the code of "unreasonable humiliation" or "national disgrace." In order to precisely grasp the historical power of the Tennô system, especially its function in regulating and structuring the social memory of war, we have to dynamically transform Major's analysis, exercising caution toward the differences in historical and cultural conditions.

> In reality, the ego ideal is an instance that is very much like a lure. It presents what is ugly, abject, and infamous under the mask of the beautiful, noble and glorious. It covers the deception of imaginary identifications of the subject who, being cornered by shame, constantly changes its disguise in order to trick the gaze that surveys it. The ultimate deceit consists of

making us believe that it is charged in a mission given by the Father God that each of us can make ourselves loved or feared for what we do not have. Chosen for the purpose of realizing the phallic ambition of the mother and extending himself among the people of the mother-country, the "great man" moves forward, masked by the divine conviction of no mistakes, and the absolute confidence that the "mission" confers on him liberates him from all scruples. Who on earth can really let themselves be taken advantage of by this weak and pitiful figure, diversely incarnated as Wilson, Stalin, or Hitler? Millions of people, indeed; yet they do not identify themselves with those laughable men who must be surrounded, pampered, flattered, reassured, and protected. If they identify with a figure, it would rather be that of the mother, imagining, in an innocent illusion, of finally conceiving in her body the assuring promise that she can swallow the total whole of his shame—this shame that the necessity will inevitably undertake to reveal.[33]

The need of covering the shame of the other—who was assimilated to God or a son of God—triggers the formation of a fantasy of "eating" or "swallowing" the shame. The fantasy that Abraham and Torok called "incorporation" is formed when we refuse to acknowledge the loss of the object we loved—be it a person, community, or thought—that is, when we avoid the painful process of mourning through which we reclaim the part of ourselves that has been projected onto the lost object and repair the resulting split within our psyche. Such a conjuncture occurs when the loss comes abruptly, and yet the loss is of a type that prohibits its being communicated (because it is caused by a humiliation of the loved object). For instance, the birth of words in infancy is an illusory fulfillment of the empty mouth, and in this sense, a figure of food. But, when the fact of loss itself is denied and the object cannot be eaten figuratively, that is, it cannot be absorbed into the ego, this relationship is inverted, and the words are objectivated literally as food. Then, the expressions concerning eating and excreting are employed by those who preserve the object in crypt, in order to forestall those who humiliate the object. It is an attempt to nullify the effects of humiliation by overtly or covertly demetaphorizing (taking literally what is meant figuratively) the words *qua* food.[34]

In the political discourses of postwar Japan, the ostentatious exhibition of shamelessness has often been observed; whose and what kind of shame has it sought to exorcise? And why can't we sense any affect of "shame" in Japanese politicians' discourses of apology? The almost exhibitionist shamelessness observed in the recent neo-nationalist discourses should be defined and analyzed in relationship with similar kinds of discourses from the past.

12

It is hard to deal with shame. As we have already seen, this is because shame itself prefers to be hidden. As our obstinate resistance to psychoanalysis is telling us, exposing shame to the light of day is itself deemed a shameless deed. And we have already seen that psychoanalysis was reluctant to thematically scrutinize shame, as if it resisted itself. But part of the difficulty lies in the fact that the word "shame" is a knotty one that easily skids from an analytical term to an offensive one. In this respect, too, we have to be cautious in treating it. Discussing shame charges the discussant him/herself with ordeals in various senses, reflecting as it does the manner in which s/he faces his/her own shame.

We have been seeking to clarify the reason as to why "shame" has to be scrutinized today despite every possible difficulty and obstacle; why we believe that we can no more develop our analysis of the social nexus without taking into consideration "shame" as the most knotty social affect, where the best and worst of all our possibilities cohabit. Notwithstanding the perpetually apocalyptic tone that "there is no longer shame for the young," and against the recent fundamentalist tone that "therefore, we now have to return to the traditional norm of shame," today, when the borders between public and private spheres as well as national and global realms are drastically collapsing because of the development of information technology, the expansion of the market economy, and the politicization of every sector of life, we declare the advent of a universal, global age of shame.

The field of analysis is vast. On the level of speakable shame alone, there are three types of analytic: (1) implications of the idiomatic expressions that involve the term "shame" in individual languages, especially in consideration of the double standard—gender and age; (2) conditions that make distinctions between public/private shames (im)possible, and various manners of their combination; (3) functions of the vocabularies akin to shame in political discourses. Above all, there must be unimaginably varied motives and forms in the shame that we cannot speak of, though we are conscious of them. And the analysis of unconscious shame has just begun in the domain of psychoanalysis, as we have seen.

This research is only possible through an inter-disciplinary collaboration. And it should always be made insecure by a double questioning: does the analysis of affect belong to ontology, and can it thus be an object of science *qua* an objectifiable being? And is affect, or the affect of shame in particular, proper to human beings? For instance, what are we really doing, as we already have been doing, when we give the name "shame" to an affect, or when we objectify it as a singular affect by reducing its original heterogeneity?[35] Aren't we anthropomorphizing affect by this act? We scrutinized the necessity of thinking of shame at the limit of humanism with respect to a moment in Deleuzian thinking. And this is also a recognition that exists as a premise of the recent work of Derrida. He begins his account on animals with a narrative of such an experience.

> Since before time, is it possible that the animal looks at us?
> which animal? Or the other.
> Often I give a try to questioning who I am—who I am at the moment when surprised, while naked, in silence, by the gaze of a cat, for instance, by the eyes of a cat, I have difficulty, yes, difficulty in overcoming a discomfort.
> Why this difficulty?
> I have difficulty in repressing a motion of bashfulness. Difficulty in silencing a protest against indifference in me . . . . It is as if I then had a shame of being naked before the cat, but also shame of having shame. Reflection of shame, mirror of a shame that is ashamed of itself, of a shame simultaneously specular, unjustifiable, and unconfessable. In the optical center of such a reflection, the 'thing' is found—and in my eyes the source of this incomparable experience called nudity. And people think this is proper to humans, namely, foreign to animals. Then people are convinced that animals are naked, without any consciousness of being so.[36]

Thus we are in front of an animal again. This cat has eyes, has a gaze, and is gazing at us, even though it is not the gaze of a human other. In contrast, the hedgehog in "*Che cos'è la poesia?*" became blind by itself. But, can we say that the hedgehog is not gazing at us? Can we determine that without eyes, it does not have a gaze? There is nothing more uncertain than this. Isn't it gazing at us as a raw figure, so modest and naked? Isn't it gazing at us by not seeing? Isn't it gazing at us by its reflex of shame? And by doing so, isn't it an allegory of poetry?

> Poetry arrives. From others. Always.
> Shame and the sense of being bashful of the shame contain not only negative images as ostensibly seen. Shame is a liminal *topos* that is finally left to us where we sense our lives by incorporating our immanent cause, immanent secret. And there cannot and should not be any thoughts, principles, and ideologies that deprive its space.[37]

According to a Japanese dictionary, "being bashful [*hanikamu-koto*]" is equal to "being embarrassed [*hazukashigaru-koto*]" or "pretending to be embarrassed [*hazukashisôna soburi-o-surukoto*]." In other words, it is a synonym, a derivative of *hajirukoto* [being ashamed of]; a mode of the expression of shame. "Being abashed and trying to avoid eye contact." (Mori Ôgai, *The Wild Goose*) "That is it. That bashful smile. That is the feature proper to a talented artist." (Dazai Osamu, *No Longer Human*) "'After getting my certification, we can get married, can't we?' Hatsue did not respond, but smiled bashfully." (Mishima Yukio, *The Sound of Waves*) These examples from masterpieces of Japanese modern literature listed in a dictionary teach us typical uses of the word as it has been internalized in Japanese culture. But, as far as we know, this word "*hanikamu*" [being abashed] has never been thrown into the turmoil of the experience of shame, in its reflex movement—essential to it—that cannot be stopped.

Even if "*hanikamu* [being abashed]" is a synonym of "*hajiru* [being ashamed of]," "being abashed of shame" [*haji o hanikamu-koto*] is a very different, almost opposite posture of "being ashamed of shame" [*haji o hajiru-koto*]. *Hanikami* is neither "undertaking" nor "overcoming" *haji* [shame]. It affirms shame, and by doing so, resists shame. For the woman who discovered this expression, nay, *affect*, life was something that could be narrated only in this manner. She discovered this in the features of elderly Korean women who had been forced to live as comfort women, as sex slaves, by the Japanese army, and finally have come out and testified after half a century.

Haji o hanikamu [being bashful of shame]. The advent of this "poematic event [*évenement poématique*]" did not come to someone whose mother's tongue is Japanese, or someone educated in a Japanese school. It was, perhaps, an impossibility.[38] The impossibility of translating this expression thus no longer belongs to the property of the culture that calls itself Japan. If there is any "proper place" for thinking of shame, the experience of translation, and words for *Traces*, it exists nowhere but this *topos* where a proper language and a proper culture no longer overlap.

Ukai Satoshi

Endnotes

1—Jacques Derrida, "Che cos'è la poesia?", in *Points de suspension* (Paris: Galilée, 1992), 303-308; in English, *Points . . . Interviews, 1974–1994*, edited by Elisabeth Weber, translated by Peggy Kamuf et al. (Stanford, CA: Stanford University Press, 1995), 288-299.
2—Walter Benjamin, "The Task of the Translator," included in *Illuminations*, trans. Harry Zohn (New York: Schocken Books, 1969), 75.
3—Ruth Benedict, *The Chrysanthemum and the Sword—Patterns of Japanese Culture* (New York: Charles E. Tuttle Company, 1946), 223-225.
4—Ibid., 114-132.
5—Ibid., 45-46.
6—See the translator's commentary to the Japanese publication of Benedict's *Japanese Behavior Patterns* trans. Fukui Nanako (Tokyo: NHK Books, 1997).
7—The most inclusive account of Watsuji's critique of Benedict is in Fukuda Yoshiya's *On Japanese Culture—Reading Benedict's The Chrysanthemum and the Sword [Nihon bunka shiron—Benedict The Chrysanthemum and the Sword o yomu]* (Tokyo: Shinyosha, 1993), 50-59. This book fully surveys and comments on the criticisms of *The Chrysanthemum and the Sword* that have appeared in Japan, and this is important for learning the history of the reception of Benedict's book.
8—*The Standard Edition of the Collection of Yanagida Kunio's Work [Teihon Yanagida Kunio shû]*, Vol. 30 (Tokyo: Chikuma Shobô), 104-105. Also see Fukuda's book (290-303).
9—Sakuta Keiichi, *Reconsideration of Shame Cultures [Haji no bunka saikô]* (Tokyo: Chikuma Shobô, 1967), 11-12. Also see Masamura Toshiyuki, *Secret and Shame [Himitsu to haji]* (Tokyo: Keisô Shobô, 1995) that meticulously describes the structure of communication in Japanese society, succeeding the reflections of Benedict and Sakuta and in reference to Niklas Luhmann.
10—C. Douglas Lummis, *A New Look at the Chrysanthemum and the Sword* (Tokyo: Shôhakusha, 1982), 21-22.
11—Ibid., 23.
12—Ibid., 57-58
13—See the two commentaries by Pauline Kent on the two books by Benedict, both published in Japanese: *Japanese Behavior Patterns [Nihonjin no kôdô patân]* (published only in Japanese) and *Race: Science and Politics* (New York: Viking Press, 1959). [*Jinshu shugi, sono hihanteki kôsatsu*] trans. Tsutsui Kiyotada, Teraoka Shingo, and Tsutsui Kiyoteru (Nagoya: Nagoya Daigaku Shuppan Kai, 1997).
14—H.D. Harootunian, "Ambiguous Silhouette: Ideology, Knowledge, and the Shape of Japanese Studies in the United States," translated from English by Endô Katsuhiko, included in *Misuzu* (May and August Issues, 1998).
15—Edward W. Said, *Orientalism*, (New York: Vintage Books, 1978).
16—Friedrich Nietzsche, *The Gay Science*, translated, with commentary by Walter Kaufman (New York: Vintage Books, 1976), 38.
17—Jean-Paul Sartre, *Being and Nothingness*, translated and with an introduction by Hazel E. Barnes (Washington Square Press, 1956), 301-303.
18—Sartre, *Situations III* (Paris: Éditions Gallimard, 1949), 33-34.
19—Tzvetan Todorov, *Facing the Extreme: Moral Life in the Concentration Camps*, trans. Arthur Denner and Abigail Pollack (New York: Metropolitan Books, 1996). There is also an important book concerning the dynamic tension between Levi's concentration camp experience and the concepts of humanity, universality, and Europe, etc: Suh Kyung-sik's *Primo Levi e no tabi* [*A Journey to Primo Levi*] (Tokyo: Asahi Shinbun Sha, 1999).
20—Karl Jaspers, *The Question of German Guilt*, trans E.B. Ashton (New York: The Dial Press, 1947).
21—Gilles Deleuze, *Negotiations*, translated by Martin Joughin (New York: Columbia University Press, 1995), 172.
22—Deleuze and Guattari, *What is Philosophy?* trans. Hugh Tomlinson and Graham Burchell (New York: Columbia University Press, 1994), 106-110.
23—Deleuze, *Spinoza: Practical*

Philosophy, translated by Robert Hurley (San Francisco: City Lights Books, 1988), 49.

24—Deleuze and Guattari, *What is Philosophy?*, 173.

25—There is only one essay by Deleuze with the word "shame" in its title. That is "The Shame and the Glory: T.E. Lawrence" in *Essays—Critical and Clinical*, trans. Daniel W. Smith and Michael A. Greco (Minneapolis: University of Minnesota Press, 1997). [*Critique et clinique*, (Paris: Editions de Minuit, 1993)]. Here "shame" is considered as rooted in a "character" precedent to the relationship with others on the deepest level, namely, "*consubstantielle à l' être* [co-substantial with being]." "Lawrence does not lie, and even in pleasure he experiences all kinds of shame in relation to the Arabs: the shame of disguising himself, of sharing their misery, of commanding them, of deceiving them. . . He is ashamed of the Arabs, before the Arabs. Yet Lawrence bears the shame within himself, for all the time, from birth, as a profound component of his Character." (124-125)

26—Serge Tisseron, *La honte, psychanalise d'un lien social* (Paris: Dunod, 1992), 1-2.

27—With respect to the positioning of affect in psychoanalysis, it is imperative to refer to André Green, *Le discours vivant; la conception psychanalitque de l'affect* (Paris: Presses universitaires de France, 1973). In contrast, Lacan always thought of shame in relationship with narcissism, and connected it to the gaze as the object *a*. I would like to write about the Green/Lacan debate concerning the status of affect in a future essay.

28—Imre Hermann, *L'instinct filial* (Paris: Denoël, 1972).

29—Tisseron, 28.

30—Ibid., 4.

31—René Major, *De l'élection* (Paris: Aubier, 1986), 162-163.

32—On the private level as well, the most eminent negative affect against Tennô was not shame, but the anger of war veterans.

33—Major, 166-167. Except that Major does not seem to actively posit affect in his theory. Major's critique of Green and Green's counter-critique are mentioned in Green, 344-346.

34—See Nicolas Abraham and Maria Torok, *The Shell and the Kernel, Vol. 1*, translated, and with introduction by Nicholas T. Rand (Chicago & London: The University of Chicago Press, 1994), especially chapter 5, "Mourning and Melancholia: Introjection versus Incorporation."

35—Tisseron pays attention to this point at the end of his book. "Finally we believe that the complexity of situations that form the basis for the origin of shame obligates us to assume that any feelings of shame *a priori* do not signify anything: neither the causes, nor the mechanisms, nor the consequences. . . This is the reason why we should always speak of shame(s) in the plural rather than the singular, or furthermore, 'feelings of shame [*sentiments de honte*]' like it is said 'feelings of guilt [*sentiments de culpabilité*]'." (182)

36—Jacques Derrida, "L'animal que donc je suis," *L'animal autobiographique* (Paris: Galilée, 1999), 253-254.

37—Lee Chong Hwa, *Tsubuyaki no seiji shiso* [*Murmuring Political Thought*] (Tokyo: Seido sha, 1998).

38—Lee Chong Hwa is a sociologist. She was born in Korea and came to Japan in 1988. It is important to note that her mother's tongue is not Japanese but Korean.

Universal Areas: Asian Studies in a World in Motion

Pheng Cheah

In recent years, the research enterprises called *area studies* have been increasingly challenged, especially by anthropologists influenced by Edward Said's critique of Orientalism, as well as by those interested in the impact of contemporary globalization on culture.[1] The primary thrust of these criticisms is directed at the organic and static understanding of the *area* as an object of scholarly inquiry. But although these criticisms have ruffled and even made indeterminate the surfaces of area studies by pointing to the mutual interpenetration of "Asia" and "the West" in global modernity, to my knowledge, they have seldom questioned the implicit conceptual determination of *area* that places it in a negative relationship to that now unfashionable but still powerful ethico-philosophical epithet and hypostatization, "universal." For it seems such an obvious fact that it is scarcely worth pointing out that an area—the object of area studies—is, that which is not universal. Or, to be more tendentious still, an area is precisely that which is not capable of universality.

What follows is primarily an outsider's attempt to understand the conceptual matrix of the formation of area studies in the United States academy, particularly its division of labor in relation to the disciplines of the humanities and the social sciences, and the constraints placed upon the work of area studies by this conceptual matrix. I argue that the conceptual definition of *world area* in the programmatic literature of key funding bodies during area studies' high-growth years in the post-Second World War era places area scholarship and the areas themselves in a subordinate relationship to the universal knowing subject of the disciplines. I trace this definition of world area back to the Hegelian idea of *Volksgeist* in order to elaborate on the underlying relationship between universal and particular. This understanding of the universal and the particular still structures critiques of the Eurocentrism of disciplinary knowledge which reject Western universalism and denounce its parochialism. I suggest that another way to reinvent area studies in contemporary globalization is to see each and every area neither as something particular that needs to be transcended to attain universality nor as concrete reality that needs to be affirmed over abstract universality, but instead, as the irreducible inscription of the universal in the singular.

I The "Area" of Area Studies and the Denegation of the West

The simplest definition of an area is the extent or measure of a surface. Today, it is generally assumed that the "area" in "area studies" refers unequivocally to a cartographically delimited region that is isomorphic with a distinctive anthropological culture.² However, many of the scholars who were involved in defining the enterprise of area studies in the U.S.A. for institutional-programmatic reasons, as well as for the purpose of attracting foundation support in the two decades following the end of World War II, were not completely insensitive to the epistemological and methodological difficulties inherent in the constitution of their field, even if they ended up papering over those very difficulties.³

Generally speaking, an area is regarded as having the two fundamental characteristics of being non-Western and being bounded. These traits are necessary corollaries of each other. *Area* is shorthand for an expanse that is spatially distinct from the academic researcher or scholar—the knowing subject— and this distinctness implies the bounded nature of the area, the impossibility of the knowing subject's confusion of the area with the location from which he or she cognizes it. Moreover, since the knowing subject is almost always explicitly nationally marked as "American," the area that is studied is also qualitatively distinct in the sense of being "alien" or "foreign" in historical, social, or cultural terms. Thus, *non-Western* is inevitably a cognate, even a synonym, of *area*. Robert McCaughey gives us a sense of this necessary coincidence of spatial distinctness and cultural foreign-ness in the definition of international studies that he places at the threshold of his historical survey of the genesis of area studies in the U.S.:

> By "international studies," I mean the serious inquiry by Americans into those parts of the world Americans have traditionally regarded as having histories, cul-

tures, and social arrangements distinctly different from their own. For convenience and in keeping with current usage, this alien world has been divided into the following components: Eastern Europe and Russia; East Asia; South Asia; the Middle East (including North Africa); Africa; Latin America; and "Other" (e.g., Canada and Oceania).[4]

But to be more precise, what is the principle according to which something becomes classified as belonging to area studies? What is it that is "non-Western"? What is it that is "alien" to "Americans"? The peculiarity of the term *non-Western* is that it is not quite a cartographical term; on the one hand, it designates something more than the parts of the world that lie outside North America, since it clearly does not refer to England or France. On the other hand, however, not all of Europe is part of the Western world. The principle for inclusion in the Western world thus seems to be the existence of a relationship of "familiarity and consanguinity" to the U.S. qua center. Western Europe would be part of the Western world and, hence, not a foreign world area precisely because of its affinity to a certain conception, vision, or myth of the U.S. as having its origin in Western Europe. It is because of such cultural and historical ties that the U.S. would need to understand Western Europe as part of its familiarity with and knowledge of itself, and by the same token, would not need to study it in the same way that it studies a foreign area that is a priori strange to it.[5]

In their preface to a 1964 volume of *The Annals of the American Academy of Political and Social Science* entitled *The Non-Western World in Higher Education*, Donald Bigelow and Lyman Legters of the U.S. Office of Education figure this principle of consanguinity as one of trans-Atlantic fraternity: "The world beyond the North Atlantic community of nations is no longer out of bounds to American scholarship."[6] What lies outside this North Atlantic brotherhood is "what, for want of a better term, we now call 'non-Western studies.'"[7] And whereas there has been a historical tendency to want to know more about what lies within this community, a tendency that is reflected in institutional structures within American universities and that is much like a desire to learn more about one's kinship or family tree, there is a deep ignorance concerning everything lying outside this community, a fact which for Bigelow and Legters constitutes an important intellectual rationale for area studies. Indeed, "non-Western" designates everything that American scholarship is ignorant of! It is what Americans do not know factually because it is not part of their community, their historical or cultural makeup. Thus,

> while the expression ["non-Western studies"] is imprecise and potentially misleading, its negative element accurately reflects the common feature that brings together highly disparate cultures under a single label—the factor of neglect. Since Latin America and Slavic Europe have been almost as badly

neglected in the curriculum as Asia and Africa, it is pragmatically justifiable to treat them as part of the "non-Western world."[8]

The establishment of a field of research on the basis of neglect begs precisely the methodological question of how each individual area within the larger domain of world areas can be clearly apprehended or delimited as a bounded unit. Thus, in a 1948 pamphlet of the Social Science Research Council (SSRC), Charles Wagley emphasizes the amorphousness of an area: "The geographic unit which is the subject of such interdisciplinary area research may vary in accordance with the specific problem which is being attacked. An 'area' may be a nation, a culture area, an ecological unit, or a subdivision of any of these."[9] Similarly, in a publication commissioned by the SSRC in 1950, Julian Steward observes that:

> Area study and area program are very inclusive terms, and area has several meanings. It may mean a world area, that is, an area of world importance (importance to the United States or its international relations), such as Russia, the Far East, South Asia, or Eastern Europe; it may mean a culture area, such as Latin America, the Near East, Middle America, or the Maya Indians, which may or may not have contemporary importance to the United States; it may be a nation, such as China, Russia, or Brazil; it may be a colony, such as the European colonies in Africa; it may be a dependency, such as the United States dependency of Puerto Rico.... These meanings of area are not necessarily mutually exclusive, but each may have distinctive methodological connotations with respect to research.[10]

In the early years of their institutionalization, such methodological doubts led to the suggestion that area divisions

> do not reflect systematic classifications derived from prolonged scholarly and scientific investigations in any discipline. They represent very rough and ready delimitations serving chiefly the practical needs of military and political operations. Whether "the Far East," "South Asia," "Southeast Asia," "Africa," and other area divisions can also serve the needs of research and training in the several social science disciplines remains to be explored.[11]

We know that these early intellectual doubts were quelled by recourse to a structural-functionalist idea of an interrelated whole that allowed a cognizable bounded unit to be aligned with or mapped onto an area of strategic interest or foreign-affairs policy.[12] In other words, area studies was inscribed into institutional existence by referring to intellectual objectives that exceeded their practical objectives, namely their relation to the disciplines and their contributions to the production of universal knowledge.

It is these extra-practical intellectual objectives that I now wish to consider in some detail, especially with regard to their continuity with power relations. In *Orientalism*, Edward Said attempted to demonstrate how European colonizers used Orientalist knowledge as a means of dominating the Orient. He articulated a complex instrumentalist view of knowledge in which the Orientalist *mode of knowing* not only served to justify colonialism as civilizing mission, but was actually a way of stimulating interest in and exerting authority over the Orient.[13] In the final chapter of his book, Said described U.S. area studies as a contemporary form of Orientalism, but also gestured towards "'decolonializing' new departures in the so-called area studies."[14] The general political criticism of area studies takes its cue from Said and points to the coincidence of area studies' rapid growth and the interdependence of their knowledge claims with U.S. national-governmental interests in the Cold War era.[15]

As necessary as this criticism of area studies seems to be, its point is also an obvious one, given that in their moment of institutionalization, U.S. area studies have never tried to hide their practical objectives.[16] But more importantly, such a criticism fails to explain how the intellectual objectives claimed by area studies in addition to its practical objectives are nevertheless continuous with the latter, without resorting to an instrumentalist account of the relationship between intellectual pursuit and practical interest, or between knowledge and power. In part, this shortcoming stems from a lacuna within Said's own understanding of the power-knowledge relationship, which is most clearly articulated in his analysis of Arthur James Balfour's 1910 speech on Egypt:

> As Balfour justifies the necessity for British occupation of Egypt, supremacy in his mind is associated with "our" knowledge of Egypt and not principally with military or economic power. Knowledge to Balfour means surveying a civilization from its origins to its prime to its decline—and of course, it means *being able to do that*. Knowledge means rising above immediacy, beyond self, into the foreign and distant. The object of such knowledge is inherently vulnerable to scrutiny.... To have such knowledge of such a thing is to dominate it, to have authority over it. And authority here means for "us" to deny autonomy to "it."[17]

In this passage Said points to the connection between Orientalist knowledge and British colonial power, but fails to elaborate on its precise nature. Instead, he assumes the connection by conflating two different meanings of the word "authority": authority in the sense of intellectual mastery and in the sense of political domination. But in what sense does the vulnerability of an object to the Orientalist mode of knowing necessarily imply its vulnerability to political subjugation? Put another way, what is the nature of Orientalist intellectual authority that makes it continuous with colonial political authority, even though it is neither identical to colonial political authority nor simply the latter's epiphenomenon or ideological reflection? To phrase the question in terms of area studies, how do the intellectual objectives of area studies articulate an intrinsic connection between the act of knowing and the well-being of the territorial site from which such knowing occurs (the national interest of the American knowing subject), a connection that places this territorial site of knowledge-production in a position of strength vis-à-vis the world area that is studied, and hence, in a position capable of exerting power, in the narrow sense, over that world area?

I should stress that the point that knowledge confers power to the knower has never been disputed, and indeed, has always been underscored as an intellectual-cum-practical justification of area studies. To quote Charles Wagley,

> Strong academic scholarship is an important national resource, and there is basically no conflict "between academic and national needs, between scholarship and government objectives, scientific progress and basic intelligence.... Where scholarship and research are involved, the academic and national needs are one and the same thing. Sound research is valuable to the nation, whereas the national need cannot be served by inadequate scholarship. Only the soundest sort of area research can be in the genuine national interest and thereby also a factor for international well-being."[18]

The question, then, is *how* the style of knowing which characterizes area studies confers power, and, indeed, expresses the essential unity of (area) knowledge and (U.S. national) power. It is too easy, I think, to point to the technical utility of area knowledge, because this begs the question of how knowledge can be a technical force and, therefore, possess a real effectivity. These issues of how knowledge can confer power and why knowledge possesses real effectivity, I want to suggest, need to be related back to a certain philosophical definition of freedom as a self-determining consciousness, a definition that underpins the conceptual matrix of area studies and its institutional position vis-à-vis the disciplines. Simply put, the nation that can treat other places as areas to be studied in relation to itself, the nation that can position other places as the objects for area studies, achieves the optimal state of freedom and power vis-à-vis others insofar as it manages to attain the highest degree of self-consciousness and self-determination. Conversely, places that can only know or cognize themselves as areas can never attain genuine self-consciousness and self-determination.

I will now turn to consider the silent workings of the two above propositions in the distinction between area studies and the disciplines that aligns the former with the particular and the latter with the universal. But first, a note of caution: my purpose here is neither to dismiss the importance of area research nor to suggest that it is an intellectually feeble enterprise. As we have seen, many crucial theoretical and methodological questions were raised at the outset of the establishment of area studies. Many of the questions being raised today regarding the continuing viability of area research in contemporary globalization—questions about the decline of the nation-state, about the obsolescence of distinct cultural areas in transnational migration etc.—can be seen as variations on these earlier concerns about how to delimit an area. My purpose is instead to examine how area studies were constrained from the very moment of its institutionalization by a certain conceptual matrix. As I will also suggest, contemporary critiques of the Orientalism of area studies and the Eurocentrism of the disciplines remain constrained by the same conceptual matrix. In a way, I am suggesting that area studies should attempt to ask more of itself than it traditionally has.

I have already pointed to two basic features of this conceptual matrix: an area is both non-Western and also clearly delimitable. These two features are governed by a principle of consanguinity that allows the subject of knowledge to distinguish between what is part of its own historical-cultural makeup, its *Weltanschauung*, and what is not. Now, the distinction between West and non-West also corresponds to a distinction between the universal and the particular and it is on this basis that area studies is separated from the disciplines. At first glance, area studies appears to be distinguished from the disciplines in at least three related ways. First, area studies are supposed to be involved in the gathering of raw empirical data or concrete factual information. They are primarily descriptive, whereas the disciplines, which engage in theoretical generalization and abstraction, further the task of pure intellection. Second, it follows from the first distinction that area studies are intellectually subordinate to the disciplines in the same way that applied knowledges are subordinate to pure forms of knowledge. The latter provides the methodological and epistemological structures necessary for the conduct of research, which the former applies or puts into practice. Area research could not be conducted without the prior intellectual groundlaying of the disciplines. The disciplines are therefore intellectually a priori to, have greater epistemological authority, and are more powerful than area studies. This is why an area-studies scholar has often been described using the metaphor of dual occupations or dual citizenship: he or she must obtain a doctorate in a department of graduate study and "also have special competence relating to a particular area." But the two jobs or citizenships are not equal, for "in general the area training is *supplementary*."[19]

The third ground of division between area studies and the disciplines is the correlation of the former with the particular and the latter with the universal. The renowned Indonesianist and theorist of nationalism, Benedict Anderson, articulates this distinction succinctly and with justifiable pique when he voices the largely unaired but tacit general opinion of his discipline of political science that its

> search for universal/global, if you prefer transcendental models, its scientific attachment to parsimony, its ever more subtle and intricate vocabulary and its methodological sophistication, all make it fundamentally beyond Southeast Asian scholars. It is as though one heard people saying: "They don't/can't think abstractly; they're uninterested in any country other than their own; they're not trained to use sophisticated mathematical or epistemological tools. They don't get the journals, and if they did, they wouldn't read them."[20]

As it turns out, the oppositions between theory-building and data-collection, between pure and applied knowledges, ultimately refer back to this opposition between universal and particular. The particular is that which is tied to the immediacy of experience—empirical evidence—whereas universality is the mark of discursive knowledge, knowledge that rises above immediacy through the mediation of abstract concepts that are universally communicable. Lucian Pye puts it this way:

Under these conditions [the spectacular growth of graduate education in the postwar period, coupled with increased funding for area research] there emerged within the social sciences a division between the ardent champions of the disciplines as the citadels of universal knowledge and the advocates of area studies as centers of highly specialized knowledge of the particular. At the most abstract and theoretical level this confrontation between the disciplines and area studies revolved around the question of how generalized or particularized scientific knowledge about human behavior can or should be. In part, thus, the division has been one between those who crave knowledge in the form of universal propositions and discount the merit of "mere description," and those who revere the unending uniqueness of human experiences and see mainly empty words in abstract formulations.[21]

It is worth noting that in this debate, the terms "universal" and "particular" have narrow meanings. They merely refer to the validity of knowledge claims according to the epistemological model of the social sciences. Consequently, the humanities occupy a curious place in this debate. For the disciplines are almost invariably associated with the social sciences. Thus, the classical association of the *humaniora* with the feeling of universality and universal communication is overturned, and the humanities here begin to accrue the connotation of particularity and are said to be naturally linked to area studies, following the rationale that they deal with language, and hence, with the multitudinous variety of human languages.[22] Indeed, the antagonism between area studies and the social sciences has been described as a displacement of the older antagonism between the humanities and the social sciences![23]

But the more important point by far is this: Insofar as the disciplines are seen as the guardians of standards for determining the universal validity of social phenomena (i.e., social-scientific laws) and these standards are formulated from evidence that is indisputably confined to the North Atlantic fraternity, there is an unspoken (but for that very reason all the more tenacious) isomorphism between the universal structures of reason and the social structures of the West. This is not exactly the commonplace criticism of the historical Eurocentrism of the social sciences.[24] I am not only saying that there has been a *historically contingent* conflation of the differentiated social structures of Western society with the divisions of the different social sciences. I am saying instead that the social sciences are inherently Eurocentric because the universality of their knowledge claims is predicated on the figure of self-consciousness, and that this necessarily sets up an isomorphism between Western social structures and the universal phenomena that are the subject of the disciplines. For if universality is defined in terms of the ability of consciousness to reflect or turn back on itself in order to abstract from and transcend what is particular in it, thereby raising itself into something that possesses unconditional validity, then this injunction to know oneself is primarily governed by the principle of consanguinity that I discussed above. What belongs to the knowing subject's historical or cultural makeup—its Western-ness—will always be raised to the level of the universal. And what lies on the side of the unknown (the non-Western world area) can only ever be the mere object of factual knowledge rather than the subject of theory. This is the conceptual matrix that governs the parameters of area studies vis-à-vis the disciplines.

We would be mistaken to see the universalism of the disciplines as dogmatically abstract and Eurocentric in a simple manner. Indeed, within the constraints of this conceptual matrix, there can be much room for variation. The most important and commonly adduced intellectual objectives of area studies are (1) the fostering of interdisciplinary cooperation and teamwork that can bridge the gap between humanities and the social sciences, and (2) the instilling of a healthy cultural relativism coupled with the accumulation of concrete material to be used as a database for testing the abstract theoretical formulations and universal generalizations of the disciplines, as a safeguard against excessive generalization. Cooperation between area research and the disciplines, between the particular and the universal is allowed, indeed, even deemed necessary to "the development of a universal and general science of society and of human behavior."[25] Thus, we learn that

> Because area studies are generally concerned with a foreign part of the world and deal with cultures very different from our own, they provide basic descriptive data without which the generalist is unable to work. Area studies bring comparative and concrete data to bear on generalization and theory, and the study of a limited area gives a concrete focus for interdisciplinary cooperation....
>
> Its preoccupation with foreign areas and non-Western cultures leads inevitably to the collection of the comparative and empirical data necessary to the development of a universal social science. Area research, then, is a natural and progressive step toward the development of an objective science of man.[26]

We are also told that the separation of theory from area research is artificial and "unfortunate because there is no basic antagonism between the two—the full development of theory depends on the accumulation of comparable data from all available sources."[27] Area research can combine "studies which illuminate the particularistic and unique elements in a society (language, literature, history, religion, etc.) with the sciences of society (the social sciences)," thereby enabling "the social sciences (and some fields in the humanities) to take into account the particular and unique as well as the universal elements in human experience."[28]

Moreover, the same conceptual matrix can also accommodate an explicit anti-Eurocentric rhetoric. Thus, Charles Wagley observes that

> the conceptual schemes upon which these disciplines [of economics, sociology, psychology, and political science] are based are, in large measure, the product of Western thought and institutions....Specialists whose training derives from this context are now attempting to apply their methods of analysis to cultures that are very different....[Their assumptions] may undergo considerable modification. At any rate, if there be a provincialism within these disciplines, it will be quickly revealed when the expert applies his formulations to alien cultures."... [Hence, i]f we are looking for a universalization of social science as well as the emergence of a body of knowledge regarding important areas of the world, we must utilize the research technicians of the areas concerned.[29]

Contemporary anti-Eurocentrism remains part of this discursive formation. But in both the explicit critique of the Eurocentrism of the disciplines and the attempt to reconcile particular and universal forms of knowledge, what we witness is merely the use of data gathered by area research to manage the crisis of Western consciousness in a post-War era when the Western belief in universal progress and the perfectibility of man had been shaken by decolonization and the rise of Communism. For instead of impinging upon and transforming the universal form of theoretical consciousness, what area research contributes is merely technical or applied know-how or even dogmatic knowledge, as opposed to the critical knowledge that is articulated in the disciplines, following Kant's distinction between dogmatic and transcendental or critical philosophy.[30] The attempt to reconcile theory and area research retains the epistemological priority accorded to theory, which is seen as something to be applied, in order to give form to raw data from non-Western world areas. The vocabulary used to describe this reconciliation is always conservative in the most literal sense: it is a testing/ checking of or tinkering with a pre-established or a priori eidetic structure, using secondary material in order to reinforce it, rather than a general rebuilding of that structure from the ground up, using bits of newly acquired comparative knowledge. Thus, Hans Morgenthau suggests that area studies needs to be grounded in the underlying universalities of human nature:

> If you know something about man as such you know something about all men…at least [about] the contours of human nature which, when superimposed upon a concrete situation, may get blurred here and there and which always lack specific interest and color. It is for area studies to provide an empirical check upon these contours' correctness and that specific content and color.[31]

But what is "man" in his "as such"? Or, better yet, what are the universal structures of consciousness that enable, first, the cognition of "man as such" and, second, the setting up of institutional research fields in which non-Western areas can be apprehended and studied in order to check the correctness of and to specify the details of "man as such"? It is precisely here that the issue of the relationship between power and knowledge needs to be raised, not as a matter of the instrumentality of knowledge, but instead in terms of *how* area studies is positioned or set up by the conceptual matrix governing its institutionalization. For this matrix predetermines that non-Western areas are a priori distinct from a self-conscious subject of universal knowledge. This has two implications. First, these areas can only gain access to universal self-consciousness through an extended apprenticeship to the West, through training in the universal knowledge of the disciplines. But second, and more importantly, since these are, by definition, particular areas, they can only know themselves through area research as empirical data and as particular bounded objects. Put another way, the only knowledge they can have of themselves comes from apprehending themselves through the eyes of the West, which amounts to saying that they can never fully know themselves. Thus these areas must either give up the aim of self-knowledge, in which case they must remain mired in self-incurred tutelage because they have not achieved self-determination, or they can attain self-determination only by being enthralled or possessed by the specter of the West, since they can only know themselves as its other.

Area knowledge thus empowers and disempowers in a very literal sense. Gabriel Almond captures only one side of the double bind when he observes that

> Third World countries, with the exception of the more advanced among them, are indeed more often objects of this knowledge search than participants in it. Among the more important themes that a survey of the political culture of foreign area studies ought to explore are the causes and consequences of this uneven distribution of cosmopolitan knowledge—in particular, the relative absence of indigenous, and the relative dominance of, American investigators for developmental prospects in various parts of the world and for international affairs generally. This concentration of foreign area knowledge in the United States, and in the advanced countries generally, and the limited knowledge in Third World areas contributes to the weakness of these countries and to their inability to relate effectively to the forces of the outside world, to develop their own agendas, and to shape and implement their own goals effectively. From this point of view, the diffusion of social science competence and foreign area studies to the Third World must have a high priority.[32]

For part of the dilemma is precisely that as U.S. area studies becomes disseminated throughout the globe, either through policy-making or through the training of indigenous area experts by the U.S. academic industry, the inhabitants of these places are constitutively made to cathect the space of the world area, the space of the particularistic object of factual information, and are thus barred from genuine self-knowledge and self-determination. The problem is not necessarily solved by the fact that there are more and more Western-trained indigenous scholars based in their "home" areas and who write in the vernacular for local audiences.[33] This in itself—physical or geographical location—is no guarantee that the conceptual matrix distinguishing areas from the universal knowing subject of the disciplines and subordinating them to it will be overturned, that these indigenous scholars will cognize the places they both inhabit and study as something other than mere areas, others of the West. One would need to ask: who is this "they" (indigenous scholars) who have become much better at studying "themselves"? How is this "they" formed by the "we" of area studies' institutional origin, and how is this "they" constitutively constrained by its conceptual matrix?

For this conceptual positioning, which is more powerful than the physical or geographical location of the area scholar, informs

Asian studies in a very profound way. Regardless of how interdisciplinary or theoretically sophisticated Asian studies are or have become, they are always concerned with a bound object. Generally, their focus is information-retrieval and not theoretical reflection and speculation pertaining to the whole of humanity. To take the most obvious example, whereas a certain strand of Christian monotheism has been sublated into universal secular ethics as such after the European Enlightenment, the great religions of Asia have been *museumized* into mere markers of "cultural difference." Because these religions are considered as predating and deviating from the secular subject of universal reason, they have rarely been seriously studied as philosophies that can provide the bases for either a universalizable secular ethics or practical action in contemporary life. At best, they are studied as "ethno-philosophy" or celebrated as mystical "nativist" exceptions to the excessive rationality of modernity that leads to Weber's iron cage.

But in order to overturn this conceptual matrix, we need to understand more fully the schema through which the subject of universal knowledge becomes isomorphic with the West and all other regions become consigned to particularity. To this end, I want to turn to an exemplary text in the history of Western philosophy: Hegel's *Lectures on the Philosophy of World History*. It is my view that this text supplies the philosophical prototype for the conceptual matrix of area studies. Unless one is a fan of Francis Fukuyama, this text is not widely read today. If it is read, it is mainly read in an accusatory or diagnostic manner: Hegel's remarks about "the Oriental World" are denounced as the Eurocentric expression of the West's will to power over Asia. But if we temper our will to diagnose, then we will begin to realize how much the discursive formation of Asian studies inhabits the folds of Hegel's text.

Hegel's teleology of world history is designed to solve the problem of how to claim universal normativity for the actions of nation-states in view of the fact that international relations exist in a state of nature. In response to the ineluctable contingency of history, Hegel maps out a path of world-historical progress in which the spirit of a certain nation (*Volksgeist*) embodies the world spirit (*Weltgeist*) in a given epoch.[34] This nation is the bearer of world-historical progress. It will lead all other nations, and its actions will have universal normative force.

> The nation [*Volk*] to which such a moment is allotted as a *natural* principle is given the task of implementing this principle in the course of the self-development of the spirit's self-consciousness. This nation is the *dominant* one in world history for this epoch.... In contrast with this absolute right which it possesses as bearer of the present stage of the world spirit's development, the spirits of other nations are without rights, and they, like those whose epoch has passed, no longer count in world history.[35]

In Hegel's view, the German *Volksgeist* embodies the modern world spirit. For present purposes, two features of Hegel's argument are important: why he regards the German nation as the embodiment of the modern world spirit—and conversely, why the different nations of Asia no longer play a part in world-historical progress—and, consequently, the fate that befalls the latter in modernity.

For Hegel, "world history is the progress of the consciousness of freedom."[36] Hegel understands freedom in an ontological sense, as a self-determining consciousness, a form of conscious being (spirit or *Geist*) that knows itself as a universal being, and in this self-knowledge, is able to determine itself in accordance with universal ends, thereby actualizing its freedom through its own actions: "freedom in itself carries with it the infinite necessity of attaining consciousness—for freedom, by definition, is self-knowledge—and hence of realising itself: it is itself the end of its own operations, and the sole end of the spirit" (*PH*, 55). It follows from this ontological understanding of freedom that the bearer of freedom and the agent of world-historical progress is a *collective* form of self-consciousness. This is what Hegel calls objective spirit, which in the court of world history takes the shape of the nation (*Volk*).

But rational consciousness or spirit can only be genuinely free if it attains complete self-knowledge. This involves not only the knowledge of oneself as a universal being but also the knowledge that one is a free individual and that one's particular ends are not opposed to universal ends but instead can be achieved only through the pursuit of these universal ends as one's own ends. In other words, to embody freedom concretely, spirit must be aware that it is, in its own essence, free, and it must have this awareness of its freedom in the element of conceptual thought.

> The substance of the spirit is freedom. From this we can infer that its end in the historical process is the freedom of the subject to follow its own conscience and morality, and to pursue and implement its own universal ends; it also implies that the subject has infinite value and that it must become conscious of its own supremacy. The end of the world spirit is realised in substance through the freedom of each individual (*PH*, 55)

The realization of freedom thus involves spirit's gradual development into self-knowledge through various stages. What is important for us is that Hegel relates these different stages in the development of collective self-consciousness in world history to different types of national spirit, each with a finite life span. Thus, not only does he divide the development of world spirit into *distinct* temporal stages or epochs of the same historical process, he also correlates each of these epochs to a *bounded* and spatially localized configuration (*Gestaltung*) by arguing that in each epoch, there is one nation whose principle embodies the spirit of the age. These configurations are then designated as quasi-cartographical/seminatural realms or worlds (*Reich*).

> The spirits of nations are the links in the process whereby the spirit arrives at free recognition of itself. Nations, however, exist for themselves—for we are not concerned here with spirit in itself—and as such, they have a natural existence. Insofar as they are nations, their principles are natural ones; and since their principles differ, the nations themselves are also naturally different. Each has its own principle which it seeks to realise as its end; if it has attained this end, it has no further task to perform in the world (*PH*, 55)

It is this underlying spiritual principle that determines the character of each nation. Each national spirit tries to understand and develop its underlying principle into actuality through its actions, and the various spiritual and cultural products of each nation—its religion, arts, and knowledge—are the different intellectual means or media through which each nation seeks to understand itself.[37]

It is important to note at this point that Hegel's idea of national spirit is not a form of cultural nationalism as is conventionally assumed, but a type of constitutional patriotism.[38] For he repeatedly stresses that it is the state and its constitution that is the primary determinant and expression of the national spirit's underlying principle. As the objective existence of the unity between individual and universal ends, the state "is accordingly the basis and focus of the other concrete aspects of national life—of art, justice, ethics, religion, and science," whose end is to attain the consciousness of freedom (*PH*, 104).[39]

It follows from this that the various aspects of national life—all its cultural products and political institutions—are related to each other and articulated into an organized/organic whole, not because they are all uniform but because they are elaborations of the same underlying spiritual principle. In turn, these various aspects enable a nation to know itself.

> [T]here is...*one* principle basic to them all, the spirit of their determinate character which permeates every one of them. This principle is the nation's *self-consciousness*, the active force at work in the destinies of all nations. The various aspects of a nation's culture are the spirit's relationships to itself; it is the spirit which shapes the nations, and we can only know these relationships if we recognise the spirit itself. (*PH*, 102)

Now, for Hegel what distinguishes the Oriental *Volksgeist* or the various national self-consciousnesses of Asia from the Germanic *Volksgeist*—and what therefore makes the latter the bearer of world spirit in modernity—is that whereas the former does "not know that the spirit or man as such are free in themselves"; "the Germanic nations, with the rise of Christianity, were the first to realise that man is by nature free, and that freedom of the spirit is his very essence" (*PH*, 54).[40] Since freedom is the unity of universality and particularity, the consciousness of freedom involves, first and foremost, the transcendence [*Aufhebung*] of particularity.[41] Through this transcendence of one's particular limits, one attains a state of being that is universal. Thus, Hegel writes, "consciousness of freedom consists in the fact that the individual comprehends himself as a person, i.e., that he sees himself in his distinct existence as inherently universal, as capable of abstraction from and renunciation of everything particular, and therefore as inherently finite" (*PH*, 144).

When this definition of freedom as the transcendence of particularity and finitude is applied to the self-consciousness of entire peoples within world history, what we see is the alignment of spatial boundaries with finitude or the limits of contingent existence. Those nations whose self-consciousness do not include the knowledge of human freedom are therefore mired in an existence that always remains limited, bounded, and particularistic. They cannot step beyond these limits into universality. Since they cannot step outside their own limits, they cannot fully apprehend themselves as objects for themselves. This means that they also cannot fully know and understand themselves. Thus, Hegel writes that "the Chinese are not yet conscious of their own nature as free subjectivity" (*PH*, 121-22), and that India and China "are lacking—indeed completely lacking—in the essential consciousness of the concept of freedom" (*PH*, 145).[42]

But more importantly, their particularistic nature also means that these nations can only have a very limited life in world history. In the contemporary era, Hegel suggests, they are no longer active bearers of progress. Because they cannot fully know themselves, they can only continue to exist as static or frozen objects to be known by others. They are the living dead.[43] In contradistinction, "the nation whose concept of the spirit is highest is in tune with the times and rules over the others. It may well be that nations whose concepts are less advanced survive, but they exist only on the periphery of world history" (*PH*, 60). Consigned to the sidelines, what these Asian nations have achieved in their moments of past glory—their contributions to world history—become raw materials that can only be fully understood and retrieved by those who are capable of universality. Thus, Hegel notes that the Oriental world "can be likened to that of childhood in general" (*PH*, 202) and that "Asia is the continent of sunrise and of origins in general" (*PH*, 190).

Much of Hegel's argument is indeed offensive to our more enlightened sensibilities. Yet, it can be argued that the taken-for-granted boundedness of the areas of area studies corresponds in a very startling way to the particularism and finitude that Hegel sees as a mark of the self-consciousness of Asian nations. I am, of course, not suggesting that the historical establishment of area studies took Hegel's charting of world history as its blueprint. My point is that there is a strong isomorphism between Hegel's arguments and the logic of area studies. This isomorphism may exist because Hegel's ideas have gained an almost axiomatic status through intellectual-historical osmosis.

I have already rehearsed many of these points in my earlier discussion of area studies, so I will be telegraphic here. First, in their implied opposition to disciplines with a universal subject-matter, Asian studies are concerned with subject matters that are empirical rather than universal. (I am using "subject" in a triple sense: first, as "topic," which is also a spatial term; second, as a topographical area; and third, as an intending collective consciousness. In my view, all these senses are braided together in the *area* of area studies.) Second, Hegel's idea that all the cultural products and political institutions of a nation can be referred back to one basic principle is, of course, conceptually identical to the structural-functionalist idea of an interrelated whole that is so crucial to area studies.[44] Third, to say that these various empirical subject matters are attributes specific to the areas being studied implies that the collective self-consciousnesses inhabiting these areas are particularistic. Fourth, the reason these self-consciousnesses cannot transcend their respective areas is because they do not know their own bounds. Since their limits have to be conferred upon them by a knowing subject, these areas and their self-consciousnesses are objects to be known by others.

The above presuppositions are most concretely illustrated by two common facts: (1) in Asian studies, Asia is regarded as the inexhaustible source of raw materials to be retrieved through fieldwork and processed for publication by scholars who are generally based in the West; and (2) Even if the Asian studies scholar is of non-Western origin, he or she is usually a native informant who comes to the West to study his or her own area of origin, because it is only through the structures and methods of Western knowledge (to which is added "native" experience, which often makes for a shorter period of field-research) that he or she can come to view this area of origin as an object of thematic knowledge.[45] In other words, Asian studies presupposes that Asia can fully know itself only through the more developed structures of self-consciousness of the West. The Indonesian novelist, Pramoedya Ananta Toer, whose work I will discuss below, captures this nicely by having his protagonist, a native youth educated in a Dutch school in the East Indies at the turn of the century, exclaim, "Only through Europe can I know my own people."[46]

As I have already pointed out, the distinction between the particularistic self-consciousnesses of Asia and the universalistic self-consciousness of the West is also reproduced in the distinction between empirical and theoretical forms of knowledge that underwrites the division of intellectual labor separating Asian studies from disciplines concerned with universal truths and ideals.

Whereas philosophy and other forms of theoretical inquiry in the Western academy continue to formulate "fundamental" concepts largely by abstracting these from evidence confined to the sociohistorical situation of the North Atlantic, Asian studies have generally remained atheoretical precisely because they are by definition concerned with the specificity and particularity of Asian cultures. At the most, scholars in Asian studies try to find equivalents for concepts such as "civil society," "human rights," and "public sphere" (*Öffentlichkeit*) in Asian cultures. Following a well-known Freudian schema, this can be called civil-society envy, human-rights envy, public-sphere envy. Or else these scholars suggest that these concepts are not in fact applicable to Asian cultures. The alternatives therein represented are either the dogmatic application of an untested universalism or a dubious cultural relativism.

But the cultural relativist's mesmerizing focus on the uniqueness of Asia is haunted by the specter of the West. Because their claims of local uniqueness are the inverted mirror-image or phantom double of the universality claimed by the West, a relativistic Asian studies is a priori barred from access to universality. At the same time, Asian materials or data are ironically processed through the concepts and methodologies of (Western) theory, which remain dogmatically unquestioned. This means that Asian studies is in fact built upon the denegation (*Verneinung*) of the West qua universal. The situation is not remedied by a recent third alternative, formed from the intersection of Asian studies and East Asian governmental cultural policy. I am referring to the East Asian chauvinism, loosely based on a repackaged Confucianism that reverses Max Weber, which sees the rapidly developing nation-states of East Asia as embodiments of a superior ideal of capitalist development capable of reconciling modernization with Asian ideals of community. This is not really an alternative form of modernity, as some scholars claim, but a displaced repetition of the chauvinism of Eurocentric modernity. It is, in fact, an Asianized version of Hegel's end of history. Its dangerous consequences are apparent in its deployment by some Asian governments to circumvent humanitarian critiques. Moreover, this alternative has been rendered implausible by the current economic crises in East and Southeast Asia, which have shown us to what degree global economic hegemony is still centered in the North Atlantic.

II Universalizing Asia: The Example of Pramoedya Ananta Toer's Buru Quartet

I want to suggest that one way for Asian studies to escape the sterile polemics that pit cultural relativism against dogmatic universalism, or, which is not quite the same thing, empiricism against theory, is neither to denegate the universal nor to claim an alternative and usually antagonistic Asian modularity, but for Asian studies to claim that their subject is a *part* of the universal, not just as a check to a pre-formulated universal, but as something that actively *shares in* and *partakes of* the universal in a specific way. In other words, instead of viewing the various phenomena and experiences that are specific to Asia as marginal to universal history, which is today sometimes explicitly discredited and coded as the history of the North Atlantic, one might consider these phenomena and experiences *as though* they were universalizable, shareable with the whole of humanity. But then, the idea of the universal will have to be transformed in such a way that it is no longer viewed as superior or antithetical to what is culturally specific or particular. Specialized research on cultural matters in area studies rarely poses problems at this level because it has generally only either accepted or denegated the concept of universality as such, and never questioned it.

But what exactly is the universal, and why has the particular been placed in a subordinate relationship to the universal in the history of modern Western philosophy, and more specifically, in Hegel's philosophy of history, which I have suggested, is a philosophical prototype for the conceptual matrix of area studies? And more importantly, why and at what point does the relationship between universal and particular have privative or exclusionary historical implications such as those exemplified by Hegel's teleology of world history?

In the history of modern Western philosophy, universality has always been regarded as the overcoming of the contingency and the finitude of human existence. It is important to remember, however, that the terms *universal* (*allgemein*) and *particular* (*besonder*) do not always necessarily refer to practical actions, and, by implication, to the ability of any particular nation to represent the whole of humanity as the bearer of universal progress. Initially, these were primarily epistemological terms used to describe the nature of the validity of cognitive judgments. When one, following Kant, speaks of universal cognitions or cognitive judgments that possess universal validity, one is referring to knowledge that has unconditional validity or objective necessity, as opposed to cognitions derived solely from mere experience or sensible sensations which lack universality because they are only valid for the particular subject of that experience.[47] To produce universally valid empirical knowledge, one must *subsume* the particular in nature under the universal rule, principle, or law that is prescribed by our understanding.

The terms are, however, used in a practical sense in Rousseau's analysis of the tension and conformity between general and individual wills in the body politic and in Kant's definition of the moral will as one that is determined by the unconditionally or universally valid moral law in contrast to a will determined by subjective maxims which only have a conditional or contingent validity because they are derived from sensuous impulses or desires. Generally speaking, in ethical and political philosophy, the particular refers to that which is one-sided, subjective, self-interested, or tied to immediate sensuous impulses. The universal is opposed to interests and attributes, that are particular or specific to a certain person or group because these interests and attributes are contingent. Consequently, the particular needs to be transcended or subordinated to a general or universal end.

It is, however, important to note that Rousseau and Kant understood these terms differently. Whereas Rousseau, who was concerned with social and political duties, understood the distinction between universal and particular in terms of a tension between the particular will/private interests of the human individual and the general will/common interests of the citizen as a member of the state, Kant, who was more concerned with defining universally valid moral actions at the level of the individual, understood universal moral willing as the transcendence of the particularity of human existence, where particularity is synonymous with the contingency and finitude of sensuous existence.[48] Rousseau's use of the term *universal* is therefore political-organizational. For him, the tension between particular and general interests within a given polity would be resolved by constraining the individual to obey the general will.[49] In contradistinction, Kant's use of the term is ontological. A being with moral universality is a being whose existence is no longer contingent because it possesses rational necessity. Moral universality thus shares a common element with universality in the epistemological sense: both involve the cognitive operation whereby the particular is raised into universality by being subsumed under the latter.

What Hegel calls objective spirit can be understood as an articulation of *universal* in the politico-organizational sense with *universal* in the ontological sense. In his critique of the abstract nature of Kant's account of moral freedom, Hegel argued that in order to be meaningful, moral universality must also be concrete and actual (*wirklich*). In other words, universal moral action needs to be embedded in an actual political community in which the individual can achieve his particular ends only through the pursuit of universal-collective ends. The corollary to this is that it is only through this actual political community that one can transcend the finitude of one's individual existence. What interests us here is how Hegel characterizes the passage from the particular to the universal. My suggestion is that Hegel's philosophy of history has privative or exclusionary implications precisely because he understands the passage from particular to universal as a movement of sublation in which both terms become reconciled in an individual body.

Now, for Hegel, particularity refers to the moment when pure thinking of self—absolute abstraction or universality—is given concrete content, when the self understands that it is a determinate being: "Through this positing of itself as something *determinate*, 'I' steps into existence [*Dasein*] in general—the absolute moment of the finitude or particularization of the 'I'" (*PR*, § 6, 39). The genuinely free will, however, is a will that pursues aims that are at one and the same time both determinate (and, hence, particular) as well as capable of self-reflection (and, hence, universal). Thus, Hegel writes that

> the will is the unity of both these moments—*particularity* reflected *into itself* and thereby restored to *universality*. It is *individuality* [*Einzelheit*], the *self-determination* of the 'I,' in that it posits itself as the negative of itself, that is, as *determinate* and *limited,* and at the same time remains with itself [*bei sich*], that is, in its *identity with itself* and universality; and in this determination, it joins together with itself alone. (*PR*, § 7, 41)

The moment of individuality is, of course, central to the understanding of the state as the primary expression of the underlying principle of each national spirit. Individuality is that which gives coherence and totality to each national spirit, allowing each to be distinguished from the others. The point that I want to make here is that Hegel sees universality and particularity as related through the moment of individuality because like Kant, he regards the particular or the finite as something that needs to be transcended by thought in order to attain genuine universality.

But then any concrete universality formed by sublating the finite inevitably involves a certain violence precisely because universality is exclusively identified with a specific body, an individuality. Because particularity is understood as a negation of abstract universality, a negation that must in turn be negated and sublated to achieve genuine universality, this leads to the internment of universality within a specific body, which is now raised to the higher level of infinity. As we have seen, in any particular world-historical epoch, the specific body which is raised to the higher level of infinity is set apart from all other specific bodies that have not been able to transcend their particularity. This elevation of one individuality, one national spirit over all others, has obvious colonialist and imperialist implications. Indeed, in the introduction to the *Philosophy of Right*, Hegel automatically resorts to the metaphor of slavery as a counter-example when he attempts to illustrate what he means by a universal self-consciousness and a genuinely free will:

> This universality is such that the immediacy of the natural and the particularity with which the natural is likewise invested when it is produced by reflection are superseded within it. But this process, whereby the particular is superseded and raised to the universal is what is called the activity of thought. The self-consciousness that purifies and raises its object, content, and end to this universality does so as thought asserting itself in the will. Here is the point at which it becomes clear that it is only as thinking intelligence that the will is truly itself and

free. The slave does not know his essence, his infinity and freedom; he does not know himself as an essence—he does not know himself as such, for he does not think himself. (*PR*, § 21R, 52-53)

The same use of the slavery metaphor is also found in his philosophy of history:

The business of spirit is to produce itself, to make itself its own object, and to gain knowledge of itself; in this way, it exists for itself. Natural objects do not exist for themselves; for this reason, they are not free. The spirit produces and realises itself in the light of its knowledge of itself; it acts in such a way that all its knowledge of itself is also realised. Thus, everything depends on the spirit's self-awareness; if the spirit knows that it is free, it is altogether different from what it would be without this knowledge. For if it does not know that it is free, it is in the position of a slave who is content with his slavery and does not know that his condition is an improper one. It is the sensation of freedom alone that makes the spirit free, although it is in fact always free in and for itself. (*PH*, 48)

Consequently, in the Hegelian gallery of world history, nations, and indeed, realms, are judged and ranked according to their capacity for genuine self-consciousness. At the endpoint of history, one nation or realm, the one that has attained the highest level of self-consciousness—Germanic or American, depending on whether one is Hegel or Fukuyama, it doesn't matter which—will stand as the ultimate judge.

To reiterate, this is precisely the conceptual matrix governing the institutionalization of Asian studies. If Asia is universalized on this basis, we get something similar to the Confucian chauvinism I mentioned earlier. In contradistinction, the idea of universality that I think is able to accommodate a non-privative universalizing of Asia is one that is marked not by the transcendence of finitude but, instead, by a radical openness to finitude, which is to say, also a radical openness to contamination by alterity.

To give an illustration of this alternative, other understanding of universality, let me look briefly at Pramoedya Ananta Toer's Buru quartet, a series of novels about the Indies national awakening published in the late 1970s and early 1980s.[50] For present purposes, what is interesting about the quartet is its suggestion that the Indies national awakening, and not the Dutch colonial state, ought to be regarded as the inheritor of the European Enlightenment. What the quartet illustrates, I want to suggest, is a certain digestion of the universal in a specific territorial body. But, this digestion is not a sublation of that body's finitude. Consequently, at the same time that the universal is concrete and specific—it is *this* particular body—it also remains radically open to the possibility of being shared with other territorially located bodies.

The quartet contains repeated references to the French Revolution. But, in the second volume, entitled *Anak Semua Bangsa* (Child of All Nations) Minke, the protagonist and the founding father of the Indies awakening is presented with other non-European models of modernity: specifically, imperialist Japan and also anti-imperialist Republican China and the decolonizing Philippines.[51] The restless energy of this chain of liberatory events is now felt in the Indies, stimulating Minke's desire for modernity.[52] Indeed, the restlessness of modernity is infectious. Minke's desire to be modern is stimulated by a comparison between the Indies and other non-European models of modernity that results in feelings of shame and frustration at the backwardness of the Indies:

> I forced myself to think through on my own the connections between them all—Japan's advance, the anxieties/uneasiness of Young China, the native Filipino revolt against Spain and later the United States.... And with my inward eye I cast my gaze around my own milieu. Not the slightest trace of movement! They were still sunk happily in dreams. And I myself was bewildered, angry, in my powerless awareness/consciousness [*Dan aku sendiri pusing, geram, dengan kesedaran tanpa daya*]. (*ASB*, 86)

These repeated juxtapositions and comparisons cumulatively suggest that the newly-born nations of decolonizing Asia, and not the colonial state or the Dutch liberals, are the true heirs of the world-historical spirit of the French Revolution. In the fourth volume, *Rumah Kaca* (Glass House), Pangemanann, a Sorbonne-educated native official of the Dutch colonial state who is Minke's destroyer, gradually comes to the same view. In his eyes, the spontaneous native awakening against European capital becomes even more powerful than the revolt in France against Louis XVI.[53] Meanwhile, beyond the Indies, the Russian Revolution indicates the actualization of a new form of power that is seen as analogous to the *pergerakan* in the Indies.

This combination of political events within and beyond the Indies compels Pangemanann to admit that these native organizations, rather than the colonial state, are the true legatees of the ideal project of modernity:

> So it's clear that this new development is not for me an adversary. It is a development that is quite natural, even though its spread/multiplication is more passionate/fiery than anything Europe itself has experienced. With the possible exception of France on the eve of the Revolution. (*RK*, 321-22)

Indeed, Pangemanann suggests that Minke is no longer Javanese but European. Even if Minke has never studied European philosophy, as the first Javanese realist, he has inherited European philosophical ideals and methods through historical osmosis and activated them in his endeavours to foster an Indies nationalism:

> With his modicum of science and knowledge, he dreamed the rise of Indies nationalism without being able to comprehend its course. Here we have a Javanese Native, dressed in Javanese costume, who is absolutely no longer Javanese. *He is a European who founds his life on reason, not on Javanese illusions, and not on Javanism....*
>
> The man beside me is possibly the only Javanese Native who has shed all his illusions as a people and as an individual. With a scientific knowledge still far from adequate he is groping, scrabbling through every twig and blade of grass to awaken Indies nationalism.
>
> ...The person beside me also has a strength/might as awesome as the ocean's, as a volcano's. A Javanese who is not Javanese is none other than a revolutionary in this age in which I live. I know he never studied Western philosophy. Only the capital of healthy reason has proved capable of liberating him from atavism.
>
> It may be that he is the first Javanese realist. (*RK*, 305-6)

But this passage of the world-historical spirit of freedom from Europe to Asia is emphatically not the sublation that interns the universal in a specific body or individuality that we saw in Hegel's philosophy of history. The quartet's narrative logic is not dialectical but aporetic. Nothing evokes the failure of dialectical sublation as suggestively as the role of Nyai Ontosoroh at the end of the narrative. Nyai Ontosoroh is Minke's spiritual mother (*ibu rohani*). The final volume of the quartet sees her reincarnated as Madame Sanikem Le Boucq, a legal resident of France, now married to Jean Marais alias Le Boucq, the French painter who fought as a mercenary in the Dutch Indies and was later a friend of Minke. A representative of the ideals of the French Revolution now embodied in a modern native person, Sanikem returns to the Indies to search for Minke and to judge Pangemanann for betraying his vocation as a person of education. Sanikem is the personification of the national spirit of modern Indonesia. As the recipient of Minke's manuscripts, she is also the trustee of its future. What her actions signify is that the future of the Indonesian nation can only be secured from outside the colonial world: in France, the nation where modern freedom was first born. But—another aporia—since the spirit of modern freedom was also betrayed by French colonialism in Indochina, Algeria, etc., it can only live on in the future of the Indonesian nation whose agent is—yet another aporia—the modern native expatriate.

The nation *qua* embodiment of universal freedom thus lives on abroad, so to speak, awaiting to be returned to itself, that is to say, repatriation. But meanwhile, it lives on uncannily (*unheimlich*), from outside its own home. At an even more mundane level, this aporia is played out by the fact that Pramoedya's own writings are banned in Indonesia and are only accessible to Indonesian readers through Malaysian imprints and English translations, as well as reviews and critical studies by commentators outside Indonesia.[54] This aporetic expatriation, I want to suggest, indicates a sharing/partaking of universality between the specific bodies of Europe (France) and Asia (the Indies/Indonesia). This means that universality is neither a static ideal of reason nor a self-conscious individuality. Instead, it is in this interminable movement of sharing between specific territorial bodies or areas that universality becomes articulated and redefined again and again.

Or better yet, universality *is* nothing other than this interminable movement of sharing. For is not this radical openness to finitude and to contamination by alterity the very "essence" of universality, the being-universal of the universal? In the obvious instance, for a given issue to be worthy of the epithet "universal," it ought to be able to accommodate every single particular example. More importantly, however, the universal must always show itself in a particular example. This is especially true of concrete or actual universality, since a concrete universal must have *exemplary* status. Yet, since to be exemplary is by definition to be both unique and also repeatable (insofar as an example is an example of some 'X' that can have other examples), any concrete universal gives itself to be inscribed in an endless series of sensible particulars. In other words, a concrete universal is constitutively open to being affected by other particulars and, hence, by alterity and particularity in general. This radical openness to alterity and particularity is a type of finitude that cannot be transcended. The relationship between universality and particularity that is implied here is therefore not the internment of universality within the proper body of an individuality but one in which a given particular answers to the call of universality in its unique way and, in so doing, remains open to other, equally singular responses to the universal. As Jacques Derrida puts it,

> the value of universality...must be linked to the value of *exemplarity* that inscribes the universal in the proper body of a singularity, of an idiom or a culture, whether this singularity be individual, social, national, state...or not. Whether it takes a national form or not, a refined, hospitable, or aggressively xenophobic form or not, the self-affirmation of an identity always claims to be responding to the call or assignation of the universal. There are no exceptions to this law. No cultural identity presents itself as the opaque body of an untranslatable idiom, but always, on the contrary, as the irreplaceable *inscription* of the universal in the singular, and the *unique testimony* to the human essence and to what is proper to man. Each time, it has to do with the discourse of *responsibility*: I have, the unique "I" has, the responsibility of testi-

fying for universality. Each time, the exemplarity of the example is unique. That is why it can be put into a series and formalized into a law.[55]

Envoi: The Universalization of Areas in Contemporary Globalization

The responsibility for testifying for the universality of each unique territorial body, each culture, and each area, is no longer a mere ethical ideal in the same way that for Marx, the global spread of capital made cosmopolitanism a material reality in 1848. Responding to the call of the universal is now an urgent imperative, because the division of intellectual labor between universal and particular knowledges, the theoretical disciplines and area studies, has become obsolete in contemporary globalization. The heightened interaction between nation-states and cultures in contemporary globalization has generated a discontinuous field of overlapping and contested universal areas.

To take Southeast Asia as a concrete example, the intensified integration of Southeast Asia by regional and global forces makes it imperative to study "Southeast Asia" as a regional entity and an important part of a shrinking world. Labor migration and foreign investment already link Southeast Asian nations. As these nations move towards the formation of an ASEAN Free Trade Area, official visions of an ASEAN consciousness, whether or not they reflect popular opinion, already abound. Moreover, the region is attracting growing attention in the spheres of world political economy and international politics.[56] Not only is Southeast Asia the destination of foreign capital from the industrialized North; it is also the source of capital flows to Africa, Latin America, the Caribbean and other parts of Asia. Before the financial crash of 1997, Malaysia and Singapore were increasingly regarded as alternative models of economic development through the attraction of foreign investment by many countries in the South.[57] But they and other Southeast Asian nations are also exemplary in the aftermath of the crash for the ways in which they have attempted to cope with the dangers of global financialization.

The challenge that lies ahead for Asian studies is to exorcize the spectre of a specifically Western universality so that they can be spectralized by the call of the universal as such. It is to develop new conceptual perspectives that will enable us to understand the impact of these globalizing/regionalizing processes on local cultures and vice versa, without sacrificing the specialist expertise and loving attention to languages and local detail that is the enduring strength of area studies. This involves a double imperative: on the one hand, from the side of Asian studies, the imperative is to treat these experiences as universalizable, shareable with everyone else—in a word, as translatable. On the other hand, what is now commonly regarded as the universal as such—the ethical concepts and normative ideals of contemporary (Western) theory—ought to be opened up by "a strategy without finality, what might be called a blind tactics, or empirical wandering" into spaces with social and political histories that are different from the North Atlantic, "if the value of empiricism did not itself acquire its entire meaning in its opposition to philosophical responsibility."[58] With this double imperative, the universal may at last become particularized into areas that possess historical effectivity at the same time as these particular areas become universalized.

Endnotes

1—For a lucid account and response by a Southeast Asianist to some recent debates on the obsolescence of area studies among area-research foundation donors, see O. W. Wolters, 'Regional Studies' in the 1990's," in O. W. Wolters, *History, Culture, and Region in Southeast Asian Perspectives* (Ithaca, New York: Cornell South East Asia Program, 1999), 206-225. I thank Carol Hau for alerting me to the existence of this article.

2—Cf. Arjun Appadurai, *Modernity at Large: Cultural Dimensions of Globalization* (Minneapolis: University of Minnesota Press, 1996), 16:

> There has not yet been a sustained critical analysis of the link, in the United States, between the emergence of the idea of culture areas in anthropology between the World Wars and the full-fledged formation after World War II of area studies as the major way to look at the strategically significant parts of the developing world. Yet there is little doubt that both perspectives incline one to a particular sort of map in which groups and their ways of life are marked by differences of culture, and in the area-studies formation these differences slide into a topography of national cultural differences. Thus geographical divisions, cultural differences,

and national boundaries tended to become isomorphic, and there grew a strong tendency to refract world processes through this sort of national-cultural map of the world. Area studies adds to this spatial imaginary a strong, if sometimes tacit, sense of the strategic importance of information gained from this perspective.

3—For a historical account of the gradual evolution of area studies in the U.S. from 1810 to 1966, see Robert A. McCaughey, *International Studies and Academic Enterprise: A Chapter in the Enclosure of American Learning* (New York: Columbia University Press, 1984). I cannot emphasize enough that my generalizations on the relationship between area studies and the disciplines in this essay refer exclusively to area studies in the U.S. and do not necessarily hold for academic institutions in Europe, Asia, Africa, or Latin America.

4—Ibid., xi-xii, emphasis added.

5—"The West" is primarily "the North Atlantic," i.e., North America and Western Europe. Eastern European studies is subjected to an analogous form of marginalization, but not to the same degree as Asian studies. These countries are considered as areas of Europe that do not have access to world history or do not give rise to (world-historical) structures of civil society, partly because these structures, which may have existed before, have been decimated by Communism. The fall of the "Eastern" bloc is then coded as their rejoining of or reintegration by the world-historical Western Europe. The governing principle is consanguinity rather than linguistic differences, since French, German, and Italian are also foreign languages in stubbornly monolingual mainstream America. This may be why McCaughey makes the interesting observation that studies of classical Greece are not part of area studies "on the ground that it is about the beginnings of the West and its cultural legacy," but that studies of modern Greece are, "on the ground that it is part of the Balkans region and is therefore properly included among the countries making up Eastern Europe." (ibid., xii) Apart from the fact that this mythology of the origins of America is highly questionable, it is also unclear whether contemporary Americans have a deeper epistemological affinity with or natural interest in classical Greece than with, say, contemporary Japan or Zaire. The current interest in *Pokemon* would suggest otherwise. As I will argue later, this conceptualization of *area* as that which is not part of the makeup of the knowing subject necessarily places area studies in a subordinate position vis-à-vis the disciplines.

6—Preface, *The Non-Western World in Higher Education*: *The Annals of the American Academy of Political and Social Science*, (November 1964): ix.

7—Ibid.

8—Ibid.

9—Charles Wagley, *Area Research and Training: A Conference Report on the Study of World Areas*, Social Science Research Council, Pamphlet 6 (June 1948), 49.

10—Julian H. Steward, *Area Research: Theory and Practice*, Social Science Research Council, Bulletin 63 (1950), 7

11—Milton Singer, "The Social Sciences in Non-Western Studies," in Donald Bigelow and Lyman Legters (eds.), *The Non-Western World in Higher Education*, 33. Singer is an area studies practitioner rehearsing arguments against his area studies. He goes on to observe that "in the 1940's our resistance to 'non-Westernization' sprang from our doubts about the availability of materials that would meet our standards of scholarship, as well as doubts about our own qualifications to deal with the newer areas. I think, too, that we were far more interested in the American and European scene than in the non-Western areas of Asia and Africa. But some of us did go on to develop serious interests in those areas," 33-34.

12—See Julian H. Steward, *Area Research: Theory and Practice*, 151-52:

Area phenomena are interrelated in the context of a structured whole. The characteristics of the whole—the patterns of economic, social, religious, political, esthetic, and other special aspects of behavior—are determined by cultural heritage, but they are interrelated within the framework of particular societies. The unit of area study therefore must be a sociocultural whole or system.

The concept of the sociocultural whole would seem to be essential to any interdisciplinary area research. The concept of the culture area has limited value, for it is based on regularities that occur among different societies in a particular area. The heterogeneous institutions and behavior patterns of any culture have a functional interdependence and reciprocity only within particular societies. As the institutions and special patterns of behavior constitute the subject matter of different disciplines, particularly in the more complex societies, the concept of the sociocultural system is the only conceivable frame of reference for interdisciplinary area research.

The concept of the sociocultural system does not of itself constitute a guide for any area research. It is simply an elucidation of the idea that area phenomena are interrelated in some sort of coherent way. Each area has its distinctive tradition and organization, which is expressed by the concept of cultural relativity. Moreover, within the cultural tradition of each area, sociocultural systems have developed through a succession of levels, each higher level being not only more complex than the lower but qualitatively different in that it has characteristics that were not evident in antecedent patterns. Finally, each sociocultural system has become increasingly linked with other systems. Area research problems and methods therefore must be adapted to the society's unique cultural patterns, to its level of development or organization, and to its dependency relations with other societies. In short, the phenomena studied by the different disciplines must be interrelated within the context of a whole, which has a sufficient degree of structural and functional unity to have some cohesion.

13—Edward Said, *Orientalism* (Harmondsworth: Penguin, 1978), 12.

14—Ibid., 300-25. The quotation is from p. 325. Said refers especially to work on the Middle East by Anwar Abdel Malek, Yves Lacoste, Noam Chomsky, and the Middle East Research and Information Project (MERIP).

15—This seems to be the general argument of Vicente L. Rafael, "The Cultures of Area Studies in the United States," *Social Text* 41 (1994): 91-111.

16—See, for instance, Charles Wagley, *Area Research and Training: A Conference Report on the Study of World Areas*, 8:

Area studies also have practical objectives. A considerable stimulus was given to area study during World War II. The wartime needs of our government and our armed forces for information regarding foreign areas and their people and for qualified personnel able to deal with people whose language and culture are different from our own especially urgent. The same needs are of even more crucial importance in this postwar period when international understanding—not military intelligence—is the goal. The kind of knowledge required concerning such areas and their people must be more profound than that which would suffice for military purposes. The roles of such areas as the Slavic countries, India, the Middle East, China, and Indonesia, for example, as important factors in the postwar international scene make it imperative that we have an economic, political, and cultural understanding of their peoples. Thus area studies are not to be regarded as military preparation for war, and the fact that some knowledge so gained can be useful in war, is not pertinent to this discussion. Such knowledge is just as necessary for international cooperation between peoples of very diverse values, ideologies, and objectives as it is for effective international competition....

Furthermore, the role of leadership in world affairs which the United States has assumed makes it obligatory that we develop our resources of science and scholarship for the peaceful conduct of international affairs.
Cf. Wendell C. Bennett, *Area Studies in American Universities*, (June 1951), 3: "[A]side from the traditional function of research training, the universities may be called upon to meet the increasing government needs for area personnel and special area training. Many government agencies are now involved in programs dealing with foreign fields. For the determination of policy and for the planning of these programs, these agencies require the services of highly trained area scholars familiar with research findings in all fields of study. Moreover, for the execution of these programs the government agencies must have numerous specialists...who have a practical working knowledge of the area concerned." (*Area Studies in American Universities* was a publication of the Social Science Research Council).

17—Said, *Orientalism*, 32.

18—Charles Wagley, *Area Research and Training: A Conference Report on the Study of World Areas*, 8-9. The quotation marks indicate Wagley's reporting of Ephraim Speiser's observations at the conference.

19—Wendell Bennett, *Area Studies in American Universities*, 4. Cf. Lucian Pye, "The Confrontation between Discipline and Area Studies," in Lucian W. Pye (ed.), *Political Science and Area Studies: Rival or Partners?* (Bloomington, Indiana: University of Indiana Press, 1975), 9: "The fact that American universities have universally agreed that after the master's degree all advanced work must be associated with a degree in a traditional discipline is generally translated in the minds of students to mean that disciplinary work is intellectually superior to area-oriented work. Therefore, some students fear that if they are overly tainted with an area specialization it may suggest to others that they are academically inferior to the regular student."

20—Benedict Anderson, "Politics and their Study in Southeast Asia," *Southeast Asian Studies: Options for the Future*, (ed.) Ronald A. Morse (Washington D.C.: Lanham, University Press of America, Asia Center, 1984), 42.

21—Lucian Pye, "The Confrontation between Discipline and Area Studies," 5-6.

22—See Harry Eckstein, "A Critique of Area Studies from a West European Perspective," in Lucian W. Pye (ed.), *Political Science and Area Studies: Rival or Partners?* (Bloomington, Indiana : University of Indiana Press, 1975), 205:

> In studies of alien societies the most obviously indispensable requisites are language and some modicum of factual, not least historical, knowledge... From the outset, therefore, programs in non-Western studies, even if principally intended for social scientific research, had to take on the internal contours of the humanistic fields, or tended naturally to do so. It happens that the internal divisions in these fields are principally geographic, simply because languages, cultures and histories differ along geographic lines. In the sciences the more "natural" division of labor is by general types of phenomena or problems, since their aim is "extensive" knowledge (nomothetic generalization); in the humanities divisions by cultural and historical entities are more apropos, since their object is "intensive knowledge" (particular "understanding"). The division of non-Western studies by geographic areas can thus be seen, in the first instance, as an outcome of the central role that linguists and historians had to play in them.

23—See George E. Taylor, "The Leadership of the Universities," in Donald Bigelow and Lyman Legters (eds.), *The Non-Western World in Higher Education*, 3:
> Theories about man and his behavior should be tested through study of man in all the rich fullness of his experience. At the same time, the growth of new conceptual tools in the

social sciences, the trend towards empirical research methods, and the strong influence of positivism explain in some measure a tendency to underrate the contributions already made by the humanists to the understanding of the rest of the world and a reluctance to believe that acceptable data could be drawn from the ancient societies of Asia and Africa. The social scientist had to have modern, not classical languages; fieldwork, not travelogues; translations, not philosophical treatises; and above all, trustworthy statistics. There was an appreciation of the desirability of universal data but sufficient skepticism of the possibility of acquiring it to discourage investment in language-learning.

24—This, for instance, is Lucian Pye's point. See "The Confrontation between Discipline and Area Studies," 6:

> The dilemma of the general and the particular in science became the source of increasing strain as the essentially Eurocentric social sciences sought to become truly global. Evidence of the inherent Western parochialism of much of contemporary social science can be found in the standard practice of giving universal, mankind-wide titles to studies based on European or American data while expecting a limiting designation for comparable studies focusing on some other part of the world. A study of, say, voting behavior or legislative practices conducted in America is normally given a title which would suggest a general investigation of the topic, while such a study carried out in an Asian or African country would almost invariably be given a title that would reveal its specific aspects.

25—Charles Wagley, *Area Research and Training: A Conference Report on the Study of World Areas*, 5.

26—Ibid., 9, 48.

27—George E. Taylor, "The Leadership of the Universities," 9.

28—Ibid.

29—Charles Wagley, *Area Research and Training: A Conference Report on the Study of World Areas*, 6-7. The sentences in quotation marks are from Pendleton Herring of the Carnegie Corporation.

30—Immanuel Kant, *Critique of Pure Reason*, trans. and ed. Paul Guyer and Allen W. Wood (Cambridge: Cambridge University Press, 1997), A 11-12, 149: "I call all cognition transcendental that is occupied not so much with objects but rather with our mode of cognition of objects insofar as this is to be possible a priori."

31—H. J. Morgenthau, "International Relations as an Academic Discipline," *The Decline of Democratic Politics* (Chicago: University of Chicago Press, 1962), cited in Milton Singer, "The Social Sciences in Non-Western Studies," 42.

32—Gabriel Almond, "The Political Culture of Foreign Area Research: Methodological Reflections," in *The Political Culture of Foreign Area and International Studies: Essays in Honor of Lucian W. Pye*, (eds.), Richard J. Samuels and Myron Weiner (Washington D.C.: Brassey's, 1992), 200.

33—This is the optimistic solution proposed by many prominent Southeast Asian scholars such as James C. Scott, Charles F. Keyes, Benedict Anderson, and Charles Hirschmann in their contributions to *Southeast Asian Studies in the Balance: Reflections from America*, (eds.) Charles Hirschmann, Charles F. Keyes and Karl Hutterer (Ann Arbor: Association of Asian Studies, 1992). See especially Anderson's contribution, "The Changing Ecology of Southeast Asian Studies in the United States, 1950-1990," 36:

> [T]here exists today in Southeast Asia a group of people who did not exist in late colonial times: a substantial indigenous academic and non-academic intelligentsia....Most are civil servants, and all, to different extents, understand their work as most relevant to a specific country (Burma, Indonesia, the Philippines), and to a lesser degree, its neighbors. They are area studies people ipso facto. They are immersed in the local

culture, are fluent in local vernaculars, and have direct access to local religious life, folk traditions, and often, pre-twentieth-century literatures. But they are also, many of them, familiar in differing degrees with the work being published on their countries in the US, England, Australia, Holland and Japan....[P]erhaps we can take advantage of an inevitable division of labor, working more intelligently than we have done hitherto to interact cooperatively with the world of Southeast Asian scholarship in the humanities and social sciences.

34—Hegel's argument is that world history is the unfolding or the incarnation of world spirit (*Weltgeist*) in finite form. But because world spirit unfolds in finitude, it must take the form of a national spirit (*Volksgeist*). The norms of a world-historical nation coincide with the direction of world-historical progress, and these norms retain their universal validity in later stages of development. Such world-historical norms cannot be revoked even though they can be modified.

35—G. W. F. Hegel, *Elements of the Philosophy of Right*, trans. H. B. Nisbet and ed. Allen W. Wood (Cambridge: Cambridge University Press, 1991), § 347, 374. Hereafter referred to as *PR*.

36—G. W. F. Hegel, *Lectures on the Philosophy of World History: Introduction*, trans. H. B. Nisbet (Cambridge: Cambridge, University Press, 1980), 54. This text is a translation of the first volume of Johannes Hoffsmeister's 1955 edition in two volumes. Hereafter *PH*.

37—In philosophical terms, the underlying principle is the content, and the various spiritual powers are the various forms this content assumes. These various forms make up the culture of the nation. See *PH*, 96-97: "A nation should therefore be regarded as a spiritual individual, and it is not primarily its external side that will be emphasised here, but rather what we have previously called the spirit of the nation, i.e., its self-consciousness in relation to its own truth and being, and what it recognises as truth in the absolute sense—in short, those spiritual powers which live within the nation and rule over it. The universal which emerges and becomes conscious within the state, the *form* to which everything in it is assimilated, is what we call in general the nation's *culture*. But the determinate *content* which this universal form acquires and which is contained in the concrete reality which constitutes the state is the *national spirit* itself."

38—For a succinct critique of the myth that Hegel is a cultural nationalist, see Shlomo Avineri, "Hegel and Nationalism," *Review of Politics* 24 (1962): 461-82.

39—Cf. *PH*, 93: "The state is the reality within which the individual has and enjoys his freedom, but only in so far as he knows, believes in, and wills the universal. This, then, is the focal point of all the other concrete aspects of the spirit, such as justice, art, ethics, and the amenities of existence. Within the state, freedom becomes its own object and achieves its positive realization."

40—For Hegel's description of the Germanic people as the bearers of the spirit of modernity, see, for instance, *PR*, § 358.

41—"[S]pirit, in its consciousness of itself, is free; in this realisation, it has overcome the limits of temporal existence and enters into relationship with pure being, which is also its own being" (*PH*, 53).

42—This lack of complete self-consciousness leads to partial and truncated development. See *PH*, 102: "[T]here are nations in which many arts have attained a high degree of perfection, as in China and India. But although the Chinese invented gunpowder, they did not know how to use it, while the Indians produced superb gems of poetry without any corresponding advances in art, freedom, and law."

43—They are literally zombies or the living dead. The universal Life of the concept has passed on into a higher sphere:

> The natural death of the national spirit may take the form of political stagnation, or what we call habit...The clock

is wound up and runs on automatically. Habit is an activity with nothing to oppose it; it retains only the formal property of temporal continuity.... It is, so to speak, a superficial and sensuous kind of existence whose profounder significance has been forgotten. Thus both individuals and nations die a natural death. And even if the latter live on, their existence is devoid of life and interest; their institutions have become superfluous, because the needs which created them have been satisfied, and nothing remains but political stagnation and boredom...In a moribund state such as this, a nation may even prosper, although it no longer participates in the life of the Idea. It then serves as material for a higher principle, and becomes the province of another nation in which a higher principle is active. (*PH*, 59-60)

44—Even in an area like Southeast Asia, where it is difficult to point to any distinct organic totality (since its cultures are historically derivative, hybrid, and lack opulent classical traditions and a core civilization), some kind of organizational coherence is always found. The coherence of Southeast Asia is either understood as coming artificially from the outside, i.e., through the encounter with colonialism in general, or "hybridity" becomes the underlying principle of the region's religious practices and its other cultural forms and spiritual powers.

45—It is probable that many Chinese, Indian etc. graduate students who become China-, India-, etc. specialists in the West would not have done so if they had remained in their countries of origin.

46—Pramoedya Ananta Toer, *Anak Semua Bangsa* (Kuala Lumpur: Wira Karya, 1982), 164, my translation.

47—Kant, *Critique of Pure Reason*, A 1-2, 127: "[Experience] tells us, to be sure, what is, but never that it must necessarily be thus and not otherwise. For that very reason it gives no true universality.... Now, such universal cognitions, which at the same time have the character of inner necessity, must be clear and certain for themselves, independently of experience; hence one calls them *a priori* cognitions." In the Third Critique, Kant also uses *universal* and *particular* to classify the types of laws we formulate in our cognition of the external world. He draws a distinction between the universal transcendental laws governing the possibility of nature as such, as an object of the senses given by the understanding and the particular empirical laws or contingent regularities that seem to issue from nature as a manifold. See Kant, *Critique of Judgment*, trans. Werner Pluhar (Indianapolis: Hackett, 1987), 18-19, Ak. 179-80.

48—See Jean-Jacques Rousseau, *The Social Contract*, in *The Social Contract and other Later Political Writings*, trans. and ed. Victor Gourevitch (Cambridge: Cambridge University Press, 1997), 52: "[E]ach individual may, as a man, have a particular will contrary to or different from the general will he has as a Citizen. His particular interest may speak to him quite differently from the common interest[.]" Also Kant, *Critique of Practical Reason*, trans. Lewis White Beck (New York: Macmillan, 1956), 89, Ak. 86: "[The moral law] cannot be less than something which elevates man above himself as a part of the world of sense, something which connects him with an order of things which only the understanding can think and which has under it the entire world of sense."

49—See Rousseau, *The Social Contract*, 53.

50—The four volumes of the quartet in chronological order are Pramoedya Ananta Toer, *Bumi Manusia* (Kuala Lumpur: Wira Karya, 1981); *Anak Semua Bangsa* (Kuala Lumpur: Wira Karya, 1982); *Jejak Langkah* (Kuala Lumpur: Wira Karya, 1986); *Rumah Kaca* (Kuala Lumpur: Wira Karya, 1988). The English translation of the first two books has been published in a volume entitled *Awakenings*, trans. Max Lane (Victoria, Australia: Penguin, 1991); *Footsteps*, trans. Max Lane (Victoria, Australia: Penguin, 1990); *House of Glass*, trans. Max Lane (Victoria, Australia: Penguin, 1992). Unfortunately, Max Lane has omitted sentences and sometimes entire paragraphs from his translations. Since it is not possible to assume that these omissions are always insignificant, I will be quoting from the Malay editions of the second and fourth volumes, hereafter referred to as *ASB* and *RK*, respectively. Translations of *ASB* are mine, and translations of *RK* are by Benedict Anderson, whom I am indebted to for correcting my translations.

51—Khouw Ah Soe, a revolutionary youth, is the personification of the nationalist youth movement in China and a model of emulation for Minke: "Learn from ... another way of thinking, one that is not European" (*ASB*, 70). He is the first to bring the example of the Philippines to Minke's attention, describing the Philippines as a world-historical example for all colonised peoples in Asia: "The Philippines is the head-teacher for all colonized nations in Asia. It established the first Asian republic. It fell. A world-historical attempt" (*ASB*, 81). Minke also learns the importance of publishing to the life of a movement from him: "In the modern age, there is no [national] movement without its own press" (*ASB*, 61).

52—Khouw Ah Soe observes that the awakening of each Asian country will have a cumulative effect on other Asian nations: "Each Asian country that begins to arise/rise up does not simply rouse itself, it also helps other peoples in the same fated backwardness to arise—including my own country." (*ASB*, 80)

53—"The State which represents Europe now faces a product of exactly that Europe: a nationalism which awakens and bursts forth.... Educated, scientific Europe, teacher of a new civilization, is now confronted by its own student, the Native, who has more will than scientific knowledge—but a will to become a new bangsa.... Disturbances/riots are occurring wherever giant European capital is planted, perhaps even more violent than those in France against Louis XVI" (*RK*, 285, emphasis added).

54—As far as I am aware, the first extensive book-length study of Pramoedya is A. Teeuw's *Pramoedya Ananta Toer: De verbeelding van Indonesië* (De Geus: Breda, 1993). Most of Pramoedya's works are published in Bahasa Malaysia (which is slightly different from Bahasa Indonesia) by the Kuala Lumpur-based publishing house, Wira Karya, run by Jomo Sundaram, a Harvard trained professor of political science at the University of Malaya. The English translation of the Buru quartet was first published by Penguin Australia. The Cornell University-based specialist journal, *Indonesia*, is the most important source for English translations of Pramoedya's shorter fiction and non-fiction prose as well as a continuing forum for critical writing on Pramoedya.

55—Jacques Derrida, *The Other Heading: Reflections on Today's Europe*, trans. Pascale-Anne Brault and Michael B. Naas (Bloomington: Indiana University Press, 1992), 72-73.

56—See Charles F. Keyes, "A Conference at Wingspread and Rethinking Southeast Asian Studies," in *Southeast Asian Studies in the Balance: Reflections from America*, 14: "International political economists have also begun to recognize Southeast Asia as an important setting for research into both the rapidly growing national economies in the region and the comparative impacts of foreign and domestic investments in those economies."

57—See, for instance, Linda Lim, "Foreign Investment, the State, and Industrial Policy in Singapore," and Chris Edwards, "East Asia and Industrial Policy in Malaysia: Lessons for Africa?", both in *Asian Industrialization and Africa: Studies in Policy Alternatives to Structural Adjustment*, ed. Howard Stein (New York: St. Martin's Press, 1995), 205-38, and 239-56, respectively.

58—Jacques Derrida, *Margins of Philosophy*, trans. Alan Bass (Chicago: University of Chicago Press, 1982), 7.

DISLOCATION OF THE WEST AND THE STATUS OF THE HUMANITIES[1]

Naoki SAKAI

I do not believe that I am the only one who has, at one time or another, pondered over the absence of any serious attempts to build ethnic-study programs dealing with Americans whose ancestors came from Europe. Why are there no urgent demands from the European Americans for European American Studies programs at universities and colleges in the United States? Why does knowledge about institutions and cultural accomplishments, which European immigrants and their successors have contributed to the well-being of the nation-state of the United States of America, not constitute an academic domain which is legitimated in terms of ethnicity?

One might think of a number of possible explanations: the European Americans compose the majority in the United States, and, the word ethnicity, is customarily not applied to the majority population. The establishment of European American Studies programs would then urge us to introduce a drastic change in our use of the term ethnicity. Or, some might point out that, since most of the human and social sciences, as they are institutionalized and practiced in higher education in the United States (with certain reservations concerning local differences, the same may be said about Western European institutional practice, as well as that in East Asia and almost everywhere else in the world today) were brought about by Europeans and their descendants, European American Studies would engulf the majority, if not the entirety, of existing fields in the humanities and social sciences. Except for certain disciplines such as ethnic studies and area-studies, some might argue, the humanities are already European American studies, instituted and still maintained mostly by European Americans themselves. The difference is in the fact that, whereas ethnic and area-studies are marked by particular ethnic names and the place-names of regions, the humanities in general are unmarked, just as European Americans are the unmarked majority in the United States. Instead of delimiting the scope of the discipline in terms of the particular identity or residential area of the people to be studied, the humanities, or the sciences of man, focus on certain general aspects of humanity in such a way that psychology and ethics, for instance, deal respectively with the "universal" psychic and ethical natures of the human being in general. In contrast, ethnic and area-studies are constituted with a view to having particular sectors of humanity as their objects of study.

Strangely enough, however, Romance and German studies are seemingly well-equipped to deal with particular regions and groups in Europe, but we do not mention them as typical of area or ethnic studies in the U.S. today. As I ponder this question, I see more and more irregularities as well as a sedimentation of historical accidents in the increasingly messy configuration of the "humanities."

I do not believe that I can present hard-and-fast rules for why there cannot be an ethnic studies program devoted to European Americans. In fact, I would not be surprised if such a program suddenly cropped up. Yet I also predict that any attempt to posit the European Americans as an object of ethnic study would meet resistance. And this probable resistance has a lot to do with a peculiar imaginary construct called the West.

It is a peculiar construct because, in the first place, "the West" may appear to be the name of a certain geographical place and by extension of the people inhabiting it. On the somewhat strained assumption that the West is a primarily geographic designation with fairly clear contours, the West could regulate our way of representing the production of knowledge, particularly in the humanities. But I do not believe that the West is either a geographic territory with an affiliated population, or a unified cultural and social formation. As I will discuss later, it is only our essentialist insistence upon its geographic and cultural uniformity that evokes the putative unity of the West.

The unity of the West seems to bestow a sense of coherence upon the configuration of disciplines in the humanities. It serves to mark a distinction between the areas and peoples that can be objects of ethnic and area-studies and those that cannot. People in the West ordinarily do not receive the attribute "ethnic," because, supposedly, they are not to be defined in terms of their status as an object of study: before being studied, known, and recognized, they are expected to take an active attitude in studying, knowing, and recognizing. Instead of being passively inspected, classified, compared, and analyzed, they are supposed to engage in applying their own means of inspection, classification, comparison, and analysis to some object, which might well be themselves. When a group of people are characterized exclusively in their communal mores and local histories—as was recently exemplified in countless articles and photographs placing refugees in the former Yugoslavia—correspondingly, they are often deprived of their subjective faculties; they are demoted to ethnicity and treated as though they were mute, passive and anonymous objects of the West's observing gaze —even if the samples are taken from within Europe. In short, in this epistemic transaction, the West insists on being determined in terms not of its characteristics as an object of knowledge but rather of its subjective faculties and productivity.

Accordingly, we could discern two radically different ways for people to relate themselves to the production of knowledge in the humanities. The group of people whose regional, civilizational, national, or ethnic identity constitutes the objective legitimacy of the discipline would participate within that discipline in the production of knowledge, primarily as suppliers of raw data and factual information. They neither need to engage in the application of a classificatory system nor of the evaluative methods in the processing of such data, nor the preparation of an epistemic framework through which the data are appropriated into a general interpretative narrative. Not engaging in those tasks, neither do they need to participate in the critical review or innovation of those means of knowledge-production. As they are supposedly not held responsible for this kind of critical review and innovation, they rarely confront the reality of existing knowledge in the humanities, namely, a reality that the presumptions and procedures circulated within the disciplines are far from being systematically coherent or complete. Indeed, these are under trenchant scrutiny and constant revision, and, moreover, the humanities are maintained and revitalized by the constant revision and innovation of their own means of knowledge-production. What keeps the sciences of man going is this insatiable movement of self-overcoming and, in this respect, the sciences are totally subordinate to the locus of modernity, an ambiguous position occupied by what Michel Foucault has called "man." Thus the humanities are produced in the element of the historicity of man, and cannot but be a part of *historical* knowledge.[2] Unless one engages oneself in the historical overcoming of knowledge, therefore, one cannot be said to be actively participating in the discourse of modern man. The suppliers of raw data and factual information are involved in the production of knowledge in the humanities, but they are not participating there as "men."

Certainly they are humans, and, in that capacity, they offer information concerning the particular cases of humanity and human nature. And, most often, they are found outside the West, or more accurately speaking, they are supposed to constitute the outside of the putative unity of the West.

On the other hand, there is another sort of people who seek to know about humanity and human nature, but who would never be content to be suppliers of information. For them, knowing is an essential part of their being, so that their way of life will be affected as their relationship to knowledge-production changes. They necessarily engage in the collection, evaluation, comparison, or analysis of raw data, but, more importantly, they are continually involved in the critical review of the existing means of knowing and the invention of new means. Their concern for their subjective conditions in knowing carries the weight of an almost moral imperative. For them, knowledge about humanity and human nature must not only consist of the variety of particular cases but must also entail a commitment to the project of changing and creating the means of knowing about humanity and human nature. They must constantly strive to overcome the limits of their own accomplishments. Everyone within the putative unity of the West is not automatically inside this group of people, but presumably they are representative of the West and can only be found in the West. The project of changing and creating the means of knowing is sometimes called "theory," and it is taken to be a distinguishing mark or even mission of the West. In this sense, "theory" is presumably the essence of Western humanity.

Thus, two different relationships to the production of knowledge presuppose two different conceptions of humanity in the Humanities. Humanity is studied through many cases of and particular manifestations of man's nature. It is presumed that, by extracting what many peoples in the world share in common, ultimately knowledge about "human nature" will be attained. In such an instance, the notion of humanity as the guiding principle is that of *general* humanity which inheres in every particular manifestation of man. Yet a completely different relationship is also possible. It relates to the production of knowledge reflectively, and tries to set the new conditions of knowing, thereby transforming both the constitution of the object for knowledge-production and the subjective conditions of knowing. In this latter relationship to knowledge-production, humanity is problematized not only as a *generality* encompassing all the particular cases but also in the aspect of subjective conditions: humanity manifests itself in self-reflective knowing about knowing and in the legislation of the new means of knowing to which "man" willingly subjects himself. The humanity that is sought in the second relationship is, therefore, not only epistemic but also practical: what is at issue here is not general but universal humanity, to use the Kantian distinction between *generality* and *universality*. And this rift of the epistemic and the practical is probably the site where modern "man" resides.

Since the nineteenth century, as Dipesh Chakrabarty and Osamu Nishitani have observed,[3] the difference between these two relationships to knowledge-production in the humanities has been hinted at by the juxtaposition of two classical analogues, *humanitas* and *anthropos*. As the historical evolution of anthropology suggests, *humanitas* has meant people who could engage in knowledge-production in both the first and the second relationships, while *anthropos* was gradually reserved for peoples who participate in knowledge-production only in the first. Humanity in the sense of *humanitas* has thus come to designate Western or European humanity, to be distinguished from the rest of humanity as long as we trust in and insist upon the putative unity of the West. This is to say that humanity in the sense of *humanitas* authorizes the very *distinction* of the West from what Stuart Hall incisively called "the Rest."⁴ This is one of the reasons why I suspect that, as an ethnic studies generally implies a disciplinary knowledge imposed on *anthropos*, the idea of the ethnic studies of European Americans would not be welcome. For it could undermine this configured division of *humanitas* and *anthropos*. It thus might just conjure up some resistance.

As if following from such a separation of *humanitas* and *anthropos,* the global circulation of information maps two different flows of academic information. The first is a centripetal flow from peripheral sites to various metropolitan centers in Western Europe and North America. This flow of factual data about *anthropos* provided by the peripheries is, however, not presumed to be immediately legible to those not familiar with local contexts. Such obstacles to transparent legibility are often attributed conceptually to the cultural and ethnic particularities of peoples in the Rest. And such information is regarded as too raw or particularistic to be understood by a non-specialist metropolitan readership because of its dense empirical content; it therefore requires translation into the more general theoretical language of *humanitas*.

The second movement is a centrifugal flow of information about how to classify domains of knowledge, how to evaluate given empirical data, how to negotiate with the variety and incommensurability inherent in the body of empirical data from the peripheries, and how to render intelligible the details and trivia coming from particular peripheral sites to "a Western audience." This is to say that the centrifugal flow roughly corresponds to the inquiry into the self-reflective "theory" about the subjective conditions of knowing. Academic information of this second kind is generally called "theory," and its production has largely occurred according to a historically specific division of intellectual labor in which "theory" is associated with that historical construct, "the West," and moves from there to the Rest of the World.

The presumption that theory is the sole provenance of "the West" presupposes various historical conditions of knowledge-production that include: (i) the disciplinary divisions in the humanities and human sciences between *humanitas* and *anthropos*, which are concerned with what is *universally* human, and area and ethnic studies, which are concerned with cultural particularity against the background of what is *generally* human; (ii) the distinction between theoretical or speculative knowledge and pragmatic knowledge; and (iii) the distinction between the ex-colonial peripheries and the metropolis, which has frequently coincided with the cultural or civilizational distinction between East and West, indeed, an extremely overdetermined distinction which is frequently enmeshed with the geopolitical and economic distinction of North and South.

Notably, these distinctions are historically aligned insofar as theoretical knowledge has always been reckoned to be the highest form of knowledge, and the colonizing metropolis has always seen itself as the West and as the site of production of this universal form of knowledge, with material from other geographical regions viewed as simply the raw material of this higher form of knowledge.

But, let me again issue a cautionary disclaimer. I am not offering a description of the state of the humanities today. There are so many instances in which such an old distinction between *humanitas* and *anthropos* has been abraded that nowadays the actual practices of ethnic studies, area-studies, and anthropology no longer abide by the expectations resulting from the putative unity of the West. Increasingly the configuration of the humanities deviates from the economy of information flow which has been regulated by the old distinction of *humanitas* and *anthropos*.

This prevailing view of global academic exchange is no longer acceptable because, clearly, its material conditions are in the process of being undermined. (The West, nonetheless, is not fading at all. But precisely because the historical conditions for the separability of the West from the Rest are being undermined, I am afraid, its *distinction* might well be emphasized all the more obsessively.) Its implicit definition of theory is inadequate in view of the academic conversations going on between and among various locations in the world. Global modernization has accelerated cultural, economic, and political interchange between different regions and brought different forms of knowledge and power into more intense interaction. These forms of "theory" which are no longer merely "indigenous" make up the power-knowledge in everyday life, not only in the Euro-American world but also in many parts of the world including East and South East Asia and Latin America. What once appeared exclusively European no longer belongs to the Euro-American world, and there is an increasing number of instances in which non-Euro-American sites are more "Western" than some aspects of North American and European life.

What, then, is the West, after all? Let me first respond to this inquiry from the standpoint of Asian Studies, an assembly of area-studies fields left over from the days of the Cold War in American higher education and the surviving legacy of even older oriental studies in European imperial centers.

Naoki Sakai

Partly because of the consequences of accelerating globalization and the emergence of what, for the last decade or two, a number of people have referred to as the postmodern conditions discernible almost everywhere on the globe, we are urged to acknowledge that the unity of the West is far from being unitarily determinable. What we believe we understand by the West is increasingly ambiguous and incongruous: the construct's immoderately overdetermined nature can no longer be shrouded.

Until recently, the indigenous or local characteristic of a social and cultural construct which is found in places in Asia, Africa, and sometimes Latin America has routinely been earmarked in contrast to some generalized and euphemistic quality specified as being "Western." Without this institutionalized gesture whereby one can identify what is unfamiliar or enigmatic to those who self-fashion themselves to be "Westerners" in terms of the Western/non-Western binary opposition, it would be impossible to understand the initial formation of Asian Studies as a set of academic disciplines in North American academia. Things Asiatic were first brought to scholarly attention by being recognized as "different and therefore Asian." Then, tacitly from the putative vantagepoint called the West, "being different from us" and "being Asian" were taken to be synonymous in an anthropologizing gesture. A similar operation could well be performed with Africa or Latin America, so as to identify Africa or Latin America as belonging to the Rest of the World, the Rest which is left over when the humanity of the West is forcibly extracted from the World.

Too often, therefore, the designation "Asian," a representative designation of the Rest, has been accompanied by the sense of "being different from us" which in a reflective manner earmarks the ethnic or racial positionality of the Asianists as Westerners. What is fundamental in the "anthropological" description of Asia is the primordial exposure of the observer to the look of the natives, what Rey Chow calls "the to-be-looked-at-ness," which precedes the self-determination of the observer as a Westerner and the native as Asian, and which discloses the position of the observer in ethnographic description primarily as the observed rather than the observer.[5] It follows that the anthropologizing observer's self-fashioning as a Westerner is essentially a reactive self-posturing, reactive precisely because, in order to posture him-or-herself as a Western observer, the observer has to disavow the initial moment of what Johannes Fabian called "coevalness."[6]

Notwithstanding the fact that the binary serves to figure out not only the non-Western or Asian "other" but also "the Western self" of North American and European Asianists, we must not overlook the fact that it also operates practically in the production and reproduction of knowledge in countries in Asia (and other sites believed to be located in the Rest). In these places the institutions of human and social sciences, such as the university sociology and English departments, have been established initially as local agents for the propagation and translation of European or North American (and one might as well include Japanese here) knowledge which is euphemistically put together as "Western"; and, even today, most of these institutions are not free from the habit of regarding themselves as secondary or derivative, that is, as imitators or importers, of Western knowledge: they have yet to rid themselves of their undue sense of indebtedness to the influence of the West and the metropolitan centers. Moreover, the binary further distinguishes the traditional from the modern, the indigenous from the transplanted, and the intimate from the alien, and thereby provides national intelligentsia on the peripheries with the ideological means to render nationality perceptible in everyday reality for a local populace. The West-and-the-Rest opposition does not only fantastically designate the boundary of one civilization from another: it is also thus interwoven into the texture of the imaginary reality of the nation as it has been formulated in Asia. In other words, the national, civilizational, and racial identity of the nation in Asia requires the implicit and ubiquitous presence of the West. Only insofar as the West is felt to be the point of counter-reference can nationality in the Rest be rendered sensible to the populace.

In this instance, let me take a moment to note that the West thus disclosed is not a determinate position which exists prior to the anthropologizing gesture of equating "being different from us" to "being Asian." An encounter between a low-ranking soldier of working-class background from Scotland and the daughter of the landlord class in Suzhou in China, or between a Jewish dancer from Berlin and a university student of medicine from western Japan, for example, could be construed in many other terms than "Western" as opposed to "Asian." It could be construed in terms of gender, economic status, profession, social class background, level of education, and so forth. Other social and personal features which are otherwise most frequently appealed to in order to describe the nature of such an encounter are overlooked when the West-and-the-Rest opposition predominates. And only where the other features are repressed could one be convinced of a gross abstraction that "to be different from us" is more or less synonymous with "being Asian." For the West is posited as a unified entity by the very synonymity of the two. The West comes into being precisely when "being different from us" is thus rendered analogous to "being Asian," "being African," and so forth. Similarly, from the viewpoint of those who fashion themselves as non-Westerners and as belonging to the Rest, the West is also postulated, in the moment that "being different from us" and "being Western" are taken as synonymous. Instead of being construed in view of many different social features, conversation and interaction about knowledge is figured exclusively in terms of a schema consisting of the two poles of the West-and-the-Rest. All the other social relations palpable in intellectual exchange are subordinated to the bi-polar co-figuration, while any cultural incommensurabilities one may come across are all reduced to figures commensurate with the schema of co-figuration.[7] So, for "the Westerners," the thematization of things Asiatic as "being different from us" is the first move to negate or exorcise "them" from "us" in such a way as to prepare the very possibility of representing "them" as Asia, and "us" as the West, according to the schema of co-figuration. The Asiatic essence of things Asiatic is thematized and isolated just like a figure separated by its frame from its background, so to speak. And one of the necessary conditions for the reality of the West is that it is assumed to be recognized as such by the Rest in a symmetrical and transferential manner.

But things Asiatic and the Asian "us" thus separated are not exterior to one another; they are not juxtaposed as parts outside other parts. An intrinsic tie puts them together because Asia is also cut out and framed up upon "us," against the background of "us," or in the place that is "us." Whereas Asia is cut off from the West, it is posited as a theme in the medium of the West. The West is not only a term in opposition to other terms; it is also a place where the very opposition between the terms occurs. The West is, therefore, a classical subject in the sense of *subjectum* precisely because it is the place or *basho* where the cutting out or framing of things Asiatic— the very negativity of the West in relation to Asia—takes place.[8] In this respect, too, Asia is framed in the West. Whereas the West, thanks to its seeming concreteness, has so frequently been taken for granted as the point of reference in determining the ethnic, national, or racial particularity of local and indigenous social formation, that it has often been claimed that it has saturated the world and expanded to cover the entire earth.

Modernity has often been defined by the historical fact that every part of the world has been in contact with the West. It is likewise said that the West has tried to reach every corner of the world for the last five centuries and that today it is virtually impossible to think of any location on the earth which has remained insulated from its persistent and penetrating reaches. As a result of its expansion, we live in an essentially modern world in which the West is ubiquitous.

What then is this implicit oxymoron, the West, which is putatively a particular locale while residing everywhere, which ardently segregates itself from the Rest but reaches all places on earth? How does the West distinguish itself from its other or others when its presence can be detected in everything in the world? And why do many still regard modernity as somewhat particular to this contradictory being called the West?

Yet, it is also necessary to keep in mind that modernity implies a historical process in which the West itself was unevenly constructed too, and that the West is essentially a modern construct. As Antonio Gramsci pointed out some seventy years ago, there cannot be any inherent reason why a certain geographical area should be designated as the West. In principle, every point on the earth could have its own west. The West could be along the Tigris and the Euphrates; it could be in the Amazon Basin; it may as well refer to the coastal area along the South China Sea. Yet, precisely because it is a *historical construct,* neither the Japanese nor the Californians are considered silly, when they refer to Tunisia—(which is located several thousand kilometers west of Japan) as the Middle East; or Japan—(which is located in the western end of the Ocean which California faces) as the Far East. Both the Middle East and the Far East are relative terms whose indexing functions would be unintelligible were they not in relations with the West, whose Middle East and Far East they are, respectively. In this regard, the geopolitical indices incorporate the particular vantage point of those who view the world from their position as the center. The master index, the West, has received its legitimacy through the hegemonic configuration of the world. The location of the West can never be divorced from the question of who came to dominate the modern world, argued Gramsci.[9]

First of all, we must acknowledge that the West is not a proper name for a geographical place which, by definition, remains identical and fixed. (Hence, it is necessary to keep the West from being reduced to Europe.[10] North America, for instance, is often referred to as part of the West but never as part of Europe. Eastern Europe, on the other hand, is regarded as being in Europe, but very often is excluded from the West. Some argue that the word Europe is etymologically traceable to the Phoenician, *Ereb,* or sunset, that is, comprehended as embodying the same directional sense as the term/construct of the West; accordingly, it cannot surgically distinguish itself from the destiny of the West. The West is an objective reality, but its reality cannot be independent of how we name it, imagine it, and relate to it. The notion of the West makes sense, directs us, and locates us in relation to other sites and other geopolitical appendages because it is a historical construct. Thus Gramsci reminded us that the location of the West was real, but that its reality was indubitably hegemonic. In short, the West makes sense because of a particular hegemonic configuration which was then and still is historically contingent. His insight was written in the 1920s. Since then, seven decades have passed, and many historical transformations have taken place in the world: today the historical construct of the West can indicate a set of very different relations, as it is based on a hegemonic configuration which may well be entirely different from that of the 1920s.

While Gramsci was perspicacious in analyzing the hegemonic reality of the West, we tend to forget that this hegemonic nature implied another diagnosis of this peculiar reality. Despite his insistence upon its historical nature, Gramsci's explanation seems to assume the unity of the West as a given. One might therefore presume that, just like the geographic area of Europe, the form of the West closed; or that, like a nation, it is composed of its members and excludes its non-members; some that, like the conventional notion of a language community, it is based upon some shared commonality; or that, like a plant or animal species, it is determined by its common features and heritages. What the globalized range of the West has rendered increasingly obvious all around the world, however, is that the unity of the West now, suspiciously, shifts and transforms according to the context of its discussion. Certainly the West is a social reality: it exists. Certainly the West is a social imaginary of global scale, but it is nonetheless existent because of its imaginary nature. It is a *real* index. Nevertheless, it does not follow from its existence that the West is an enduring tradition, a discernible collectivity based upon common physiognomy or a social group with any recognizable stability. The West can be defined in so many different and contradictory ways that we can hardly persuade ourselves that its unity can ever correspond to some substance. It is increasingly difficult to discover an organizing coherence among the varying definitions of the West, and its spectral character can no longer be overlooked.

From the mass media, let me cite at random several general statements about the West which contain the above definitions as uncritically accepted given. (1) Democracy could develop only in the West, thanks to its tradition of individualism, as well as its Judeo-Christian historical consciousness, which views World History as a court of judgment. (2) As a member of the West, Japan must contribute to the maintenance of world peace. (3) The world is not moving inevitably toward Western values, as the West's victory in the Cold War seemed to promise, but, on the contrary, it is moving toward a clash of cultures in which the Western model is confronted by increasingly assertive civilizations of the East—Islamic, Chinese, Indian, Japanese and Orthodox. (4) The U.S. was built upon the traditions of Western culture and the heritage of Western civilization, so it is inevitable that non-Western cultures and civilizations cannot be allowed to have dominant status there. (5) No solution for the civil war in Bosnia will be in sight unless the West intervenes in the region. (6) Once the West has ceased to provide aid to Russia, the Russian economy will face the crisis of probable collapse; it is then highly likely that it will have an extreme-rightist government which will pose an imminent danger to the West.

A cursory review of these examples clearly shows how arbitrarily the semiotics of the West follows a vastly disparate variety of semes. According to the first statement, which evokes the ancient notion of Europe as Christendom, the West characteristically consists of those societies where Christianity and Judaism are dominant, so that Ethiopia, Peru, Israel, and the Philippines are subsumed under the heading of the West, while other countries and regions actually within Europe (such as Bosnia, Bradford in Yorkshire, England, and Albania) are excluded. And let us not forget that, generally speaking, until the end of the Second World War, Judaism was taken to symbolize what was most immediately heterogeneous to Western Christianity. The second statement is used to define the

West as the group of countries whose governments have declared, in one way or another, their military and political affiliation with the United States and which included Britain, France, the Republic of China, and South Korea but not the old Communist Soviet Union, the People's Republic of China, the former East Germany, Poland, and so forth. According to the premises of the third statement, the West is no longer characterized by Christianity in general. Only those countries where Catholicism and Protestantism dominate are now admitted into the West. Similarly exclusively, the fourth statement seems to assume the familiar dogmas that the cultures and civilizations of the white people in the United States are evidently Western and thus distinguished from those of the non-white population. And the fifth statement refers to the West vaguely as the membership of NATO, minus some Eastern European countries. In addition to the United States and Germany, other wealthy countries with surplus capital to invest in Russia, such as Japan, the ROC, and South Korea, are also in the West, as the sixth statement suggests.

Depending upon the context of comparison, then, the West could be inclusive or exclusive of many regions, social groups, economic features, or cultural characteristics. In one instance, it spreads over five continents of the world. In another, it excludes many ethnic communities living in the United States. It is finally simply impossible to presume the existence of some substratum able to accommodate a collection of all the various definitions of the West. Of course, the name of every singular reference gives rise to exceptions; accordingly, every proper name of a social group or a geopolitical area exceeds its own definition and proves itself to be overdetermined. Even so, in the case of the West this overdetermination is too excessive to pass as the name of a geographic region. The West is, above all, only *a* west, a relative direction where, seen from a certain vantage point, the sun seems to set: every place is a west for somewhere else, so that a west, in principle, cannot designate an immovable place. Even when it is treated as though it were a proper noun, it fails to anchor itself in the sturdy and physical map of the world precisely because it is not the name of a bounded surface area. Nevertheless, it cannot be substituted for with general terms—such as industrial capitalism or consumer society—whose application is not limited by the singularity or propriety of a geopolitical place.

In this respect, it is important to keep in mind that Stuart Hall specifically talks about the West-and-the-Rest as a discursive formation in the Foucauldian sense, arguing that the West must first be understood in reference to this discursive formation of the West-and-the-Rest in which an individual is constituted as a subject of either the West or the Rest by occupying certain positions. In other words, the West owes its putative unity to various statements about itself and its differences from the Rest, statements regulated under that discursive formation. From this insight too, I believe, it should follow that the West is neither a geographic closure nor a cultural whole since, for Foucault, a discourse is dispersed in such a way as to evade existence in a fixed location in a homogeneous continuity, either of geographic space or of calendar time. When discourse is dispersed spatially, how can the West as a construct in discourse possibly serve as a spatial index? It must be doubly dispersed so that it can never be conceived of as a spatial unity at all. And a corollary of our postulate is that the West is variously posited whenever a difference between the West-and-the-Rest is invoked—that is, in many different places on many disparate occasions with a vast variety of actors. As a whole, the West can never be a unity: it is a composite or assemblage of disparate contexts.

Though it is generally believed to designate a place, the West is a name whose indexing function is evoked in order to *spatially* represent a particular social relationship which exists—say, between the traveler and the resident, the colonizer and the native, the educated upper-class elite and the peasants from the countryside—in the guise of spatial direction at the very site where reference to or distinction regarding either the West or the Rest is enunciated. Here it is important to keep in mind that it is equally possible to conceive of this social dynamics *temporally*, without spatial representation. Time and time again, modern man's temporal relation to himself has been conceptualized as a form of transcendence or self-overcoming. It goes without saying that the ecstatic form of aporetic or self-contradictory temporality has been recognized as the essential feature of "modern subjectivity."[11] But, when spatially represented, the aporetic temporality inherent in modernity is bound to be neglected. What I cannot emphasize enough here is that the opposition between spatial representation and temporal form derives from a deliberately alternative mode of grasping the social dynamics of modernity. Just as I have elsewhere argued about disjunctive relation between the representation of translation and the work of translation,[12] spatial representation and temporal form are connected to one another in a disjunction: if social dynamics is represented as a spatial direction, its temporality cannot be conceived; if it is grasped as an instance of aporetic temporality in modern subjectivity, it is irrespective of spatial representation. And disjunction between the temporal conception of "man's" relation to himself and the spatial representation of this relation in terms of the West-and-the-Rest binary is logically incompatible with the distinction between *humanitas* and *anthropos*, a distinction which is not disjunctive at all— and yet it is displaced and projected onto this binary. As a consequence, it is through this displacement and confusionism that Western humanity was to gain the status of "man," as if they could relate to themselves exclusively in terms of self-transcending temporality, while the Rest are destined to remain anthropologized and thus deprived of this "modern" historicity.

In short, the West is one term of the West and the non-West binary which serves to co-figure spatially the relation of one subjective position to another. Rather than designating a bounded territory, it expresses the orientation or *gradient* at a specific place. A vector at one site does not necessarily indicate the same orientation it would at another one. Furthermore, even at the same place, the West can easily be associated with multiple vectors, each of which may well have a different gradient. For instance, a Chinese American businessman might well be regarded as a Westerner in relation to most of the residents in Taiwan, but he would be an Asian in relation to French tourists visiting there. Likewise a Japanese visitor to India on his way to Europe in the 1920s might have described the residents there in almost the same way as the British colonial administrators did. His viewpoint and his anthropologizing attitude toward the Indian populace were unambiguously those of someone desiring to fashion himself as a Westerner in contrast to the non-Western natives. But, the same person began to describe himself as a representative of Asia as soon as he reached France. Essentially, as a gradient, the West-and-the-Rest opposition can be associated with so many different and unequal social relationships. This is one of the reasons why the West can be such a powerful trope demonstrating a historical tendency or orientation in a given social relationship. Furthermore, a gradient always comprehends a derivative function, so that, even if it were subordinate to spatial representation, it retains some aspect of temporal change. And this also explains why the West has so frequently been taken as a synonym for modernity and progress, as a projected trajectory for the subject's self-transcendence.

Because it expresses a historical orientation in a particular relationship, the West-and-the-Rest opposition has been duplicated in many regions and sites in the world, involving a different set of people each time.

In the late nineteenth and early twentieth centuries, Japanese elite were sent to Western Europe to study and learn about what was then thought of as the most advanced civilization. The sight of metropolitan glory and the growing racism in European societies overwhelmed these visitors, who subsequently began to identify themselves ethnically and racially according to the civilizational hierarchy of the Eurocentric worldview. Even while this experience of confronting a powerful and sophisticated civilization gave rise in them to a resolve towards Japan's progress and modernization, they were made to realize how oriental and non-Western they were. Precisely because they experienced living the reality of the West, they were acutely aware of their exclusion from the West and their Japanese ethnic identity. Yet returning to Japan, they were expected to civilize and modernize the local commoners (who knew little or nothing of the Eurocentric world order) and took upon themselves the mission of creating national subjects of these commoners. In this novel orientation, they now had to play the role of "Westerners" and to duplicate the hierarchical relationship between themselves and the "uncivilized masses." Far from believing in an immediate relief from the haunting power of the West, their sense of being excluded from the West induced them to duplicate the anthropologizing attitude in the local community (which they supposed was in the Rest) and to locate the presumably "primitive" reality of the local within the ethnographic framing of modernity.

As Rey Chow demonstrates, however, the "primitive" is not something chronologically precedent to the modern age. It is, rather, a mark of modernity in the local:

> Because it is only in this imaginary space that the primitive is located, the primitive is phantasmagoric and, literally, ex-otic. This exoticizing of what is at the same time thought to be generic and commonplace characterizes the writing of history within a culture as much as the writing between cultures, such as the practices of orientalism.[13]

Most striking in Chow's lucid illustration is that what she refers to as the primitive appears to be a variation of modern temporality in the visual field rather than a formation particular to China. Underlying the exoticizing is the movement of negativity, which objectifies what has socially been given (and thus reflectively posits the subject) and transforms it into something, which has yet to come: "...What makes it possible for a Chinese audience to become not simply inheritors of but also foreigners to their 'tradition' is the act of transmission—the fact that whatever they experience, they experience as a passing-on."[14] To see the socially given as primitive is a necessary step to viewing it as what can be transformed, to recognizing a social formation not as naturally given but as something that is manufactured. Let me construe the concept "primitive passions" in terms of its temporality rather than the spatial externality of one culture to another, and one can see that to view the local reality as primitive is correlative to the formation of a subject which constitutes itself by transforming its environment as well as itself.[15]

Similarly to this Chinese exoticizing, Japanese intellectuals began to view their local reality as primitive. Their sense of being Japanese and Asian was thus closely interwoven with their contradictory aspiration for the West, on the one hand, and their resentment against it, on the other.[16] As some literary historians have noted,[17] it is astonishing that exactly the same orientation can be detected in the aspiration and resentment of those Asian elite from the annexed territories of imperial Japan towards the metropolises of Tokyo and Kyoto during the heyday of Japanese colonialism. Just as Paris and Berlin symbolized "the West" to Japanese intellectuals, Tokyo and Kyoto embodied the image of "modernity" towards which Taiwanese elite, who were educated in Japanese at Japanese universities, for instance, turned, as they accepted the mission of transforming their own, local and indigenous "primitive" reality.

Thus, the same Japanese intellectual can be a typical representative of the Rest in one gradient, but in another, is expected to play the role of the "Westerner." Multiple gradients coexist even within the same person. And this is evidently not limited to the case of Japanese. The doublet of *humanitas* and *anthropos* seems to be duplicated in many sites in the world—hence, let me repeat, it is fundamentally misleading to map the distinction between *humanitas* and *anthropos* onto the world's geographic configuration—and, along with the global circulation of industrial commodities and the expansion of Euro-American-Japanese military domination, this is one of the reasons the West was and still is felt to be ubiquitous throughout the world. As I argued in terms of the complicity of universalism (more specifically, it should be called generalism) and particularism, what may appear to be the universality of the West consists in its capacity to generate at a remote site, far from European metropolises, a certain orientation or gradient by means of which something like the West-and-the-Rest binary distinction is duplicated.

And each of those orientations or gradients is, let me note, always associated with a certain qualification. In order for a highly educated engineer to play the role of the Westerner as distinct from the indigenous habitants in a remote region of the Japanese Empire, for instance, a specific opposition of qualities—such as a contrast between the ability to think and behave rationally and its lack—is highlighted. The relationship of Japan proper and Taiwan was often represented by some vague contrast between the two groups of people: those who supposedly possessed scientific rationality and those who still dwelled in superstitious premodernity. And in this chronologically-measured orientation from pre-modernity to modernity, one would have to exhibit the signs of scientific rationality in order to be qualified to be a Japanese and to fashion oneself as a Japanese—although it should have been glaringly evident that the vast majority of the Japanese population in Japan proper lacked scientific rationality in comparison with many well-educated Taiwanese.

Similarly, in an orientation from premodernity to modernity, one has to demonstrate the signs of individualistic autonomy—as opposed to collectivist deference—in order to be qualified to be and to fashion oneself as Westerner. Yet in another orientation, the ability to speak one of the Western European languages is taken to be a qualification for belonging in the West, just as the ability to speak Japanese was once considered to be an emblem of modernity in some Japanese colonies. As is obvious, however, scientific rationality, the quality which has long been ascribed exclusively to the West, is totally independent of another quality, the ability to speak French or English. Moreover, if both qualities are taken to designate Westernness, they are neither necessarily co-possible nor mutually exclusive or antinominal. We cannot infer, in other words, that, if one has one quality of the West, one will then have the other, any more than we can assume that, if one does not have one, one cannot have the other.

Naoki Sakai

Clearly, a great number of different qualifications and orientations are taken to be characteristic of the West. Neither the West nor the modern is ever determined by one single qualification or gradient. The gradients in which one is caught are never single, and one always engages with multiple gradients. Yet the inference regarding the two qualities applies to the other co-existing qualities with the result that, even if a number of qualities are supposed to refer to the same West, they are neither necessarily compossible with nor contradictory to one another. This is to say that, as I see it and many examples have already amply shown us, the West is never an internally coherent substance. At first glance, the West may appear to be a subject consisting of an organically systematized set of predicates; yet, as my argument has demonstrated, the West should be regarded as an accidental composite of such predicates which are in fact independent of each other. The West is a composite of many variables, none of which remains constant. At the risk of repetition, *there is no single quality which is adequate to define the identity of the West.* Neither Christianity, economic superiority, democratic values, nor whiteness of skin—nor, indeed, all of these together—would suffice. Neither the West nor the Rest is, therefore, a coherent systematicity of qualities: neither of them can be presumed to be a substance.

Therefore, one rarely exists either in the West or in the Rest consistently and coherently, except for the fact that, just as with social class, the means and resources to acquire certain qualifications and their qualities are not equally distributed. In fact, the means and resources are concentrated in certain groups in such a way that it is easier for those in certain privileged groups to acquire the qualifications for Westernness than others.

Those historical conditions which have induced us to overlook the heterogeneity and overdetermination inherent in the concept of the West are fast disappearing; the social and economic realities which allowed those qualities characterizing the identities of the West-and-the-Rest to appear anchored in solid ground have melted into thin air. It is not surprising that around the world many are overwhelmed by anxiety concerning their social, economic, and cultural identities. Fundamentally, what has been called into question is the status of the West as a single and unified referent. Particularly since Asia has traditionally been defined as the negative of the West (or of the Occident) the overdetermined nature of the West, which expresses many forms of social and economic anxiety in a condensed manner, is acutely felt in the production of knowledge in Asian Studies today.

And yet, curiously, nowhere in the world does the term "the West" seem to have lost its universal appeal and immediate intelligibility. Nowhere in the world has it lost the force of an objective reality. In this respect, the West has continued virtually to remain ubiquitous for the last seven decades since Gramsci. Particularly in East Asia, the West has continued to play the role of the master index in relation to local nationalism, which has tried to determine its ethnic, cultural, and racial identity in contradistinction to the West. At the same time, however, a growing number of social groups and aspects of everyday life in East Asia may well be located inside the West rather than in the Rest, depending upon the choice of contexts.

But how can the West manage to hold on to its immediate intelligibility? How can people in many places in the world continue to believe in the West despite the glaring evidence of its instability, transience, and overdetermination? Let us now return to our own examples of the overlapping of the colonial relationship and the West-and-the-Rest binary. To the exemplary observation about the Western/non-Western oscillation of a Chinese American businessman in Taiwan, one might plausibly respond by claiming that he is only figuratively and not really a Westerner. In this claim, one would presume that there must necessarily be "natural" Westerners, who are originally Western in themselves and among whom the Chinese American businessman is not in the first place included: one would insist on being able to posit the substance of the West beyond any and all historical vicissitude. This is an essentialist claim which attempts to naturalize, as well as root and ground the pedigrees of the West (as well as the Rest) on certain properties assumed to be solid, unchanging, and natural.

In terms of the concept of fixity, Homi Bhabha has analyzed the processes of subjectification for the colonizers as well as the colonized and the ideological construction of otherness in colonial discourse.[18] We also know that such an obsession with this presumed fixity can easily be appropriated into that nationalist yearning for an eternal "peoplehood," particularly in post-independence countries, where the memory of subjugation to the Euro-American-Japanese colonial administrations is still vivid. What I want to envisage with regard to the presumptive and essentialist claim to the West's pedigree, however, is slightly different from this desire for fixed essence and immemorial past. For this presumptive claim of nationalism is intended to countervail a recognition of the fundamental facticity of the identities of the West-and-the-Rest, a facticity such that, with no good reason and without knowing why, a person happens to be Western simply by virtue of some "qualifications" and non-Western by virtue of other qualifications; it is an almost instinctive reaction compensating for the dissolution of those historical conditions which once allowed those qualities characterizing the identities of the West-and-the-Rest to appear to emanate from essences, to disavow the dissolution which may well be brought about by globalization.

The claim is essentialist in the sense that, as Pierre Bourdieu has argued,

> aristocracies are essentialist. Regarding existence as an emanation of essence, they set no intrinsic value on...deeds and misdeeds.... They prize them only insofar as they clearly manifest, in the

nuances of their manner, that their one inspiration is the perpetuating and celebrating of the essence by virtue of which they are accomplished.[19]

Unlike the social-class distinction on which Bourdieu focuses, the distinction of the West from the Rest is often imposed by both thus separated parties upon themselves. The West-and-the-Rest are both anxious to naturalize their distinctive qualities and qualifications. Therefore, the presumptive and essentialist claim to the respective pedigrees of the West-and-the-Rest calls for a sort of naturalization. Let me cite Bourdieu again on natural taste here:

> The ideology of natural taste owes its plausibility and its efficacy to the fact that, like all the ideological strategies generated in the everyday class struggle, it *naturalizes* real differences, converting differences in the mode of acquisition of culture into differences of nature: it only recognizes as legitimate the relation to culture (or language) which least bears the visible marks of its genesis, which has nothing 'academic,' 'scholastic,' 'bookish,' or 'studied' about it, but manifests by its ease and naturalness that true culture is nature—a new mystery of immaculate conception.[20]

It is through this urge to naturalize that the disparate, overdetermined, and heterogeneous West (like the Rest) appears unified. The unity of the West, therefore, is always its *putative* unity: it is something to be called for, and yet, in the presumptive and essentialist investment, it is naturalized and presumed to be a given. This explains why the West-and-the-Rest distinction can never be free of the aura of racism. Here, we need not comprehend racism narrowly, that is, in terms of reduction of the social and cultural qualities of an individual to his or her physiological features such as skin color, hair type, and the distribution of cerebral functions. What constitutes racism is a foundationalist investment, a demand that the perceived qualities and differences must be naturalized, rooted and grounded in essentialized properties such as ethnic culture, whiteness, national tradition, and language. In this respect, the West is another sort of fictive ethnicity after Etienne Balibar's terminology.[21] As goes without saying, none of these grounding terms is more reliable and less contingent than the perceived qualities and differences. It is no accident that the most pervasive form of racism is today found in national/ethnic culturalism, in which social differences are naturalized in terms of the essentialized culture of a nation or ethnos.

In spite of its constant dispersal, fragmentation, and mutation, the distinction of the West from the Rest appears intact only because this effort to countervail the dissolution of the historical conditions, an effort which has encouraged us to overlook the dispersal and overdetermination inherent in the very distinction of West/Rest, is always at work. In other words, the distinction of the West from the Rest is reactive to vicissitude; it is an attempt to repress historical changes. No wonder that those who obstinately insist on their Western identity are more often than not the ones who feel most uncertain about their own qualifications to be Western. For what is preserved in the distinction are the historical conditions of the encounter of unequal powers which gave rise to bourgeois Europe and in which colonial forces progressively dominated what would summarily be lumped together as the Rest. There is no doubt that the West is a historical construct and as such is constantly exposed to historical change, but the putative unity of the West which is also at work in that countervailing tendency is not historical in the sense of continually registering historical mutation. Rather it represses the historical. In short, the putative unity of the West is *not in time*. It is instead in the topography of the colonial unconscious that the proper understanding of the distinction of the West from the Rest must be sought.[22]

We now find ourselves in an extremely precarious situation, in which the production of "theory" and the flow of knowledge no longer follow the economy of humanistic disciplines regulated by the putative unity of the West. Thousands of scholars outside Western Europe and North America engage in the studies of *humanitas*, reading and writing about European heritages in philosophy, sociology, psychology, European literatures, and so forth. Of course, *humanitas* is today far from being the exclusive possession of Western Europe and North America. Increasingly, are we not discovering that those with fair skin, who are deprived of bourgeois taste or Enlightenment secular values, qualify as *anthropos* even in the urban centers of Western Europe or the Deep South of the United States? Just as the West is dispersed all over the world so the Rest is also scattered even through the heartland of European civilization.

From this, however, we cannot conclude that the West will cease to be distinctive from the Rest. Nor would I ever claim that, because of its increasing fragmentation and dispersal as an inevitable consequence of globalization, the West will soon cease to be a reality. Just as it would be inane to presume that the social category of race will soon be irrelevant to one's perception of social reality simply because the notion of race is so abstract, incoherent, fragmented, arbitrary, historically contingent, geographically mutable, and, in short, irrational—just so I would commit a fatal mistake if I expected the West to be dissipated by increasing commerce in the world.

Indeed, in view of the location of the West in the varieties of colonial unconscious, certain people are probably all the more tempted to naturalize the putative unity of the West. But might not the obsessive insistence on this unity lead to the further racialization of the concept of the West? On so many occasions, has Western not clearly been synonymous with white? And might not the essentialist presumption of the unity of the West lead to the acting-out of the repressed memory of colonial violence?

Naoki Sakai

I believe that the globality of theory calls for a new definition of the Humanities and a comparative cultural theory which is not in the sole possession of European humanity. By this, I mean a form of theorizing that is attentive to the transcultural dissemination and global traces within theoretical knowledge produced in geopolitically specific locations and which explores how theories are themselves transformed by their practical effects when they are performed in other sites. This comparative enterprise, which is no longer regulated by the opposition of *humanitas* and *anthropos*, is also political insofar as it seeks to examine the theoretical bases and conflicting desires at the heart of contemporary politics which manifests itself in forms of violence. The form of comparative cultural theory envisaged here is already being produced by many intellectuals and cultural workers firmly located in the South and the "non-West"—Asia, Africa and Latin America—as well as those from the North Atlantic regions who are concerned with the transformative dissemination and living-on of Euro-American ideas in non-Euro-American sites, as well as the legacies and political futures of non-European theories in Northern locations. It is a form of theorizing based on the acknowledgment of the traces of the other in a specifically local text.

We are not at all hesitant to acknowledge our indebtedness to the intellectual and cultural legacies of Europe. In this respect, we are willing to find the traces of European inventions in all of us. In the project of Traces, however, we will not seek to distinguish ourselves from the West or from the Rest but rather to re-articulate the very distinction between the West-and-the-Rest in such a way as to allow us to see the traces of the West as well as of the non-West in all of us.

Just as Itô Jinsai, scholar of the Confucian classics of the seventeenth century, once remarked, virtues are to realize themselves only as traces;[23] virtues are never properties confined to the individuality and indivisibility of a person, a tribe, an ethnos, a nation or of a race, but are always traces of encounters and interactions, that is, of dispersion and openness.

Endnotes

1—Parts of this article have been delivered on several occasions. The first half was presented at Goldsmith College of the University of London on 10 November 1998. The title "Dislocation of the West" was first suggested by Hiroki Ogasawara, who helped organize my talk there. I thank him for his suggestion and Paul Gilroy from whose comments I learned much. A slightly different version was delivered at Cornell University on 2 February 1999.

2—According to Michel Foucault who deployed the Heideggerian problematic of the finitude in his archeological analysis of "human being," man is fundamentally historical precisely because man can never be exhaustively determined in its positivity, because the limitlessness of history, which is inherent in the modern determination of the human being, "perpetually refers certain positivities determining man's being to the finitude that causes those same positivities to appear" (*The Order of Things* [New York: Vintage Books, 1973], 371). The modern positivity of man is characterized by the man's mode of being, that is, the mode of "repetition—of the identity and the difference between the positive and the fundamental" "within the figure of the *Same*" (315). "Man became that upon which all knowledge could be constituted as immediate and non-problematized evidence; he became, *a fortiori*, that which justified the calling into question of all knowledge of man. Hence that double and inevitable contestation: that which lies at the root of the perpetual controversy between the sciences of man and the science proper—the first laying an invincible claim to be the foundation of the second, which are ceaselessly obliged in turn to seek their own foundation, the justification of their method, and the purification of their history, in the teeth of 'psychologism,' 'sociologism,' and 'historicism'" (345).

Let me note in passing that, despite an alluring analysis of "the empirical—transcendental doublet" called man, the notion of Western culture or its unity is never under suspicion throughout Foucault's book, and that the putative unity of the West has never been interrogated in relation to modern humanism.

3—See: Dipesh Chakrabarty, "Marx after Marxism: Subaltern Histories and the Question of Difference" in *Polygraph* 6, no. 7. Also see: Osamu Nishitani, translator's Postface II for *Le Crime du caporal Lortie* (Rorthi gochô no hanzai; The Crime of Corporal Lortie), by Pierre Legendre (Kyoto: Jinmon Shoin, 1998), 287-88; Osamu Nishitani & Naoki Sakai, *Sekaishi no kaitai* (Deconstruction of World History) [Tokyo: Ibunsha, 1999] 20-2, 103-8. Also see: Philippe Lacoue-Labarthe, "The awakening of the power of myth—the auto-poietic act—becomes a necessity once the inconsistency of the abstract universals of reason has been revealed and the beliefs of modern humanity (Christianity and belief in humanity itself), which were at bottom only bloodless myths, have collapsed. But here again we should be careful: Nazism is a humanism in so far as it rests upon a determination of *humanitas* which is, in its view, more powerful—i.e. more effective—than any other. The subject of absolute self-creation, even if, occupying an immediately natural position (the particularity of the race), it transcends all the determinations of the modern subject, brings together and concretizes these same determinations (as also does Stalinism with the subject of absolute self-production) and constitutes itself as the subject, in absolute terms. The fact that this subject lacks the universality which apparently defines the *humanitas* of humanism in the received sense, still does not make Nazism an anti-humanism" (Heidegger, *Art and Politics*, Chris Turner trans. [Oxford, Basil Blackwell, 1990], 95.

4—See: Stuart Hall, "The West-and-the-Rest: Discourse and Power" in *Modernity*, Stuart Hall, David Held, Don Hubert, and Kenneth Thompson ed. (Cambridge, MA, and Oxford: Blackwell Publishers, 1996), 184-227.

5—Rey Chow, *Primitive Passions*

(New York: Columbia University Press, 1995), 176-82. The notion of the "to-be-looked-at-ness," introduced in *Primitive Passions* is a conceptual development of Chow's earlier assertion about the colonial encounter.

6—Johannes Fabian, *Time and the Other* (New York: Columbia University Press, 1983).

7—For a more detailed discussion on the schema of co-figuration, see: Naoki Sakai, "The Problem of 'Japanese Thought': The Formation of 'Japan' and the Schema of Cofiguration," in *Translation and Subjectivity* (Minneapolis and London: University of Minnesota Press, 1997), 40–71.

8—Here, I refer to the vocabulary of Kitaro Nishida (1870–1945). Adopting the Aristotelian term *hypokeimenon*, Nishida pursued a philosophical investigation concerning modern subjectivity. He modified the concept of *hypokeimenon* and introduced his own term *basho* which means "place" in modern Japanese.

9—See: Antonio Gramsci, *Selections from Prison Notebooks*, Quintin Hoarse and Geoffrey Nowell Smith trans. (New York: International Publishers, 1971), 447.

10—Christopher GoGwilt notes that the term "Europe" was called into question early in the twentieth century when the term "the West" gained a new rhetorical force. In reference to Heidegger's discussion of "Nihilism," he shows that, in discussing "Nihilism" Nietzsche never ascribed the word "Western" to nihilism. Citing passages from Heidegger's *Nietzsche*, however, GoGwilt writes, "Heidegger here translates Nietzsche's term 'European' ('europäish') into the post-Nietzschean terminology 'Western history' ('abendländischen Geschichte'). Heidegger was lecturing in Nazi Germany, and his terms are of course inflected in complex ways by debates of the 1930s. Yet precisely the distance between the contested terms of Nietzsche's Europe and those of Heidegger's indicates that the term 'Western' had acquired a rhetorical force between the 1890s and the 1930s" (*The Invention of the West - Joseph Conrad and the Double-Mapping of Europe and Empire* [Stanford, CA: Stanford University Press, 1995], 232).

After the emergence of such a use of the term "the West" which originated from the Russian Slavophile-Westerner controversy over nihilism, GoGwilt argues, Oswald Spengler could make the following claim about "Europe" and "the West" in the Introduction to *The Decline of the West*: "The word 'Europe' ought to be struck out of history. There is historically no 'European' type …. It is thanks to this word 'Europe' alone, and the complex of ideas resulting from it, that our historical consciousness has come to link Russia with the West in an utterly baseless unity—a mere abstraction derived from the reading of books—that has led to immense real consequences."

11—For the term "aporetic" see: Paul Ricoeur: "The Aporetics of Temporality," Section 1, in *Time and Narrative*, vol. 3, Katheleen Blamey and David Pellauer trans. (Chicago and London: The University of Chicago Press, 1985), 11–96.

12—See: Naoki Sakai: *Translation and Subjectivity*, 12–16, 51–63.

13—See: Chow, Rey, *Primitive Passions—Visuality, Sexuality, Ethnography, and Contemporary Chinese Cinema* (New York: Columbia University Press, 1995), 22–23.

14—Ibid., 199.

15—As Rey Chow notes, primitive passions are politically ambivalent. It is no doubt concerned with the invention of the national origin "which is now 'democratically' (re)constructed as a common place and a commonplace, a point of common knowledge and reference that was there prior to our present existence" (ibid., 22).

16—A very informative analysis of the attitude of Japanese intellectuals towards the West can be found in "*Higashi kara nishi e, nishi kara higashi e*" in Komori Yô'ichi's *<Yuragi> no nakano Nihon-bungaku* [Japanese Literature in Oscillation] (Tokyo: NHK books, 1998), 170–98.

17—See: Chen Wangyi: "*Yume to genjitsu*" [Dreams and Reality] in *Yomigaeru Taiwan bungaku* [Resurrecting Taiwan Literature], edited by Shimomura Sakujirô, Nakajima Toshio, Fujii Shôzô, & Huang Yincuo (Tokyo: Tôhô Shoten, 1995), 389–406; Tarumi Chie, *Taiwan no Nihongo bungaku* [Japanese language literature in Taiwan] (Tokyo: Goryü Shoin, 1995), 51–101. It is worthwhile noting that the colonized intellectual's commitment to modernity is frequently interrogated as to whether or not it was a form of collaboration with the colonial rule after the colony's independence. Beyond specific historical contexts, there seem some intimate connection between modernity and the colonization of the world.
18—Homi Bhabha, "The Other Question—stereotype, discrimination and the discourse of colonialism," in *The Location of Culture* (London and New York: Routledge, 1994), 66–84.
19—Pierre Bourdieu, *Distinction—Social Critique of the Judgment of Taste,* Richard Nice trans. (Cambridge, MA: Harvard University Press, 1984), 24; also see, Ghassan Hage, *White Nation—Fantasies of White supremacy in a multicultural society* [West Wickham, UK: Comerford and Miller Publishers, 1998), for brilliant deployments of Bourdieu's insights in the analysis of anti-immigrant racism in Australia.
20—Ibid., 68.
21—See Etienne Balibar's "Racism and Nationalism" and "The Nation Form: History and Ideology" in *Race, Nation, Class—Ambiguous Identities,* ed. E. Balibar and I. Wallerstein (London and New York: Verso, 1988).
22—Cf. John Kraniauskas, "Beware Mexican Ruin," in *Walter Benjamin's Philosophy: Destruction and Experience,* Andrew Benjamin and Peter Osborne (London and New York: Routledge, 1994), 139–54.
23—Itô Jinsai, "*Gomôjigi*" in *Nihon shisô-taikei,* vol. 33 (Tokyo: Iwanami Shoten, 1971), 36.

TRANSLATION AND THE WORK OF TRANSCULTURATION

John KRANIAUSKAS

The most important innovation of Homi Bhabha's *The Location of Culture* is its use and generalization of the idea of 'disjunctive enunciation.'* With it Bhabha produces his key critical concepts such as 'third space,' 'postcoloniality,' and 'time lag,' concepts which account for the ways in which discourses of modernity are haunted and interrupted by the history of colonialism. Grounded psychoanalytically in disavowal, and philosophico-linguistically in deferral, 'disjunctive enunciation' also suggests a more universal and constitutive hauntology. The problem with such a generalization is that it tends to mythify the present experience of colonialism. Strategically mobilized, however, the idea of 'disjunctive enunciation' undermines the authority of colonial power—indeed, any authority—at the very moment of its articulation while, as ideology critique, it also shatters the historical mirrors of colonialism. The latter is particularly important, for *The Location of Culture* suggests that even critical accounts and conceptualizations of colonial power have taken it at its word and thus possibly served to symbolically reduplicate and sediment it in our theoretical imaginations, reifying its effects. In this sense, Bhabha may also be read as articulating something like retrospective, postcolonial—and knowingly voluntaristic—revenge on the history of colonialism, particularly at the level of its self-presentation, now virtually 'defeated,' at its very inception.[1] In what follows I intend to revisit this critical space by way of other conceptual and historical routes.

Translation and the Work of Transculturation

The ideas of transculturation and translation have recently become part of the lexicon of metropolitan cultural studies, traces of its transnationalization as it critically shadows overlapping capital-cultural formations. The idea of transculturation is a Latin-Americanist one, but it has been conceptually subordinated to an extent, firstly, by the similar but now hegemonic term in the field, 'hybridity,' and, secondly, by recent powerful articulations of subalternist perspectives. This is not the place to reflect upon these issues in any detail, but my preference for transculturation over hybridity, at least in its classical Néstor García Canclini and Homi Bhabha versions, has to do with the fact that 'transculturation' keeps an eye—albeit a problematic, dependent one—on capital as 'development' with a possible view to its eventual overturning, whilst 'hybridity' seems to have emerged in opposition to such consideration.[2] Subalternist perspectives, meanwhile, while sharing in this critical concern for the logics of development—subalternism is, in my view, a critique of the total apparatus of 'development' considered as the 'time of capital'—have highlighted both the national-populist and culturally elitist complicities that ideas of transculturation can also share with the processes they criticize.[3] To an extent, I agree with some of these criticisms. Here I will argue, nevertheless, that such complicity hardly exhausts the concept of transculturation's potential critical content.

Translation is, of course, not so locatable, but has entered the domain of a transnationalized cultural studies animated particularly by postcolonial criticism and critical anthropology, rearticulating Romantic aesthetic and ethical concerns paradigmatically established by, for example, Friedrich Schleiermacher. The work of both Lawrence Venuti and James Clifford is important in this regard. Indeed Clifford evokes the practices of translation as a model for thinking through and across cultures ('travelling'), warning against the identitarian logic of conceptual equivalence. As Peter Osborne argues in this issue, however, his notion of 'translation terms' presupposes the very otherness of the other that arguably only emerges in actual processes of transculturation and translation.[4]

There are thus two dimensions to what follows. Firstly, I read transculturation against the grain of recent trends which either critically disarm it through institutionalisation or confine it to the history books through radical—historicist—critique, in an effort of critical retooling which foregrounds the concept's historical content. I do so by sketching what I call the *work* of transculturation. Secondly, I hope to produce an historical example of the apparent 'defeat' (through 'disjunction') of colonial authority as evoked by Bhabha, albeit in a very different context from the ones he reflects upon in his work. Such a defeat emerges from the work of translation in transculturation. More specifically, I intend to look at a colonial Latin American instance of interlingual and intersemiotic translation. In other words, at absolutist and imperial acts of translation prior—but crucial—to the constitution of European bourgeois or modern nation-states in the equally imperial eighteenth century which is so important to postcolonial theory today.[5] Here, disjunction makes its appearance by breaking the logics of colonial equivalence in translation. Paradoxically, however, it does so only to reenforce *conjunction*—and colonial power—at another level, creating the conditions of politico-cultural alliance. From this point of view, transculturation may be thought of as the dialectics of disjunction and conjunction.

The Work of Transculturation

The idea of transculturation was incorporated into English-language cultural studies mainly via Mary Louise Pratt's deservedly influential book *Imperial Eyes: Travel Writing and Transculturation*. 'Transculturation,' she points out, 'is a phenomenon of the contact zone' where 'subordinated or marginal groups select and invent from materials transmitted to them by a dominant or metropolitan culture.'[6] The materials privileged in this text are representations and languages, for example, pidgen and creole frontier languages. Such zones, borders, of mutual transformation and interaction are surely also key historical sites of translation; and, indeed, we shall be turning to one below. Although important, however, I do not want to reduce transculturation to representations, language, even to translation, nor to insist on its one-directional, bottom-up character, as we shall also see below, but to scrutinize language and representation in translation as part of a cluster of practices and social relations.

The concept of transculturation was invented by the Cuban anthropologist Fernando Ortiz, having emerged from his analysis of the social and cultural effects of the production of tobacco and sugar in Cuba. He put the concept into circulation in his book *Cuban Counterpoint: Tobacco and Sugar*, first published in Spanish in 1940 and appearing in English translation in 1947 with a preface written by Bronislaw Malinowski. 'Tobacco and sugar,' says Ortiz, 'are the two most important figures in the history of Cuba.'[7] This is because they have shaped Cuban history. The production of sugar is an imperial phenomenon, the form too in which plantation slavery and the black Atlantic passes through the island. Tobacco meanwhile is originally indigenous, local, and 'gave rise to the small holding.' 'Always in contrast!' (6), exclaims Ortiz, each emerges from the specific combination of 'land, machinery, labor and money' (5) with a particular plant and their properties. This, then, is one kind of work—forms of labor, social relations, and surplus appropriation—associated with processes of transculturation in Cuba. The fundamental differences associated with both processes of production have been tendentially lost, however, as they are subordinated to the regime of mass industrial production—particularly important here for the production of tobacco is the emergence of the cigarette as a mass luxury form—and finance capital (71, 78-9, 93). Even tobacco (like sugar, Ortiz regrets) comes under foreign control. The concept of transculturation thus emerges here with a sharpened sense of subordination within the international economy, but also nostalgically, in the form of a critique of modernity and a perceived sense of national loss. Which brings us to another kind of work performed in transculturation, its symbolic work. However different tobacco and sugar may be, says Ortiz, each 'gives to man not only its complete usefulness but at the same time its unbroken continuity.' (8) Hence their common cultural importance. Each plant-product is, however, color- (i.e., race-) and gender-coded: 'If tobacco is male [… springing erect from the lips…], sugar is female'[8] (15-6). The following passage further underlines both the racializing and class dimensions of Ortiz's reading:

> Tobacco is dark, ranging from black to mulatto; sugar is light, ranging from mulatto to white. Tobacco does not change its color; it is born dark and dies the color of its race. Sugar changes its coloring; is born brown and whitens itself; at first it is a syrupy mulatto and in this state pleases the common taste; then it is bleached and refined until it can pass for white, travel all over the world, reach all mouths, and bring a better price, climbing to the top of the social ladder.(9)

The reference to 'passing' is interesting, serving to underline the fact that the binaries constructed by Ortiz do not all fall into conventional gendered patterns, but cross them: if tobacco is a '*he*' and 'hairy,' it is also stands for 'love and reproduction' (6, 15, 17). But, insofar as these attributes and processes configure the history of Cuba, the cultivation and transculturation of tobacco and sugar symbolize nationality: rooted and dispersed, organic and changing, male and female, miscegenating. Such is Ortiz's counterpoint, a 'dialogued composition,' as exemplified in the folk ballads and vernacular verses on which the author models the dispute of 'Don Tobacco and Doña Sugar' (3-4) in his extraordinary essay; and, in which, it transpires, black 'savage' tobacco is more national than is the once Eastern, then colonial, but now rooted (and Western?) Cuban white sugar. There is, of course, much more to Ortiz's reflections, but this is enough to give a sense of the symbolic work of transculturation, in which, on the one hand, the *culture* of transculturation is territorial, linked to agriculture and the land—cultivation—and, on the other hand, heavily marked by questions of race. In response to the denationalization of tobacco and the emergence of the cigarette, the properties of each plant are thus extended into culture and class, entangling them in their attributes. In other words, his is an early anthropological organic and positivist notion of culture which has not quite yet—of course, by definition—been separated from certain ideologies of nature. But there is more to transculturation than simple ideological reproduction.[9]

This is Ortiz's definition and justification of the idea of transculturation, as well as its generalization to the rest of the continent:

> I am of the opinion that the word *transculturation* better expresses the different phases of the process of transition from one culture to another because this does not consist merely in acquiring another culture, which is what the English word *acculturation* really implies, but the process also necessarily involves the loss or uprooting of a previous culture, which could be defined as deculturation. In addition it carries the idea of the consequent creation of new cultural phenomena, which could be called neoculturation…
>
> These questions of sociological nomenclature are not to be disregarded in the interests of a better understanding of social phenomena, especially in Cuba, whose history, more than that of any other country in America, is an intense, complex, unbroken process of transculturation of human groups, all in a state of transition. The concept of transculturation is fundamental and indispensable for an understanding of the history of Cuba, and, for analogous reasons, of that of America in general… (102-103)

Societies and cultures in transition, involving both loss and innovation, in historical contexts of Spanish colonialism and U.S. imperialism: it is also clear that Ortiz's idea takes a critical Latin-Americanist perspective on the dominant Eurocentric paradigm of 'acculturation' for thinking cultural change in anthropology at the time.[10] And, indeed, it is also possible to recognize Pratt's 'contact zones' here. But in Ortiz's work the models used to think through their dynamics are not linguistic ones, but rather tend towards the biological and ethno-racial. What follows are the passages that complete the paragraphs cited above:

> In the end, as the school of Malinowski's followers maintains, the result of every union of cultures is similar to that of the reproductive process between individuals: the offspring always has something of both parents but is always different from each of them…
>
> But this is not the moment to go into this theme at length, which will be considered in another work in progress dealing with the effects on Cuba of the transculturation of Indians, whites, Negroes, and Mongols. (103)

It is at this point that it is also important, however briefly, to recall an intertext and a context. Firstly, Ortiz's early anthropological works, influenced by Cesare Lombroso, on the topic of race and crime in Cuba—for example, *The Black Witchdoctors*, published in 1906—in which a highly embodied and racialized schema of cultural development is fundamental to his analysis.[11] By 1940 his racist views had changed, at least to an extent, and especially with regard to its valorization, but the *mechanics of his reading*—that is, the over-symbolization of supposed natural properties[12]—remains very similar, if botanically displaced. Secondly, it appears that the background to this displacement from racialized criminal bodies to the sociocultural life of plants, as well as Ortiz's foregrounding of the importance of black tobacco for the constitution of Cuban identity, was a crisis in race relations in Cuba which saw the emergence of the Independent Party of Colour in 1908 in response to the perceived piecemeal institutionalization of racism on the island, and a short 'race' war in 1912—known as the 'little war'—in which, the available research suggests, approximately 3,000 black people were killed. This would also endow Ortiz's reflections on transculturation with a politics. In this context, might it be that Ortiz's symbolic displacement (of 'race'), read as the response to such racist violence, *is* the cultural work of transculturation in *Cuban Counterpoint*?[13]

Needless to say, Malinowski did not take up Ortiz's term despite its translation and his own apparent enthusiasm: there would be no changes to the evolutionary paradigm of acculturation in dominant anthropology and thus no troubling of the denial of coevalness nor breach in the international division of theoretical labour. Of course, transculturation, as we have seen, is also itself partially structured by the racism it displaces, the developmentalism it still secretly contains, and the national populism it adopts. To this extent it might hardly merit critically retooling. But the critical concept of culture that emerged with cultural studies in the U.K. has also been so marked, for example, as has, more obviously, the notion of 'hybridity.'[14] Critique, however, it seems to me, means precisely working with the historical experiences written into ideas as a form of self-reflexivity. All of which, moreover, make real demands—a politics of theory—on the uses to which they are put. The concept of transculturation, meanwhile, did circulate in Latin America, particularly in the work of the novelist and anthropologist José María Arguedas. In the 1970s it was rediscovered there and reelaborated by the critic Angel Rama, who used it to rewrite the coordinates of the history of Latin American literature from the point of view of its various regionalisms, as these both reflected and responded culturally to the metropolitan-dominated experience of modernization as it passed through the cities into the peasant and Indian hinterlands. 'Race' is dropped as a dimension of cultural analysis, although the idea of transculturation remains marked by the practices and experiences of racism in the world from which it emerged to reflect upon; while a concern for cultural form is highlighted—particularly, as in the case of Arguedas, who was a bilingual Quechua- and Spanish-speaking anthropologist, the ways in which novelists 'select' (Rama's word) and reuse aspects of popular culture. This 'transcultural avantgarde' experimented with and transformed the novel by incorporating popular peasant and Indian ways of narrating, their media (fields of vision and sound), and cosmologies as compositional principles (rather than mere content) without, furthermore, the exoticism and epistemic subalternization associated with magical realism. Located culturally and emotionally in what Pratt calls 'contact zones'—historically the place also of missionaries and anthropologists—these transculturating writers prefigure, in Rama's account, the cultural regrounding, sublation, and overturning of the metropolitan-led forms of capitalist modernization and development they nevertheless depend on. In this sense, a key criticism of such a rural-centric conception—which Pratt's formulation quoted above redeploys—is its populism, advancing a cultural politics of hegemonic extension and incorporation rather than transgression.[15] Indeed, it is clear that for the most part the novelists Rama was concerned with were more critically aware of the contradictions and relations of power they were involved with than was Rama himself. The important point, however, is that this evident tension in Rama's use of the concept of transculturation—a tension between the dynamics of developmentalism, on the one hand, and its dependency-theory-inspired national-populist critique, on the other—should not be lost through falsely identifying them. Rather, this tension calls out to be theoretically grasped as a moment of potential reflexivity that simultaneously opens up the idea of transculturation to further elaboration in new contexts, as well as enhancing the sense of the contradictory work of culture-as-process which the concept historically contains.

Translation and Reduction

In the above section I have attempted to bring out the key historical contents of the concept of transculturation associated, firstly, with Ortiz and, secondly, as it was subsequently developed by Rama, hinting also at its English-language usages (including non-usage) by Malinowski and Pratt, that is: labor processes within an international political economy, on the one hand, and displacements in the notion of culture associated with 'development,' on the other. These are the practices I call the 'work of transculturation.' I would like to add another here, in a brief account of translation in the political or, even more so, governmental work of transculturation: specifically, the so-called 'spiritual conquest' of the Guaraní Indians in the Jesuit Missions of Paraguay from the mid-seventeenth to the mid-eighteenth century. I am assuming that the struggle against idolatory in the context of Christian conversion may be considered a kind of 'premodern,' colonial form of 'development'; in other words, paradigmatically (trans)cultural in its attempt to (re-)form subjectivities according to European models. In this regard, the Jesuit Missions were also known as 'Reductions'. What is meant by Reduction here? This is the definition given by the pioneer Jesuit priest in the region at the time, Father Antonio Ruiz de Montoya in his *The Spiritual Conquest of Paraguay*:

> We call *reductions* those towns of Indians, who having lived in their customary ways in mountains, hills and vales, by hidden streams, in three, four, or six houses alone, separated from one another by one, two, three, and more leagues, were reduced through the diligence of the Fathers to large settlements and political and human life, benefiting from cotton in which to dress.[16]

The colonial literary form known as the chronicle was in fact a legal document, a letter to the State (Crown) narrating—and accounting for—particular acts of colonization. The text from which the above definition is taken, traces the history of the Jesuit Reductions with a view to obtaining permission for the Fathers to arm them. They were founded on the colonial borders between the Spanish and Portuguese Empires in the New World, serving as colonial outposts. And as the letter makes abundantly clear, the Jesuits carried out their mission of conversion-reduction of the Indian population in this 'contact zone' structured by the ongoing process of colonization, but which also included the resistance of some Guaraní and other Indian groups, incursions by bands of slave-traders capturing Indians to be sold over the colonial border, and competition for Indian bodies to put to work on the farms and plantations of the local *encomendero* lords. The Jesuits, for their part, were of course interested in both bodies *and* souls. The main local produce was not tobacco, as in Ortiz's Cuba, but included some sugar, vine and, above all, the local tea leaf, *yerba mate* or Paraguayan tea, which served the regional colonial market from the mines of Potosí, to the west, to the port of Buenos Aires to the south. The Jesuit Reductions were an important part of this Paraguayan tea production and exportation sector, and competition for Indian labor was intense. The work of transculturation indeed.[17]

Labor and religion were the central coordinates of life in the Jesuit Reductions. As the above quotation suggests, apart from the dress code, 'reduced' Indians were to experience a dramatic change in way of life. The organization of housing and family type were radically transformed, as were rituals of community, such as dance. Here is a passage from Alberto Armani's 1972 book *The City of God and the City of the Sun* describing a process to which it is clear the author himself is blind, and in which the apparent socialization referred to by Montoya clearly involves forms of planned cultural or "spiritual" individuation:

> On such festive occasions, the Indians were carried away by their ancient passion for dance, and the missionaries, against their better judgment, allowed their charges to externalize their vitality in

the rhythms of choral dance and music. The missionaries' respect for this form of Indian culture (ordered rhythmic dance, the natural complement of music) did not change over time. Even weekly dance lessons were organized in which the most gifted trained the young in symbolic and figured dance, a form of artistic expression into which the Jesuits attempted to direct the exuberance of the Guaranis. Only in 1689, when the Second General Rules of the Reductions were passed, was this form of entertainment restricted, with the number of dances that could be performed in each festival being limited to four, while promiscuity between the sexes... was prohibited.[18]

The majority of the Mendicant orders that arrived in the New World to combat idolatry and save souls, including the Jesuits, initially did so in the local languages of the Indian peoples. Indeed, the first book produced in the Americas was a Nahautl catechism printed in 1529 in New Spain.[19] Montoya's 'spiritual conquest' was thus carried out in Guaraní. For this reason, the practice of translation became fundamental to colonization and conversion in the Reductions, as did the production of books.

According to Bartomeu Meliá, 'the Jesuits exercised on the Guaraní language a reduction of the same order as politico-religious reduction...'[20] This particular 'reduction' took three forms: firstly, the translation of spoken Guaraní into alphabetical script; secondly, the invention of a grammar (mainly, in the first instance, for the teaching of the language to Europeans); and thirdly, the compilation of a bilingual dictionary, conceived as a 'treasure' of both the Guaraní language and culture. I will refer here briefly only to the first and third forms of reduction as these clearly involve practices of translation—intersemiotic, in the first instance, and interlingual in the second—that are fundamental to the very processes of colonization.

The relation of Spanish alphabetic script to the Guaraní voice it overcodes might be thought of as being similar to the well-known colonial image of the church built on top of a Mexican pyramid: the strategy involved the reuse of pregiven forms of ritual, appropriating them into new circuits of signification. Deleuze and Guattari use the term *miraculation* for this process, because such an appropriation tends also to suggest that what has been overcoded is in fact an effect of what has been imposed; in other words, that the Guaraní voice is an effect of alphabetic Spanish language script. I say this because it has been pointed out by Meliá that the Guaraní alphabet thus created was notable for its 'phonological systematization [and] characterized by its simplicity and the almost univocal correspondence between graphism and phoneme' (265). In this sense, the overcoding might be thought of as totalizing, subordinating and incorporating the Guaraní soundscape and connecting it to the signifiers of Jesuit pedagogy, especially via the catechism. In the words of Deleuze and Guattari: '[T]he triangle has become the base for a pyramid, all of whose sides cause the vocal [the Guaraní voice], the graphic [alphabetic script], and the visual [the book] to converge toward the eminent unity of the despot.'[21] Alphabetic writing itself, linked as it was to Latin, was considered an organizing, civilizational value at the time, taming the body and voice, and was mobilized as such both in Spain and the colonies.[22] Such a process also acted to standardize the Guaraní language, while the printing presses made it reproducible. In contrast to the grammar books, which were read mainly by priests learning language, the catechism circulated more widely among the 'reduced' Guaraní population. The catechism was to be both learned and repeated aloud. And the sounds, now returning and transculturated, bore the imprint of their capture.

Naoki Sakai's critique of Jakobsen's notion of interlingual translation is surely correct insofar as the latter presupposes the unity of language that is only produced in the practice and relation of translation and, I would add, in the compilation of mono- and bilingual dictionaries and grammars.[23] From among the varieties of local languages and dialects, a dominant form was sought and worked upon such that, for example, a particular version of Guaraní also became a language of colonial incorporation, as well as prolonging its existence in postcolonial Paraguay—notably in the form of 'classical' Guaraní—as the language of everyday life, intimacy, in a diglossic relation with the dominant 'public' Spanish.[24] Indeed, some have argued that what in fact has emerged is a third, mixed language known as *yopará* (which means 'soup' or 'stew'). In this regard, a history of imperial bilingual dictionaries produced in such 'contact zones'—Nahuatl-Spanish, Quechua-Spanish, Guaraní-Spanish—might be crucial to reflecting on the constitution of European-national-state languages. In *A Treasure of the Guaraní Language*, for example, also compiled by Montoya, he praises the language for its 'elegance which with reason might compete with those [languages] of fame.'[25] It was also a powerful language. Among the Guaraní, power and nobility were attributed to its good use: many chieftains, Montoya reports in his *The Spiritual Conquest*, 'were ennobled with their eloquence in speech (so do they value their language, and with reason, because it deserves praise and celebration)' (76). All very good reasons, of course, for its reduction. He further notes that they even had a word for *Dios* (God): 'They knew of God, and in a sense of his Unity, as evidenced in the name they gave him, which is *Tupá*; the first word *tu* is "admiration," the second *pá* is "interrogation."'[26] Which does not mean that they are not cannibals, an act he goes on to describe. And *Tupá* is the word offered as the Guaraní word for '*Dios*' in Montoya's *Treasure*. Here, therefore, is an excellent example of the making of translatory 'equivalence' in colonial cultural contact, a caption point for transcultural transformation as it 'reduced' *Tupá* to *Dios*. But it is also, of course, the possible site of the kind of 'ambivalence' in colonial authority with which I began. The enunciation and circulation of the voice *Tupá* in the Reductions could only have been, I suggest, disjunctive. Which "God" was being referred to as the signifier *Tupá* was enunciated, *Tupá* or *Dios*? And when spoken, was not the authority of Christian theology fractured by Guaraní cosmology and, indeed, vice versa? It seems, moreover, that Tupá was in fact a minor deity in Guaraní cosmology, suggesting that—again, when enunciated—*Dios*/God was in reality in the process of being overcoded and reduced (even haunted) by the god *Tupá*. This might partially explain Montoya's own anxieties as to his ability to communicate with the Crown, as expressed in *The Spiritual Conquest*: 'With all this, of having for so many years no relation with the Spanish and their language, obliged perforce to use the Indian, an almost rustic man is formed, foreign to polite language, a circumstance not helped,' he goes on to complain, 'by the food the Indians commonly use, and perforce we too, being roots, squashes, herbs, beans, and the like, [and by] even hostile invasion, the burning of churches, the wounding of priests....' (46) Who, in fact, is conquering whom?

The words of Father Montoya bear witness to what Bhabha might refer to as the disjunctive production of ambivalence, the signs of colonial Christian authority seemingly breaking down even as they are enunciated. There is some truth in this. But from the perspective of the practice of translation, the colonial work of transculturation—linked, as noted above, to the production of Paraguayan tea (economics) and the conversion of souls (culture)—was slightly more complex. For disjuncture itself, that is, translatory *nonequivalence* within imposed equivalence (*Tupá* = *Dios* [God]) acted as a caption point in which colonial authority was indeed consolidated (politics). The signifier Tupá is thus better approached as a hinge, linking cosmologies which may, indeed, facilitate moments of fracture, but which may also, within non-identity facilitate moments of co-existence, alliance, and even identification. For the Jesuit Missions were not only centers of 'reduction,' but also military outposts. And although the missionary authorities were ordered to take great care of the arms and munitions, many of the 'reduced' Indians became formidable soldiers. Alberto Armani writes:

> The Guaraní armed forces... were at the service of the Spanish authorities not only for reasons of public order but also for participation in veritable military operations against the Portuguese and Indian tribes that had not submitted.... Between 1644 and 1766 the Guaranís took part in approximately seventy military interventions alongside the Spanish. Among the most significant, ...the repression of the autonomist rebellion by Paraguayan creoles led by José Antequera and Fernando Mompox between 1722 and 1735 (on which occasion more than twelve thousand Guaranís were mobilized). (113-114)

From the point of view of transculturation, however, the question must always return: But were they soldiers of Christ?

Endnotes

I would like to thank Carol Watts and Elizabeth Grosz for their help in writing this article.

1—See, for example, the following statement of intentionality: 'I attempt to represent a certain defeat, or even impossibility of the "West" in its authorization of the "idea" of colonization.' Homi K. Bhabha, *The Location of Culture* (London: Routledge, 1994), 175. See also John Kraniauskas, 'Hybridity in a Transnational Frame: Latin Americanist and Postcolonial Perspectives on Cultural Studies', *Nepantla. Views from the South* (1, 2000): 117-144

2—Néstor García Canclini, *Culturas híbridas. Estrategias para entrar y salir de la modernidad* (Mexico City: Grijalbo, 1989).

3—See, for example, important articles by John Beverley, 'Los límites de la cuidad letrada: subalternidad, literatura, y transculturación', *Historia y Grafía*, no. 12 (1999): 149-176, and Alberto Moreiras, 'Hybridity and Double Consciousness', *Cultural Studies*, Vol. 13, No. 3 (July, 1999): 373-407.

4—See Lawrence Venuti, *The Translator's Invisibility: A History of Translation* (London: Routledge, 1995), and James Clifford, *Routes: Travel and Translation in the Late Twentieth Century* (Cambridge and London: Harvard University Press, 1997). See also, Friedrich Schleiermacher, 'On the Different Methods of Translating', in Rainer Schulte and John Biguenet (eds.), *Theories of Translation: An Anthology of Essays from Dryden to Derrida* (Chicago: University of Chicago Press, 1992), 36-54.

5—For 'interlingual' and 'intersemiotic' translation, see Roman Jackobsen, 'On Linguistic Aspects of Translation' in Rainer Schulte and John Biguenet, 144-151. For reflection on the relation between translation and the constitution of nation-states, see Naoki Sakai, *Translation and Subjectivity: on 'Japan' and Cultural Nationalism* (Minneapolis: University of Minnesota Press, 1997), 1-17; on the problems of considering the relation of national-imperial languages without including the Spanish language and its imperial history, see Walter Mignolo, *The Darker Side of the Renaissance: Literacy, Territoriality, and Colonization* (Ann Arbor: University of Michigan Press, 1995) and *Local Histories/Global Designs: Coloniality, Subaltern Knowledges and Border Thinking* (Princeton: New Jersey: Princeton University Press, 2000).

6—Mary Louise Pratt, *Imperial Eyes: Travel Writing and Transculturation* (London: Routledge, 1992), 6. For a mention of transculturation that subordinates it to hybridization, see Paul du Gay, Stuart Hall, Linda Janes, Hugh Mackay, and Keith Negus, *Doing Cultural Studies: The Story of the Sony Walkman* (London: Sage/Open University, 1997), 72. It should be obvious that my intention is to reverse this theoretical relation.

7—Fernando Ortiz, *Cuban Counterpoint: Tobacco and Sugar* (1940), trans. by Harriet de Onís (1947) and Introduced by Bronislaw Malinowski and Fernando Coronil (Durham and London: Duke University Press, 1995), 4 (all subsequent references to this work will be made in parenthesis in the text).

8—In this regard, for Ortiz, cigarettes are 'perverted' and tendentially female!

9—For culture and agriculture, see Raymond Williams, *Marxism and Literature* (Oxford: Oxford University Press, 1977), 11. According to Gabriela Nouzeilles, 'the emergence of the concept of "transculturation" opened up a critical perspective from which it is possible not only to reconstruct the discursive genealogy of Latin American positivism... but also to account for its agonic relation with scientific systems of representation which ordered the world, from a European perspective, according to racial hierarchies.' See her 'El espejo transculturado de la ciencia: raza y autorepresentación en Latinoamérica' in *Latin American Literary Cultures: A Comparative History* (Oxford: Oxford University Press, and Mexico City: Fondo de Cultura Económica, forthcoming).

10—See Angel Rama, *Transcultur-*

ación narrativa en América Latina, Siglo XXI editores, 1982, 32-34.

11—See Fernando Ortiz, *Los negros brujos* (1906) (Havana: Editorial de Ciencias Sociales, 1995). Discussing the cultural experience of the wage form, he says of 'free men of color' that 'the primitiveness of their psychology deprived them of certain virtues which whites had acquired…' (40).

12—In his new Introduction to *Cuban Counterpoint*, Fernando Coronil suggests that what I am calling 'oversymbolization' is in fact a 'counterfetishism,' 'a critique of reification.' It is true that Ortiz traces a kind of social history of commodities; he does not, however, have a concept of 'commodity form.' This is why, as Coronil points out, Ortiz does not 'mak[e] a reference to Marx' (xxx, xxvii). This does not mean, of course, that he has no concept of fetishism, but rather it is one derived from anthropology and used to designate so-called primitivism, as in *The Black Witchdoctors* (*Los negros brujos*). Indeed, Coronil displaces onto Ortiz his own excellent critical extension of the latter's account of transculturation.

13—See Rafael Fermoselle, *Política y color en Cuba: la guerrita de 1912* (1974) (Montevideo: Editorial Colibrí, 1998). I would like to thank John Beverley for mentioning the possible relevance of this war to me.

14—See my 'Globalisation is Ordinary: The Transnationalisation of Cultural Studies', *Radical Philosophy*, 90 (July/August, 1998): 9-19.

15—See Rama's posthumous *La cuidad letrada*, Ediciones del Norte, Hanover, 1984, where he states: 'Although isolated in a foreign and hostile spatial and cultural immensity, the cities had to dominate and civilize their surroundings;… what at first was called 'evangelizing' and then 'educating'… [was] a matter of the same effort of *transculturation* according to European models.' (17-8; my emphasis) This is the space of 'conversion' that I will be looking at below. The most important critique of Rama's idea of 'narrative transculturation' remains Neil Larsen's, in his *Modernism and Hegemony: A Materialist Critique of Aesthetic Agencies* (Minneapolis: University of Minnesota Press, 1990), 49-71. His discussion is, however, so entangled in a reading of the short stories of Juan Rulfo that I cannot give it the attention it deserves here.

16—Antonio Ruiz de Montoya, *Conquista espiritual hecho por los religiosos de la compañía de Jesús en las provincias de Paraguay, Paraná, Uruguay y Tapé* (1639) (Rosario: Equipo Difusor de Estudios de Historia Iberoamericana, 1989), 58 (my translation). All subsequent references to this work will be made in parenthesis in the text.

17—For the importance of Paraguayan tea, see J.C. Garavaglia's outstanding, *Mercado interno y economía colonial* (Mexico City: Grijalbo, 1983). In this regard, it should also be noted that Asunción was at the time the regional colonial administrative capital.

18—Alberto Armani, *Ciudad de Dios y ciudad del sol: el 'Estado' jesuita de los guaraníes (1609-1768)* (Mexico City: Fondo de Cultura Económica, 1982), 148. All further references to this work will be included in the text in parenthesis.

19—See Louise M. Burkhart, *The Slippery Earth: Nahua-Christian Dialogue in Sixteenth-Century Mexico* (Tucson: University of Arizona Press, 1989), 20. I assume Burkhart is referring to books printed in alphabetic characters. I would like to thank Eleanor Wake for bringing this book to my attention. For the books of the Indian cultures of the Americas, see Gordon Brotherston, *Books of the Fourth World: Reading the Native Americas through their Literature* (Cambridge: Cambridge University Press, 1992).

20—Bartomeu Melià, *El guaraní conquistado y reducido: ensayos de etnohistoria* (Asunción: Universidad Católica, 1986), 264, my translation. (All subsequent references will be included in parenthesis in the text).

21—Gilles Deleuze and Félix Guattari, *Anti-Oedipus: Capitalism and Schizophrenia* (1977), trans. by Robert Hurley, Mark

Seem and Helen R. Lane (New York: The Viking Press, 1977), 205.

22—See Walter Mignolo, *The Darker Side,* 29-67.

23—Naoki Sakai, *Translation and Subjectivity,* 2.

24—On diglossia, see Martin Leinhard, 'Of Mestizajes, Heterogeneities, Hybridisms and Other Chimeras: On the Macroprocesses of Cultural Interaction in Latin America,' *Journal of Latin American Cultural Studies*, Vol. 6, No. 2 (November, 1997): 183-200 (which offers a critique of transculturation among other terms).

25—Antonio Ruiz de Montoya, *Tesoro de la lengua Guaraní* (Madrid: n.p.,1639) (my translation)

26—See also both Antonio Ruiz de Montoya, ibid., pp. 402-3 and *Arte y Vocabulario de la lengua Guaraní* (Madrid: 1639), 323.

INTERLUDES

TRACES

1. Of necessity, a trace is the trace of something. Of a painting, for example, which has long been hanging on a wall, and which, before having been withdrawn, slowed through its presence the yellowing of the wall caused by light. But more often, it is the trace of a movement conducted by a living being, or by a machine: for example, the trace designates that which remains from the passage of any living being or engine: the traces left by tires in the sand, for example. In each case, the trace implies the disappearance of the very thing of which it is the trace.

2. Hence it traces at the same time both something and its disappearance. It is not that which remains of the thing, for even if the trace itself is something—for example, lipstick left on a cigarette rolling paper—this thing itself is properly not the trace: it is another thing. For example, the imprint of a tire is a thing other than the tire itself. Or again, the trace left by lipstick is certainly made of the same substance as lipstick, yet in a state and in a dispersion (*éclats*) quite different.

3. As thing, the trace is a type of thing like any other (for example, it is the dried ink deposited by a pen or a printer). The trace as trace, however, is something other than a thing. It is the presence of an absence indicated as such: as absence, and most often also as an absence which remains incompletely determined and still to be imagined or reconstituted.

4. In this sense every trace is at the same time the trace of something and the disappearance of that thing. It is thus at least just as

Jean-Luc NANCY

translated by
Jon SOLOMON

Interludes

much the trace of emptiness, an emptying out or a pre-empting (*d'un vide, d'un vidage ou d'un évidement*). As a tract—for the trace is a tract (*trait*), a passage *drawn out* from the thing of which it is a trace—the trace is the thing in retreat (*retrait*) or retraction. Or again, it is an abs-traction.

5. In the chemical sense of the word, the trace is an evanescent state of the thing: the impalpable presence, the infinitesimal last identifiable elements of the thing, on the edge of complete disappearance. It is in this sense that one may say that such and such bodies are not present in a solution "except in trace form." The trace is the threshold of dissolution.

6. A trace is thus made of something and of nothing: its future and its past are both a disappearing. The trace is between negations, both of which are negations of the same thing, a thing which has withdrawn since the very start before retracting, later on, from its proper retreat, erasing even its own traces.

7. Every trace must be considered not only as a traced line (*trait*), but also as the tracing of a line which begins to erase itself in the moment of tracing. Every trace is a movement of tracking (*trace*), and every tracking movement is similar to the steps of a sly warrior who advances by doubling back on her own tracks to cover her footprints.

8. In a sense, a trace has always-already begun to erase itself, but in another sense, in erasing itself, it produces other traces which are the traces of erasure and which can be interpreted as such by an opposing warrior even more sly than the first. Hence, a trace never stops, perhaps, erasing itself.

9. The trace is the interminable passage from one disappearance to another—just like a unique—yet infinite—stroke of the pen in the blank middle of a page. The passage is interminable because it never exactly begins: there is always something of the thing and already nothing more of it—and, more precisely, it never ends: Always, there is already nothing more, and still something left.

10. Let us consider an existence in general—or the existence of the world in totality—as a trace: a passage from disappearing to disappearing. Birth and death, flaring up (*déflagration*) and flaring out (*conflagration*)… In the sense of the logic just exposed (*exposée*), finite existence is thus properly infinite.

11. In the trace, there is necessarily something—which is, if you will, the figure of the trace—and something other which is not something: the *nothing* for which the trace, in its function, makes way. This *nothing* is not only situated (to infinity) behind and ahead of the trace: it also accompanies the trace along its entire route. The tracing of it is the trace: the nothing between the two frayed extremities of the thing.

12. The trace is constituted by two borders between which this *nothing* draws or withdraws. Hence, a trait, a line, has two sides but nothing in between the two because it is without thickness. The trace is a groove of emptiness at the interior of an empty space. In this manner, it is also infinitely finite: completely and continually open along its entire

length—and completely and continually closed throughout all of its self-reticulated density.

13. The trace strives to abolish itself in tracing itself: it has no other destination nor other representation of its being as trace. It traces an abolition and it abolishes itself in its proper tracing. Such is the essence or such is the sense of the trait in general: a tract of writing, the track of an arrow, a schematic outline, a flash of wit. In French, the saying *"d'un seul trait"* designates a shot-gun like action, very rapid and animated: to drink in a single go (*boire d'un seul trait*), to recite all at once (*réciter d'un seul trait*)… The trace is both the vector and the velocity of crossing a threshold (*vitesse de franchissement*). The trait abolishes itself in its own traction, attraction and abstraction.

14. The trait is the speed of tracing. In the tracing, the trait appears, but what it shows is but the speed of its appearing and disappearing: the trace of its vanishing unicity. Such is the trace of a calligraphic art or of a thought of painting as movement and not as tableau.

15. On the painting which has just been hung upon a wall, the trait of the artist has already broached the disappearance of the painting. On the wall which one will discover upon removing the painting, the trait will have left an absence of trace in the midst of the dim trace of the painting itself, which the light of long days, or that of eternity, will end by extinguishing in turn.

FRAGMENTS FOR RESTANCE

MORINAKA Takaaki

translated by Naoki SAKAI

Restance ------- in what language does this word offer itself to be read and listened to? As soon as we receive this word, we will have an unmistakable feeling that something has begun to unravel, slightly but irredeemably, in the place of our belonging; that already an event which will open us to the multitude of other people is under way. That is, an experience of the remnant, of what remains, what cannot be appropriated. Yet, against what does it refuse to be appropriated? It is, above all, against an abstraction called the system of a language, against forces inherent in the system which confine the heterogeneous within its boundary or expel it. REST-ANCE is, no longer or not yet, either in French or English (or German). In order to read this word one must work on it: one must actualize it in specific languages, rendering it in the contexts relevant to each of the languages. To read it, therefore, one must necessarily translate it. The word calls for a translation as an experience of deforming languages and as a listening to the murmuring of languages thus distorted, a translation which will destroy any illusion that a text can ever be reduced to a signification, concept, or thesis, and also raze a dream of the resistanceless communication. Such a translation will call into question the assumed autonomy of a linguistic system, and trace what overflows the limits of such a system—tracing a movement of that which remains / resists (the suffix—ANCE—indicates this movement, which oscillates between activity and passivity, and space - time opened up by such a movement). To this very extent, this word designates "us" of today: it will mark the pronoun to come. The subjects of contemporary theoretical discourse and of contemporary artistic acts can find their position of enunciation only in the non-presentable place of intersection and interruption, that is, in the place which only translation can possibly disclose. Thus we must not lose sight of a politics concealed in the concept "*universalitas*," of the desire to orchestrate various differences in one—*unus*—direction—*versus*—. Wherever the solicitation to oneness is in operation, regardless of whether it is of "Western" or "non-Western" thought, we will demonstrate the movement of RESTANCE thereby trying to create a space of communication that is irreducible to one. Rather than representing ourselves as a *unified* subject, as RESTANCE we will offer ourselves to translation, to an endless process of re-translation. This is the condition as well as the end for us: after all, we are the multitudes of traces.

MULTIPLICITY

Coming from "the West" and accompanied by the expansion of capitalism, the concept of "Theory," just as Hegel's *Geist,* which is a process of *Aufhebung* from particular to universal, appropriates all heterogeneities and transforms others into its resources in the process of its self-externalization. The uniqueness and the absoluteness of "Theory" are founded not only by "the West" in taking itself as the point of reference and considering the differences as a kind of differentiation, but fundamentally it is also constructed by "the Local," which ignores other local experiences and constitutes itself directly in opposition to "the West." Most of all, the others that we perceive are always through the western intellectual market and theoretical framework.

In the instance of deconstructing the vertical and temporal relation between "the West" and "the Local," the linkage with other locals should be built up horizontally and spatially. Rather than constructing an "Asian" theory to confront the "West," this attempt no longer tries to consider the "West" as the only Other, but to create the MULTIPLICITY of interlocutors and finally to go beyond the binary opposition of "the West" and "the Rest."

Yu Chi-chung

Contribution to the Inaugural Issue of *Traces*

Who will be the readers of *Traces*? Preparing a short contribution for the inaugural issue, I find it difficult to know which is the greater constraint: the requirement for brevity or the necessary disorientation involved in addressing a *potential* reader/readers. I want to write about the everyday, where (believe it or not, reader!) my sense of obscurity and the marginal is powerful. I have watched barns in this area corrode, motionless, for twenty-three years. Yet this week, teaching my class entitled "Virtual Orientalisms" (and somewhere amid the barns) I observed how a text by Roland Barthes, commencing with a call to readers ("us") to "write the history of our own obscurity" ends with a description of "the Japanese eye" as a calligraphic product, a "comma painted sideways," a "brief point" at the end of a brush line, punctuating the ideograph. One could ask, particularly in the context of a requirement for brevity, why give *this* example weight? I must want to locate myself somewhere in relation to it, some place in which the text and myself are empowered by the same gesture with which I criticize and reject it. At the same time, why feel smug in the face of such an artifact, rare in its extravagant elegance and crudity? Am I writing in/from the West? That question is already old hat. Am I writing in/from a post-Orientalist, post-feminist discursive space? ("Well," I keep thinking "the men have produced these statements for *Traces* a lot more casually than I have.") But how, then, *does* an anti-Orientalist aspiration, like Barthes', transmute into a disquisition on

| Brett DE BARY

Interludes

the epicanthic fold? Almost thirty years after the publication of the text in question, the problems of writing "the history of our obscurity" have been clearly analyzed, have they not? Erase the "our" (but where does it go?), and stop assuming that one is the center to be decentered, circling in ever narrowing spirals around the same monuments---traces, to be sure. But doesn't the expression "stop assuming one is the center" assume that one ("I"?) is ("am"?) precisely that ("there"?)... and so on and so forth: this is the everyday. At any rate, whoever we are, and wherever we are, my space is filled, so, *Traces* readers, hello!

Ithaca, New York, February 2000

Sign: Inspired by a Letter

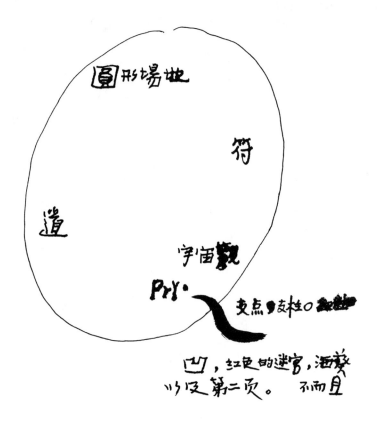

CHE Qianzi

translated by
Yunte HUANG

Interludes

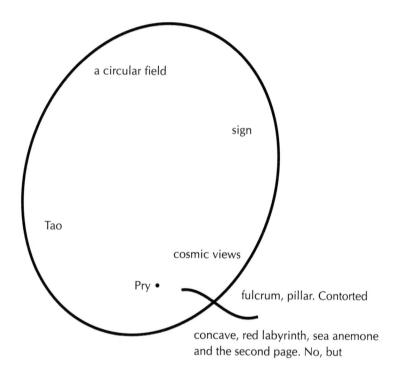

Translator's note: The Chinese word for "letter" in the title is *zimu*, which, literally, means "mother of words." Hence, the title may be translated as "Sign: Imaginations Given Birth by Mother of Words."

II

THEORY AND THE POLITICS OF LOCALE

MIMICRY AND DIFFERENCE: A SPECTRALOGY FOR THE NEO-COLONIAL INTELLECTUAL

KANG Nae-hui

translated by KANG Nae-hui

1. The Neo-colonial Intellectual

The expression "neo-colonial" in the title of this essay is chosen rather deliberately to reveal my theoretical and political position. I say this to clarify at the outset that the perspectives and opinions to be presented here have been deeply influenced by my involvement in the current politics of intellectual life in South Korea. Of course, theoretico-political positions do not automatically derive from the fact that one belongs to a particular society, but rather have to be constituted or even won through various kinds of intellectual struggles. This claim to be a neo-colonial intellectual, however, is my attempt to open up a perspective from which to intervene in a controversial theoretical terrain. To be specific, this terrain is brought into being by the question of "decolonization," a theoretical issue which has recently received much critical attention, thanks to the rise of "post-colonialism" as an important field of academic debate. I want to approach this question from the position of a "neo-colonial." We all know that the "terrain of theoretical debate" is located in the metropolitan centers of the West, which are currently at the heart of theory production. Is it not the case that even theorists of post-colonialism, often intellectuals from Third World societies, take the Western metropolitan centers to be the home ground of their own theory production? My confession as a "neo-colonial," then, is an attempt on my part to interrogate the discourse of decolonization from a different perspective, from the position I have come to take within South Korea where I have to engage in various social practices.

In an essay written in 1993, Chungmoo Choi suggested the need to interrogate the discourse of decolonization in South Korea. While admitting that "[t]he discourse of decolonization...is ever more relevant in the post-colonial era," and endorsing the "*minjung* [people's] movement's critique of the imperialist hegemony of the capitalist superpowers,"[1] she remains suspicious of the movement's discourse. What she takes issue with is the strategy of "representation" which subversive intellectuals of the movement have been promoting since the early 1980s. While the intellectuals may have fancied themselves as representatives of the people, there was a serious problem: "[the] workings of hegemony could be disguised in the structure of representation, especially in the act of self-abnegation, to embody the people it represents."[2] According to Choi, the intellectuals have made an idealization of the *minjung* for "self-serving" purposes.[3]

This analysis seems accurate, for, since the collapse of the Soviet Union in 1989, many *minjung* intellectuals have left the movement and begun to accept government jobs. They may have had an excuse, for after 1993, the Korean government was consecutively under the control of Kim Young-sam and Kim Dae-jung, formerly self-proclaimed democracy-fighters against the military dictatorships of Park Chung-hee, Chun Doo-whan and Roh Tae-woo. Once in power, however, the rule of the two Kim's, though no longer military, was not so different from that of their predecessors, for they continued to practice anti-democratic policies. The participation of intellectuals in these civilian governments was thus a surrender of the movement in favor of pursuing personal interests, Choi suggests. I believe that this betrayal has to do with the fact that intellectuals were prone to depend on the strategy of "representation." While allowing progressive intellectuals to act as the representatives, if not the leaders, of the movement, this attitude of representation tends to ignore the fact that their discursive practices and calculations are themselves objects of analysis and interrogation.

Notwithstanding my sympathy with Choi's critical assessment of the discourse of decolonization, however, I believe that there is a different way to interrogate it. I do not want to call into question the entirety of the movement from an outsider's viewpoint, but rather to risk locating my own locus of discursive enunciation within the theoretical debate over the question of decolonization. It is true that Choi's critique comes from a deep interest in the minjung movement, but its locus of enunciation is inevitably outside South Korea. Perhaps her location in the Western center of theory production makes it difficult for her to side with any of the competing positions within the movement. In addition, it is probably normal that making a choice between opposing political positions does not arise for someone not directly involved in a social movement.

However, for one who wants his/her own theoretico-practical position to produce "political and other actual consequences," it seems more important to conceive of the decolonization discourse as a terrain of theoretical debate in which different strategies and calculations compete with one another.[4] This is something very different from considering it as an object of totalizing criticism. Once within that terrain, it is always necessary to make political calculations, since practical judgments, hostile or friendly affiliations, controversial decisions need to be made continuously. This shows that not only the "representation" of the people by the discourse of decolonization, but also the difference in positions and ways of resistance within the movement require critical interrogation. From this perspective, to confess to being a neo-colonial intellectual is not only to take the position of one who "represents" the people—not that we should give up the work of representation. As Spivak pointed out, there always remains the question of interests which cannot do without representation and which do not disappear easily.[5] At the same time, however, the role of the intellectual participating in the *minjung* movement cannot be reduced to representing the people. Intellectuals produce discourses not only to represent the interests of the subordinated people, but also to intervene intellectually in the movement. This intervention necessarily takes the form of theoretical practice of the type Louis Althusser has insisted distinguishing from other social practices. Moreover, it is because s/he has the profession in which to produce theoretical positions that an intellectual can engage in this intervention.[6] I believe this practice necessitates an "embodied" participation on the part of the intellectual in the movement. To create a position in the battleground of decolonization, the intellectual must risk committing him/herself to the movement, rather than critically observing it.

The theoretical frontiers which I want to intervene in are twofold: the discourse of decolonization produced by the inter- or trans-national community of intellectuals as well as the discourse of decolonization produced by progressive intellectuals in South Korea. My intervention in the first frontier, no doubt, is affected by the fact that my theoretical position is determined by my participation in social practices in South Korea. Although this might go without saying, I am repeating it to suggest the possibility of addressing questions of decolonization in a different way from those of the "post-colonial" intellectuals who are active in the Metropolitan centers of the West. Nevertheless, the more important question for me is how to intervene in the second frontier, the ongoing debate going on the question of decolonization within South Korea. My way of participation in this debate is to deal with the problem of liquidating the colonial past, probably the most serious issue for those involved in decolonization.[7]

I have taken the position of "neo-colonialism" to call attention to the questions and issues often neglected in the previous work on decolonization done in South Korea. The concept of "neo-colonialism" presupposes a particular judgment of the social character of South Korea. I prefer the term "neo-colonial" to "colonial," since I believe that the latter is inadequate to describe present-day South Korea, a highly-developed capitalist society with an energetic economy fueled by monopoly capital. To be sure, it is still suffering from the colonial past, but since the 1980s it has become a highly-developed consumer society in which commodities are not merely the object of fetishism, as in colonial days, but a staple, too. I also prefer "neo-colonial" to "post-colonial," since I do not believe that South Korea has overcome the traumas of its colonial past: as we shall see, the liquidation of the vestiges and dregs of colonialism remains an incomplete social project. In addition, it should be pointed out that South Korea has not yet been fully liberated: Even after the Liberation in 1945, it has remained occupied by foreign troops. To be sure, one can argue that the US military presence is required because of the hostile relationship between South and North Korea, but this itself is a sign that Korea has not yet achieved full independence. While South Korea is a country with its own apparatus of government, its national sovereignty is limited, to say the least. For instance, crimes committed against Koreans by US military personnel, civilian employees, and their families cannot be prosecuted by Korean law officers. Recently, South Korea has come to find itself in a deeper subordinate position. Hit by an economic crisis due to a shortage of foreign currency in 1997, it was forced to promise the implementation of a neo-liberalist restructuring of the whole society in order to receive bailout from the International Monetary Fund. As the IMF and transnational monetary capital came to have a stronger say in the South Korean economy, there is little doubt that the recent economic crisis will deepen the extent to which South Korea's economy and political autonomy remain subject to foreign influences. Thus to define South Korea today as a post-colonial society is to engage in a "premature celebration of the pastness of colonialism,"[8] and to obscure "the faces of neo-colonial structure in the process of reconstructing global capitalism."[9] Of course, This is not to say that the theory of post-colonialism is without value. I myself have learned a lot from it, as my subsequent discussion will abundantly show. Nevertheless, I think it important to define South Korea's social character as "neo-colonial" rather than "post-colonial" to emphasize that the conflicts and contradictions formed in the colonial past and the neo-colonial present still haunt South Korea so that the society still needs to be decolonized.

That Koreans are still suffering from the colonial past and the neo-colonial present is reflected in the fact that Korea is the only great nation (as large as seventy-five million) that has not succeeded in forming a nation state. Therefore, South Koreans naturally take reunification and national liberation to be important social projects. At the same time, having been incorporated into the capitalist world system, they now face a class struggle as probably their most serious social problem. Moreover, South Korea is no exception to those new social conflicts surrounding such issues as sexual difference, the generation gap, and the ecological crisis. To describe present-day South Korea as "neo-colonial," therefore, is not to disregard these issues, but rather to distinguish my own position from the theories of colonialism and post-colonialism. I hope that "neo-coloniality" will be effective to describe the connectedness of various social issues: the way in which the "old" social issues of nation, region, and class interconnect with the "new" social issues of gender, sexuality, generation, and environment.

2. The Aporia of Decolonization

Now I want to turn to a difficulty, or rather an *aporia* facing the neo-colonial intellectual who is engaged in decolonization. Decolonization is the kind of work that will allow the neo-colonial to overcome the colonial past and the problems caused by it, and to achieve the historical progress previously prevented by the dregs and vestiges of a colonial past. Decolonization naturally strives after an alternative way of life. There can be no doubt that this alternative is radically different from the social order imposed on the Third World by the modern world system. To construct this alternative order, which may be viewed as a "counter- or oppositional order," members of a neo-colonial society would have to be able to dispense with those colonial remains. For, how could decolonization be accomplished without relying upon a social energy independent of the modern world system and its domination? In the process of decolonization, however, this obvious principle seems to be challenged by a conundrum: the fact that the neo-colonial intellectual cannot but depend upon the products of the colonial past, even while erasing it.

The work of decolonization is a de-demystification. It attempts to overcome the consequences of colonization, of the modernization of pre-modern societies, which often takes the form of enlightening, disenchanting, and demystifying those communities, ethnic groups, and nations forcibly subordinated in the process. We know that colonial subjects are forced to abandon their traditional ways of life since they have been caught up in superstitions, pseudo-sciences, or mysticism. Thus they enter into a new discursive space in which Western modernity and scientific reasoning dominate. Decolonization as a critical project functions as a deconstruction of this demystification, hence a de-demystification. De-demystification, however, has to rely upon that which it needs to criticize, for it cannot do without the project of enlightenment and modernity. At stake here is a certain solar mythology, for operating in this project is a "darkness of light," a "mythical" space which the enlightenment causes. A "lightened darkness" which the West has seduced the non-West into worshiping, the enlightenment operates as another superstition, but it now consists of scientism and rationalism rather than mysticism and pseudo-science. De-demystification, therefore, is an attempt to get out of the Western system of knowledge which, in the name of modernity and science, has been accusing the non-West of being trapped inside such limitations as Oriental mysticism, historical lag, and the Asiatic mode of production. Although de-demystification thus attempts an escape from capture by the solar mythology of the West, the problem remains that it must depend upon what it has to overcome.

How does this *aporia* of decolonization arise? It is because the colonial past continues to function as a universal perspective from which the neo-colonial has to see things, and because s/he cannot be free from it. In addition, once something becomes a universal framework in your life, it is impossible to locate yourself outside it. Universalism is such that you have to rely upon it in order to criticize it. The work of decolonization that I want to attempt in this essay is no exception. How would it be possible without those concepts, theories, and critical attitudes that I have acquired in my own neo-colonial subjectification? The neo-colonial intellectual can only depend upon the imperialistic and universalistic theoretical framework produced by the colonial suzerain. S/he is like Caliban in *The Tempest* who has to use the language Miranda has taught him. Of course, Caliban uses it very differently from the way Miranda uses it. "You taught me language; and my profit on't / Is, I know how to curse. The red plague rid you / For learning me your language!"[10] My point, however, is that he has to depend upon the language of his dominators even when he attempts to curse them. It is because he is not yet free from the effects of domination that the colonized cannot but adopt the colonizer's language or conceptual framework. Just as the West's domination has been universal, so has the non-West's dependence upon Western knowledge.

The neo-colonial intellectual is no exception in his dependence upon Western universalism. S/he has undergone a process of ruthless neo-colonial subjectification, as a consequence of the demystification caused by colonization. This process, which coincided with the change of the fields of subject formation, included a dismantling of the traditional system of knowledge and the introduction of a new mode of knowledge production. In Korea, Confucianism, which the old elite had to learn, came to be replaced by New Learning and, with this change, private homes and traditional schools lost their importance as places of education. Of course, such a tendency was already evident even before the annexation of Chosôn Dynasty by Japan in 1910.

After 1905, there was a nationwide educational movement to establish new-style schools, since intellectuals participating in it had come to believe that "the enlightenment of the nation through (new-style) education is the way to overcome difficulties which our nation is facing."[11] This was a sudden change of opinion, because when the Ministry of Education of the *Taehan Cheguk* (The Great Empire of Koreans, the new name for the dying Chosôn Dynasty), had attempted to enforce modern education with the help of Japanese advisors, the administrators met with obstinate resistance among the people. After annexation, the "enlightenment" of Koreans by Koreans was no longer possible, since a series of new subjectification processes and new practices of educational policies began. In brief, one may say, that the Japanese occupation of Korea brought about a massive transformation of the *chõsenjin* (Koreans) into colonized but modern subjects. While Japanese colonialists insisted on the idea of *naesôn ilche* (*naisen ittai* in Japanese), the "one-bodiment of the inner land (Japan) and Chosôn," there actually was no equality between Japan and Chosôn. For Koreans *naesôn ilche* meant such things as the dismantling of the traditional system of knowledge, the prohibition of the public use of the Korean language, or the enforced enlistment and drafting of Korean youths. During the Occupation, Koreans had to face pervasive colonial disciplinary power and endure extensive militarization, ideological indoctrination, and disciplining through almost all the social apparatuses. It goes without saying that the habitus acquired through this subject constitution was colonial. The school child, for instance, was taught to believe that s/he was a *hwangguk sinmin*, "subject of the Japanese Empire," or *kukmin* (*kokumin* in Japanese) for short. This kind of subjectification was also encouraged through such social institutions and activities as fashion, the legal system, censorship, housing, and an administration whose vestiges still remain in South Korea today.

Colonization has not disappeared since Korea was supposedly liberated, because the United States, the "benefactor" who terminated Japanese rule, made South Korea into a neo-colony in order to create an anti-communist stronghold against the communist regime in the north. Under American military rule, a new type of subjectification appeared, this time with the intention of Americanizing the lifestyle of the Korean people. In 1946, two years before the installation of the Korean government, the US military government introduced the "Plan for Seoul National University." There was a massive popular resistance to this foreign intervention in the national education system, but the military government reacted by expelling over 100 professors from colleges and was able to introduce the American-style university model into South Korea.[12] As a result, studying in the United States became a shortcut to joining the new ruling elite. "America" was a model not only in knowledge production; as American power turned out to be insurmountable, the American way of life became an inevitable model for Korean people. In the mid-1950s, domestic musicians active in the music clubs of the Eighth Army in Yongsan,

Seoul, began to introduce American popular music, and Hollywood movies also made people feel the American way of life as the most viable.

The Americanization of the Korean way of life was full-fledged when General Park Chung-hee came to power in 1961 through a military coup. He began to adopt the modernization strategy, devised by Walter W. Rostow to turn areas other than the Unites States into capitalist societies, in the form of the Five-Year Economic Plan.[13] Park promoted massive urbanization in order to prepare the workforce necessary for the modernization and capitalization of South Korea. With the onset of this urbanization came a mass culture, and people began to imitate the American lifestyle, by watching such cultural products as *Blondie*, the comic series that began to appear in a leading newspaper in the early 1970s. Obviously, this Americanization through imitation remained superficial. For instance, while people were living in apartment buildings whose outside features were similar to the international style of modern buildings, on the inside they were still using briquette furnaces for heating. However, about this time, especially after television-viewing became widespread, American mass culture began to flood into Korean society, and it became impossible to reverse the trend. As a result, not only South Korean intellectuals' language and knowledge products, but so many cultural activities and products, such as popular music and the film industry, have either carried American brand names or tried to look American.

I am mentioning these facts not simply to say that, while Japan had ruled in colonial days, the United States now exerts a determining impact on the lives of South Koreans. Rather, what I want to stress is that we are faced with vestiges of (neo)colonialization everywhere so that they constitute an objective living condition which, as a result, neocolonial intellectuals have to live with, in the very process of decolonization. In the neocolonial situation, the colonial period, insofar as it is in the past, has gone, but it still lingers on since the effect of colonial domination has not disappeared. Can one deny that colonial vestiges remain a "heritage" and that this heritage has an undeniable materiality or is even a necessity? These vestiges sometimes manifest themselves very clearly and sometimes remain hidden; but, they appear at almost every level and, in almost every field of South Korean society so that they naturally constitute the habitus and unconscious of South Koreans. Moreover, if their habitus, or "inner selves" are thus constituted by colonial vestiges, are they not "traitors" to the nation? For have they not become Japanized and Americanized?

Vestiges are traces. The trace belongs to that aspect of the sign, which C. S. Peirce called "indexical." "An Index is a sign which refers to the Object that it denotes by virtue of being really affected by that Object ... In so far as the Index is affected by the Object, it necessarily has some Quality in common with the Object, and it is in respect to these that it refers to the Object."[14] The index can be distinguished from the symbol and the icon in that it is more closely connected than the latter two to the bodily, physical aspect of the sign. Indexes such as smoke and footprints, unlike the symbol (the cross, for instance) and the icon (picture), are linked to their original objects in the very physical world and have causal relationships with them. Smoke signals a fire; footprints are a symptom that someone has trodden on the beach. The vestige-sign as index is a resultant of an historical event, namely the invasion of the world by logistically capable imperialist powers.

The fact that the dregs and vestiges of Western universalism and imperialism are widespread in South Korea today is a sign, or rather an index that Korea has had a physical encounter with the West and its "surrogate," Japan. Of course, the countless vestige-signs that remain today are not composed only of those products that came into Korea at the time of the encounter. They include all sorts of products and commodities that South Korea, a society already incorporated deeply into the capitalist world system, is now able to produce. New social products include such newly constituted subjects as students, lawyers, medical doctors, ministers, businessmen, brokers, and imposters. They include not only the neo-colonial, monopoly capitalist, social regime with its fascist government and its ideological state apparatuse, but also, micro-social machines such as classrooms, streets, and time-schedules which determine the way teachers and students, doctors and patients, cars and passersby interact with each other. In that they operate physically or mechanically, all these are "machines" rather than symbolic systems or iconic signs. These vestige-signs or indexes are as physical as footprints, as machine-like as cogwheels.

What does it mean that indexes have such a characteristic? I believe that it requires us to take a close look at the materiality of the vestiges, to conceive of vestige-signs as belonging to the level of the trace, and to take a new perspective on the way we see a sign. It is true that the trace, insofar as it is a sign, reminds us of the "original" object, but insofar as it remains always a vestige-sign, or an index, it seems necessary to understand the relationship between the original and the trace in terms of a reverse causality. The vestige-sign, the trace, is the only checkpoint through which one has to pass in order to get to the original that has always already disappeared. It is a barrier gate one has to get through even before the original.

This is because the vestige-sign is "spectral" in the sense which Jacques Derrida understood this word. The specter is a thing that comes again, that which comes after the death of a certain being, or the trace that appears after the original has disappeared.[15] The specter is thus a remnant, a vestige, and since this vestige is spectral in its own turn, it follows the way the specter comes and goes. Once it begins to appear, the specter has its own kind of frequentation, appearing anytime and anywhere as Hamlet says of the Ghost: "*hic et ubique.*"[16]

The colonial vestiges are ubiquitous today in South Korea, just like ghosts—a trait that comes from their "logistic" capacities. This capacity is not metaphorical, since it was proven by the power and attraction of cannon balls, curiosities, modern gear and goods which Western warships and commercial ships carried. The neo-colonial intellectual who has taken up the task of eradicating colonial vestiges cannot but face this specter which has been haunting almost every part of the world. To confront specters is not an easy task, for they may possess you; but, confronting them is something that cannot be avoided, since they are already here in their strange materiality. The neo-colonial intellectual can only belatedly "face" them as traces, and when s/he recognizes them as such, it is already after being somehow affected by them. Is this not an indication that s/he is indebted to the enlightenment, demystification, and universalism of the West? This indebtedness is another sign of the *aporia* that the work of decolonization has to rely upon the colonial past. How can decolonization find a way around this? Perhaps the only option left for the neo-colonial intellectual is to admit this *aporia* and live with it, as the only condition with which s/he can have the possibility of giving birth to something new, a condition s/he has to live through in order to begin again.

3. Exorcism

Of course, it is not easy to recognize the *aporia* as such, not easy at all, especially when the specter to be lived with is felt as a deeply begrudged enemy, someone who devastated the beautiful land of our ancestors, the national spirit and pride. Did not the Japanese imperialists drive iron piles into the peaks of the mountains along the Great Range of Paektu, that starts from Mount Paektu and continues to the southern end of the Korean Peninsula, in order to block the flow of energy and vitality (ch'i)? Did they not commit a "symbolic rape" by building the Ch'ongdokpu (government-general) Building right in front of Kyŏngbok-kung, the central palace of the Chosôn Dynasty?[17] If these reproaches cannot be disregarded, it would be natural to agree that we have to eliminate the specter-vestiges immediately. While I agree that their liquidation is indeed necessary, the question still remains: how many ways to eliminate are there and which should be chosen?

First, there is the strategy of "eradicating" by preserving the colonial past, understandably the strategy which former collaborators with the Japanese colonialists usually preferred. Since nobody could openly object to cleaning up colonial dregs and traces, their eradication has naturally become a manifest social objective in South Korea. Even those who would want to preserve colonial disciplinary apparatus cannot but agree on its necessity. Nevertheless, their way of doing the job is by letting people forget the "painful traumas of the past." The justification is that reconciliation and unity need to be forged for the well being of the whole nation. This, of course, is an excuse, fabricated to prevent the disclosure of their anti-nationalist activities, which might lead to the loss of their vested interests. This is why popular requests to remove former collaborators from high office used to be promoted as an attempt to divide the nation and were often suppressed. A prominent example can be found in the stubborn attempt of the *Chosôn Ilbo*, undoubtedly the most influential and reactionary newspaper in South Korea, to accuse nationalists or progressives who ask for the liquidation of the past of being pro-North leftists. Not surprisingly, its founder is known to have been a collaborator.[18]

Secondly, there is the attitude that would not allow any continuation of colonial remains; this I would call the strategy of exorcism. It is an attempt to expel whatever dregs there are. From the perspective of this typically nationalistic attitude, vestige-specters are traces of invaders from outside; they are represented as alien substances or impurities that should not be allowed to mingle with the national culture, if its purity is to be preserved. From the perspective of this strategy, then, no vestige-specters or vestige-signs should be tolerated, for only after their total elimination can the "real identity" of the nation be recovered. The third way of liquidating vestiges and traces is to endure them and, as we shall see, this is the strategy I think we need to take; but before discussing it, I would like to consider the strategy of exorcism in more detail.

Exorcism may be found in various forms, but it very often appears as the rejection of, and the repulsion and antipathy to anything foreign, especially Japanese. One typical example can be found in the on-line responses of Koreans, to the fact that Japan advanced to the final game in the World Youth Soccer Championship, held in April, 1999. Many Koreans, including teenagers who have little memory of the colonial days, argued that the Japanese soccer players, often underdogs in recent games with Korean players, could have only advanced to the finals by a fluke rather than on their own merits. This kind of response shows how unwilling Koreans are to recognize the athletic competency of their former colonizers. Similar examples can be found very easily, for instance in Koreans' response to books on Japan published in the 1990s. In Kim Jin-myung's novel, *Mugunghwa kkoch i p'iôssûmnida* (Althaea flowers have blossomed), the chauvinistic hatred for Japan seems to have reached its apex. When a war breaks out between Korea and Japan in 1999, the Korean government, in order to make a comeback after military humiliations, uses a secretly developed nuclear warhead. The nuclear weapon achieves a bull's-eye strike on the target, "Mikurajima, an uninhabited island 100km south of Tokyo." The warhead does not hit

Tokyo, which is the heart of Japan; but this is not a mistake on Korea's part. To hit an island close to the heart of Japan is to "hide sufferings and sorrows caused by Japan for a long time in our heart, and to stab the enemy to his armpit, not the heart."[19] Chôn Yô-ok's collection of essays, *Ilbon ûn ôpta* (There is no Japan) also became a bestseller by capitalizing on nationalistic sentiments. She does not hide her own anti-Japanese feelings: "I decided to write because I could never forgive Japan and the Japanese."[20]

At this point, one can see that belittling and condemning former colonizers has become a practice which many Koreans have no scruples about revealing. This is also closely connected to the attitude that refuses to accept anything foreign, and to the blind trust in things Korean. While Kim Young-sam's *munmin chôngbu* or "civilian government" was pushing forward economic policies for globalization, "things truly Korean are truly global" used to be a popular slogan. Intellectuals are no different in their thinking. A personal example of this is that while attending academic conferences, I have often heard such reprimands as "Stop being an importer of foreign-made theories!"

This tradition of rejecting Japan or the West as the other has a long history. It would not be an exaggeration to say that the history of nineteenth-century Korea was interspersed with attempts to expel the "Western ghosts." Among such attempts are: the Persecutions of Catholics, early nineteenth-century movements to exclude "Western Learning"; battles against invading French and U. S. warships in 1866 and in 1871; the seclusion policies instituted by King Kojong's father Yi Ha-ûng (Taewôn'gun) against foreign countries; the *Chôksa wijông* ("Expel Evil, Defend Right") Movement; the rise of "Eastern Learning" against "Western Learning" and the Peasants' War(1894) associated with it; and a series of the *Ûibyông* ("Righteous Soldiers") wars against the invasion of Japanese imperialism in the late nineteenth and early twentieth centuries. In the process of all these, the West and its "surrogate" Japan were perceived of as "evil spirits." A nomenclature was invented to label the new others. The traditional way of describing barbarians, of course, was not given up, since people preserved the expression *i* or "barbarians" by distinguishing between *yang-i* (Western barbarians) and *so-i* (little barbarians, that is, the Japanese). According to the new nomenclature, however, foreigners, especially Westerners, were perceived to be subhuman: they were either *gûmsu* (brutes), *yanggui*, (Western ghosts), or g*uich'uk*, (ghostly beasts).

The tendency, mentioned above as prevalent among Koreans, to disapprove the worth of Japan and of the West and to recover things purely Korean no doubt derives from this historic tradition of exorcism. Exorcism works to expel the evil spirit from the nation and to return to that "original state" of the nation before the national spirit was injured and corrupted by colonization. This attitude, however, is ahistorical in that it wishes to participate magically in the historical present without passing through the vestige-signs. In operation here is the antithesis between "us" and "them," the Manichaean opposition between good and evil, which demonizes the other, making it the object of expulsion. This attitude of exorcism treats possession by the evil spirit; a state in which one has to live with specters, as that which cannot be tolerated, as a state tainted by some satanic elements. Possession is thus presented as a suffering, a state to be overcome. Of course, the South Korean *minjung*, former colonials, have every reason to maintain such an attitude. They have not forgotten that when Western forces such as France and the United States, and Japan came to Korea, they obviously had the objective of invading and occupying it. Their tendency to disapprove the worth of Japan in advance or to look upon Western-made theories with distrust has to do with the subaltern status they came to assume in the capitalist world system. Social forces that promote Westernization in neo-colonial societies are usually anti-democratic. In a society where the degree to which you are Westernized often determines how close you can get to the source of power, and in a society which has adopted "the logic of modernization which privileges Western culture," explanations of social problems on the basis of Western theories can hardly be of benefit to the *minjung*.[21]

However, the question persists: is exorcism indeed a realizable objective? *Chôksa-wijông-ron* (the theory of expelling evil and defending right), a version of exorcism in the mid-nineteenth century, insisted on the theory of *wha-i-ron*, arguing for a fundamental difference between China and barbarians. According to this theory, China was the center of civilization, while Chosôn was "Little China." At first glance, the *wha-i-ron* seems to have idealized Chinese culture; actually, it thought Chosôn to be the only civilized society left: "[a]s Ming had been destroyed by Ching, the thread of Chinese culture had been cut off and, as a result, the center of civilization had shifted from China to Chosôn." As Chosôn was now the only China left, "the destruction of Chosôn" was the same as "the disappearance of the only civilized country on earth."[22] From the perspective that saw Chosôn as the only China left that could realize the right way of life (Tao), foreign forces were nothing but evil spirits, threatening the Confucian order which represented the only civilization. It may be natural for an evil spirit to have become the object of expulsion, but the problem was that such understanding was based on a complete ignorance of the contemporary international situation. Worse than that, some proponents of *Chôksa-wijông-ron* who later participated in the *Ûibyông* Movement are known to have participated in the subjugation of the revolutionary peasants who followed Eastern Learning. If this was the case, the anti-foreign sentiments that connected the *Chôksa* Movement and the *Ûibyông* Movement were not completely free from anti-democratic attitudes. Exorcism was, then, an attitude of those who wanted to attribute causes of domestic problems to foreign invasion. Therefore, the Confucian intellectuals, who believed that Chosôn was "the only China" left, had little recognition of the fact that the society was problem-ridden, and that too many people were being discriminated against on the basis of sex, caste, and class. The appearance of Western specters' appearance in this situation is perhaps a sign that Chosôn needed to know how things were going on around the world, that its problems arose also from within, not only from outside, and that "time was out of joint".[23] The West had appeared unexpectedly, but its spectral appearance was a configuration formed by a surplus produced by a historical reality that could not be represented through the symbolic order of Chosôn. The appearance of the Western specter was therefore a historical necessity.[24]

This is not to say that the appearance of the specter was a desirable phenomenon. Specters are always a nuisance for those who "face" them. However, the way specters become a nuisance depends on what kind we are talking about. It seems to me that there is a need to distinguish between colonial specters and the "specters of Marx" referred to by Jacques Derrida. In a later study on Marx, Derrida has maintained that it is absolutely necessary to have a certain Marxism today, that is, at the very moment when the death of Marxism has been officially announced, arguing that "there is no future without Marx."[25] "Marx" here seems to be a promise of democracy. Democracy according to Derrida is "a promise that can only arise in such a *diastema* (failure, inadequacy, disjunction, maladjustment, being 'out of joint')." This democracy is "a democracy *to come*," not "a future democracy in the future present," that is, not in the "temporal of a *future* present, of a future modality of the living present."[26] It is not easy to have a clear idea of Derrida's democracy. Nevertheless, one can hardly deny that it is something desirable, and that Marx's specters are harbingers of it. The vestige-specters of the colonial past on the other hand have a different function. For do they not prevent democracy from coming? Hence the necessity to approach them from a different perspective. At stake, here is the question: how does the "river of history" flow? Is the flow unitary? If so, the way to deal with vestige-specters would have to converge with Western spectralogy. Nonetheless, is there no possibility that the neo-colonial intellectual can constitute her own spectralogy? I will discuss this possibility later on; in the meanwhile, let us proceed with the problem of exorcism.

In the exorcist theory, the ghost or specter is conceived of as that which should not come inside and that which, once inside, does nothing but damage. One such theory presents the thesis of colonial exploitation, which has been the position of many progressive historians since the Liberation. According to this theory, Japanese colonization robbed Korea of the opportunity to develop, independently into a fully-developed capitalist society, and prevented its modernization. This theory has similarities to the "colonial semi-feudalism" or "colonial semi-capitalism" theories, which constitute the theory of "colonialism" and have attracted more than a few supporters from among the intellectuals involved in the decolonization movement. Just as the exploitation theory argues that the capitalization of Korea under Japanese colonial rule did not progress at all, so the theory of "colonial semi-capitalism" puts forward the thesis that South Korea under American imperialism has failed to develop a full-fledged capitalism. Against this thesis, one can ask if it is true that no real capitalism has appeared in South Korea. At issue here is the question of whether modernization and capitalization are possible in a colonial society and if possible, how they take place. Marx's "primitive accumulation" seems to be useful in this context, for it explains that capital accumulation can take place in the process of violent exploitation. I have already mentioned that colonial disciplinary power institutionalized the process of subjectification, and that, as a result, there was a massive formation of Koreans into "modern" subjects. I take this to mean that modernization and capitalization can take place even in a colonial situation.

My argument may cause a misunderstanding. It may seem that I am siding with the "theory of semi-developed capitalism" which has recently been at odds with the thesis of exploitation over the question of modernization in the colonial age. According to the semi-developed capitalism theory, Korean society, having achieved capital accumulation and modernization in the colonial period, is progressing toward a full-fledged capitalist society.[27]

However, both the theory of colonial semi-capitalism with its exploitation thesis and the theory of semi-developed capitalism with its colonial modernization thesis seem to share a common theoretical presupposition that I find difficult to accept. At first glance, the exploitation thesis and the modernization thesis seem to oppose each other, for the former argues that Japanese occupation prevented Korea's capitalization, whereas the latter maintains that it helped Korea achieve capitalization and modernization. However, this opposition notwithstanding, both theories stand on one and the same ground: they assume that convergence with world capitalism is desirable. I admit that there was a colonial modernization, but it is one thing to recognize modernization as a historical fact and it is another to say that it is desirable. The point here, I think, is to see modernization as a problem to interrogate rather than to consider it as desirable.

Modernization and capital accumulation in a (neo)colony is a social transformation fraught with problems. As Michel Foucault has shown in his analysis of the disciplining of inmates in the Panopticon, the effect of power is such that one gets empowered to the extent that one gets disciplined. In this machine-like apparatus, "the inmates should be caught up in a power situation of which they are themselves the bearers."[28] The result of this is a kind of self-inspection, an internalization of domination. Its effects are contradictory, for, while the inmates, like students and soldiers caught in similar situations, can cultivate capabilities, at the same time they fit into the machine of domination through that cultivation insofar as their capabilities function to operate the Panopticon. The subjectification of the (neo)colonial has a similar function. Through participation in the (neo)colonial-ruling machine, the (neo)colonials acquire modern capabilities that will contribute to their subjection to the machine. In addition, we know that in a non-Western, Third-World society, the process of subjectification creates a problem that would not arise in the West. The subjectification of the citizens of the suzerain countries produces metropolitan citizens who may, in one way or another, engage in, or depend upon, the colonization of colonial subjects. The subjectification of colonials, on the other hand, is the process of their marginalization, since it happens through their becoming other than themselves, through their Westernization. The result of this is the international division of labor and the (re)production of the colonial subjects as subalterns. Nevertheless, it is true that their modernization takes place—but along with their exploitation. In this case, "modernization" refers to the colonized becoming modern through participation in social apparatus and modes of behavior specifically developed to oppress and exploit them. When I mention "colonial modernization," I have in mind the reality in which, for instance, the accumulation of capital through exploitation requires the operation of social institutions and apparatus as well as the formation of a working class.

After the 1945 Liberation, South Koreans reopened the tradition of exorcism in the name of the "liquidation of the colonial past" and set up the Special Committee for the Prosecution of the Anti-Nationalists in 1948, in order to punish the collaborators with Japanese imperialism. This elimination, however, met with all sorts of interference and was finally interrupted by Rhee Syngman, the first South Korean president, who planned to oppose the communist regime of North Korea with the assistance of these collaborators. For many people, the breakup of the committee meant the destruction of the only social machine that could perform the liquidation job properly. Since the breakup, the elimination of collaborators was never pursued seriously, although it remained a manifest object of decolonization. One consequence of this is that the work of eradication repeats itself over and over again. In a sense, this is inevitable, for how can liquidation stop when no real and serious punishment was inflicted on the "traitors to the nation," and when they still retain their power?[29] The vestiges are like ghosts. "A ghost never dies."[30]

Without dying and disappearing, the vestige-specter haunts, it surfaces frequently. As a consequence, the conjuration of exorcism repeats itself indefinitely, but in this repetition something important is omitted and lost . It is the mourning process that is omitted, a process that should accompany any eradication or death. Mourning is a necessary, indispensable process at a funeral. We should not avoid it, if we want to bury the dead properly, or if we want to identify the dead in order to prevent burying someone alive. The strategy of exorcism, in contrast, is to proceed hastily, haphazardly with the burial, without an examination of the identity and condition of the dead. It is an attitude that tries to erase colonial vestiges and traces without negotiating with them, without facing their *aporia*.

4. The Accident of Event

The neo-colonial intellectual, who is engaged in the work of cleaning up the vestiges of colonialism and imperialism, faces a real problem. This problem seems to arise from the fact that s/he inevitably has to work with those vestiges even in the very act of attempting to erase them. This creates an enormous difficulty for the intellectual: s/he has to work in order to eliminate the dregs of the past, but the fact of the matter is that s/he is possessed, in one way or another, by imperialist/colonialist specters from, which liberation is necessary. Continuously haunted by vestige-specters, the neo-colonial intellectual thus faces an *aporia* that cannot be resolved either logically or experientially. How should the responses to this *aporia* be? Is evasion possible? Can one put it aside in a safe place so as not to have to see or acknowledge it? It seems, however, that the more uncritically blind one remains to the necessity of those specters, the more shackled one becomes by their haunting. Korean nationalists, for instance, have been adamant about the necessity of liquidating the past in order to recover *minjok chônggi*, "the spirit of the nation," but they have to "live on" those vestiges in order to be able to undertake the work of liquidation. Of course, the necessity of this "sleeping with the enemy" is rarely acknowledged, and the result is that they almost always fail to achieve their objective, because it is impossible to remove something without acknowledging its materiality.

A prominent example of such a failure was the demolition, of the former Ch'ongdokpu Building, the Japanese governmental-general building on the fifteenth day of August 1995. The purpose of this demolition, from the nationalist point of view, was to eradicate the Korean nation's shameful past, to restore *minjok chônggi*, and to inaugurate a new historical era. The building was completely destroyed by the end of 1996, and on the very same site now stands Hongryemun, which had been the gate to Kûnjông-jôn, Chosôn's administration building in the Kyôngbok-kung Palace. It was dismantled to give room for the colonial administration building. The dismantling of the Ch'ongdokpu Building and the restoration of the Hongryemun Gate must have represented, at least for the nationalists, a real event, a historical turning point, at which a transition was made from a temporality in which colonial dregs still survived to another in which they had disappeared. With the restoration of the Hongryemun Gate of the very same place where the Ch'ongdokpu Building used to stand, a shameful period, in which Koreans, even after the Liberation, had to use the colonial administration building first as the Government Building, then as the National Museum, came to an end. At last, a new era, in which the national spirit was finally restored, seemed to have begun.

However, it would be an illusion to believe that the dismantling of a building could bring about a change in history, no matter how significant it might be. As a matter of fact, there was no illusion. Who could have believed that the demolition of this building would result in the liquidation of the colonial vestiges? It is true that there was a solemn ceremony for the occasion. Furthermore, it is also true that a storm of applause arose at the very moment when the dome of the building was removed. At that ceremony, just as at other ceremonies, there were a lot of promises, oaths, and prayers; but there was no event that inaugurated a new beginning, that could match the announcement of "We proclaim the end of the colonial past and the beginning of a new history." What, then, about this "dismantling"? If it was conducive to the liquidation of the dregs of the colonial past, it was only fractionally so. For the Ch'ongdokpu Building was only one of so many colonial remains and traces that should disappear. What, moreover, about the restoration? Of course, there is no way back to the glorious past. The restoration of the Kyông-bok-kung Palace was not a restoration of the "consistency" of the past, of the lost world of the *wha-i-ron* by which the civilized Little China ought to be distinguished from the "ghostly beasts." No "new plane of consistency" was created, despite the dramatic production of a dismantling-restoration event. This event could only manage to be inserted temporarily into the neo-colonial plane of consistency where colonial dregs and vestiges are still rampant.[31]

The effect of the illusion is to foreground what Homi Bhabha has called the "pedagogical" which he distinguishes from the "performative." The performative of a dismantling-restoration produces a promise for a certain imaginary experience, such as the promise of the restoration of the national spirit. As there is a wide gap between the pedagogical and the performative, however, the dismantling-restoration cannot produce its material effect at the very place where it is promised.[32] The restoration work, or the enunciation of this particular performative occurred at the very place where the Ch'ongdokpu Building stood. However, there was no significant, epochal change in the distribution of power to make things fundamentally different from the days when the liquidation efforts had not yet started. The decision to dismantle the Ch'ongdokpu Building and to restore the Kyôngbok-kung Palace was made by Kim Young-sam, the head of the "civilian government," in the midst of strong objections from various sectors of the population. Kim's decision was part of a political maneuver to "redeem historical justice" in order to establish the legitimacy of his government, which was not a little tarnished by his participation in the military regime of Roh Tae-woo. This maneuver first proceeded in earnest, because it got the former presidents Chun Doo-whan and Roh arrested and sentenced to severe punishment (death for Chun and life in prison for Roh). Nevertheless, the political character of the maneuver was soon exposed, for Chun and Roh were set free before Kim was relieved of his presidency. Is this not a postponement of the new beginning of history promised in the pedagogical, a proof that the dismantling-restoration was only a "re-territorialization" taking place within the same series of things, the same assemblage, the same plane of consistency and not a "de-territorialization" cutting across two different temporalities?

What has happened here? Something epochal was promised, but no such thing materialized. There must have been a fundamental problem at the spot where the change was supposed to take place, where the colonial administration building was demolished to make room for the now-restored Hongryemun Gate. If the historical change that should have taken place did not, something must have "happened." What is this "happening"? Is this "happening" an event? The term "event" does not sound appropriate, for what matters here is something that did not take place. If anything, it is a non-event. What does this conversion of a possible event into non-event say to us? Does it not mean that a certain accident has taken place; that is, the accident of an event? If the event that should have taken place, namely, the inauguration of a new historical series, has been cancelled, that event must have met with an accident. What has "happened" through this accident of an event? What else can it be, if not the disappearance of colonial vestiges and traces? The expression "disappearance," however, calls for an explanation. By "disappearance" I do not mean something like the dismantling of the Ch'ongdokpu Building. Of course, the disappearance of the building may be seen as the disappearance of a very important colonial trace. Nevertheless, this disappearance may be an optical illusion. For do not colonial dregs still remain in abundance? When they "disappear," we, therefore, need to examine how they disappear. It may be those colonial traces and vestiges disappear without actually disappearing. The "disappearance of vestiges and traces," in this case, does not mean that the vestiges and traces have been liquidated, nor that we have succeeded in overcoming the colonial past, but rather that our sense of their materiality has been somehow lost. The "disappearance" refers to this loss of our sense of their materiality, not their actual disappearance. This strange, ghostly phenomenon takes place since these vestiges and traces are signs for us. As long as they are perceived to be symbols, the vestiges and traces can always disappear without disappearing. Of course, what disappears, what is lost sight of, is the sign as index which has materiality. Unless we deal with this indexical aspect of the sign, we will not be able to prevent this ghostly disappearance of colonial vestiges and traces.

Now it seems necessary to note the fact that the colonial vestiges in question are "things" that call attention to their surfaces. The vestige-sign as a trace is a thing that is very evident, for its materiality is never denied, never concealed. The Ch'ongdokpu Building, for instance, was always there for people to see. But this nakedness or evidence of the vestige-sign will disappear, as soon as the symbolic aspect of the sign begins to represent the entirety of the vestige-sign, as soon as the Ch'ongdokpu Building symbolizes all the vestiges of the colonial past. Why does the vestige-sign disappear at the very moment when the Ch'ongdokpu Building is determined to represent the dregs of the past? It is probably because the light produced during the dismantling of the building was too bright. The glitter of the optical instruments deployed to document the moment of the dismantling, the splendor of the fiftieth anniversary of the *kwangbok* (literally "restoration of light"), and the sunlight of August were such that they must have produced a "darkness of light." The dregs have disappeared in the darkness of this light. Rather, with a magical power to disappear in the very moment of their dismantling, these vestiges always reappear, just as before with the same consistency, in the power structure controlled by collaborators and their patronage. This disappearance and reappearance of the vestige-sign is the non-event that "took place" between the eradication of past colonial dregs and the restoration of the national spirit.

The "non-event" does not mean, therefore, that nothing has happened. Things that are non-events continue, very quietly, without attracting attention. Many important decisions were made, but mostly behind the scenes, when the Ch'ongdokpu Building was being demolished. As the building functioned as the National Museum for some time, the dismantling of it created an opportunity to construct a new National Museum building as well as to restore the old palace gate. Strangely, or naturally enough, the building of the new National Museum—which will cost about 200 million dollars, and the restoration of the Kyôngbok-kung Palace, have not attracted people's attention, whereas the dismantling of the colonial administration building caused a great stir among ordinary citizens as well as among opinion leaders. While the dismantling of the building which could be recognized easily as an event, as an epochal break from a historical period, the construction of a new building and the restoration of the old palace buildings were considered part of the normal procedure of things. Important policy choices, decisions, and measures were made and taken, but as these were part of the "normal procedure," there was no need for popular debate. In this process policy decisions concerning the demolition, construction, and restoration of public buildings, and enunciative acts concerning the distribution of politico-economic and cultural interests and power aroused no serious controversy.

If we pay attention to these enunciative acts, we may have a different perspective on the claim that this dismantling-restoration has brought in a new historical period. The claim presented in the statements of the discourse of decolonization is not important. Rather, there was a different kind of event, that is, the very act of making such a claim. What we need to pay attention to are, then, real-political moves which individuals and collectives with their particular subject positions, come to take. Important now is not only the fact that the dismantling of a building has produced a different symbolic order, a new era of the national spirit, but also that it has created a rare opportunity for architects, developers, and cultural experts to participate in large-scale public projects.

5. Pulverization and Umfunktionierung

It is time to change the strategy of elimination. The alternative that I offer is enduring. This strategy is possible only when we admit the materiality of colonial dregs and vestiges, when we recognize the vestige as a trace. To perceive the vestige as trace is to pay attention to its surface character. The reason why we cannot see the vestige, even while seeing it, is that we tend to see it almost always as a depth, an inside, or a secret. The vestige, then, is perceived as hiding somewhere else, and this "somewhere else" is always not the place where it actually is. Nonetheless, these dregs and vestiges, insofar as they are traces, do not hide themselves but belong to a system of visibility, and operate according to a "normal procedure." Does not the repeated failure of nationalist decolonization derive from the lack of countermeasures to this normalcy? Can we deny that colonial dregs and vestiges will survive even after the dismantling of such important symbols as the Ch'ongdokpu Building? As long as the site of such a dismantling does not coincide with the site of these vestiges that still remain, the liquidation of the colonial past will be incomplete. In addition, this failure will repeat itself as long as the nationalist discourse of decolonization avoids an interrogation of real-political decisions and moves, even while making utterances and promises of dismantling and restoration.

It is not that the nationalists (usually theorists of colonialism) do nothing real-political. The decolonization discourse of the colonialism theory attempts to call attention to its pedagogical level. Just like any other discourses, this is precisely the work this discourse does. There is a dislocation between the "intention" and "the function" in the strategy of the "colonialism" theory; a dislocation residing between "story" (*histoire*) and "discourse" (*discours*), or between "statement" (*enoncé*) and "enunciation" (*enonciacion*).[33] Nationalists who adopt the colonialism theory appear to maintain that the liquidation work can be accomplished on the level of the "story" alone. However, insofar as they too produce a discourse, a very controversial discourse at that, nationalists cannot avoid being subjects of enunciation just like their opponents. For the nationalists to dissimulate their enunciatory position by concentrating only on the story of their discourse is, then, to conceal that they are themselves making real-political moves in the process of discursive enunciation. In order to get a proper understanding of the question of liquidation, then, it is crucial to interrogate the nationalists' enunciatory positions, and the problems that accompany them.

The merit of taking note of the enunciatory subject rather than the subject of the statement seems obvious. It becomes possible to understand the discourse of nationalism in terms of the difference between the story and the enunciation, and to analyze the nationalists' performative acts in terms of their positions on such issues as conflicts and differences in class, gender, region, race, or generation. It is also possible to understand the actual function and position of nationalism by examining not what pedagogical message it carries, but what event, or rather nonevent it causes. Thus, if the "discourse," not the "story" is, foregrounded, it becomes important to ask how the statements belonging to this discourse are deployed.[34] And this means that it is necessary to observe nationalism from the perspective of the discourse rather than that of the story; to conduct a topological analysis that examines the enunciatory position of the discourse, the condition of the emergence of statements.[35] A statement, according to Michel Foucault, is deployed in a discursive archive, and the discursive formation it belongs to is determined by the distance it has from other statements dispersed in the archive, by their frequency or scarcity. According to what discursive formation and to which subject of enunciation it belongs to, in other words, depending on its discursive position, the meaning and function of the statement changes. It follows that the statement is never neutral and has no independent meaning separate from the condition of its emergence.

The nationalist believes in the capacity of the nation to integrate various identities, but this integration disregards their differences. Always insisting upon "our own things," "the unique tradition," "the national spirit," he—the nationalist is very often male—is a purist who remains blind to the fact that his enunciatory position and activities can be "tainted" by his own class, gender, regional, generational identification. His pedagogical position is that nothing alien should remain in his "body politic," so that he insists upon the restoration of the national spirit, the reunification of the nation, the restoration of past glory, and the purity of the nation. While thus believing in the imaginary "nation," he usually conceals the fact that the question of the nation is articulated according to the questions of class, gender, region, race, nationality, sexuality, generation, and environment, and, also, that he is pursuing the nationalization of this articulation. What we need to note, then, is that the real function, work, and effect of the nationalist's call for the "eradication of the past" is to institute a subject position in the neo-colonial situation and, through that institution, to intervene in that situation and to appropriate it to his own advantage. From the perspective of the colonialism thesis, the enemy is either foreign forces like those of Japan and the United States or the internal "betrayers" of the nation.

While I do not think that this kind of understanding is totally wrong, it reveals an ignorance of the fact that we are all more or less betrayers of the nation, and that in a neo-colonial situation most people are subject to general dependence on colonial vestiges. As a matter of fact, it is impossible to deny the fact that colonial dregs and vestiges are our unconscious or habitus. This may mean that they are not merely evil spirits that have come from outside to possess the pure spirit of the nation. Oppositions surrounding the vestiges of colonialism originate not only from outside the nation; they also derive from the conflicts and contradictions between different enunciatory positions within the nation. The "enemy" here cannot be fixated, stabilized, or identified as a particular social force; if it has an identity, its formation is flexible in that it is open to the complex articulation of class, gender, regional, racial contradictions and differences arising in the process of the actual constitution of the nation.

The nation itself, then, is not a community but rather a *force-field* traversed by class, gender, generation, region, and race. To deny that the nation is not a unitary community, but always a fissured collectivity is to accept the position that the nation represents various groups, collectivities and minorities; but this project of representation is usually conservative and reactionary. Of course, we cannot blame the entirety of the nationalist line for being reactionary since it can contribute to the anti-imperialist front. Nevertheless, as soon as the common enemy disappears, nationalism tends to become conservative and to become the ruling ideology of the national bourgeoisie.

At this point, I want to clarify that the object of my interrogation is not only the nationalist standpoint of the colonialism thesis, but also the strategy of decolonization put forward by the theorists of post-colonialism. Post-colonialists in South Korea no longer consider the question of the colonial past seriously, as if the eradication work were over. Alternatively, perhaps they have simply given up on the project because of its difficulty. I say this because this has finally become the official position of the South Korean government. In October, 1998, while visiting Japan, President Kim Dae-jung announced that he would not make a political issue of the question of the past, exhibiting an attitude very different from that of his predecessor Kim Young-sam who had embarrassed several Japanese prime ministers by saying at official meetings that Japan should apologize for its past atrocities. A former champion of democracy, Kim Dae-jung seems to believe that with his takeover as president a new era has begun, and that now a truly civilian government has replaced the military governments first started by the former Japanese Army officer Park Chung-hee, and which had inherited the colonial power structure. However, Kim's conciliatory statement that the past is no longer a problem for the relationship between Japan and South Korea rings hollow, since Japan, for instance, has made no official apology for the "comfort women" who had been forcibly conscripted by the colonial authorities.

Kim's attitude must be interpreted in terms of the policy line he has taken since his election. In contrast to Malaysian Prime Minister, Mahathir Mohamad, who resisted international pressures to receive bailout money from the International Monetary Fund and to take belt-tightening measures, President Kim did his best to receive the IMF fund and to implement most neo-liberalist policies recommended by the organization. To be sure, neo-liberalist policies had been introduced into South Korea before Kim Dae-jung's presidency, for they were included in his predecessor Kim Young-sam's Segyehwa (globalization) policies. However, Kim Young-sam's neo-liberalist policies, especially his attempt to introduce new labor-related laws in order to make labor flexible, met with a massive resistance in a national general strike led by the Korean Confederation of Trade Unions. Since the time when Kim Dae-jung won the presidency in December 1997, in the middle of an economic crisis, the situation has changed, and so the President elect took the initiative of implementing neo-liberalist policies. What would it mean for a Third World country to adopt neo-liberalism as the basic social policy line? In most societies, the United States and Britain, for instance, where neo-liberalist policies have been introduced, the result has been disastrous, bringing in the "society of 20% vs. 80%."[36]

Moreover, we all know that, consequently, the welfare system that used to characterize Western countries has suffered a great blow. Because the country has been providing little welfare in the first place, South Korea's adoption of neo-liberalist policies must produce severely devastating results. I suspect that in this context, post-colonialism acts as a new strategy of domination and subjection, for it can produce, among other things, the illusion that South Korea is now in a condition which is neither colonial nor neo-colonial. The position of post-colonialism seems to adjust well to neo-liberalist policies in that it averts the social problems arising from the neo-colonial condition.

To emphasize the spectral character of colonial dregs and vestiges, and to consider different strategies of liquidating them is to adopt a strategy distinguishable both from that of colonialism theorists and post-colonialists. While theorists of colonialism, their desire and wishes notwithstanding, are unable to map out a proper strategy of elimination, post-colonialists announce the accomplishment of the elimination without actually accomplishing it. I believe we can find the way to the liquidation of the past only when we acknowledge the actuality of colonial dregs, when we admit that they survive in the form of traces, and that we retain them as our own habitus. One can, I think, take issue with the position of post-colonialism, since Koreans, who have been suffering from the division of the nation for more than half a century, still have the task of national liberation. At the same time, however, it is necessary to interrogate the nationalist position of those who conceive of the liberation and reunification of the nation as their mission. I think that unless "the nation" is understood as a "minority," "national liberation" cannot constitute a progressive project.[37]

As long as imperialism still remains in power, as long as many Third World societies which have suffered colonialist domination still find themselves in a neo-colonial condition, the concept of "the nation" can indeed have a critical function in the world in which the axiomatic of imperialistic capitalism dominates. If "the nation" is conceptualized as a "majority," however, it immediately becomes the main cause for internal colonization, as evidenced in the fact that the national bourgeoisie develops into the ruling class in many Third World countries.[38]

If we have to take into account this instability of the historical function of the nation, we need to engage in the work of identifying the enunciatory position of the discourse of decolonization, and of examining the mode of the emergence of discursive statements and their functions. One way of achieving this, I think, can be found in the spectralogical approach.

The specter is a nuisance. Once it appears, it does not disappear and is very difficult to expel. Spectralogy pays attention to this fact. In order to be able to practice exorcism, a specter needs to be visible. While this is a fact that people tend to ignore, spectralogy acknowledges that exorcism presupposes cohabitation with the specter, and that the vestige-specter should be with us, even for us to engage in the work of expelling it. Jacques Derrida thus suggests "to learn to live *with* ghosts."[39] Moreover, this is the strategy I am also employing. To live with ghosts is to endure them. In addition, to endure ghosts is a strategy radically different from that of exorcising them. To endure ghosts is not to get rid of them but to bear up and resist the afflictions caused by them. This endurance is a condition that cannot be avoided once specters have appeared. It is also a precondition for us to be able to deal with them properly. How could we deal with ghosts without enduring them?

At the same time, however, this endurance should not be taken to be the toleration of the ghosts. Enduring vestige-specters does not mean leaving them as they are, letting them survive forever. To suggest that we should endure colonial dregs is not to suggest that we should leave the Ch'ongdokpu Building alone; that we ought to never have tried to punish anti-national collaborators; and that the setting of the Committee for the Prosecution of the Anti-nationalists was misguided. The purpose of tolerating colonial dregs and vestiges is to prevent the "accident of event," or the "disappearance of vestiges," by acknowledging the materiality of vestige-specters and the trace-ness of vestige-traces.

Vestige-specters exist as a reality. Without acknowledging this reality, there is no way of dealing with them. To deal with specters, therefore, is not to leave them alone. Hence the necessity for the neo-colonial intellectual to interpret Derrida's advice "to learn to live with ghosts" from a different angle. The specters of the West and Japan should be distinguished from "specters of Marx," since the former are oppressive forces imposing modernization and colonization rather than harbingers of "democracy to come." If confluence with Western modernity is not what the Third World ought to aim for, if the ultimate goal for humankind is not incorporation into world capitalism, this cohabitation with specters cannot be taken for granted. To learn to live with ghosts, then, is to learn how to deal with them, not to ignore them.

Thus, we need to examine carefully the suggestion that "we need to endure ghosts." Vestige-specters are traces in that they are, as suggested above, indexical signs. The indexical signs can, I think, be seen in terms of "simulacra" as Gilles Deleuze understands them. According to Deleuze, simulacra belong to the surface: "Sounds, smells, tastes, and temperatures refer especially to the emissions from the depths, whereas visual determinations, forms, and colors refer to the simulacra of the surface."[40] The "surface is the locus of sense," sense here being the same as event.[41] "The event is sense itself, insofar as it is disengaged or distinguished from the states of affairs which produce it and in which it is actualized."[42] In that the surface is where event and sense take place, in that the event's "essence is that of the pure surface effect,"[43] simulacra are where events take place, and indexical signs or vestige-ghosts, in that they are the site of traces where the accident of the event takes place, are not different from simulacra.

It is because of this link between vestige-ghosts and simulacra that the endurance of colonial ghosts can be viewed as having a positive meaning. When vestige-specters are understood as simulacra, to endure them becomes a necessary process in starting a "real" event. Having to endure specters does not necessarily mean that it is hard to make them disappear. Enduring them is now necessary because the locus of vestige-specters corresponds to that of simulacra where the event can take place. We need to see colonial vestiges as indexical signs and simulacra, since it is on this surface locus, where enunciatory acts of discourse take place, that history will either make progress or fail.

There are at least three ways in which the strategy of endurance treats vestige traces. The first is to wait upon or worship them. This is typically the way former collaborators endure colonial dregs and vestiges, but actually few Koreans can avoid them, since most South Koreans have been living with colonial ghosts in one way or another. As a result, we cannot do without the skills, methods, and even objectives of demystification, for these will have to be employed in the project of decolonization. The same can be said of the tools, techniques, and concepts of universalism and modernity, which we have come to employ. For instance, can we dispense with such terms and concepts as *ch'orhak* (philosophy), *munhak* (literature), *munhwa* (culture), *kwahak* (science), and *kyoyuk* (education) for the reason that they are Japanese-made? Of course, this is not to say that worshipping and preserving colonial dregs and vestiges is problem-free. To worship them is not merely to make use of needed concepts and products; it is also to continue the environment of their use, the ritual in which they appear, and their "aura."[44]

The continuance of this aura allows the "darkness of light" and the "unreason of the enlightenment" to reign over the participants involved in the ritual, and makes it impossible to liquidate colonial dregs. While waiting upon and preserving them is one way of enduring them, we cannot tolerate the continuance of their aura. Hence comes the second way that I would like to call "pulverization." Apparatus and mechanisms of political power, and social domination under the control of former collaborators should be eliminated through their pulverization. It goes without saying that such apparatus of social capture as the national security law, frequently used to suppress political and labor activists and such violations of human rights as torture and censorship should be dispelled. This strategy of pulverization needs to combine with what Benjamin, borrowing from Brecht, has called "*Umfunktionierung*" or "functional transformation."[45]

Umfunktionierung as the third way of endurance is to go beyond the preservation and waiting upon colonial vestiges suggested by the academic terms mentioned above to a transformation of their discursive functions. While it would be honest to admit that at least certain vestiges and dregs cannot but be preserved, the combination of the pulverization and functional change of colonial dregs and vestiges is probably the only viable way toward the eradication of the past. The materiality of colonial dregs must be acknowledged, but some of them need to be eliminated, as in the case of the dismantled Ch'ongdokpu Building, or at least removed from the places where they now stand, while some others have to undergo changes in their function so that they might contribute to decolonizing Korean society. Among the social apparatus, systems of representation, or "desiring machines" which allow colonial dregs and vestiges to survive, some should be deployed in a new way, while others should be broken down. The dregs and vestiges in this respect are "bricks" which may or may not be needed to build a new "house of history," to start the event of historical progress. Bricks from the old house will be pulverized when found useless, but when found useful, they are incorporated into the new house. To conceive of colonial dregs and vestiges as traces, as simulacra, in other words, as things whose materiality cannot be denied, is to use them as building blocks in the work of decolonization.

6. Mimicry and Difference

While the neo-colonial intellectual attempts to make new historical progress through his/her cohabitation with vestige-signs, this cohabitation is always tenuous, and a prediction of its results is extremely difficult. S/he has to experience vestige-ghosts' frequentation and endure the sufferings it causes. In doing this, s/he has to crush a lot of the remaining "bricks" of the past, while deploying some of them in a new way; but all this requires a complex calculation. How should the neo-colonial intellectual pulverize the vestiges or change their functions? While insisting upon the need to comprehend the spectral character of these vestiges, I want to emphasize that the way spectralogy will function is to be determined by the individual's enunciatory position, and in the case of the neo-colonial intellectual, by his/her "belatedness." The penalty inflicted upon one who comes belatedly is to mimic those who come before.

Mimicry becomes a general lifestyle in former colonies or present-day neo-colonial societies, because people there often do things belatedly. Of course, this mimicry is of colonialist other's way of life, and it is always possible since people in neo-colonies have already become subjectified through the problematic ways of colonization, modernization, and Westernization. It should be noted that this subjectification very often involves having to become a contaminated, corrupt, mixed-up subject, a betrayer, a hybrid; that is, an undesirable subject-form.

However, becoming a hybrid should be seen as a necessary foundation upon which a new historical progress can be constructed, a progress which neither nationalistic separatists nor "integrationists" like the theorists of colonial modernization can imagine. Being belated, the neo-colonial intellectual must take mimicry as the basic mode of activity; exactly for this reason, however, s/he comes to have the opportunity or obligation to have a dream fundamentally different from that of those who went before. Mimicry is no mere repetition. An imitation, insofar as it is an imitation, cannot be the same as the original. All imitations are necessarily imperfect, supplementary, and, thus, always have the possibility of making a difference. Perhaps this is why a new beginning comes at the last moment. The "last," according to Gilles Deleuze and Félix Guattari, comes as a penultimate. Thus, the "last" should be distinguished from the "threshold." Once an assemblage has arrived at the threshold, it is already in the phase in which a different assemblage has begun. It is by taking the risk of going one step further at the very last moment, before a new assemblage or series begins, that the subject attempts at becoming an other than itself. As mimicry is a game that occurs in a temporality in which the position of the leader and that of the follower should involve certain pre-established rules, the moment of mimicking the other belongs to that temporality. Nevertheless, as this moment is the last, that is, a moment that coincides with the last moment of that temporality, it can lead to the threshold where differences can appear.⁴⁶

I would like to argue that mimicry can make a difference because it can produce what I call "*Malttuk-i* (fool) effect." In *madang gûk*, a traditional style of Korean theater, the most important theatrical figure and action, epistemologically and ethico-politically, is *Malttuk-i*, or the fool figure and his foolery. What is important about *Malttuk-i* is that he both belongs and does not belong to the world of *Yangban* or the nobleman figure. His best skill, of course, is to mimic. *Yangban* struts with his long pipe in mouth; *Malttuk-i* follows him, and uncontrollable laughter immediately comes from the audience. The laughter has an epistemological significance in that it is touched off by the audience's recognition of the resemblance and the difference between the two figures. No doubt, there is a shared knowledge of the stupidity of the swaggering *Yangban*, between the audience and *Malttuk-i*. This sharing is not guaranteed, as *Malttuk-i* is frequently punished by the audience. Important for us, however, is that the laughter, or the moment of the audience's ethico-political awakening, takes place only while *Malttuk-i*'s mimicry is in progress; when it can perceive both the resemblance and the difference between him and *Yangban*.

This aesthetics of mimicry, deeply rooted in the *minjung* tradition, which often appears in the neo-colonial condition, can, I think, be given a new name: that of "follow," after the typical position of *Malttuk-i* who follows *Yangban* and of the neo-colonial intellectual who always comes after the Western intellectual. This "follow" phenomenon comes into being due to the "noncontemporaneity of the contemporaneous," to the fact that "time is out of joint" in a neo-colony. That our time is out of joint means that things have become topsy-turvy; that the social order has been utterly shaken. Hence, the neo-colonial intellectual finds himself in situation of experiencing that he has come to his own society later than the colonialist other, for he feels forced to accept the present of the latter as his own future. If he finds that his future is already prepared by the colonialist, can it not be said that the neo-colonial intellectual has come to his society later than the colonialist has?

However, a new beginning can happen in the neo-colony precisely because it is in such a jumble. This beginning owes its possibility to that singular gesture of the mimicry of those who follow in a topsy-turvy situation. The point of this mimicry is to come behind but to proceed differently from the one who goes ahead. The role of the neo-colonial intellectual, like *Malttuk-i*, is to create a vectorial variance in the *Figurenposition* of the figures who appear in *madang gûk*.⁴⁷ *Malttuk-i* is the one who causes changes in the direction of the characters' movement in *madang*, "the open ground of performance," and he does this simply by being in it. New relationships that will ensue among theatrical figures or characters thus remain exposed to the resonance of the *carnivalesque* laughter whose democratic potential Mikhail Bakhtin best understood.⁴⁸

Mimicry has its own pitfalls, though. There are two modes of mimicry: the one follows the leader as a model, and the other also follows, but to parody and to criticize. The former aims to reproduce the model or to converge into the main stream. It goes without saying that most typical social problems of present-day neo-colonial societies derive from this "integrationist" attitude. Attempts to modernize themselves like their suzerain model countries, known as convergence, cannot but fail as a strategy of social development. When convergence is insisted upon, what happens is a "phantasmagoria," a term which Chungmoo Choi borrows from Walter Benjamin to describe a colonial society. A phantasmagoria comes into being when the "commodity on display," which the colonized want but cannot possess, becomes a pure illusion so that it only has a representational, symbolic value.[49]

This phantasmagoria is the result of the proliferation of what Jean Baudrillard has called "simulacra" and the effect of it is the frequent occurrence of the "accident of event." However, as we have seen, there is a different view of "simulacra." The Deleuzian concept of "simulacra" prevents us both from seeing the trace merely as a phenomenon of the absence of the original and from believing that no fundamental change can take place on the level of the trace. On the contrary, it allows us to see that the transformation of traces themselves can become an event. The mimic is necessarily someone who follows. The follower follows in the predecessor's footprints. In that s/he follows others, s/he cannot ignore or nullify the footprints. Like all the other belated, s/he can infer about the predecessor only in terms of the materiality of the footprints, and add a certain supplementarity to the absent original. The supplementarity here is a strategic effect which, by adding "to," does not necessarily "add up" but "may disturb the calculation."[50]

The follower can produce this supplementary effect because following on the predecessor's heels is almost always a process of erasing the footprints, of flattening the remaining traces under foot. To follow and flatten the footprints perhaps includes the possibility that mimicry can make a difference from the original. This flattening, just like mimicry, presupposes a bodily participation. Moreover, insofar as the footprints as indexes are physical, following and flattening them will happen at some place other than the symbolic or iconic levels of the sign. The actor who takes up the role of *Malttuk-i* often mingles with the audience in the *madang*. He sometimes gets beaten, while squeezing himself between spectators and exchanging epithets with them. We know that similar things could happen to the fool-actors in Shakespeare's age. Hence, the warning against the Fool, who appears to have the sole right to ridicule Lear: "Take heed, sirrah, the whip."[51] The Fool's foolery, like Kent's loyalty, can be a matter of life and death. As a mimic, the neo-colonial intellectual is similarly engaged in a struggle of life and death. However, his struggle is a risk to be distinguished from that of the Fool or Kent. Whereas the latter challenge the authority of Lear in order to preserve it, the neo-colonial intellectual is engaged in the risky work of creating a world different from the one created by Western modernization and capitalism. This adventure is an attempt to make a difference from the dominating West; an experiment to do things differently from the dominator, even while borrowing things from the colonizer. Here one might recall Michel de Certeau's contention that the domination of the ruling classes does not always succeed and that subordinated groups employ "tactics ... to win small victories from larger, more powerful, and ultimately determining systems."[52]

In a similar way, the colonized can utilize things belonging to the colonizer in his or her own way and develop new uses radically different from the original. It is almost inevitable for the neo-colonial intellectual to mimic and employ Western culture, but its ultimate meaning will be determined by its uses. Only when there is a different use of colonial vestiges and dregs can the mimicry of the neo-colonial intellectual produce meaningful differences that will materialize into historical progress. Moreover, it is an illusion to believe that s/he will be able to assume full autonomy in determining the uses. The enunciatory position of the neo-colonial intellectual is not given automatically and cannot be chosen easily. It follows complex dynamics of reality and is only made possible by a certain discursive territorialization that will enable an utterance of some statements while prohibiting some others. It is necessary for the neo-colonial intellectual to recognize that the influence of the enunciatory position of the discourse of the West on neo-colonial society is still very strong, that this enunciatory position is complex in that there are various positions in the West, that their very relation to the non-West can only be determined by the power struggle going on in non-Western societies, and that this determination should be made through a complex calculation. This process will be a nuisance but if we ignore its necessity, we shall end up with what Homi Bhabha has called the "missionary position."[53]

To get out of the neo-colonial condition—this flight would be neither a return to the pre-colonial days nor a rise to the position of an empire. In South Korea, it will have to be a movement that experiences national reunification, but the achievement of the status of a nation state cannot be its only goal. National reunification can have validity insofar as it also functions as a flight from the neo-colonial condition and containment within the capitalist world order. The possibility of taking a third road that will coincide neither with convergence with the capitalist world order nor with a return to the pre-colonial past seems to reside in *Malttuk-i*'s mimicry. As s/he creates variance in the positions of theatrical figures, what his/her mimicry does is effect changes in the dynamism of the *madang* stage as a totality, make differences in relationships among the figures, construct the possibility of changing the direction of the totality's movement, and finally produce a transformation of that totality. Mimicry thus is an opening in the historical present. Its possibility, as we have seen, lies in living with vestige-ghosts and enduring them. As Derrida says, "this being-with specters would also be, not only but also, a politics of memory, of inheritance, and of generations." There would be no point in talking about the future, "[w]ithout this *non-contemporaneity with itself of the living present*, without that which secretly unhinges it, without this responsibility and this respect for justice concerning those who *are not there*, of those who are no longer or who are not yet *present and living*."[54] In a neo-colonial society, this respect for justice needs to take the form of *Malttuki*'s mimicry. With his presence in the *madang*, arises the possibility of constructing a heterogeneous time-space, of introducing a radically different outside into the *madang*, which would otherwise remain unitary.

My point, then, is that the mimicry of the neo-colonial may bring something quite unexpected, namely the possibility of opening up a future that will be more just. This mimicry should be different from the repetition of the Same. Decolonization of the neo-colonial condition is not a return to the neo-colonial's original self, but rather a work of producing the "non-contemporaneity with itself of the living present." Considering that this present is a globalized, Westernized present, the work cannot take the form of a convergence with Western modernity, either. Is there a new way which is neither the return to the past nor a convergence with the axiom of Western modernity? If flight can take place at the last moment, as Deleuze and Guattari have argued, this last is the very moment when we can take the risk of entering the threshold of a new series of things. While this moment remains one when the established assemblage of things is still exerting a determining power, it is nonetheless open to a different world, perhaps to a democracy to come. It is an opening that comes into being thanks to the fact that such "last" things as vestiges and dregs are simulacra. The last belongs to the inside of the assemblage or the series that contains it as a moment, but it is already turned toward the outside. Being inside, but facing outside, the last is the moment when vestige-signs and traces can be found, and is the way vestige-ghosts exist. In this sense, this "last" moment belongs to the territory in which spectralogy needs to operate. It seems that neo-colonial intellectuals must take this territory as their own in order to engage in mimicry, to consider a new historical beginning, or a democracy yet to come.

Endnotes

1—Chungmoo Choi, "The Discourse of Decolonization and Popular Memory: South Korea," *positions: east asia cultures critique* vol. 1., no. 1 (Spring 1993): 96.

2—Ibid., 98.

3—Ibid.

4—Rashmi Bhatnagar and Rajeshwari Sunder Rajan respond to Gayatri Spivak who defines them as the "post-colonial" intellectuals in an interview: "Perhaps the relationship of distance and proximity between you and us is that what we write and teach has political and other actual consequences for us that are in a sense different from the consequences, or lack of consequences, for you." Gayatri Chakravorty Spivak, *The Post-colonial Critic: Interviews, Strategies, Dialogues*, Sarah Harasym ed. (New York: Routledge, 1990), 68.

5—Gayatri Spivak has criticized the position taken by Michel Foucault and Gilles Deleuze who, taking the oppressed as the subjects of power and desire, argue that they have knowledge and can speak for themselves. She argues that subalterns cannot speak for themselves. "Can the Subaltern Speak?" in Patrick Williams and Laura Chrisman, eds., *Colonial Discourse and Postcolonial Theory: A Reader* (New York: Columbia University Press, 1994), 66-111.

6—"Theoretical practice falls within the general definition of practice. It works on a raw material (representations, concepts, facts), which it is given by other practices, whether 'empirical', 'technical' or 'ideological'. In its most general form theoretical practice does not only include scientific theoretical practice, but also pre-scientific theoretical practice, that is, 'ideological' theoretical practice (the forms of 'knowledge' that make up the prehistory of a science, and their 'philosophies')." Louis Althusser, *For Marx* (London: Verso, 1977), 167.

7—The importance of the question of decolonization cannot be exaggerated enough. Here I provide some examples that will show the persistence of the question. In 1998, a great-grandson of Yi Wan-yong, the most notorious traitor to the Korean nation, sued for the return of Yi's land property, known to have been bought with the gift money awarded to him for "serving" his country. When the descendent finally won the case, people got furious and demanded the legislation of a special law that would deprive the traitors and their descendents of rights to the properties they came to possess for anti-national activities. In 1993, 173 members of the National Assembly had proposed passing such a special law but failed to legislate it. In 1999, the Institute for National Problems Studies started a fund-raising campaign to publish a Who's Who of the pro-Japanese. More than 10,000 college professors have shown their support for the campaign.

8—Anne McClintock, "The Angel of Progress: Pitfalls of the Term 'Post-colonialism'," in Patrick Williams and Laura Chrisman, eds., *Colonial Discourse and Post-Colonial Theory: A Reader* (New York: Columbia University Press, 1994), 294.

9—Kuan-Hsing Chen, "Not Yet the Post-Colonial Era: The (Super) Nation-state and Transnationalism of Cultural Studies: Response to Ang and Stratton," *Cultural Studies* vol. 10, no. 1(1996): 50.

10—William Shakespeare, *The Tempest*, Frank Kermode, ed. (London: Methuen, 1954), I, ii, 365-67.

11—Hong Il-p'yo, "Chuch'e hyôngsông ûi chang ûi pyônhwa: kajok esô hakkyo ro" (Changes in the fields of subject formation: from the family to the school), in Kim Chin-gyun and Chông Kûn-sik, eds., *Kûndae chuch'e wa sikminji kyuyul kwonryôk* (The modern subject and colonial disciplinary power), (Seoul: Munwha kwahaksa, 1997), 292-95.

12—The Publication Committee, *Sôul Taehakkyo kyosu minjuhwa undong osimnyônsa* (A history of the democratic movement of the professors at the Seoul National University for the last fifty years), (Seoul: Seoul National University Press, 1997), 6-16.

13—Five-Year Economic Plan was a strategy Park Chung-hee adopted for the economic development of South Korea. There were six Five-Year Economic Plans: the first series started in 1962, and the sixth one ended in

1992.

14—C. S. Peirce, *Philosophical Writings of Peirce*, Justus Buchler, ed. (New York: Dover Publications, 1955), 102.

15—Jacques Derrida, *Specters of Marx: The State of the Debt, the Work of Mourning, & the New International*, tr. Peggy Kamuf (London: Routledge, 1994).

16—William Shakespeare, *Hamlet, Prince of Denmark*, Philip Edwards ed. (Cambridge: Cambridge University Press, 1985), I. v. 156.

17—On the symbolic rape of Chosôn by Japan, see Chungmoo Choi, "Sorcery and Modernity" in *Proceedings of '97 Kwangju Biennale International Acdemic Symposium: Unmapping the Earth* (October 30 to 31, 1997): 3.1-3.17.

18—In 1998, The Chosôn Ilbo launched, for instance, a dirty press campaign to oust Professor Choi Jang Jip from the chairmanship of the National Policy Planning Committee. Choi was singled out by the newspaper as a typical high-ranking official of the Kim Dae-jung Government who was suspected of holding a dubious, that is, leftist, position on the communist regime of North Korea. Although press-related NGO's as well as progressive intellectuals supported Choi, he finally lost his position. Choi's defeat occurred at a turning point when Kim's government gave up pursuing reformist policies.

19—Kim Jin-myung, *Mugunghwa kkoch i p'iôssûmnida*, vol. 3 (Seoul: Haenaem, 1993), 281-82. This trilogy has been the best seller in the 1990s. It is estimated that more than 4 million copies were sold.

20—Chôn Yô-ok, *Ilbon ûn ôpta*, vol. 2 (Seoul: Chisik kongjakso, 1995), 7.

21—Chungmoo Choi, "The Discourse of Decolonization and Popular Memory," 82-3.

22—Pak Sông-su, "Ûibyông chônjaeng" (The Ûibyông War), Yi Ka-wôn, et. al., eds., *Han'gukhak Ipmun* (Introduction to Korean Studies), (Seoul: Chisiksan psa, 1981), 421.

23—William Shakespeare, *Hamlet*, Act I. sc. v. l. 189. Derrida seems to have noticed the importance of these words, for he repeatedly cites them in his *Specters of Marx*.

24—"[R]eality is never directly 'itself', it presents itself only via its incomplete-failed symbolization, and spectral apparitions emerge in this very gap that forever separates reality from the real, and on account of which reality has the character of a (symbolic) fiction: the spectre gives body to that which escapes (the symbolically structured) reality." Slavoj Zizek, "Introduction: The Spectre of Ideology," in Zizek, ed., *Mapping Ideology* (London: Verso, 1994), 21.

25—Derrida, *Specters of Marx*, 13.

26—Ibid., 64; emphasis in the original.

27—The "theory of semi-developed capitalism" has been presented by An Pyông-jik, who argues that "there are only three kinds of countries in the capitalist world-economy: advanced, semi-developed, and under-developed capitalist countries" (291) and that South Korea belongs to semi-developed capitalism. He believes that "conditions for the development of South Korea's capitalism had been formed under the colonial regime and the regime of dependency"(303). An Pyông-jik, "Chungjin chabonjuû irosô ûi Han'guk kyôngje" (The South Korean economy as semi-developed capitalism), Pak Hyôn-ch'e and Cho H i-yôn, eds., *Han'guk sahoe kusôngch'e nonjaeng* (Debates on South Korea's social character) vol. 3, (Seoul: Chuksan, 1991), 286-304.

28—Michel Foucault, *Discipline and Punish: The Birth of the Prison* (New York: Vintage Books, 1979), 201.

29—The "traitors" include: cat's paws of the Japanese police, informants against independence fighters, intellectual celebrities who urged Korean youths to go to the front to show gratitude for the "Emperor's kindness," and leading newspapers like The Tong'a Ilbo and The Chosôn Ilbo which collaborated with Japanese imperialism.

30—Derrida, *Specters of Marx*, 99.

31—According to Deleuze and Guattari, "*consistency*" is "the 'holding together' of heterogeneous elements. "The problem of *consistency* concerns the manner in which the components of a territorial assemblage hold together....[F]rom the moment heterogeneities hold together in an assemblage or inter-assemblages a problem of consistency is posed, in terms of coexistence or succession, and both simultaneously." Gilles Delueze and Félix Guattari, *A Thousand Plateaus: Capitalism and Schizophrenia*, tr. Brian Massumi (Minneapolis: University of Minnesota Press, 1987), 327.

32—For a distinction between the pedagogical and the performative, consider the following: "The scraps, patches and rags of daily life must be repeatedly turned into the signs of a coherent national culture, while the very act of the narrative performance interpellates a growing circle of national subjects. In the production of the nation as narration there is a split between the continuist, accumulative temporality of the pedagogical, and the repetitious, recursive strategy of the performative. It is through this process of splitting that the conceptual ambivalence of modern society becomes the site of writing the nation." Homi Bhabha, *The Location of Culture* (London: Routledge, 1994), 145-6.

33—I am borrowing "story" and "discourse" from Emile Benveniste, and "statement" and "enunciation" from Michel Foucault. See Jonathan Culler, *Structuralist Poetics: Structuralism, Linguistics, and the Study of Literature* (Ithaca, NY: Cornell University Press, 1975), 197-99; and Foucault, *The Archaeology of Knowledge*, tr. A. M. Sheridan Smith (New York: Harper Torchbooks, 1972).

34—A statement "is linked to a 'referential' that is made up not of 'things', 'facts', 'realities', or 'beings', but of laws of possibility, rules of existence for the objects that are named, designated, or described within it, and for the relations that are affirmed or denied in it. The referential of the statement forms the place, the condition, the field of emergence, the authority to differentiate between individuals or objects, states of things and relations that are brought into play by the statement itself; it defines the possibilities or appearance and delimitation of that which gives meaning to the sentence, a value as truth to the proposition." Michel Foucault, *The Archaeology of Knowledge*, 91. I have to admit here that Foucault's "statement" does not correspond to Benveniste's "story."

35—"[I]n the nineteenth century, psychiatric discourse is characterized not by privileged objects, but by the way in which it forms objects that are in fact highly dispersed. This formation is made possible by a group of relations established between authorities of emergence, delimitation, and specification. One might say, then, that a discursive formation is defined (as far as its objects are concerned, at least) if one can establish such a group; if one can show how any particular object of discourse finds in it its place and law of emergence, if one can show that it may give birth simultaneously or successively to mutually exclusive objects, without having to modify itself." Michel Foucault, *The Archaeology of Knowledge*, 44. In his book on Foucault, Gilles Deleuze has pointed out that Foucault's concept of discourse needs to be understood from a topological perspective: "A statement always represents a transmission of particular elements distributed in a corresponding space. As we shall see, the formations and transformation of these spaces themselves pose topological problems that cannot adequately be described in terms of creation, beginning or foundation." Gilles Deleuze, *Foucault*, tr. Seán Hand (Minneapolis: University of Minnesota Press, 1988), 3.

36—Hans-Peter Martin and Harald Schumann, in their *Die Globaliesierung*, maintain that, in a "society of 20 vs. 80," 80% of the population get rejected from society and have to survive barely with a sparse means of living allocated to them. Martin and Schumann, *Die Globaliesierung*, (Hamburg: Rowohlt Verlag, 1996). Korean translation: *Segyehwaui tôtt: minjujuûi wa salmûi chil e taehan konggyôk* (Seoul: Younglim Cardinal, 1997), 28.

37—According to Deleuze and Guattari, "minorities are not necessarily defined by the smallness of their numbers but rather by becoming or a line of fluctuation, in other words, by the gap that separates them from this or that axiom constituting a redundant majority. Understood in this way, the "minority" is a possibility of change, of creating differences, while the "majority" is a determining framework that will capture every one or thing within its own purview and power." Deleuze and Guattari, *A Thousand Plateaus*, 469.

38—Kuan-Hsing Chen's following remark seems apt, in this regard: "[If] the energy of nationalism cannot be channeled into liberating political consciousness and social forces, once the common enemy (colonizer) has disappeared, the most resourceful group, the national bourgeoisie, would take the leading position; in the process of fighting for control of the state apparatus under the name of new nation building, they will cooperate closely with the previous colonialist state, making the colony a neo-colony, and launching an internal colonization, suppressing the working class, peasantry, aboriginal, and women, or worse, moving to other evil ends." Kuan-Hsing Chen, "Not Yet the Post-colonial Era," *Cultural Studies* 10.1 (1996): 156.

39—Derrida, *Specters of Marx*, xviii; emphasis in the original.

40—Gilles Deleuze, *The Logic of Sense*, tr. Mark Lester with Charles Stivale (New York: Columbia University Press, 1990), 273.

41—Ibid., 104.

42—Ibid., 211.

43—Ibid., 182.

44—According to Benjamin, "the existence of the work of art with reference to its aura is never entirely separated from its ritual function. In other words, the unique value of the 'authentic' work of art has its basis in ritual, the location of its original use value." Walter Benjamin, *Illuminations*, Hannah Arendt, ed., (New York: Schocken Books, 1969), 223-24.

45—Walter Benjamin, *Reflections: Essays, Aphorisms, Autobiographical Writings*, tr. Edmund Jephcott (New York: Harcourt Brace Jovanovich, 1979), 228.

46—Deleuze and Guattari, *A Thousand Plateaus*, 437-38.

47—"Figurenposition," a concept borrowed from Robert Weimann, is "the actor's position on the stage, and the speech, action, and degree of stylization associated with that position." Robert Weimann, *Shakespeare and the Popular Tradition in the Theater: Studies in the Social Dimension of Dramatic Form and Function*, tr., Robert Schwartz (Baltimore: Johns Hopkins University Press, 1978), 224.

48—Mikhail Bakhtin, *Rabelais and His World*, tr. Héléne Iswolsky (Cambridge, Mass.: M.I.T Press, 1968).

49—Chungmoo Choi, "Sorcery and Modernity," 3.13.

50—Mimicry is "supplementary" as Bhabha understands it. "Coming 'after' the original, or in 'addition to' it, gives the supplementary question the advantage of introducing a sense of 'secondariness' or belatedness into the structure of the original demand. The supplementary strategy suggests that adding 'to' need not 'add up' but may disturb the calculation...The supplementary strategy interrupts the successive seriality of the narrative plurals and pluralism by radically changing their mode of articulation." Bhabha, *The Location of Culture*, 155.

51—William Shakespeare, *King Lear*, Kenneth Muir, ed., (London: Methuen, 1972), I, iv, 108.

52—Graeme Turner, *British Cultural Studies: An Introduction* (New York: Routledge, 1990), 216. See, Michel de Certeau, "General Introduction," *The Practice of Everyday Life* (Los Angeles: University of California Press, 1984).

53—"There is for instance a kinship between the normative paradigms or colonial anthropology and the contemporary discourse of aid and development agencies. The 'transfer of technology' has not resulted in the transfer of power or the displacement of a neo-colonial tradition of political control through philanthropy—a celebrated missionary position." Bhabha, *The Location of Culture*, 242.

54—Derrida, *Specters of Marx*, xix; emphasis in the original.

EUROPE AS A PROBLEM OF INDIAN HISTORY

"Europe... since 1914 has become provincialized, ... [O]nly the natural sciences are able to call forth a quick international echo."
Hans-Georg Gadamer, *Philosophical Apprenticeships* (1977)

"The West is a name for a subject which gathers itself in discourse but is also an object constituted discursively; it is, evidently, a name always associating itself with those regions, communities, and peoples that appear politically or economically superior to other regions, communities, and peoples. Basically, it is just like the name "Japan," ... [I]t claims that it is capable of sustaining, if not actually transcending, an impulse to transcend all the particularizations."
Naoki Sakai, *Translation and Subjectivity: On "Japan" and Cultural Nationalism* (1998)

Dipesh Chakrabarty

I once wrote an article calling for a project of "provincializing Europe."[1] The Europe I wanted to provincialize is only tenuously connected to the region of the world we call "Europe." That latter Europe, one could say, has already been provincialized by history itself. Historians have long acknowledged that the so-called "European age" in modern history began to yield to other regional and global configurations towards the middle of the twentieth century.[2] As such European history is no longer seen as embodying anything like a "universal human history."[3] No major Western thinker, for instance, has publicly shared Francis Fukuyama's "vulgarized Hegelian historicism" that saw in the fall of the Berlin wall a common end for the history of all human beings.[4] The contrast with the past seems particularly sharp when one remembers the cautious but warm note of approval with which Kant detected in the French Revolution a "moral disposition in the human race" or with which Hegel saw the imprimatur of the "world spirit" in the momentousness of that event.[5]

I am by training a historian of modern South Asia, which forms my archive and is my site of analysis. The Europe I seek to provincialize or de-center is an imaginary figure that remains deeply embedded, in *clichéd and shorthand forms*, in the everyday habits of thought which invariably subtend attempts in the social sciences to address questions of political modernity in South Asia.[6] The phenomenon of "political modernity"—namely, the rule by modern institutions of the state, the bureaucracy and capitalist enterprise—is impossible to *think* anywhere in the world without invoking certain categories and concepts, the genealogies of which go deep into the intellectual, and even theological, traditions of Europe.[7] Concepts such as citizenship, the state, civil society, public sphere, human rights, equality before the law, the individual, distinctions between public and private, the idea of the subject, democracy, popular sovereignty, social justice, scientific rationality, and so on all bear the burden of European thought and history. One simply cannot think political modernity without these and other related concepts that found a climactic form over the course of the European Enlightenment and the nineteenth century.

These concepts entail an unavoidable—and in a sense indispensable—universal and secular vision of the human. The European colonizer of the nineteenth century both preached this Enlightenment humanism at the colonized and at the same time denied it in practice. But the vision has been powerful in its effects. It has historically provided a strong foundation on which to erect—both in and outside Europe—critiques of socially unjust practices. Marxist and liberal thought are both legatees of this intellectual heritage that is now global. The modern Bengali educated middle classes—to which I belong[8]—have been characterized by Tapan Raychaudhuri as "the first Asian social group of any size whose mental world was transformed through its interactions with the West."[9] A long series of illustrious members of this social group—from Raja Rammohun Roy, sometimes called "the father of modern India," to Manabendranath Roy, who argued with Lenin in the Comintern—warmly embraced the themes of rationalism, science, equality, and human rights promulgated by the European Enlightenment.[10] Modern social critiques of caste, of oppressions of women, of rights denied to labouring and subaltern classes in India, and so on,—and, in fact, the very critique of colonialism itself—are unthinkable except as a legacy, partially, of how Enlightenment Europe was appropriated in the subcontinent. The Indian Constitution tellingly begins by repeating certain universal Enlightenment themes celebrated, say, in the U.S. Constitution. And it is salutary to remember that the writings of the most trenchant critic of the institution of "untouchability" in British India refer us back to certain originally-European ideas about liberty and human equality.[11]

I too write, then, from within this inheritance. Postcolonial scholarship is committed, almost by definition, to engaging the universals—such as the abstract figure of the human or that of Reason—which were forged in eighteenth-century Europe and which underlie the human sciences. This engagement marks, for instance, the writing of the Tunisian philosopher and historian Hichem Djait, who accuses imperialist Europe of "deny[ing] its own vision of man."[12] Fanon's struggle to hold onto the Enlightenment idea of the human—even when he knew that European imperialism had reduced that idea to the figure of the settler-colonial white man—is now itself a part of the global heritage of all postcolonial thinkers.[13] The struggle ensues precisely because, in the condition of political modernity, there is no easy way of dispensing with these universals. Without them there would be no social science addressing issues of modern social justice.

This engagement with European thought is also called forth by the fact that today, the so-called European intellectual tradition is the only one alive in the social-science departments of most, if not all, modern universities. I use the word "alive" in a particular sense. It is only within some very particular traditions of thinking that we treat fundamental thinkers who are long dead and gone not only as people belonging to their own times but also as though they were our own contemporaries. In the social sciences, these are invariably the thinkers one encounters within the tradition that has come to call itself "European" or "Western." I am aware that an entity called "the European intellectual tradition" stretching back to the ancient Greeks, is a fabrication of relatively recent European history. Martin Bernal, Samir Amin, and others have justly criticised the claim of European thinkers that such an unbroken tradition ever existed or that it could even properly be called "European."[14] The point, however, is that, fabrication or not, this is the genealogy of thought that social scientists find themselves inserted into. Faced with the task of analyzing developments or social practices in modern India, few if any Indian social scientists or social scientists of India would argue seriously with, say, the thirteenth-century logician Gangesa or with the grammarian-cum-linguistic-philosopher Bartrihari (who straddled the fifth and sixth centuries) or with the tenth-through-eleventh-century aesthetician Abhinavagupta. Sad though it is, one result of European colonial rule in South Asia is that the intellectual traditions once unbroken and alive in Sanskrit or Persian or Arabic are now only matters of historical research for most—perhaps all—modern social scientists in the region.[15] They treat these traditions as truly dead, as history. Categories once subject to detailed theoretical contemplation and inquiry now exist as practical concepts, bereft of any theoretical lineage, embedded in the quotidian practices South Asia. Contemporary social scientists of South Asia seldom have the training that would enable them to turn these concepts into resources for critical thought for the present. And yet past European thinkers and their categories are never quite dead for us in the same way. South Asian(ist) social scientists would argue passionately with a Marx or a Weber without feeling any need either to historicize them or to place them in their European intellectual contexts. Sometimes—though this is rather rare—they would even argue with the ancient, medieval, or early-modern predecessors of these European theorists.

Yet the very history of politicization of the population, or the coming of political modernity, in countries outside of the Western capitalist democracies of the world produces a deep irony in the history of the political. This history challenges us to rethink two conceptual gifts of nineteenth-century Europe, concepts integral to the idea of modernity. One is historicism—the idea that understanding anything necessarily means having to see it both as a unity and in its historical development—and the other one is the very idea of the political. What historically enables a project such as that of "provincializing Europe" is the experience of political modernity in a country like India. European thought has a contradictory relationship to such an instance of political modernity. It is both indispensable and inadequate to help us to think through the various life-practices that constitute the political and the historical in India. Exploring—on both theoretical and factual registers—this simultaneous indispensibility and inadequacy of social science thought is the task this essay has set itself.

The politics of historicism

Writings by poststructuralist philosophers such as Michel Foucault have undoubtedly given a fillip to global critiques of historicism.[16] But it would be wrong to think of postcolonial critiques of historicism (or of the political) as simply deriving from critiques already elaborated by postmodern and poststructuralist thinkers of the West. In fact, to think this way would itself be to perform historicism, for such a thought would merely repeat the temporal structure of the statement, "First in the West, and then elsewhere." In saying this, I do not mean to take away from the recent discussions of historicism by critics who see its decline in the West as resulting from what Jameson has imaginatively named "the cultural logic of late-capitalism."[17] The cultural studies scholar Lawrence Grossberg has pointedly questioned whether history itself is not endangered by consumerist practices of contemporary capitalism. How do you produce historical observation and analysis, Grossberg asks, "when every event is potentially evidence, potentially determining, and at the same time, changing too quickly to allow the comfortable leisure of academic criticism?"[18] However, these arguments, while valuable, still by-pass the histories of political modernity in the third world. From Mandel to Jameson, nobody sees "late capitalism" as a system whose driving engine may be in the Third World. The word "late" has very different connotations when applied to the developed countries and to those seen as still "developing." "Late capitalism" is properly the name of a phenomenon that is understood as belonging primarily to the developed capitalist world, though its impact on the rest of the globe is never denied.[19]

Western critiques of historicism that base themselves on some characterisation of "late capitalism" overlook the deep ties that bind together historicism as a mode of thought and the formation of political modernity in the erstwhile European colonies. Historicism once enabled European domination of the world.[20] Crudely, one might say that historicism itself was one important form that the ideology of progress or "development" took from the nineteenth century on. Historicism is what made modernity or capitalism look not simply global but rather as something that became global *over time*, by first originating in one place (Europe) and then spreading outside it. This "first in Europe, then elsewhere" structure of global historical time was historicist; different non-Western nationalisms would later on produce local versions of the same narrative replacing "Europe" with some locally constructed centre. It was historicism that allowed Marx to say that the "country that is more developed industrially only shows, to the less developed, the image of its own future."[21] It is also what authorised historians such as Phyllis Deane to describe the coming of industries in England as *The First Industrial Revolution* (and I emphasise the concept of "First").[22] Historicism thus posited historical time itself as a measure of the cultural distance (at least in institutional development) that was assumed to exist between the West and the non-West.[23] In the colonies it legitimated the idea of civilization.[24] In Europe itself it made possible completely internalist histories of Europe in which Europe came to be described as the site of the first occurrence of capitalism, modernity or Enlightenment.[25] These "events" in turn are all explained mainly with respect to "events" within the geographical confines of Europe (however fuzzy its exact boundaries may have been). The inhabitants of the colonies, on the other hand, were assigned a place in the latter part of the "First in Europe and then elsewhere" structure of time. This move of historicism is what Johannes Fabian has called "the denial of coevalness."[26]

Historicism—and even the very modern, European idea of history—one might say, came to non-European peoples in the nineteenth century as somebody's (in this case, the European's) way of saying "not yet" to somebody else.[27] Take the classic liberal but historicist essays by John Stuart Mill, *On Liberty* and *On Representative Government* both of which proclaimed self-rule as the highest form of government and yet argued against giving Indians or Africans self-rule on grounds that were indeed historicist. According to Mill, Indians or Africans were *not yet* civilised enough to rule themselves. Some historical time of development and civilization (colonial rule and education, to be precise) had to elapse before they could be deemed suitable for such a task.[28] Mill's historicist argument regarding self-government or democracy consigned Indians, as well as African and other "rude" nations to an imaginary waiting room of history. In doing so, it converted history itself into a version of this waiting room. We were all headed for the same destination, Mill averred, but some people were to arrive earlier than others. That was what historicist consciousness was: a recommendation to the colonized to wait. Acquiring a historical consciousness, acquiring the public spirit that Mill thought absolutely necessary for the art of self-government, also meant learning this art of waiting. Moreover, this waiting was the realisation of the "not yet" of historicism.

Twentieth-century anti-colonial democratic demands for self-rule, to the contrary, harped insistently on a "now" as the temporal horizon of action. From about the time of the First World War to the decolonization movements of the fifties and sixties, anti-colonial nationalisms were predicated on this urgency of the "now" of the present. At the century's end, historicism has not disappeared from the world but its "not yet" exists today in tension with this global insistence on the "now" that marks all popular movements towards democracy. This had to be so, for in their search for a mass base, the various anti-colonial nationalist movements introduced into the sphere of the political, certain classes and groups who, by the standards of nineteenth-century European liberalism, could only look ever so unprepared to assume the political responsibility of self-government. These were the peasants, tribals, semi- or unskilled industrial workers in non-Western cities, men and women from the various subordinate social groups, in short, the subaltern classes of the Third World.

A critique of historicism therefore goes to the heart of the question of political modernity in non-Western societies. As I shall argue in more detail later, it was through recourse to some version of a stagist theory of history—ranging from simple evolutionary schemas to sophisticated understandings of "uneven development"—that European political and social thought made room for the political modernity of the subaltern classes. This was not, as such, an unreasonable theoretical claim. If "political modernity" was to be a bounded and definable phenomenon, it was not unreasonable to use its definition as a measuring rod for social progress. Within this thought, it could be always be said with reason that somebody was less modern than somebody else and that the former "somebody" needed a period of preparation and waiting before they could be recognized as full participants in political modernity. But this was precisely the argument of the coloniser, the "not yet" to which the colonized nationalist opposed his or her "now." The achievement of political modernity in the Third World could only take place through a contradictory relationship to European social and political thought. It is true that nationalist elites often rehearsed to their own subaltern classes—and still do where the political structures permit—the stage-theory of history on which European ideas of political modernity were based. However, there were two developments in nationalist struggles that made it necessary to produce at least a practical, if not theoretical, rejection of any stagist, historicist distinctions between the premodern or non-modern and the modern. One was the nationalist elite's own rejection of the "waiting room" version of history when faced with the European's use of it as a justification for denying "self-government" to the colonized. And the other was the twentieth-century phenomenon of the peasant becoming a full participant in the political life of the nation (that is, in the nationalist movement itself at first and then as a citizen of the independent nation) long before he or she could be formally educated into the doctrinal or conceptual aspects of citizenship.

Quite a dramatic example of this nationalist rejection of historicist history is the Indian decision, taken immediately after the attainment of independence, to base Indian democracy on universal adult franchise. This was directly in violation of Mill's prescription. Mill had counselled exactly the opposite: "universal teaching," he said in the essay on *Representative Government*, "must precede universal enfranchisement."[29] Even the Indian Franchise Committee of 1931, with several Indian members, stuck to a position that was a modified version of Mill's argument. The members of the Committee agreed that while universal adult franchise would be the ideal goal for India, the general lack of literacy in the country posed a very large obstacle to its implementation.[30] And yet in less than two decades India opted for universal adult suffrage for a population that was still predominantly non-literate. In defending the new constitution and the idea of "popular sovereignty" before the nation's Constituent Assembly on the eve of formal independence, Sarvepalli Radhakrishnan, later to be the first Vice-President of India, argued against the idea that Indians were not yet ready to rule themselves. As far as he was concerned, literate or illiterate, Indians had always been suited for self-rule: "We cannot say that the republican tradition is foreign to the genius of this country. We have had it from the beginning of our history."[31] What else was this position if not a national gesture of abolishing the imaginary waiting room in which Indians had been placed by European historicist thought? Needless to say, historicism remains alive and well today in the all the developmentalist practices and imaginations of the Indian state.[32] Much of the institutional activity of governing in India is premised on a day-to-day practice of historicism. There is a strong sense in which the peasant is still being educated and developed into the citizen. Nevertheless, every time a populist/political mobilisation of the people on the streets of the country makes a version of "mass democracy" visible in India, historicist time is put in temporary suspension. In addition, once in every five years—or more frequently, as seems to be the case these days—the nation produces a political performance of electoral democracy that sets aside all the assumptions of the historicist imagination of time. On the day of the election, every Indian adult is treated practically and theoretically as someone already endowed with the skills of making a major citizenly choice, education or no education.

The history and nature of political modernity in an ex-colonial country such as India thus generates a tension between the two aspects of the subaltern/peasant-as-citizen.[33] One is the peasant who has to be educated into the citizen and who therefore belongs to the time of historicism; and the other the peasant who, despite his or her lack of formal education, is already a citizen. This tension is somewhat akin to the tension between the two aspects of nationalism that Homi Bhabha has usefully identified as the pedagogic and the performative.[34] When we write history in the pedagogic mode, we see the peasant's world, with its emphasis on kinship, gods, and the so-called supernatural, as anachronistic. But the "nation" and the political are also performed in the carnivalesque aspects of democracy: in rebellions, protest marches, sporting events, and in universal adult franchise. The question is: How do we *think* the political at these moments when the peasant or the subaltern emerges in the modern sphere of politics, in his or her own right, as a member of the nationalist movement against British rule or as a full-fledged member of the body-politic, without having had to do any "preparatory" work in order to qualify as the "bourgeois-citizen"?

I should clarify that in my usage the word "peasant" refers to more than the sociologist's figure of the peasant. I intend that particular meaning but I load the word with an extended meaning as well. The "peasant" acts here as a shorthand for all the seemingly non-modern, rural, non-secular relationships and life-practices that constantly leave their imprint on the lives of even the elites in India and on their institutions of government. The peasant stands for all that is not-bourgeois (in a European sense) in Indian capitalism and modernity. The section below elaborates a little further on this idea.

Subaltern Studies and the critique of historicism

This problem of how to conceptualise the historical and the political in a context where the peasant was already part of the political, was indeed one of the key questions that drove the historiographic project of *Subaltern Studies*.[35] My extended interpretation of the word "peasant" actually follows from some of the founding statements Ranajit Guha made when he and his colleagues attempted to democratise the writing of Indian history by looking on subordinate social groups as the makers of their own destiny. I find it extremely significant, for example, that *Subaltern Studies* should begin its career by registering a deep sense of unease with the very idea of the "political" as it had been deployed in the received traditions of English-language Marxist historiography. Nowhere is this more visible than in Ranajit Guha's criticism of the British historian Eric Hobsbawm's category "pre-political" in his 1983 book *Elementary Aspects of Peasant Insurgency in Colonial India*.[36]

This category "pre-political" revealed the limits to how far historicist Marxist thought could go in responding to the challenge posed to European political thought by the entry of the peasant in the modern sphere of politics. Hobsbawm recognized what was special to political modernity in the Third World. He readily admitted that it was the "acquisition of political consciousness" by peasants that "made our century the most revolutionary in history." Yet he missed out on the implications of this observation for the historicism that underlay his own analysis. Peasants' actions, organized, more often than not, along the axes of kinship, religion, caste and involving gods, spirits, and supernatural agents as actors alongside humans, remained for him symptomatic of a consciousness that had not quite come to terms with the secular-institutional logic of the political.[37] He called peasants "*pre-political* people who have not yet found, or only begun to find, a specific language in which to express themselves. [Capitalism] comes to them from outside, insidiously by the operation of economic forces, which they do not understand" In Hobsbawm's historicist language, the social movements of the peasants of the twentieth century remained "archaic."[38]

The analytical impulse of Hobsbawm's study belongs squarely to a variety of historicism that Western Marxism has cultivated ever since its inception. Marxist intellectuals of the West and their followers elsewhere have developed a diverse set of sophisticated strategies allowing them to acknowledge evidence of the "incompleteness" of the capitalist transformation in Europe and other places while retaining the idea of a general historical movement from a pre-modern stage to that of modernity. These strategies include, first of all, the old and now-discredited evolutionist paradigms of the nineteenth century—the language of "survivals" and "remnants"—sometimes found in Marx's own prose. But there are some other strategies as well, and they are all variations on the theme of "uneven development," itself derived, as Neil Smith shows, from Marx's use of the idea of "uneven rates of development" in his *Critique of Political Economy* (1859) and from Lenin's and Trotsky's later use of the concept.[39] The point is, whether it is "uneven development," or Ernst Bloch's "synchronicity of the non-synchronous," or Althusserian "structural causality," these strategies all retain elements of historicism (and in spite of Althusser's explicit opposition to historicism). They all ascribe at least an underlying structural unity (if not an expressive totality) to historical process and time which makes it possible to identify certain elements in the present as "anachronistic."[40] The thesis of "uneven development," as James Chandler has perceptively observed in his recent study of romanticism, goes "hand in hand" with the "dated grid of an homogenous empty time."[41]

By explicitly critiquing the idea of peasant consciousness as "pre-political," Guha was prepared to suggest that the nature of collective action by peasants in modern India was such that it effectively stretched the category "political" far beyond the boundaries assigned to it in European political thought.[42] The political sphere in which the peasant and his masters participated was modern—for what else could nationalism be but a modern political movement for self-government?—and yet it did not follow the logic of secular-rational calculations inherent to the modern conception of the political. This peasant-but-modern political sphere was not bereft of the agency of gods, spirits, and other supernatural beings.[43] Social scientists may classify such agencies under the rubric of "peasant beliefs" but the peasant-as-citizen did not partake of the ontological assumptions about the human that the social sciences take for granted. But Guha's statement recognized this subject as modern and hence refused to call the peasants' political behaviour or consciousness "pre-political." He insisted that instead of being an anachronistic remnant in a modernising colonial world, the peasant was a real contemporary of colonialism. Peasants were a fundamental part of the modernity that colonial rule brought to India. Theirs was not a "backward" consciousness—a mentality left over from the past, a consciousness baffled by modern political and economic institutions and yet resistant to them. Peasants' readings of the relations of power that they confronted in the world, Guha argued, were by no means unrealistic or backward looking.

Of course, this was not all said at once and with anything like the clarity one can achieve with hindsight. There are, for example, passages in *Elementary Aspects of Peasant Insurgency in Colonial India* where Guha follows the tendencies general to European Marxist or liberal scholarship. He sometimes reads undemocratic relationships—issues of direct "domination and subordination" involving the so-called "religious" or the supernatural—as survivals of a precapitalist era, as not quite modern, and hence as indicative of problems of transition to capitalism.[44] Such narratives often make an appearance in the early volumes of *Subaltern Studies* as well. Nonetheless, these statements, I submit, do not adequately represent the radical potential of Guha's critique of the category "pre-political." For if they were a valid framework for analyzing Indian modernity, one could indeed come back and argue in favour of Hobsbawm and his category "pre-political." One could point out—in accordance with European political thought—that the related category "political" was inappropriate for analyzing peasant protest, for the sphere of the political hardly ever abstracted itself out from the spheres of religion and kinship in pre-capitalist relations of domination. The everyday relations of power involving kinship, gods, and spirits that the peasant dramatically exemplified could, then, with justice be called "pre-political." In addition, the persisting world of the peasant in India could be legitimately read as a mark of the incompleteness of India's transition to capitalism—and the peasant himself seen rightly as an "earlier type," active no doubt in nationalism but really working under world-historical notice of extinction.

What I build on here, however, is the opposite tendency of thought signalled by Guha's unease with the category "pre-political." Peasant insurgency in modern India, Guha wrote, "was a *political* struggle."[45] I have italicized the word "political" in this quotation to highlight a creative tension between the Marxist lineage of *Subaltern Studies* and the more challenging questions it raised from the very beginning about the nature of the political in the colonial modernity of India. Examining, for instance, over a hundred known cases of peasant rebellions in British India between 1783 and 1900, Guha showed that practices that brought gods, spirits, and other spectral and divine beings into presence were part of the network of power and prestige within which both the subaltern and elite operated in South Asia. These presences were not merely symbolic of some of deeper and "more real" secular reality.[46]

South Asian political modernity, Guha argued, fundamentally brings together two non-commensurable logics of power, both modern. One is the logic of the quasi-liberal legal and institutional frameworks that European rule introduced into the country and which in many ways were desired by both the local elite and the subaltern classes. I do not mean to understate the importance of this development. Braided in with this, however, is the logic of another set of relationships involving both the elites and the subalterns. These are relations that articulate hierarchy through practices of direct and explicit *domination and subordination* of the less powerful by the more powerful. The first logic is secular; in other words, it derives from the secularised forms of Christianity that mark modernity in the West and shows a similar tendency towards first making a "religion" out of a medley of Hindu practices and then secularising forms of that religion in the life of modern institutions in India.[47] The second has no necessary secularism about it. This second set of practices is what continually brings gods and spirits into presence in the domain of the political. This is to be distinguished from a secular-calculative use of "religion" that many contemporary political parties make in the subcontinent. To read these practices as a hangover or survival of an earlier mode of production would inexorably lead us to stagist and elitist conceptions of history. It would, then, take us back to a historicist framework. Within that framework, historiography has no other way of responding to the challenge presented to political thought and philosophy by the involvement of peasants in twentieth-century nationalisms, and by their emergence after independence as full-fledged citizens of a modern nation-state.

Guha's critique of the category "pre-political," I suggest, fundamentally pluralises the history of power in global modernity and separates it from any universalist narratives of capital. What subaltern historiography questions is the assumption that capitalism necessarily brings to a position of hegemony bourgeois relations of power.[48] If Indian modernity places the bourgeois in juxtaposition with that which seems pre-bourgeois, if the non-secular supernatural exists in proximity to the secular, and if both are to be found in the sphere of the political, it is not because capitalism or political modernity in India has remained "incomplete." Guha does not deny the connections of colonial India to the global forces of capitalism. His point is that what seemed "traditional" in this modernity were "traditional only in so far as [their] roots could be traced back to pre-colonial times, but [they were] by no means archaic in the sense of being outmoded."[49] This was a political modernity which eventually would give rise to a thriving electoral democracy even when "vast areas in the life and consciousness of the people" escaped any kind of "[bourgeois] hegemony."[50]

It is the pressure of this observation that introduces into the *Subaltern Studies* project a necessary—though sometimes incipient—critique of both historicism and of the idea of the political. My argument for provincializing Europe follows directly from my involvement in this project. A history of political modernity in India could not be written as a simple application of the analytics of capital and nationalism available to Western Marxism. One could not, in the manner of some nationalist historians, pit against the story of a regressive colonialism an account of a robust nationalist movement seeking to establish a bourgeois outlook throughout society.[51] For, in Guha's terms, there was no class in South Asia comparable to the European bourgeoisie of Marxist meta-narratives, a class able to fabricate a hegemonic ideology which made its own interests look and feel like the interests of all. The "Indian culture of the colonial era," Guha argued in a later essay, defied understanding "either as a replication of the liberal-bourgeois culture of nineteenth-century Britain or as the mere survival of an antecedent pre-capitalist culture."[52] This was capitalism indeed but without bourgeois relations attaining a position of unchallenged hegemony, a capitalist dominance without a hegemonic bourgeois culture—or, in Guha's famous terms, "dominance without hegemony."

One cannot think this plural history of power and provide accounts of the modern political subject in India without at the same time radically questioning the nature of historical time. Imaginations of socially-just futures for humans usually take the idea of single, homogenous, and secular historical time for granted. Modern politics is often justified as a story of human sovereignty acted out in the context of a ceaseless unfolding of inert historical time. However, this view is not an adequate intellectual resource for thinking about the conditions for political modernity in colonial and post-colonial India. We need to move instead away from two of the ontological assumptions entailed in secular conceptions of the political and the social. The first is that the human exists in a frame of a single and secular historical time, which *envelops* other kinds of time. The task of conceptualising practices of social and political modernity in South Asia often requires us to make the opposite assumption: that historical time is not-one, that it is out of joint with itself. The second outdated assumption is that the human is ontologically singular, that gods and spirits are in the end "social facts," and that the social somehow is prior to both. I try to think *without* the assumption of even a logical priority of the social. One empirically knows of no society in which humans have ever existed without the company of gods and spirits. While the God of monotheism may have taken a few knocks—if not actually "died"—in the nineteenth-century European story of "the disenchantment of the world," the gods and other agents inhabiting the practices of "superstition" have never died anywhere. I take gods and spirits to be existentially coeval with the human, and I think from the assumption that the question of being human involves the question of being with gods and spirits.[53] Being human means, as Ramachandra Gandhi puts it, discovering "the possibility of calling upon God [or gods—D.C.] without being under an obligation to first establish his [or their] reality."[54]

In conclusion let me reiterate that provincializing Europe is not a project of rejecting or discarding European thought. Relating to a body of thought to which one largely owes one's intellectual existence cannot be a matter of exacting what Leela Gandhi has aptly called "postcolonial revenge."[55] If European thought is at once both indispensable and yet inadequate in helping us to think through the experiences of political modernity in non-Western nations, provincializing Europe becomes the task of exploring how this thought—which is now everybody's heritage and which affects us all—may be renewed from and for the margins.

I recognize that Europe appears differently when seen from within the experiences of colonisation or inferiorisation in specific parts of the world. Postcolonial scholars, speaking from their different geographies of colonialism, have spoken of different Europes. The recent critical scholarship of Latin Amercanists, Afro-Caribbeanists, and others points to the imperialism of Spain and Portugal, triumphant at the time of the Renaissance and in political decline by the end of the Enlightenment.[56] The question of postcolonialism itself is given multiple and contested locations in the works of those studying South East Asia, East Asia, Africa, and the Pacific.[57] Yet, however multiple Europe's loci and however varied colonialisms, the problem of getting beyond Eurocentric histories remains a shared problem across geographical boundaries.[58]

A key question in the world of postcolonial scholarship will be the following. The problem of capitalist modernity cannot any longer be seen simply as a sociological problem of historical transition (as in the famous "transition debates" in European history) but as a problem of translation as well. There was a time—before scholarship itself became globalized—when the process of translating diverse forms, practices, and understandings of life into universalist political-theoretical categories of deeply European origin (such as capital), seemed to most social scientists an unproblematic proposition. That which was considered an analytical category—be it Marx's "capital," Weber's "rationalism," or Geertz's "experience-distant" concepts—was understood to have transcended the fragment of European history from which it may have originated.[59] At most we assumed that a translation acknowledged to be "rough" was adequate for the task of comprehension.

The English-language monograph in area studies, for example, was a classic embodiment of this presupposition. A standard, mechanically put-together and least-read feature of the monograph in Asian or area studies was a section, called the "glossary" which came at the very end of the book. No reader was ever seriously expected to interrupt their pleasure of reading by having frequently to turn pages in order to consult the glossary. The "glossary" reproduced a series of "rough translations" of native terms, often borrowed from the colonialists themselves. These colonial translations were rough not only in being inaccurate and approximate but also in that they were meant to fit the rough and ready methods of colonial rule. To challenge that model of "rough translation" is to pay critical and unrelenting attention to the very process of translation itself.

The project of provincializing Europe therefore turns toward the horizon that many gifted scholars working on the politics of translation have pointed to. These scholars have demonstrated that what translation produces out of seeming "incommensurabilities" is neither an absence of relationship between dominant and dominating forms of knowledge, nor equivalents that successfully mediate between differences, but precisely the partly opaque relationship we call "difference."[60] The global project of provincializing Europe thus has to turn to philosophies of difference to explore what it might mean to renew European thought for and from the margins of the very globe that that thought has historically helped to create.

Appendix: A Note on the term "Historicism"

The term "historicism" has a long and complex history. Applied to the writings of a range of scholars, who are often as mutually opposed and as different from each another as Hegel and Ranke, it is not a term that lends itself to easy and precise definitions. Its current use has also been inflected by the recent revival it has enjoyed through the "new historicist" style of analysis pioneered by Stephen Greenblatt and others.[61] Important in particular is a tension between the Rankean insistence on attention to the uniqueness and the individuality of a historical identity or event and the discernment of general historical trends that the Hegelian-Marxist tradition foregrounds.[62] This tension itself is a now an inherited part of how we understand the craft and the function of the academic historian. Keeping in mind this complicated history of the term, I try to explicate my own use of it below.

Ian Hacking and Maurice Mandelbaum have provided the following, minimalist definitions for historicism:

> [historicism is] the theory that social and cultural phenomena are historically determined and that each period in history has its own values that are not directly applicable to other epochs.[63] (Hacking)

> historicism is the belief that an adequate understanding of the nature of any phenomenon and an adequate assessment of its value are to be gained through considering it in terms of the place it occupied and the role which it played within a process of development.[64] (Mandelbaum)

Sifting through these and other definitions as well as some additional elements highlighted by scholars who have made the study of historicism their specialist concern, it may suffice to say that "historicism" is a mode of thinking with the following characteristics. It tells us that in order to understand the nature of anything in this world we must see it as a historically-developing entity, i.e. firstly, as an individual and unique whole, as one thing—as some kind of unity at least *in potentia*—and, secondly, as something that develops *over time*. Historicism typically can allow for complexities and zigzags in this development; it seeks to find the general in the particular; and it does not entail any necessary assumptions of teleology. Nonetheless, the idea of development and the assumption that a certain amount of time elapses in the very process of development are critical to this understanding.[65] Needless to say, this passage of time that is constitutive of both the narrative and the concept of development is, in the famous words of Walter Benjamin, the secular, empty, and homogenous time of history.[66] Ideas, old and new, about discontinuities, ruptures, and shifts in the historical process have from time to time challenged historicism's dominance, but much written history still remains deeply historicist. That is to say, it still takes its object of investigation to be internally unified and sees it as something developing over time. This is particularly true—for all their differences with classical historicism—of historical narratives underpinned by Marxist or liberal views of the world, and this is what makes for descriptions/explanations in the genre "history of"—of capitalism, of industrialization, of nationalism, and so on and so forth.[67]

Endnotes

1—Dipesh Chakrabarty, "Postcoloniality and the Artifice of History: Who Speaks for Indian' Pasts?'", *Representations*, no.37, (winter, 1992): 1-26.

2—See, for instance, Oscar Halecki, *The Limits and Divisions of European History* (Notre Dame, Indiana: The University of Notre Dame Press, 1962), chapter 2 and *passim*. The impact of "America" on educational institutions, practices of (sub)urbanism, military and industrial technology throughout the world is attested to by two contrary global movements: the desire for, and the simultaneous fear of, Americanisation. Reading and speaking to Bernard Cohn and Arjun Appadurai has made me aware of the post-war impact of the United States on knowledge-institutions around the world. The "mythic banality" of "America" is explored in Jean Baudrillard, *America*, trans. Chris Turner (London: Verso, 1993).

3—Such histories have, of course, been challenged by several historians in the last two decades: Janet Abu-Lughod, *Before European Hegemony: The World System A.D. 1250-1350* (New York and Oxford: Oxford University Press, 1989); Eric Wolf, *Europe and the People Without History* (Berkeley: The University of California Press, 1982); K.N. Chaudhuri, *Asia Before Europe: Economy and Civilisation of the Indian Ocean from the Rise of Islam to 1750* (Cambridge: Cambridge University Press, 1990). See also Talal Asad, "Are there Histories of Peoples Without Europe? A Review Article," *Comparative Study of Society and History* (1987): 594-607. Recent books and essays on "world history" exemplify further the trend toward moving away from Eurocentric orientation in the writing of history. See, for example, Sanjay Subrahmanyam, "Connected Histories: Noted towards a Reconfiguration of Early Modern Eurasia," *Modern Asian Studies* XXXI. 3 (1997): 735-762; J.M. Blaut, *The Colonizer's Model of the World: Geographical Diffusionism and Eurocentric History* (New York and London: The Guilford Press, 1993); Martin W. Lewis and Karen E. Wigen, *The Myth of Continents: A Critique of Metageography* (Berkeley: The University of California Press, 1997).

4—See the discussion of Fukuyama in Michael Roth's essay, "The Nostalgic Nest at the End of History" in *The Ironist's Cage: Memory, Trauma and the Construction of History* (New York: Columbia University Press, 1995), 163-174.

5—Immanuel Kant, "An Old Question Raised Again: Is the Human Race Constantly Progressing?" in *The Conflict of Faculties*, trans. Mary J. Gregor (Lincoln and London: University of Nebraska Press, 1992), 153. Hyppolite's summary of Hegel's responses to the French Revolution reads:

"in 1807 Hegel no longer thought of the French Revolution as he had during his years at Tubingen; ... the Terror of 1793 and the Napoleonic Empire, led him to change his views .... But Hegel continued to affirm that there was in that political revolution a prodigious effort on the part of the world spirit to realize "the rational, in-and-for-itself' on earth."

Jean Hyppolite, *Genesis and Structure of Hegel's* Phenomenology of Spirit trans. Samuel Cherniak and John Heckman (Evanston, Ill: Northwestern University Press, 1974), 426. See also Charles Taylor, *Hegel* (Cambridge: Cambridge University Press, 1978), 416-421.

6—It is important to keep in mind that it is not my purpose here to discuss the long history and genealogy of the fundamental categories European social and political thought. Habermas's book on the "public sphere" or Colas's book on the "civil society" provides such detailed genealogies. My engagement with European-thought-as-the-cliches of modern South Asian history does not deny the rich and diverse origins and careers of the fundamental categories that this body of thought has produced. Jurgen Habermas, *The Structural Transformation of the Public Sphere: An Inquiry into a Category of Bourgeois Society,* trans., Thomas Burger and Frederick Lawrence (Cambridge, Mass: The MIT Press, 1989) and Dominique Colas, *Civil Society and Fanaticism: Conjoined Histories*, trans. Amy Jacobs (Palo Alto, Ca: Stanford University Press, 1997) provide two exemplary genealogies of two crucial categories of European social and political thought. But these genealogies are completely "internalist" accounts of European history. My project of "provincializing Europe" is not as such as project in European history but I see possibilities for fruitful conversation in the recent research of some younger Europeanist interested in tracing the role of colonialism in the origins of modern European thought. See, for example, Alice Bullard, *Constellations of Civilization and Savagery: New Caledonia and France 1770-1900* (forthcoming).

7—I distinguish here between thought and practice. To be a member of the parliament or a similar legislative body in a country such as India does not require one to know the history of anything called "the parliament" in any depth. And that it is how it perhaps should be. Yet imagine having to write a text-book explaining to the children of India what the role of "the parliament" is in the life of the nation. It would be impossible to address this task without some engagement with European history. It is at the level of thought, not practice, that I raise the question of provincializing Europe.

8—Fragments of whose history I recount in my, *Provincializing Europe: Postcolonial Thought and Historical Difference* (Princeton, N.J.: Princeton University Press, forthcoming).

9—Tapan Raychaudhuri, *Europe Reconsidered: Perceptions of the West in Nineteenth Century Bengal* (Delhi: Oxford University Press, 1988), ix.

10—On Rammohun Roy, see V.C. Joshi ed., *Raja Rammohun Roy and the Process of Modernization in India* (Delhi: Nehru Memorial Museum and Library, 1973); on M. N. Roy see Sanjay Seth, *Marxist Theory and Nationalist Politics: The Case of Colonial India* (Delhi: Sage Publications, 1995).

11—See the discussion of B.R. Ambedkar in the last chapter of *Provincializing Europe*.

12—Hichem Djait, *Europe and Islam: Cultures and Modernity*, trans. Peter Heinegg (Berkeley: The University of California Press, 1985), 101.

13—See the Conclusion to Frantz Fanon, *The Wretched of the Earth*, trans. Constance Farrington (New York: Grove Press, 1963).

14—See Martin Bernal, *The Black Athena: The Afroasiatic Roots of Classical Civilization* volume 1 (London: Vintage, 1991); on "the myths of Greek ancestry" Samir Amin, *Eurocentrism* trans. Russell Moore (New York: Zed, 1989), 91-92 Bernal's whole volume bears the subtitle "The fabrication of ancient Greece, 1785-1985." I understand that several of Bernal's claims are being disputed in the scholarship today. I am not competent to comment on these debates. But his point about the contributions made by Egyptians and other non-Greek persons to so-called "Greek" thought remains.

15—This is not to deny the fact that Sanskrit learning enjoyed a brief renaissance under British rule in the early part of the nineteenth century, inspired by a coming together of both British interest in European scholarship and eighteenth-century institutions of India that lingered on into the nineteenth. But this revival of Sanskrit should not be confused with the question of survival of an intellectual tradition. Modern research and studies in Sanskrit have on the whole been undertaken within the intellectual frameworks of the European human sciences. Sheldon Pollock's forthcoming book on *The Language of the Gods in the World of Men: Sanskrit and Power to 1500* directly engages with the problematic intellectual legacies of this practice. See also the collection of essays in Jan E.M. Houben ed., *Ideology and Status of Sanskrit* (Leiden, New York, and Koln: E.J. Brill, 1996), in particular the following illuminating pieces: John D. Kelly, "What was Sanskrit for? Metadiscursive strategies in ancient

India" (87-107); Sheldon Pollock, "The Sanskrit Cosmopolis, 300-1300 C.E.: Transculturation, Vernacularization, and the Question of Ideology" (197-247); Saroja Bhate, "Position of Sanskrit in public education and scientific research in modern India" (383-400). The very use of the word "ideology" in the title of this book would appear to support my thesis. The issue receives further discussion in two other essays of Sheldon Pollock's: "The Death of Sanskrit," *Comparative Studies in Society and History* (forthcoming) and "The New Intellectuals of Seventeenth Century India," in *Indian Economic and Social History Review* (forthcoming). Similar points could be made with respect to scholarship and intellectual traditions available, say, in the eighteenth century in Persian and Arabic. I am, unfortunately, less aware of contemporary research of this problem with respect to these two languages. I also acknowledge the highly respectable line of modern scholars of Indian philosophy who over generations have attempted conversations between European and Indian traditions of thought. Two contemporary exemplars of this tradition would be J. N. Mohanty and the late B. K. Matilal. But, sadly, their thinking is yet to have any major impact on social-science studies of South Asia.

16—Robert Young, *White Mythologies: History Writing and the West* (London and New York: Routledge, 1990).

17—Frederic Jameson's path-breaking study of postmodern culture ascribes the decline of historicism to postmodernism's resistance to depth-perspectives, its promotion of a certain aesthetic of depthlessness. Frederic Jameson, *Postmodernism or, the Cultural Logic of Late Capitalism* (Durham: Duke University Press, 1991), chapter 1.

18—Lawrence Grossberg cited in Meaghan Morris, "Metamorphoses at the Sydney Tower," *New Formations*, 11 (summer, 1990): 5-18. See the larger discussion in my "The Death of History? Historical Consciousness and the Culture of Late Capitalism," *Public Culture* 4.2 (spring, 1992): 47-65. Meaghan Morris has now set forth her views on the problem of "history" in cultural studies in greater and considered detail in her recent book *Too Soon Too Late: History in Popular Culture* (Bloomington: Indiana University Press, 1998). Lawrence Grossberg's own reactions to this discussion are forthcoming in a new essay of his (personal communication).

19—Interesting in this respect is Jameson's response to Mike Davis who in his essay "Urban Renaissance and the Spirit of Postmodernism," *New Left Review* 151 (May-June, 1985), criticised Jameson for overlooking connections between postmodern architecture in Los Angeles and a ruling-class desire to forget "the great Hispanic-Asian city" with its sweatshops and "smog-poisoned" reality. Jameson's response reproduces a certain familiar schema of historicism. On the one hand, he argues that the sweat-shops are part of capitalist production ("Lessons in economics from someone who thinks sweatshops are 'precapitalist' are not helpful," he writes angrily) but on the other hand he posits a temporal lag between capital and the growth of resistance to it: "capital (and its multitudinous 'penetrations') comes first, and only then can the resistance to it develop, even though it might be pretty to think otherwise." *Postmodernism*, 421. The time of this "lag" is nothing but the time of historicism. The temporal relation Jameson posits between "capital" and the resistance it encounters in the Third-World inside the First - the sweatshops of Los Angeles - is no different from the temporal lag that, in historicist narratives, separates the Third World from areas where "late capitalism" is first supposed to come into its own. Late capitalism may spread to the Third World through processes such as "post-Fordism" and "flexible accumulation," and through globalisation of the media. Nevertheless, the expression refers primarily to events in countries in the West or in countries that are deemed to have caught up with or outpaced the West at its own game. See David Harvey, *The Condition of Postmodernity: An Enquiry into the Origins of Cultural Change* (Oxford: Basil Blackwell, 1990), chapters 8 and 9.

20—See the "Introduction" to David Lloyd and Lisa Lowe eds., *The Politics of Culture in the Shadow of Capital* (Durham: Duke University Press, 1997). Gyan Prakash urges similar reconsideration of historicism in his introduction to Gyan Prakash ed., *After Colonialism: Imperial Histories and Postcolonial Displacements* (Princeton, N. J.: Princeton University Press, 1995).

21—"Preface to the First Edition" in Karl Marx, *Capital: A Critique of Political Economy* vol. 1, trans. Ben Fowkes (Harmondsworth, UK & New York: Penguin Books, 1990), 91. A similar position is worked out in Marx's famous 1853 essay, "The Future Results of the British Rule in India" in K. Marx and F. Engels, *On Colonialism* (Moscow: Foreign Languages Publishing House, n.d), 83-90. Bob Jessop and Russell Wheatley eds., *Karl Marx's Social and Political Thought: Critical Assessments – Second Series* volume VI (London and New York: Routledge, 1999) is an excellent collection of recent essays (reprints) on the issue of Eurocentrism in Marx.

22—Phyllis Deane, *The First Industrial Revolution* (Cambridge: Cambridge University Press, 1979).

23—Both Naoki Sakai, in his *Translation and Subjectivity: On "Japan" and Cultural Nationalism*, (Minneapolis: University of Minnesota Press, 1997), and Samir Amin in *Eurocentrism* make this point.

24—Uday Singh Mehta, *Liberalism and Empire: A Study in Nineteenth-Century British Liberal Thought* (Chicago: The University of Chicago Press, 1999), 99-100 offers a relevant reading of John Stuart Mill's essay on "civilization." For an analysis of the role of the idea of "civilization" in the American academic organization of "area studies," see Andrew Sartori, "Robert Redfield's Comparative Civilizations Project and the Political Imagination of Postwar America" in *positions: east asia cultures critique* 6.1 (spring, 1998): 33-65.

25—"The West's self-fashioning as the self-made center of world history," writes Coronil, "should be seen as the mystifying effect of power relations." Fernando Coronil, *The Magical State: Nature, Money and Modernity in Venezuela* (Chicago: The University of Chicago Press, 1997), 387-88. Enrique Dussel, *The Invention of the Americas: Eclipse of "the Other" and the Myth of Modernity*, trans. Michael D. Barber (New York: Continuum, 1995) is a powerful attempt to question Eurocentrism.

26—Johannes Fabian, *Time and the Other: How Anthropology Makes Its Object* (New York: Columbia University Press, 1983), chapters 1 and 2. Of course, the target of Fabian's analysis is the language of anthropology rather than historicism as such. But the anthropology he criticises was often historicism in another guise. For a related and powerful reading of nineteenth-century anthropology that furthers this line of argumentation, see Patrick Wolfe, *Settler Colonialism and the Transformation of Anthropology: The Politics and Poetics of an Ethnographic Event* (London and New York: Cassell, 1999).

27—There are many existing studies of the European origins of the academic knowledge-form we call "history." One does not have to enter into interminable debates as to whether or not the Arabs or the Chinese or some other non-European peoples also had a sense of history. One can say "yes" to these questions and still speak of the European origins of the discipline in its contemporary academic form. See Peter Burke, *The Renaissance Sense of the Past* (London: Edward Arnold, 1969); J. G. A. Pocock, *The Ancient Constitution and the Feudal Law: A Study of English Historical Thought in the Seventeenth Century* (Cambridge: Cambridge University Press, 1990); and Reinhart Koselleck, *Futures Past: on the Semantics of Historical Time*, trans. Keith Tribe (Cambridge, Mass: Massachusetts Institute of Technology,

1985). Koselleck writes (200) : "Our contemporary concept of history, together with its numerous zones of meaning ... was first constituted towards the end of the eighteenth century. It is an outcome of the lengthy theoretical reflections of the Enlightenment. Formerly there had existed, for instance, the history that God had set in motion with humanity. But there was no history for which humanity might have been the subject or which could be thought of as its own subject."

Before 1780, Koselleck adds, "history" would have always meant the history of something particular. The idea of being, say, a "student of history"—that is, the idea of a history-in-general which is what this book engages at one level—is clearly a modern, post-Enlightenment exercise.

28—"On Liberty," chapter 1 (especially 15) and "Considerations on Representative Government," chapter 18 (409-423 in particular) in John Stuart Mill, *Three Essays* (Oxford and New York: Oxford University Press, 1975). See also the stimulating discussion on Mill in Mehta's *Liberalism and Empire*, chapter 3.

29—Mill, "Representative Government," 278. Mill produces a list of topics knowledge of which "could be required from all electors."

30—*Report of the Indian Franchise Committee* (Calcutta: Government of India, 1932), vol.1, 11-13.

31—Radhakrishnan's speech to the Constituent Assembly on 20 January 1947 reprinted in B. Shiva Rao et al. eds., *The Framing of India's Constitution: Select Documents* (Delhi: The Indian Institute of Public Administration, 1967), vol. 2, 15.

32—See Akhil Gupta, *Postcolonial Development* (Durham: Duke University Press, 1998), James Ferguson, *The Anti-Political Machine: "Development," Depoliticization, and Bureaucratic Power in Lesotho* (Minneapolis: University of Minnesota Press, 1994), and Arturo Escobar, *Encountering Development: The Making and Unmaking of the Third World* (Princeton, N.J.: Princeton University Press, 1995) document the historicism that underlies the language of development administration.

33—I use of the word "peasant" in two senses: to refer to the group of people whom we could call "peasants" in the language of sociology, but also as a figure that stands for a certain other of modernity. The connections between the urban middle classes in India and the rural world of the peasant are too complicated to detail here but they exist. My use of the word "peasant" is not unmindful of those connections.

34—Homi Bhabha, "DisseMiNation: Time, narrative and the margins of the modern nation," in H. Bhabha, *The Location of Culture* (London: Routledge, 1994), 139-170.

35—Ranajit Guha ed., *Subaltern Studies: Studies in Indian Society and History* (Delhi: Oxford University Press, 1983-1993), vols.1-6; Later volumes, 7-10, have been edited, respectively, by editorial teams consisting of Gyan Pandey and Partha Chatterjee, David Arnold and David Hardiman, Shahid Amin and Dipesh Chakrabarty, and by Susie Tharu, Gautam Bhadra and Gyan Prakash.

36—Ranajit Guha, *Elementary Aspects of Peasant Insurgency in Colonial India* (Delhi: Oxford University Press, 1983) "Whatever its validity for other countries," wrote Guha, "the notion of pre-political peasant insurgency helps little in understanding the experience of colonial India."

37—I ignore here the figure of the peasant in rational choice theory as few historians use rational choice theory in writing histories of human consciousness or of cultural practices. Rational choice has been a more dominant framework in economics and political science departments.

38—E. J. Hobsbawm, *Primitive Rebels: Studies in Archaic Forms of Social Movement in the 19th and 20th Centuries* (Manchester: Manchester University Press, 1978; first pub. 1959), 2-3.

39—Neil Smith, *Uneven Development: Nature, Capital and the Production of Space* (Oxford: Basil Blackwell, 1990). Smith's own understanding and application of the concept remains historicist. Marx's distinction between "formal" and "real" subsumption of labour, for example, is treated by Smith mainly as a question of historical transition. See p.140. James Chandler, *England in 1819* (Chicago: The University of Chicago Press, 1998), 131 dates the idea of uneven development back to the Scottish Enlightenment.

40—Ernst Bloch's powerful and imaginative discussion of Nazism in terms of the "synchronicity of the non-synchronous" assumes a "totality" within which the "now" belongs to the capitalist mode and the peasant remains an "earlier type," an example of the "genuinely non-synchronous remainder." Bloch's is a version of "uneven development." Ernst Bloch, "Nonsynchronism and the Obligation to Its Dialectics," *New German Critique*, trans. Mark Ritter 11 (spring, 1977): 22-38. Bloch, as Martin Jay points out, developed later his own critique of empty, secular historical time in the same way as Benjamin did, by seriously thinking through the so-called religious. See Martin Jay, *Marxism and Totality: The Adventures of a Concept from Lukacs to Habermas* (Berkeley: The University of California Press, 1984), 189-190.

41—James Chandler, *England in 1819*, 131.

42—For an explication of Guha's use of the category "consciousness," see my, "A Small History of Subaltern Studies" Sangeeta Ray and Henry Schwartz eds., *Companion to Postcolonial Studies* (Oxford: Blackwell, forthcoming).

43—See "Minority Histories, Subaltern Pasts" in my *Provincializing Europe* (forthcoming).

44—Ranajit Guha, *Elementary Aspects*, 6.

45—Ibid., 75.

46—Ibid., Chapters 1 and 2. Conservative historians ignored this phase of peasant rebellion as the "traditional reaching out for sticks and stones" and therefore devoid of politics. See, for example, Anil Seal, *The Emergence of Indian Nationalism: Competition and Collaboration in the Later 19th Century* (Cambridge: Cambridge University Press, 1968), Chapter 1. Marxists historians of India, on the other hand, typically emptied religion of all its specific content by assigning to its core a secular rationality. For Guha's critiques of these positions, see his essay "The Prose of Counter-Insurgency" in Ranajit Guha and Gayatri Chakravorty Spivak eds., *Selected Subaltern Studies* (New York: Oxford University Press, 1988).

47—Talal Asad's essays collected in his *Genealogies of Religion: Discipline and Reason of Power in Christianity and Islam* (Baltimore and London: The Johns Hopkins University Press, 1993) contain perceptive remarks on the many "secularised" forms in which Christianity presents itself in the public institutions and rituals of Western democracies. I must record here my gratitude to Saba Mahmood for helpful discussions on these questions.

48—For its many limitations, this was one of the arguments attempted in my book *Rethinking Working-Class History: Bengal 1890-1940* (Princeton, N.J.: Princeton University Press, 1989).

49—Ranajit Guha, "On Some Aspects of Indian Historiography" in *Selected Subaltern Studies*, 4.

50—Ibid., 5-6. Emphasis in original.

51—This is how Indian nationalist leaders such as Jawaharlal Nehru argued in the 1930s. See Jawaharlal Nehru, *India's Freedom* (London: Unwin, 1962), 66. Bipan Chandra reproduces a similar argument in his *Nationalism and Colonialism in Modern India* (Delhi: Orient Longman, 1979), 135.

52—Ranajit Guha "Colonialism in South Asia: A Dominance without Hegemony and Its Historiography" in his *Dominance Without Hegemony: History and Power in Colonial India* (Cambridge, Mass: Harvard University Press, 1997), 97-98.

53—I say the "the *question* of being human" because this question, as we know from Heidegger, could only ever be asked as a question and not posed as an answer. Any attempted answer based on the positive sciences would end up dissolving the category "human." Yet, as a question, the question of being human, *dasein*, always remains even if it is not answerable in a positivist manner. See the section entitled "How the Analytic of Dasein is to be Distinguished from Anthropology, Psychology and Biology" in Martin Heidegger, *Being and Time*, trans. John Macquarrie and Edward Robinson (Oxford: Basil Blackwell, 1985), 71-75.

54—Ramachandra Gandhi, *The Availability of Religious Ideas* (London: Macmillan Press, 1976), 9.

55—Leela Gandhi, *Postcolonial Theory: An Introduction* (Sydney: Allen and Unwin, 1998), x.

56—Walter Mignolo powerfully draws attention to the renaissance in his *The Darker Side of the Renaissance: Literacy, Territoriality, and Colonization* (Ann Arbor: The University of Michigan Press, 1995). Fernando Coronil's "Introduction" to Fernando Ortiz's, *Cuban Counterpoint: Tobacco and Sugar,* (Durham: Duke University Press, 1995) alerts us not only to the presence of renaissance Europe in Latin America but also to the ways the Spanish mediated the circulation of modern European philosophical traditions in Latin America ("Introduction," xix). Also see Fernando Coronil, *The Magical State: Nature, Money, and Modernity in Venezuela* (Chicago: The University of Chicago Press, 1997); Sara Castro-Klaren, "Historiography on the Ground: The Toledo Circle and Guaman Poma" (unpublished); Peter Hulme, *Colonial Encounters: Europe and the Native Caribbean 1492-1797* (London and New York: Routledge, 1986); Enrique Dussel, "Eurocentrism and Modernity," *Boundary 2* 20.3 (1993): 65-76.

57—Xudong Zhang's *Chinese Modernism in the Era of Reforms* (Durham: Duke University Press, 1997), chapter 2 contains a lively discussion of the disputed status of postcolonial studies among China scholars. See also his "Nationalism, Mass Culture, and Intellectual Strategies in Post-Tiananmen China," *Social Text* vol. 6, no. 2 (summer, 1998): 109-140. Rey Chow's writings, significantly, mark a somewhat different trajectory. See her *Women and Chinese Modernity: The Politics of Reading between East and West* (Minneapolis: University of Minnesota Press, 1991).

58—See, for example, Stefan Tanaka, *Japan's Orient: Rendering Pasts into History* (Berkeley: The University of California Press, 1993), Chapter 1; Vincente L. Rafael, *Contracting Colonialism: Translation and Christian Conversion in Tagalog Society Under Early Colonial Rule* (Durham: Duke University Press, 1993); Tessa Morris-Suzuki, *Reinventing Japan: Time, Space, Nation* (New York and London: M. E. Sharpe, 1998), Chapter 7; Ann Stoler, *Capitalism and Confrontation in Sumatra's Plantation Belt, 1870-1979* (Ann Arbor: The University of Michigan Press, 1995), see in particular Stoler's new "Preface"; idem., *Race and the Education of Desire: Foucault's History of Sexuality and the Colonial Order of Things* (Durham: Duke University Press, 1995); V.Y. Mudimbe, *The Idea of Africa* (Bloomington, Indianapolis, and London: Indiana University Press and James Currey, 1994). Naoki Sakai's work would clearly belong to this list, and I myself have attempted to raise the question of non-Eurocentric history in Japan's case in my brief "Afterword" to Stephen Vlastos ed., *Mirror of Modernity: Invented Traditions of Modern Japan* (Berkeley: The University of California Press, 1998), 285-296.

59—I have in mind Clifford Geertz's discussion of the basics of anthropological method in his *The Interpretation of Culture* (London: Fontana Press, 1993).

60—Here I echo what Meaghan Morris has said with great clarity and sensitivity in her "Foreword" to Naoki Sakai, *Translation and Subjectivity: On "Japan" and Cultural Nationalism* (Minneapolis: University of Minnesota Press, 1997), xiii: "… Sakai clearly shares with other theorists a conception of translation as a practice producing difference out of incommensurability (rather than equivalence out of difference)." See also Gayatri Chakravorty Spivak, "The Politics of Translation" in her *Outside in the Teaching Machine* (London and New York:

Routledge, 1993), 179-200; Vincente L. Rafael, *Contracting Colonialism*, chapter 1, "The Politics of Translation"; Talal Asad, "The Concept of Cultural Translation in British Anthropology," in his *Genealogies of Religion*, 171-199; Homi K. Bhabha, "How newness enters the world: Postmodern space, postcolonial times and the trials of cultural translation" in his *The Location of Culture*, 212-235.

61—See H. Aram Veeser, ed., *The New Historicism Reader* (New York and London: Routledge, 1994).

62—See Georg G. Iggers, *The German Conception of History: The National Tradition of Historical Thought from Herder to the Present* (Hanover, New Hampshire: University Press of New England, 1983).

63—Ian Hacking, "Two Kinds of `New Historicism' for Philosophers" in Ralph Cohen and Michael S. Roth eds., *History and ... Historians within the Human Sciences* (Charlottesville and London: University of Virginia Press, 1995), 298.

64—Maurice Mandelbaum, *History, Man and Reason* (Baltimore, 1971), 42 quoted in F.R. Ankersmit, "Historicism: An Attempt at Synthesis" in *History and Theory* (1995): 143-161.

65—I depend here on Ankersmit "Historicism"; Friederich Meinecke, *Historism: The Rise of a New Historical Outlook*, trans. J.E. Anderson (London: Routledge and Kegan Paul, 1972); Hayden White, *Metahistory: The Historical Imagination in Nineteenth-Century Europe* (Baltimore: The Johns Hopkins University Press, 1985) and "Droysen's *Historik*: Historical Writing as a Bourgeois Science" in his *The Content of the Form: Narrative Discourse and Historical Representation* (Baltimore: The Johns Hopkins University Press, 1990), 83-103; Leopold von Ranke, "Preface: *Histories of Romance and Germanic Peoples*" and "A Fragment from the 1830s" in Fritz Stern ed., *The Varieties of History: From Voltaire to the Present* (New York: Meridian Books, 1957), 55-60; Hans Meyerhoff ed., *The Philosophy of History in Our Own Time: An Anthology* (New York: Doubleday Anchor Books, 1959), see "Introduction," 1-24 and the section entitled "The Heritage of Historicism"; and Paul Hamilton, *Historicism* (London and New York: Routledge, 1996). James Chandler's discussion of historicism in *England in 1819* is enormously helpful. I choose not to discuss Karl Popper's formulations on "historicism" as his use of the term has been acknowledged to be rather idiosyncratic.

66—"History is the subject of a structure whose site is not homogeneous, empty time, but time filled by the presence of the now." Walter Benjamin, "Theses on the Philosophy of History" in his *Illuminations*, trans. Harry Zohn (New York: Fontana/Collins, 1982), 263. For a perceptive critique of Benjamin in terms of his failure to deal with the question of why constructing a chronology retains its significance for the historian, see Siegfried Kracauer, *History: The Last Things Before the Last*, (Princeton: Markus Wiener Publishers, 1995), chapter 6 in particular.

67—A revised and extended version of this essay will be reprinted as a chapter in my book, *Provincializing Europe* (forthcoming).

INTELLECTUAL APPROPRIATION NO PIRACY

Intellectual activities seek understanding the way pirates capture booty. It is all about pulling up alongside, finding and holding the rhythm of the other vessel, fixing the grappling hooks in order to board and to appropriate. This is not the way understanding is usually depicted, even if appropriation is its intended aim. Philosophers in particular characterise understanding more gently, as a kind of welcoming of distant truth, held out to the foreign past. However, gentleness is an illusion in hermeneutic thought, philosophical or ethnological, as I wish to show in reflecting on "dialogue" and "story" as two major intellectual grappling hooks.

I Illusion and reality of dialogue

Most intellectuals cherish the idea of conversation when they are asked how their ideas will work in real life. They want to engage in dialogue with their peers, with artists, with scientists, or with society as a whole. Such dialogues are meant to be peaceful relations, based on mutual recognition of the interlocutors. For intellectuals, such exchanges seem to symbolise the reality of thinking itself within the world they live in. They consider a dialogue to be the perfect way of communicating, reason itself in action. However, clearly this idea differs greatly from any given practice. Real dialogues are one-sided, or begin under incompatible assumptions; they are conducted badly, or

Ulrich Johannes SCHNEIDER

translated by Ulrich Johannes SCHNEIDER

exert pressure. The shiny image of respectful dialogue does not even seem applicable to exchanges among intellectuals themselves. We learn as much from our history books. All relations between intellectuals and artists, scientists, or other members of society, are marked by many, often insurmountable, differences, resulting from divisive interests and cultural discrepancies.

This is no news to most of us, and when philosophers today still put forward communication–via-dialogue they are no idealistic fools. The American philosopher Richard Rorty pleads for dialogue by saying that we ought to have a conversational attitude in articulating our ideas. We should be aware of the fact that our discourse is a language with a limited vocabulary which can only be fully applied and understood "at home," within the cultural area in which it originated. There is a humanistic touch in this position, but it also reveals a considerable amount of despair regarding ongoing discursive relations. Rorty implicitly admits that it is impossible to qualify the relations among intellectuals all over the world as ideal conversations, and even less so the relations of intellectuals to their respective societies. Rorty realizes that the idea of dialogue is tainted by experience, but still sees its significance as the object of a prudent recommendation to those who want to converse.

Others believe in the effect of counterfactual ideas. They discount experience altogether, enjoying admittedly non-working ideals, like the hope for a domination-free dialogue advocated by the German philosopher Jürgen Habermas. I believe it to be a common feature of intellectual exchanges that both sides have some idealistic misconceptions about their mutual relationship. It is, in fact, the very assumption that all parties are equal which makes dialogue so attractive to everybody. We like to wallow in the illusion that dialogue brings us together, that it produces some kind of "we" following the initially different "I" which starts it off. Here the illusion is first one of activity: that I am having a conversation with somebody else should mean that I am doing something, not having something done to me. It is this dream of initial and sustained reciprocity that never works in reality, neither for individuals nor for collective bodies. Exchanges do affect all participants, and they do it according to the situation in which they take place. No conversation ever starts among equals; there is always some asymmetry, between teacher and pupil, between dominant cultures and other ones, between an aggressive discourse and a defensive one, etc.

Yet, the illusion has more faces than just that of equality, since real dialogues are rarely a simple exchange of views and more often there is something else at stake. Let us take an example from the history of philosophy. When philosophers met in Paris in the year 1937 to converse about philosophy, especially the philosophy of René Descartes (in celebration of the four hundredth anniversary of his discourse on method), one might have expected discussions, for instance, of the

Ulrich Johannes Schneider

importance of method in Descartes. Such discussions did of course take place. Nevertheless, the occasion was the Ninth World Congress for Philosophy, the last to be held before World War II, and political differences were played into the academic meeting. There were, for instance, certain Polish philosophers present, among them Roman Ingarden and Alfred Tarski. They represented not only a strong philosophical school, but also a new national identity based on a regained national sovereignty barely twenty years old. There were only a few Russian participants, and none from the Soviet Union, probably because Marxists were not invited, but certainly also because Stalin was, at that same time, "purifying" the elite of his country. The significant number of exiled Russian philosophers living in Paris was also poorly represented. Their only voice was Nicolaj Berdiaev, who spoke in a session on the more or less general topic of reason. In addition, there were German philosophers present, some from Germany, some from their places of exile in Switzerland or France. One "official" German speaker openly demanded some sort of new philosophy to serve the "new" Germany. The exiled thinkers never mentioned politics. They almost all kept strictly to their professional concerns and dealt with their topics as if nothing were happening. Karl Loewith was alone in publicly condemning nationalism in philosophy.

It is difficult to know much about what really happened at this World Congress for philosophy in Paris in 1937. What is not in the documentation of the papers we have to guess: Nazi philosophers in uniform talking party politics to their Italian colleagues, and ignoring former German colleagues who had been pushed out of their universities and their country. Politics must have been an issue in the hallways in those days, with fascism in Italy, Nazism in Germany and the Spanish Civil War raging. The following episode provides a good illustration. Martin Heidegger, undoubtedly a well-known German philosopher of the time, was not coming to Paris, because he felt he had been invited too late. Interestingly enough, Heidegger had not been waiting for an invitation from the organisers—who had written to him repeatedly—but, rather, for the German government's invitation to represent Germany in Paris, as head of the official delegation. What do we learn from his attitude? In philosophy and elsewhere, intellectual activity is more than enacting an idea. Some term "external factors" those things that influence intellectual life, but this is probably too simple. Was it external to philosophy when Heidegger chose not to join the Paris meeting because he felt insulted? Was it external as well when a member of the German delegation asked for a new philosophy to suit the new social order in Germany? Moreover, was it merely internal to philosophy when exiled Germans omitted mention of the circumstances of their philosophizing?

When we think about rooting the idea of discussion in the real world, we must acknowledge that everything said has implicit meanings that can be easily deciphered within the situation itself, at the time of the utterance, but which in contrast have to be reconstructed on the basis of context and comparison later on. Let us go back to the two antagonistic German groups of philosophers in Paris in 1937. The fact that the exiled thinkers did not refer to the general political situation in Europe, nor even to their own shattered lives, has to do with the fact that they believed philosophy was a purely intellectual and even scientific enterprise. Otto Neurath and Rudolf Carnap were opposed to metaphysics, which they found in Husserl; to the philosophy of history which they found in Hegel; and to the philosophy of existence which they found in Heidegger, and their interest in keeping philosophy pure made them restrain themselves from making political statements. For their counterparts the opposite was true, because these thinkers defined philosophy in relation to social life and thus, for philosophical and other reasons, did not separate philosophy from politics.

So, then, what we see is that the opposing concepts of philosophy itself were as likely to provide an equally compelling reason for not engaging in dialogue as was the political divide. In effect, there was politics within philosophy. Even when there were no overt criticisms from one or the other, both sides believed very strongly in their own ideas and deeply mistrusted those of the others. Nonetheless, the scientifically oriented philosophers, who did not include politics in their professional discourse, all embraced the idea of unhindered conversation and favoured the unrestrained discussion of methods and findings, no matter where and when or with whom. For them, the congress was just another professional meeting which they attended without regard for their own plight. On the other side, those philosophers who believed in the social significance and practical relevance of their intellectual endeavours wanted to stress the conditions and requirements that needed to be fulfilled before dialogue could begin. Thus, they did not see much sense in a dialogue in which they were automatically cast as "the bad guys." For them, from the very beginning the Paris Congress was a meeting of political importance. Therefore, when these two groups of philosophers met and did *not* talk to each other in Paris in 1937, it was because of both political and intellectual oppositions. It was the importance that both sides attributed to the idea of philosophy that made them unable to converse with each other. The very idea of philosophy produced enemies, and it still does, even in relatively more peaceful times than pre-war Paris.

At this point, let me summarise my argument thus far. Starting with the somewhat naive assumption that the ideal dialogue seems to be a possibility only for angels, I found that real communication "here on earth" is marked by contradiction and dispute right up to the level of metaphysical last thoughts. This led to a second assumption that the distortion of dialogue was due to external factors, such as politics. External factors explain a good deal, but not everything. What the story of the 1937 World Congress for Philosophy should have hinted at, is the impossibility of assigning distorting factors merely to "external" circumstances. The act of philosophising itself produces differences, disputes and bitter opposition; and such is the case, I think, for all intellectual activities.

There is no solution to this problem. Rather, our reflection only leads to some point of no return. Dialogue can be realised, that much is true. However, every step in its direction increases its idealistic, nay illusionary, character as something yet to come, as well as enforcing the very conditions that prevent its ever being achieved. Naturally, there is always hope that we can say in some future time that we have had a dialogue in which we were involved as much as we engaged in it. Yet to intentionally start a dialogue is very much like casting the grappling hooks: it means dominating the situation of intellectual exchange by creating it. On the other hand, there would be no exchange at all without somebody creating a situation for it. So we are left with the ambiguity of dialogue, and this ambiguity is not between idea and practice, between activity and receptivity, nor between wishing for a dialogue and enduring a conversation; it is simply an ambiguity inherent in the concept of dialogue, a concept that inseparably binds the illusion of communication to the realities of its realisation.

Put more clearly: there is not just one illusion involved in dialogue (that of unhindered and unforceful communication), rather many more, and more concrete illusions built into dialogue once we take into account the different cultural backgrounds of its reality. To take once more the example of philosophers: Ever since their history has been written, it has been presented as an endless story of misunderstanding, misrepresentation, and intellectual distortion. (My account of the 1937 Congress may count as an example.) At the same time, the histories of philosophers display many dialogical features: they tell us that ideas were discussed, that they were taken up from one thinker by another whose philosophy "responded" in some way to the former, and so on. Intellectual quarrels can be recounted as conversations, so that bitter oppositions turn out to be only voicing different points of view, once these disputes are moulded into a story.

II Story and geography

Sticking to philosophy as a prime example of intellectual activity, we see its history providing plenty of stories of the "dialogical type," and it has done so for so long that it has become a kind of master narrative for intellectual life as a whole. The history of philosophy tells us, for instance, stories about philosophical schools, shared metaphysical orientations, scientific preferences, and the like. Moreover, it shows us that intellectual life is ever-changing, that is, any proposition *in philosophicis* is only stated to be left behind. When we introduce a story line into our idea of philosophical conversation, ideal or real, we can view the differences together with their solutions, the dispute together with its outcome. Once we look to see what it is all about in the long run, we find fierce opposition and stubborn contradiction resolved by change and transformation. Conversations among intellectuals, whenever they are told as stories, seem to process differences rather than allowing them to stay the same as they were. The story combines the diversity of positions, even open and relentless political conflict, with a long-term perspective on how such diversity and conflict comes to a crisis and how it was overcome. Storytelling shows discrepancies as moving forces of intellectual productivity. Wherever there is an idea, there is also a mind to change it just by taking it on. So the story stretches diversity out in time, makes dissent appear as productive rather than as an impediment to intellectual life. As we live intellectually by the stories we read and write their permanent consumption shapes our judgement profoundly.

Traditional historiography helps us to understand how one philosopher's ideas were considered, modified, or contradicted by another philosopher. It makes us understand the sequence of philosophical debate in outlining a consequential string of thought. Some sequences are, of course, better suited for close follow-up stories than others are. German idealism exemplifies almost ideally the hard work of one philosopher on the system of his predecessor. Kant claimed to have understood Leibniz better than Leibniz had understood himself, and Fichte said the same thing about Kant, as Schelling did about Fichte, and Hegel could not help but feel much the same about Schelling. We can find even earlier examples of this consecutive appropriation when looking at Descartes and his followers, or even earlier in the schools of Greek philosophers, although what we know about them is limited by the historical accounts. Stories of consequential linkage between philosophies are never quite untrue, even when we are able to establish counter-narratives, which highlight internal distances and often rather loose references by later thinkers to former ones.

However, the fact that we cherish continuity, stories with vectors and factors all working in the direction of *progress* may not be at all contingent upon their "reality." Cartesianism, German idealism, and more recent philosophical movements like philosophical phenomenology, analytic philosophy (as well as smaller orientations like those of the constructivists, the utilitarians, and so on) may be represented truly as successions of thoughts, but nothing really tells us that succession alone should be the model for historical understanding. There are a great many thinkers with no affiliation close enough to allow their being seen as participating in any movement, and there is, most of all, the undeniable fact that even successions of an intimate nature, as in so-called philosophical schools, have a beginning and an end. There is discontinuity not so much inside the stories but

Ulrich Johannes Schneider

around them. In the nineteenth century, the historian Leopold von Ranke laughed at Hegel's world spirit winding its way from Asia to the Mediterranean scene and from there to Northern Europe. However, nobody laughs in the twentieth century when philosophy is thought of as universally accessible and, at the same time, as inevitably bound to national linguistic and cultural conditions.

If, indeed, there is little problem in accepting Fichte as a German thinker and Victor Cousin as a French one, what, then, about others? Very early on we have a French Leibniz and a German one, an English Kant in addition to the German one, and a German Hume besides the English thinker. In the twentieth century, there is a German Heidegger who is close to Nazism, and a French Heidegger who is read as a radical phenomenologist and valued by leftists. In all these cases, we have an original thinker, only not with a single, but with two or more traditions built upon his work. It is not very hard to see—even if we do not want to see it this way—that some geographic jumping is necessary to enable the smooth telling of a story. Thus, by enjoying the story of philosophy from Kant to Hegel, we voluntarily forget about philosophers in England and France, Scotland, and Italy. Adjust to any major narrative are untold stories positioned "aside." To any intelligent observer, however, the history of philosophy is rich in simultaneities typically covered up by seemingly evident divisions along the lines of national cultures.

Opposition to the major narrative of Western intellectual history has its own small tradition. A somewhat extreme example of a story about Western philosophy based on place rather than time is provided by a book published in 1943 by Max Wundt. The son of Wilhelm Wundt, he had made his name as a historian of early modern philosophy and, apparently, believed not only in the links between place and philosophy, but also between race and philosophy. The title of his book *Die deutsche Philosophie nach Stamm und Rasse* (The tribal and racial roots of German philosophy) obviously points to the special (and by implication superior) character of German thought. Max Wundt limits his examples to the eighteenth and early nineteenth centuries and to German thinkers, thus his argument has a small scope. His main goal is to point out the different birth-places of eminent figures of the German Enlightenment and of the Romantic period. This valid study, yet has questionable purposes. In positive terms, it is not clear exactly what Wundt tries to show: is it that the region of one's upbringing determines one's thinking? The point seems to be rather more implicit here, since he does little to avoid the suggestion that place and even race may divide European intellectual life as a whole, since other peoples do indeed have other thoughts and not everybody can be of Nordic Germanic origin.

The main feature of historical stories is that they are organised chronologically, while at the same time also displaying a map, a place-order of intellectual production. The most general map of cultural areas such as Asia - Africa - The Mediterranean - North Europe - America is also the most commonly told story about Western predominance. Within Europe, smaller and more detailed maps offer regional differences, such as the Italian Renaissance and North European humanism, the Vienna and the Frankfurt Schools, French Postmodernists and American Pragmatists. Moreover, when different regions and places are further explored and understood separately, we get particular maps which guide us through them, but show little or no connection with other maps of equal resolution. The dilemma seems to be that place and time cannot be reconciled except by introducing hierarchy into storytelling. In addition, even the most general, all-embracing story of philosophy is faced with strong marks of area-specified, regional, and local particularities, a fact which has always called for some explanation. The nineteenth century brought forward the idea of national identity, the twentieth century the sterner concept of race, and after World War II the subtle concept of culture. The thought of inevitability, however, seems to be linked to all three forms of explanation: It is the inevitability of belonging to the nation, the race, or the culture from which you stem, and although these three notions differ greatly in meaning and plausibility, they are all intended either to highlight or to stigmatise. It all depends on who is issuing a particular judgement. If it is a "we" then its purpose is to highlight; if it is a "they" then it is to stigmatise.

Undoubtedly, the philosophical scenes are situated in places and can be described geographically, even if this is no simple task.

Still, in terms of intellectual history, we tend to think geography as a negative factor, complicating the ideally straightforward line of one basic story. More importantly, we tend to think in proprietary terms. We arrange thinkers in groups according to what is considered to be "their" thinking. There must also be something "there" which can be taken up or argued against. The history of philosophy becomes a grand register of intellectual property the moment we feel free to declare "that is a Marxist thought," "here I sense the influence of Wittgenstein," or "this is clearly nominalistic thinking." We think of philosophy as being "owned" by some original thinkers and then "preached" or "disseminated" by pupils. I do not want to say that discerning properties within the history of philosophy is a bad thing in itself. We need to know whose idea a certain concept it was, if anybody's, and that the order of things is structurally identical to the order of ideas, that being determines consciousness, that existence precedes essence and so on. And we have to handle the mass of information by occasionally attributing "isms." However, listening to these stories of philosophy also makes us believe that differences are in some way objective or non-controversial.

Therefore, here we come to realise the ambiguity of storytelling with regard to intellectual life. We understand intellectual history only through stories told about the succession of thought, because we interpret succession as progress, standstill or backlash, which means we judge it and thereby establish the history we live by, day in day out. We per-

Ulrich Johannes Schneider

ceive our own lives to be part of some future story to be told, and accordingly project this kind of understanding backwards and sidewards. Wherever we feel the need to understand something we try to organise it in to a simple story, grouping text and context, cause and effect, implicit and explicit meaning within the stretch of time we need in order to tell these complex relations to ourselves or to others. Yet the very success of storytelling, as visible in the European tradition of intellectual history, has led to hierarchy and to ranking of what counts as part of a major story and what can be regarded as marginal. The whole implicit geography within the history of philosophy is an explicit sign of the limits of story-like understanding.

Again, this problem has no solution. Many historians have tried to discover whether they tell their stories from the sources or for an audience. However, this seems to be no real alternative: sources are identified by interests, which are common to the cultures the audiences belong in. Not wishing to minimise the variety of stories told, there is no "story of all stories," no master narrative which sums it all up. We are left with charts and maps, regional insights, and local knowledge. As much as geography contradicts the claim of philosophers to work for a universal reason, the massive number of minor stories makes it impossible to establish just one major one. When an unhindered dialogue can be called an illusion (an illusion nevertheless necessary for everyone ready to converse) we can call the construction of cultural stories ideology (which is necessary for everyone willing to understand).

III Intellectual Appropriation

As I have tried to suggest in the first two parts of this paper, dialogue and story are ambiguous concepts. As clearly structured as the idea of a dialogue seems to be, it never matches the corresponding practice, which in reality entails the initial separateness of both sides involved, the enactment of substantial interchange, which thereby transforms profoundly whatever was given in the beginning. A dialogue links two sides—they may be persons or cultures—which cannot stay the same if dialogue is really happening. Therefore, the very idea of two independent sides is more a construction than a reality. A similar ambiguity haunts the concept and practice of story: It may appear a simple thing to tell a story, but its sequential structure exposes the very ruptures, loose ends and gaps which it was called to overcome in the first place. Story is meant to combine events consecutively, even as they fall apart geographically.

Hence, conceptual ambiguity has important consequences, most of all for those of us intellectuals who use dialogue and story in describing or even advocating interchange between individuals or cultures. There is a permanent danger of using these concepts in a naive way, in which they are made to mean simply an exchange of opinions (points of view in a dialogue) or just an interpretation (a story of something). Furthermore, a more informed use, conscious of the ambiguities at work, cannot help but fall into oppositions and dichotomies, while distinguishing between a true and free dialogue and other more complex and mixed forms of communication such as in politics, i.e., between a straightforward story and its dissolution into charts and maps of regional significance. There seems to be no clear-cut line between a successful story and the events it is excluding, just as there is no exact definition of the threshold where dialogue gets loaded with "secondary" purposes. No dialogue can be enacted untouched by politics (which is to say that a communication is always distorted by its situation), and no story can avoid being shaped by its margins.

Intellectual adventurers intoxicated by the high sea of floating meanings may be indifferent to these ambiguities. They may throw their grappling hooks toward whatever they want get hold of, and just rejoice in what comes next within their grasp. Intellectual pirates are by definition free to "converse" and free to tell a story about it. They do not recognise proprietary laws, as any settled culture must do. Their business is trade for trade's sake, a freedom no educated intellectual can live by successfully for a very long time. Dialogue and story are culturally framed concepts, and they work according to contexts that cannot immediately be overcome or suspended. Another way of putting this dilemma would be to say that intellectual understanding is no piracy, if and only if it is not appropriation for appropriation's sake. In a dialogue, each side (an individual or a culture) appropriates what is said by the other, and in a story, events and facts are appropriated in order to be made part of it. Appropriation has degrees, it is accomplished in steps, and it can be exercised by anyone. However, it is never a free trade.

Ambiguity of dialogue and story means that opinions are forever shifting in a dialogue and that references are reorganised in a story, but it also means that there are things "owned" which have to be bought, laid hands on, or taken over completely. This we can call proprietary thinking: it starts with the assumption that we own our opinions and that we in turn are owned by our culture. The whole business of "we" and "you" or "they," so important for any culturally advanced dialogue and so essential for any elaborate intellectual history, become a burden and a weight once proprieties are thought of as properties. If what "we" say, think, or do is something which defines us in such a way that no one else can say, think, or do the same, it is thought of as "our" property as opposed to the property (in opinion, philosophy, or culture) of others. The same is true for stories: Once a story is supposed to be a full and valid account of something, it is thought to be owned by the culture which adopts it, which implicitly means that no other culture can own it nor even have a similar story.

The illusion that there is such a thing as

Ulrich Johannes Schneider

dialogue we actually engage in and the ideology of stories we live by are relatively easy to deconstruct in comparison to the proprietary thinking inherent in any culture of dialogue and story. It is a fairly common assumption we make with regard to all kinds of intellectual "goods," namely that we can easily appropriate them, make them our own. This assumption works almost automatically when we think of "our" tradition, that is the kind of history we use to explain ourselves to ourselves, European history for Europeans, German history for Germans, the history of the cities we live in, of the religious cults we grew up with and so on. We also assume, just because we think knowledge in general to be expandable at will and property to be found everywhere, that we can appropriate all kinds of things. Appropriation means acceptance, recognition, which we ourselves bring to bear on foreign places, distant cultures, and unknown regions. It is to us that these are foreign, distant and unknown, but it is also to us that they are accessible and thus understandable.

I do not want to say that this assumption of universal comprehensibility is wrong, nor even that it is commonly exaggerated. It just works whenever we "read," because we can never acknowledge that we do not understand what we feel is "talking" to us. This assumption works so successfully, I believe, because there are different degrees of our understanding. Take historical thought: we understand recent history as immediately accessible to us, so that we do not even tend to call it historical knowledge, even if we know the bulk of it only through secondary sources. We see the history of twentieth-century intellectual production as a broader background to what we are trying to achieve in the present, and, in the large sense of the notion of tradition, the history of modern thought in general is identified for us with the kind of tradition we stem from.

Hence, the smooth running of the practice of appropriation is due to the fact that we are no pirates, or, put it differently: that dialogue, story, and their in-built techniques for appropriation are well-established practices. There is always a logic of appropriation already in place wherever we deal with intellectual life. Nonetheless, there is a feature common to both pirates and culturally established appropriators: they always disown somebody somewhere. The techniques of appropriation are also affected by some ambiguity, insofar as acquiring knowledge or understanding ideas always means making them familiar within a context that is different from their original place. So appropriation in intellectual life is always bringing "home" as well as destroying some other "home," it is making one's "own" what was once someone else's. There is of course only a suspicion thrown upon ourselves when we seem to drown in overwhelming understanding; it is exactly then that we realise we have gone too far and reached the point where our dialogue is not wanted and our stories are not believed. Moreover, it is then that we have to acknowledge the "piratical" character of our understanding, and then only because we experience the force of pirates brought to bear upon ourselves. What is taken away from us has no meaning except in our imagination and in our dreams, and it is from these places that we long to get it back. Nevertheless, the thought of loss and deprivation does not belong to any idea of piracy (or understanding) which I have put forward in this paper. It is something altogether different to consider the ambiguities of intellectual activities such as dialogue or storytelling and to face the idea of thinking beyond the intellectually "mine" and "thine." We should leave behind what is ours and live as pirates to qualify for this new way of thinking. But who wants to leave behind what is his or hers? There are too few real pirates around these days, as always.

Spheres of Debt and Feminist Ghosts in Area Studies of Women in China

> while. In the whiteness
> no distinction her body invariable no dissonance
> synonymous her body all the time de composes
> eclipses to be come yours
>
> —Theresa Hak Kyung Cha[1]

Tani E. Barlow

This essay is wrapped around a thesis and a question. The thesis holds that, in all their local, historical haunts, feminist studies are foundationally spectral, since their discourses arise as gendered logics in relation to geopolitical others. Writing histories of gendered subjects requires sensitivity to feminist ghosts and spheres of debt, lest the project devolve into repetitious, neo-colonial forms of imperial outreach. This is not an unfamiliar point. The question is, so what? My answer: It is valuable to discard the presumed relation of feminist theory and local case, and rewrite theory/case historically, disarming and displacing what are patently colonial Enlightenment logics. In this paper I look primarily at logics structuring the theoretical feminisms of Li Xiaojiang, a Chinese nationalist, and Dai Jinhua, a Chinese Marxist-feminist. I also introduce logics informing the work of Partha Chatterjee and Joan Scott that highlight the decentered quality of liberal,

Western, enlightened theory projects. Such proximation enables the insight that theoretical feminism emerges in the "transnational world," not at one "Western," place, but at many historically delineated sites; that the liberalizing power of global finance capital forms the contemporary world's horizon; that theory is a resource of transnational feminisms; that the nation is *not* in fact the singular template for histories of feminist theory.[2]

And East Asia. A simple academic limit, marked by a promise of future work.

Gayatri Chakravorty Spivak[3]

Actually there is lots of action at the site Spivak is denoting as a limit and a promise (how else to explain its liminal in/visibility?). The causes of the commotion are the crude ones of political economy in the transnationalized world. Reemergence of Eastern Asia gender politics on the screen of institutional feminists situated in the US is transpiring at a conjucture where a post-Cold War economic restructuring of US area studies meets a partially–Ford-funded, partially post-Mao women's movement underway in the PRC, in a media domain opened up through the offices of the United Nations.[4] This nexus includes expatriate scholar networks of PRC feminists (also Ford Foundation grantees) who translate US feminism and gender theory into Chinese; Hong Kong-, Singapore-, Japan-, and Taiwan-based research projects; interregional meetings like the Chinese University of Hong Kong's "International Conference on Gender and Development"; semi official PRC institutionalization of "women's theoretic studies"; PRC-government-sponsored liaison with transnational corporate interests; and many, many other initiatives that I do not know about.[5]

Obviously such events *should* be more visible in transnational or cosmopolitan feminist theories.[6] However, for the moment, I will simply assume that there will eventually exist a history of these peripheralizing feminisms now as yet unwritten, because I want to pursue instead the question of what happens when feminism is thought through other circuits. Though my work emerges out of an encounter with feminist problematics in relation to Chinese writers, I am not claiming exclusive specificity for the Chinese theorists considered here, i.e., I do not think there is something essentially Asiatic about these feminist logics. Rather, there is political value in rethinking feminism through another (East Asia) circuit.[7] Of course, many have called attention to the instability of the term Asia and the ludicrousness of assembling all our projects under one umbrella term, Asian Studies. Yet between the gesture of dismissal and the defensive gesture of counter-dismissal lie other stratagems. So I proceed at once in two directions.[8] On the one hand, toward the question of what specters are haunting the logic of "Western feminism" *and* Asian studies.⁹ And on the other hand, what logics are available *in* feminisms, and offer a haunting reminder of what remains to be done again about the extraordinary coincidence of persistent, gendered inequality globally. This disruptive logic, one that is persistently interested in emancipatory critique of social reality embedded in foundational discourses, must rest on problematics of various kinds: the assumption that there even *is* a relation of "Asia" to "Western feminism" as such; a suspicion that "Western feminism" may be such a vacuous notion that the differences constituting it will overwhelm any hope of ever using it as a proper noun; that "Western feminism" in the PRC marks a complex of movements that are now so thoroughly localized as to be simply unremarkable; that this foundational instability holds for "Asia" as well as for "Western feminism," and so on.[10] In the meantime my objective stays afloat: in all the commotion of arguments and counter arguments, the habitual impulse to distinguish "not Western" and "Western" feminism is persistently deferred.

Li Xiaojiang and the Logic of the Universal and Particular

> You read you mouth the transformed object across
> from you in its new state, other than what it had been.
>
> Theresa Hak Kyung Cha, *Dictee*, 131

> one always rebuilds the monument in
> his own way. But it is already something gained to have
> used only the original stones.
>
> Walter Lew, *Excerpts From Dikte: For Dictee (1982)*, 12[11]

In the 1980s a generation of new scholarship on feminist issues surfaced in the PRC. Activist-scholar Li Xiaojiang exemplifies the early group, which found inspiration in Simone de Beauvoir's *Second Sex* and Betty Friedan's *Feminine Mystique*. Particularly, Simone de Beauvoir. But which Simone de Beauvoir? The one H. M. Parshley translated to English? The same Parshley, whose view was that *The Second Sex* was "on woman, not on philosophy," and who thus produced a "text that was to become a mainstay of early women's studies in the United States and Canada," but which, according to Mary Dietz, "was in many significant respects not the text Simone de Beauvoir wrote."[12] The answer is that it does not matter which *Second Sex*. The power of Beauvoir for the influential Li seems to have lain in a logic of the particular and universal that fueled Li's critique of the Chinese revolutionary and women's movements. Li set out her initial position in *Sex Gap* (*Xing gou*), though one can see a preoccupation with the dynamics of universal and particular throughout her oeuvre.[13]

Sex Gap begins with a consideration of the logic of sexual relations in an agonistic relation to logics of sexual emancipation. While it may be the case, Li argued, that under the conditions of the social emancipation of the sexes a logic of "substantially the same" prevails, this logic of similitude rests on a subordinated recognition that in fact the sexes are simply not the same. Indeed, the allegedly universal principle (*gongli*) of equality is in actual fact foundationally unstable, since it is contradicted by the very sexual gap which makes the whole notion of universality seem a hoax.[14] Universality actually lies in another quarter altogether. If it is anything it is the universal ground formed out of a historically necessary degradation of Women into masculinized extensions of Man. Rooted in Nature, universal degradation is nonetheless expressed historically, which is to say that the human sexes evolved on independent tracks.[15]

Sex Gap sought a way to mobilize feminine difference against what Li and many Chinese theorists in the mid-1980s felt was the Communist Party's instrumental use of a practical logic of similitude to reinforce Chinese women's degraded, masculinized status. And yet Li did not distinguish ontology from the existential logic that one is not born, but rather becomes, Woman. Rather, she concerned herself with establishing foundational status for biological difference and the creative potential she felt lay in natural, sexed embodiment (50-7). It is, Li argued, "in her existence as a biological entity that woman is a concrete incarnation of each link in the teeming mass of Humanity; which is to say, Woman's natural destiny is to guarantee the biological continuation of Humanity through time" (10). If anything, this is the universality of human existence. Yet, until a female subject (*renge*) emerges that is sexual and social, practical, and theoretical, Humanity as an undifferentiated whole will have to remain *un*selfconscious, the dissynchronous evolutionary paths of male and female will continue to diverge, and genuine female emancipation will remain out of reach. Objectively, not only will social development and human evolution retain the impress of the sexual gap, also, until that emancipatory event, "women [will remain] without doubt, men."[16]

Li Xiaojiang's project, therefore, is to link her discovery of the universal foundation of difference (the sex gap in Nature and History) to a historical teleology, familiar in Mao, Bebel, Marx, and Engels. This requires her to shift her analytic interests from social division of labor to what she argues is the natural division of *r*eproductive labor. Much of *Sex Gap* is devoted to tracing evolutionary Historical stages from matriarchy to patriarchy, the middle eras to modernity, and on into the premature or pseudo-emancipation of women into productive labor and so on. At each step, Li goes to pains to point out that because masculinity-Humanity-History coincide and because it is the duty of the unpredicated female body (*feiwo* or *feirenge*) to provide a material base for mindless human reproduction, there is no historical uprising of women. History for women lies in their infinite particularization within the regimes of social gender (*shehui xingbie*) where the immobilizing and particularizing reproductive functions—wife, mother, marriageable daughter, and so on—substitute for any female autonomous subjectivity. Objectified and enthralled in this patriarchal web, women not only contribute nothing to History; they have not benefited even now from the efforts made by states on their behalf for a host of reasons, beginning with the fact that woman as a subject does not exist for herself in theory in any sense.

Yet, Women—even in a state of pre-predication—is an irreducible albeit ahistorical entity. And it is this particularity that preoccupies Li Xiaojiang. Analytically and theoretically (she wrote at a time when the Cultural Fever of the mid-1980s had yet to completely burn itself out), the particularity of the feminine is momentous. Women cannot be enfolded into either mere class abstraction, nor be reduced to a simple category of social economy. The task facing Chinese women and theorists is, therefore, to articulate a feminine subjectivity that is appropriately gendered, i.e., is truly feminine rather than being an ersatz version of a masculinized woman. Men will be men and women will be finally and truly women only when the special, sexual, particular difference of women is acknowledged as universal, foundational fact (40-43). The law of heterosexual dualism prescribes no other nature for the (two) genders than the one grounded in sexual reproduction.[17]

In outline, *Sex Gap* precisely parallels Simone de Beauvoir's *Second Sex*, and another historian might be forgiven for suggesting that *Sex Gap* is a derivative copy. In *Sex Gap* Li contemplates briefly but bluntly the priorities of the sexed body, particularly its grotesque physiology, and provides an extraordinarily negative characterization of feminine deficiencies within the established, masculine order. Like Beauvoir, Li too dwells at length on the relation of interiorization that Man establishes with his projected other, Woman. Indeed, Li claims the same scholarly and political tradition and vocabulary (Engels, Bebel, Victorian ethnography and stage debates) as Beauvoir; posing an agonistic dilemma of feminist pseudo-emancipation and presuming that history is a global flow of economistic transformation that somehow ranges through time and space around a barely differentiated, globalized, "universal history." And yet these are not the same book. For whatever reason (perhaps because of the deficiencies of the English translation, perhaps because the Chinese translators did attend to these matters), Li Xiaojiang substitutes "active" and "passive" for the terms immanent and transcendent (16-17). She also skips any consideration of questions of difference in social, national, or cultural codes, choosing instead to fold social difference into her grand corporeal anatomical divide. Into the sexual gap she collapses all other considerations of differentiation, writing only that "there are only two social sexes (*xingbie*) in Humanity," but that "in different societies at different times gendered behavior has been remarkably different in [those] two genders (*liangxing xingbie*)" (24).

Mostly, Li Xiaojiang's undertaking re-encodes a logic of the universal and particular through the immediate conditions of post-revolutionary gender crisis that Li describes in greatest detail in a chapter called "The Great Rupture of Yin and Yang." There she notes, that globally, at least in all nations that really count, the 1960s were a time of conflict between the sexes (registered in rising rates of divorce and sexual promiscuity, problems stemming from the same cause) which Li attributes to failures in gendering the human personality (*renge*). Until *renge* is split, gendered or shared, the particularized and othered female subject will remain derivative and indexed to male re/productive drives. Failure is likely. The evidence, Li asserts, is all around: and she cites a passage from Zhang Jie's "The Ark":

> Probably they [the women] would all remain single until they died. Why was this? There seemed to be a yawning abyss where there should have been reciprocal understanding between themselves and men, an abyss similar in nature to the "generation gap" plaguing older and younger people. Could it be that a gender gap troubling the relation of women and men? Could it be a "sex gap" (*xing gou*)? In this stage of historical development it might well be that women were simply more evolved than men were, or perhaps the reverse was true. Or was it that men were so much more evolved than women that they had forfeited the possibility of engaging in any dialogue from the same starting point?

Zhang Jie's story denotes an unbridgeable sexual antagonism. Surely Li was suggesting, in her articulation of fiction into theory, that theory and not fiction was the appropriate idiom of the present moment.

This raises two further points. First, Li Xiaojiang forges an intimate bond between literature and theory when she cites as key evidence a classic in contemporary Chinese women's fiction. Second, the rhetoric and riddles of predication or subjectivity that Li extracts out of *The Second Sex* long predate *Sex Gap*, since the problem of female *renge* or personality arose at the heart of enlightened thinking about social emancipation in the early May Fourth era. Consequently, as per Chatterjee, Li's is not a derivative discourse. The sphere of debt is very broad; the spectral presence of the Algerian Other haunting the perimeter of the *Second Sex* finds its logical analogue in the ghost of passive Beauvoirean femininity in *Sex Gap*. Moreover, it is worth saying that nowhere in these complex lines of enchainment does an atavistic West surface as the measure of Chinese difference. An angry (and Joan Scott would probably say, a paradoxical) book written in the angry years of the late 1980s suggests Zhang Jie's feminist story "The Ark" as its exemplar and thus rests its case on the bloody text of *Chinese* social history.

Am I suggesting, then, that Li Xiaojiang is applying Western theory to a Chinese case, and am I enjoining social scientists to follow her lead? Li's rigid preoccupation with the play of universal and particular does lend a predictable familiarity to the book. The universal is imposed through a web of historicist categories—civilization, Man, historical progress, individuation, and liberty. The particular coincides with the Other and the remaindered, female, barbaric, static, de-individuated, material, and passive. Like de Beauvoir, Li Xiaojiang makes this logic of male primacy and female secondariness foundational historically, theoretically, psychoanalytically; and reading de Beauvoir through Li certainly has the effect of refracting deficiencies in the former.[18] But the point I wish to draw has to do with the question of what is "Western feminism" and thus what the relation of *Sex Gap* is to this purported entity. And who is more "Western" than Simone de Beauvoir? Her repudiation of bourgeois feminist claims is well known, and yet *Second Sex* is a major text in the history of enlightened feminist theory. Analogously, Li Xiaojiang is a major contributor, even perhaps a founder, of the renewed Chinese women's movement and a prolific contributor to its theoretical world. As Li Xiaojiang initiated her project of a resurgence of theoretical writing about the oppression of women, she reinvented by translating the matrix that she identified in Simone de Beauvoir. This is not the same as applying theory to a case. There is no sense of any need in Li's writing to particularize the case of Chinese women. Quite the contrary, the matrix that Li Xiaojiang shares with de Beauvoir is the same as—yet distinct from—*Second Sex*. Locked together through the force of translation, *Second Sex* and *Sex Gap* nonetheless form a *mise en abyme*, a discontinuous linkage that can never be grounded in similitude.[19]

The Formation of the "West" in Chinese Theoretic Feminism

> The new Chinese womenism is taking shape by reading its differences from Western feminism.
>
> Lin Chun, 18[20]

Before moving on, I want to make several further peripheral points. First, Li Xiaojiang's interlocutors do not share her preoccupation with logics of particular and universal. Although Li, like Nawal El Sadawi, is alleged by some critics to be a maternalist or "monster" feminist, Li is still just one of a big cohort.[21] The events that brought Li Xiaojiang to "international" visibility are quite complex and include local PRC Communist Party agitation; early access to the pre-Maoist, Chinese feminist archive in translation; the outflow of female scholars to universities in Japan, Europe, and the US and other points in the First World; Li's travels outside the PRC; the endorsement of Ford Foundation; early collaboration with international feminists; and many other factors. Moreover, the work of the post-Mao women's movement in China has been more than philosophical. That much is widely documented and can be illustrated with reference to writing that elite scholars call "*funü lilun yanjiu*" or women's "theoretic studies," which might also be translated as women theory or policy studies on women. Those who publish under that rubric hold that the post-1981 economic reforms initiated a wave of theoretic studies of women and that this initiative is symptomatic of staggering social transformation. An elite compendium of theoretic writing published in 1991, *Zhongguo funü lilun yanjiu shinian*, argues that "it was the times that hailed people into responding to the women's movement with historical and theoretical answers." Additionally, it argues, "as women's theoretic writing is a response to the reality of the women's movement, it also can critically reflect on history, traditional culture, the entire history of civilization."[22] In other words, a nascent scholarly community should accelerate theoretical research in response to given conditions and use this call as a raised platform for critical reflection on current affairs, as a scholarly means of predicating female subjects in research and practical politics and a way of stabilizing professional niches for scholars like themselves.

Second, one senses particularly in *Zhongguo funü lilun yanjiu shinian* that the call for a theoretic study of women coincided exactly with the movement in the elite academy to reconstitute traditional social science disciplines. Reports from feminist and womenist scholars Tan Shen (sociology), Yu Yan (anthropology), and Tan Lin (demographics) echo thematics raised in humanist scholarship by Li Meige (aesthetics), Luo Qunying (ethical philosophy), and Li Huiying (literature). These long, often bibliographically rich discussions disclose theoretic scholarship staking out protocols for gendered research at a moment of wholesale restructuring and recuperation of pre-1966 academic disciplines. Yu Yan's critique of Li Xiaojiang's women's studies model, "Anthropology of Women: Construction and Prospects" (*Nüxing renleixue: jiangou yu zhanwang*) for instance, makes the point that the academic discipline of anthropology, long quiescent in the PRC, already possesses the necessary intellectual resources for gendered scholarship; this not only vitiates the need for an institutional form of Women Studies, it suggests that gendered disciplines are actually intellectually superior to Women Studies. Li Meige's "A Brief Introduction to the Study of Female Psychology" (*Nüxing xinglixue yanjiu jianjie*) does something similar in her theoretic discussion of the discipline of "women's psychology" as a globalized form of truth, at the same time as she traces its reentry into the PRC in 1981, its major canonical texts and its most significant subdisciplines, e.g., the study of gender difference, family psychology, psycho-physiology, and comparative psychology. Humanist Li Huiying's "Commentary on Research in Women's Literature" (*Nüxing wenxue yanjiu shuping*) is less delicate about the source of theoretical insight. Li Huiying states clearly that feminist theory infuses studies of female literature globally and, increasingly, China, too. She expresses uneasiness. How can feminist critique from the West be "applied" in China, since Chinese women secured their basic political rights (the sine qua non of Western feminism) long ago? Li cites as evidence the two canonical texts most commonly found in this cohort's bibliography, Simone de Beauvoir and Betty Friedan.[23]

In other words, as they participate in reestablishing disciplinary standards and divisions, these scholars (who are also Li Xiaojiang's interlocutors) resituated gender difference as an *open* question in a globalized form of social-science scholarship. This in itself is a remarkably powerful move. First, it erodes Li's pessimistic, fundamentalist, heterosexual matrix. Second, it writes "Women" into the project of restructuring the social sciences. Of course, these theorists also do not question a basic assumption upholding social-science scholarship, which is that "theoretic work" is an analogue of scientific theory. They assume "Women" in the social science disciplines is a source of obscured truth; the project of including "Women" in the representational order is remedial and practical for them, since once the truth of women is revealed scientifically, efforts at social remediation can be undertaken. (This assumption is why I would prefer to translate "*funü lilun*" *in*correctly as "policy on women.") Second, the gendering of the social sciences and traditional disciplines may, as Tan Shen has argued, have had precious little practical effect on boosting the real numbers of female sociologists working in the discipline or the number of sociologists working on sociology of gender, but what it does do is to render conventional disciplines foundationally uncertain. The strategy adopted by female scholars such as Chen Ping and Tan Shen is to demonstrate that one cannot proceed in demographic work or sociological research without a clear grasp of the split subject of disciplinary knowledge.[24]

These scholars pose a question of feminist *enchaînement*. They suggest to me a nicely disruptive logic that links together "women's theoretic studies" and a resurgent, normalizing, and triumphalist masculinist academic, social science disciplinarity.[25] But they do not solve—either in theory or political agitation—the question of how to join China and the West in scholarship that takes as its predicate the subject of "Chinese women." Indeed, the intellectual history of the rise into global circuits of a body of writing stipulated as "Chinese feminism" is foundationally split over the perceived perimeter that is said to separate China and the West. In other words, present in the debates among feminist social scientists in China and many scholars in U.S.-dominated "Asian Studies" is the presumption of a constitutional relationship between universal scholarly theory and particular social science case: this same case is made in the relation of Weberian universalism and Chinese instance, Euro-Marxism and Chinese revolution, feminism and Chinese women.[26] As a reminder of how thoroughly these presuppositions inhabit our minds, it is useful to briefly inquire at this point: Why is a Li Xiaojiang, broadly dismissed in the U.S.A. side of the Pacific as "an essentialist," admitted into the Western feminist-theory pantheon as a worthy primitive, an instance of minoritarian, grass-roots or local feminism, and never, for better or worse, a legitimate contender for the Enlightenment mantle? Why do the internationalized conventions of the logical relation of particular and universal in Asian Studies (and in the existing practices of international feminism as noted above) make Dai Jinhua *un*acceptable as a feminist theorist to area studies scholars in the US, and mark a Joan Scott as *not un*acceptable? Why, conventionally, is Gayatri Spivak not perceptible as a feminist critic with anything to say to the Association of Asian Studies—or not in the way that Allison Jagger and Ann Ferguson are routinely held to be?[27]

Actually, it is not possible to cast Li Xiaojiang or Dai Jinhua (or for that matter Tan Shen, Chen Ping, Li Meige, et al.) as exclusively "native" or "local" theorists. Each woman, the nationalist, Mao-style feminist and the post-Mao, post-Lacanian critic, has sidestepped standardized, Ford Foundation-style "international feminism" with its area studies scholarly format, to draw instead on a century-old heritage of international Marxist-feminist thinking. Problematics of universal and particular, presence and lack, normalized now in transnationalized theoretical feminism are acceptable, even valuable, as analytic logics of feminist projects in Asian Studies and beyond. This is not so much because they encourage native women to represent themselves—though of course they sometimes also have that effect—or because they bind Western feminism and Asian studies in some new and improved way. Rather the logics in play in transnationalized theoretical feminisms are valuable because they are syncretic and unmistakably spectral. They are postcolonial in the broad sense of being constitutionally heterogeneous. They are also valuable because in the transnational boom-bust cycle of Asian development and global late capital, feminist logics offer elaborate, flexible, and variable methods of grasping how gendered political subjects articulate with global capitalism in crisis.[28] This holds true across the board, of course. Whether the ghosts of Western feminism inhabit the transnationalizing feminist theoretical scholarship rethought by the likes of Dai Jinhua in the PRC, or whether, as Joan Scott notes, these ghosts also inhabit that shiftless ideological formation, the "West" itself, feminism cannot be reduced simply to a homogeneous ideological effect of national politics. Empirically as well as theoretically (as though these were divisible), it is impossible to reduce feminism as such. What does this have to do with the geopolitics of theory and the specters of the West in Asian studies? Two things. First, the spectral qualities of Chinese women's studies (and even Lin Chun's "womenism") are saturated with so-called Western feminism. Second, there is little recognition in U.S.-dominated area studies of the complex theoretic positioning of Chinese feminist scholarship, a site where predication of "women" is particularly rich. Where collaboration unfolds it is through either projects that translate "Western feminism" into Chinese, or projects that excavate for nonChinese scholars archives of primary-source documents. I am not arguing either for considering Chinese theory as particularity or as an alternative universal; rather, like all scholarship, Chinese academic and social science writing is already mediated through theoretical work, and theory is the dwelling place of ghosts.

Partha Chatterjee, Derivation, and the Will of the Imagination

> Still, the appearance of survivals is by no means just a trick of the eye. Many bricks of the old structure are still around—but not the structure. Fragments may still survive because they meet a modern taste, not because (more than the fragments forgotten) they must be conveying the essence of an invincible tradition. . . . the language of the culture, cannot be explained as created by the fragment.
>
> Joseph R. Levenson, Volume 3, p. 113

A distinction should be drawn between the romance of the universal and particular, around which Joseph Levenson—like Li Xiaojiang—wove his claustrophobic web, and the related logic of Partha Chatterjee's discourse of derivation. Interest in Levenson is on the rise again. And perhaps it is possible to see a coalescence here between the liberal rhetoric of an orthodox Jewish Levenson and the cultural nationalism of a post-Mao Li Xiaojiang. What else do we do with classic statements of liberal political ideology like this one:

[T]he way back is the way out .... [I]n a genuinely Confucian China, a China that *was* the world, to cite the Classics was the very method of universal speech. The Confucian Classics were the repositories of value in the abstract, absolute for everyone, not just Chinese values relevant to China alone. When the Classics make China particular instead of universal, it is a China *in* the world—still China, but really new, even as it invokes (indeed, precisely as it invokes) what connects it to the old.[29]

In Levenson's famous logical vise, a complex negotiation was held to characterize Chinese modernity. This event, modernity, involved a libidinal-emotional rerouting as disenchanted Chinese intellectuals resituated themselves in a historically reduced nation, in relation to a totalizing West. Disenchantment (according to Levenson) led to a virtual nervous breakdown. A surfeit of desire: intellectuals sought at the same time to "own the ground they stood on" while they also needed to "attract" alternatives to particularity now that "Confucianism repelled" (I:xii). Commentators recently have drawn attention back to Levenson in order to rethink what is an essentially liberal view that history is a multiplicity in which differences resides, and difference is a matter of the metaleptic extension of linguistically distinctive terms, i.e., the cultural essence of each nation in a system (same) of nation states (difference).[30]

I draw attention to this legacy, probably only of interest to historians of modern China, in order to suggest a relation of difference-in-similarity linking Li Xiaojiang and Joseph Levenson. But also so that I can distinguish the logic of derivation in Partha Chatterjee. For Chatterjee (particularly in his most recent book, *The Nation and Its Fragments: Colonial and Postcolonial Histories*) the historical project of the discourses of nationalism is *an appropriation of universals on condition of nonidentity*, e.g., our (nascent) nation is not like Britain.[31] Unlike Levenson, whose sense of historical agency is limited to Chinese acquiescence or repudiation of the inexorable unfolding of liberalism and attention to the consequent impaction of (semi)colonial desire, Chatterjee predicates a subject or *agent of nationalism* who thinks about the postcolonial nation within what Chatterjee calls a framework of the marriage of Reason and Capital. It is not simply that the nationalist in Chatterjee discriminates a singularity in relation to universalizing colonial power. Rather, Chatterjee's nationalist subject instantiates something that is neither a particular of the universal nor the opposite of a universal, a mere particularity. Because the process barely alluded to in Levenson is stipulated as capitalism in Chatterjee, nationalism according to *The Nation and Its Fragments* is an economic and social as much as a cultural project. But the book's primary, underlying object is to develop a retooled notion of particularity through the metaphor of the logic of the fragment. Distinguishing nation/particularity from *inter*national/ universal, Chatterjee argues that far from being a mere metaleptic projection, "the domain of the 'national' was defined as one that was different from the 'Western'": nation*alism* made the nation a particularity, in other words. Difference is a thought or imagined *relation*. Thus what Levenson saw as a replacement of one universality with another, Chatterjee understands quite differently. In the political domain, Chatterjee claims, "the hegemonic movement of nationalism was not to promote but rather, in a quite fundamental sense, to resist the sway of the modern institutions of disciplinary power" (75). Which is to say that nationalism turns colonial difference into cultural difference; the newly formed cultural subject, based on its particularity, launches itself against the putative universal of the colonizer and the modernist. What has been "forcibly suppressed" in the process of the colonial discourse, may in the future be mobilized as alternative. Difference is strategy.

Why call this a logic of derivation? What about that movement Chatterjee calls "the possibilities of opposition as well as encapsulation" (234)? Chatterjee's argument in the chapters dealing with the "fragmentary" in the anti-colonial nationalist discourse, precisely those "forcibly suppressed" elements he hopes may be mobilized sometime in the future, focuses on what he calls the paradox of the women's question. His point being simply that in the name of nationalism "women" was posited "not on an identity but on a difference with the perceived forms of cultural modernity in the West," which enabled women and men to situate "the women's question" in what Chatterjee calls "an inner domain of sovereignty, far removed from the arena of political contest with the colonial state ... constituted in the light of the discovery of 'tradition'" (117). Nationalists took up the vexed question of women, but in a way that defeated the notion of simple derivation. And it turned out that difference under domination, not simple derivation from the norms of the colonizer, proved a flexible logic of differentiation: "a marked *difference* in the degree and manner of Westernization of women, as distinct from men, in the modern world of the nation" (126). I will not follow out the intricacies of Chatterjee's argument concerning the realm of autonomy for political women during the anti-colonial struggle, except to say that his suggestion that the home "was not a complementary but rather the original site on which the hegemonic project of nationalism was launched" (147) is an excellent sociological means of demonstrating the shortcomings of simple notions of derivation.

How does this work in relation to feminism and area studies? Whether or not one accepts his sentimental thesis that possibilities of community are lodged in repressed form in the narratives of capital, Chatterjee's belated answer to his own question—Are nationalism, and by extension feminism, derivative discourses?—is still instructive. For his premise is that no foundational discourse is immune to political deconstruction and thus no strict derivation à la Levenson can ever be demonstrated empirically. In Chatterjee's own words, his strategy is to give logical relations an "unmanageable complexity" (169) and to ground historical consciousness "in the immanent forms of social development" that must relegate "the universal categories of social formations into a temporary state of suspension, or rather a state of unresolved tension" so that the "relation between history and the theoretical disciplines" is "constantly disturbed and refashioned." In doing this, he argues, the relation of something called "West" to specificity is impossible to discern, since the entire question eventually extrudes out of the disciplinary boundaries (since no one discipline can contain it) and out of the liberal framework, because no one, single trajectory in history can bind to itself all fragmentary or archival specificity, even the trajectory of globalizing capital.

Most significant for my purposes here, however, is Chatterjee's focus on the suppressions and absences in modern European social theory. And that is why I have included Chatterjee's logics of derivation in this discussion. Exemplary of the value of the Subaltern Studies initiative as a whole, Chatterjee represents a means of reworking the assumption prevalent in even very good area studies (the critique that Chatterjee levels at Benedict Anderson is widely applicable), whereby scholars presume that Culture or Capital work magically and without the willed expression of intent that Chatterjee calls "agency." The logics of derivation suggest ways of reworking problems long embedded in area studies. Area studies often ratify the presumption that the so-called "areas" consist of far-flung units in a universal, progressive history of modernity or globalizing capital in which European models are adapting to Asian ends. The weakness of this diffusion model has long been understood. I draw us back to the problem only as a reminder that not only are representations social facts (i.e., signifier and signified are inextricable), but also that *theories* are themselves empirical, social facts. Chatterjee's concern with suppression within the domain of theoretical "facts" calls attention to what is made to disappear. That is, liberal historiography yields, in Chatterjee's critique, a simplistic local problem of original and copy. And what is unspeakable in liberal theory is well known: (1) the possible existence of anticolonial national agents, (2) the existence of negotiated "Wests" that actually are shaped in relation to their intercourse with their own colonies, (3) imaginaries that may be other than simply distilled versions or reductions to the terms of models generated in European, genetic universal histories, (4) the pressures of the heterogeneous field where the surfacing of agents or "predication" takes place in a contradictory terrain, (5) recognition that not only is universalizing theory itself full of unexplored heterogeneous spots but also that universalizing theories are thinkable elsewhere and that the ideological relation of universal and particular is always and by definition in crisis.

Dai Jinhua and the Modernist Logic of the Presence and Absence

Li To: It's not just China. Intellectuals in all Third World nations chronically confront chagrin (*ganga*), which the thrust of postcolonial theory has magnified. In the history of eruptions and development in capitalism over the last few centuries, an unequal situation has emerged within the dissemination of knowledge, which is that in the processes of modernization, when Third World nations form a discourse of "modernity," it originates in Western modernity and is standardized by it. When intellectuals resist and attempt to transform the unequal relation, they discover that since the language they use belongs to everyone (*renjia*) it is unclear where their own subjectivity is located. We absolutely cannot avoid taking on this chagrin in the process of doing cultural studies. . . . [Moreover] it is simply impossible from the perspective of modern Chinese's historical formation to talk about indigenization (*bentuhua*). I joke around with friends and say that if you really want to indigenize Chinese you're going to have return to writing in Classical Chinese . . . . Relations of power infiltrate language, particularly modern Chinese . . . . It is impossible to separate ourselves from the West.[32]

Airborn. Here, this speck and this speck you have missed.
Nominative. Numbers in cell division. Spheres of debt. The paradigm's
stitchery of unrelated points.

Myung Mi Kim, "Exordium"[33]

Li Xiaojiang's initial theoretical contribution to Chinese feminist letters came in the mid- and late 1980s in the heat of the resurgence of enlightenment criticism imprecisely called "cultural fever." Dai Jinhua, professor of literature and cinema studies at Beijing University, has moved feminist discussion in a different direction in the 1990s. Since publication (with literary critic Meng Yue) of the influential Lacanian feminist rereading of Chinese women's literary tradition in the modern era, *Women on the Horizon of History: Research on Modern Women's Literature*, Dai Jinhua has developed a style of critique that rests on developments in current Chinese cultural studies.[34] She has shifted her own focus from literature per se to film criticism and most recently to investigation into popular culture including TV serials and advertising styles.[35] While clear about the centrality of feminist criticism, her psychoanalytic optic, and preoccupation with the historical depth of representational practices situates her in a space that is adjacent to the feminist theory establishment that I have described in connection to Li Xiaojiang.

Dai's work has been most consistent in its use of a psychoanalytic logic of presence and absence. Much of her analysis reads like this translation below.

Thus, when women substituting for men become the heroes of Su Tong's historical allegory, Su Tong has already dispelled the predicament of women in 1990s writing: woman, the perpetual image of the other in masculinist culture (*nanquan wenhua*) is the one who sustains the castrating force of history and the extinction of the allegory, who comes to successfully bridge the differential abyss of the "generation of sons" [post-GPCR male culture] as they write the history of the Other. The appearance on the scene of a female/Other (*Yige nüxing/taren dechuchang*), effectively assimilates the other sex (*taxing*) into the historical allegory, enables such an assimilation of elements of the different sex, which is to say that it constitutes the other into its own successful organization as a constituent part. Woman (*nüren*), always selected by the historical unconscious as the hitman (*shashou*) and sacrificial lamb, this form (*xingxiang*), Woman, is constructed both as transcendence and as the link over the historical abyss. Spatialized history/the circular dance of death (*kongjianhua de lishi/ siwang huanwu*) invokes a spatialized image—that is what constitutes the long, unbroken line of the emergence (*chengxian*) of Woman; spreading and extending, in this long emergence of Woman into the world, a chain of linear temporality.[36]

This underlying ratio rests, as it must, on the presupposition that the field of analysis is not simply visual or viewable, but, in a conceptual sense, is spatial. In her 1995 volume *Breaking Out of the City of Mirrors: Women, Cinema, Literature*, Dai's conceptualization rested primarily on space as an extension of the cinematic screen image; much of her concern with framing derived from the optic of the mise-en-scène and its technologies, and she was drawing inspiration from philosophers of photoimage—Walter Benjamin and Teresa de Lauretis, Lacan, Metz, and Doane as well as Bakhtin, Eagleton, Jameson, and the Western Marxist tradition.

Dai had developed in the course of writing and rewriting the essays that make up the chapters of her book a notion of space/time as a central datum in the discourse of cultural history.[37] In the mid-nineties Dai was talking about a conceptualization of space that was broad and flexible, allowing her to rethink basic ideological formulae imported earlier, during the late 1980s.[38] As she has shifted further away from her preoccupation with film history and film culture and toward a new interest in television, she has expanded the notion of space a step further. In an analytic style already marked by complexity, she has begun arguing recently that TV is now the multilayered repository of the national space; idealist analytic categories such as public sphere, civil society, and so on do not apply because they cannot properly frame any discrete, material analytic space.[39] In a very important essay, "Redemption and Consumption: Depicting Culture in the 1990s," Dai lays the groundwork for her materialist conception of spatialities of consumption, arguing that the desacralization of culture and the proliferation of the realization that culture is not spiritual wealth but owned property opens up a space of consumption where the desacralized sign—in this case, images of Mao Zedong—is exchangeable, purchasable, edible.[40] Certainly, this sustained analytic interest in visible spatialization is congruent with another line of critique that Dai shares with current Chinese cultural criticism, that is, that historical, modern, elite Chinese *language* is constitutionally heterogeneous.[41]

Her concern that analysis be situated spatially is also linked to Dai's interest in retooling the effusive theoretical preoccupations of the 1980s. In the various chapters of her deeply difficult work Dai expanded on arguments that she had previously published in article form elsewhere. Elliptical about a personal, spiritual breakdown after the failures of the popular uprising in Beijing, Dai is now writing about the need to confront a post-1989 upsurge in popular culture, commodity culture, pleasure-seeking and mass cultural production generally. She takes the position that theorists in the eighties, herself included, had sought to situate their present as a certain point in a narrative of modernization. Now, looking back she sees that all cultural work then did was to project desire—for a better future, for a manageable past—through cinema and literature that refused the immediate present, anchoring itself in archaism, debates over matriarchal antiquity, and so on. Facing the present squarely and widening her optic to include the carnival of the popular moment requires self-criticism and immediate attention. A major issue confronting her in this attempted reorientation is the problem of the gendering of "communal space."

The logic of presence/absence also infused *Breaking Out of the City of Mirrors*. In this deeply difficult work Dai made a series of arguments in chapters that appeared in various forms in many venues over the years. The volume recasts the theme of historical patricide that she and Meng Yue had established in *Women on the Horizon of History*: the patricidal psychic events of imperialism and colonial war ruptured the machinery of patriarchal cultural transmission that had conventionally precluded the subject "women" from coalescing as such. Thus the national trauma—loss of the patriarchal literary language, cultural tradition, son-to-son transmission—lead to the historic emergence of "women" as a social subject onto the horizon of modern history. *City of Mirrors* focuses on the era of the seventies and eighties. It argues that cultural work undertaken in the immediate era after the Great Proletarian Cultural Revolution was not an extension of the patricidal historical rupture initiated by imperialism in the 1920s, but rather can be understood as a carnivalesque burlesque in which the orphaned sons who during the Cultural Revolution had destroyed in the Name of the Father, Mao Zedong, retooled themselves in cinematic innovation. The attempt to bridge the abyss of past and present was an agonistic event. On the one hand, the Fifth-Generation filmmakers, particularly, reinvented an entire rhetoric and technique—a virtual Lacanian new Symbolic for the cultural iteration of modern, gendered subjects. On the other hand, in the process of the de-apotheocizing one Great Father, they reapotheocized their own fathers, restoring to them their dream of unfettered transmission of culture from father to son in an unbroken historical line. How did this reknitting of a new Chinese patriarchy through the restoration of the Symbolic occur? In the absence of a genuinely worked-out aesthetic modern (given the havoc wreaked since the May Fourth by Japanese invasion, ideological asphyxiation, and cultural revolution) culturally orphaned men like Zhang Yimou, Tian Zhuangzhuang, and Chen Kaige invented a fresh new cinematic language.

This healed one historical rupture, supplying a language of representation that could process the inchoate experience of trauma. But it reinflicted even older violations when the experimental cinema of the Fifth Generation collapsed. The tragedy of the Fifth Generation for masculinity was the reinstantiation of male desire in patriarchal terms, which meant male auteurs could choose only whether to continue the old order's preoccupation with Fatherland and patriarchal transmission or be rendered speechless and fatherless. In a historical filmic analysis of the castration of the nation in the Japanese invasion, Dai argued that Red *Sorghum*'s historical breakthrough—the narrative construction of a Chinese individual (*geti chengren shi*)—is predicated on a savage resacralization of father and nation which forces the subject "women" back into its orbit around the eye of the desiring man. After 1987, as the market economy and the cultural effusion of popular consumerism overcame the immediate concerns of the Fifth Generation, signification of urbanity and future plenty resituate literature and film as mere entertainment and the repatriarchalization of gendered subjects continues relentlessly.

Rephallicization of the cultural symbolic is only half the argument, however. Subsequent chapters focus on the efforts that gender-sensitive work consequently undertakes to narrativize the condition of women. When the neopatriarchal sons of the contemporary moment turned toward the West for their cinematic markets, manufacturing representations for the pleasure of the Western gaze, Chinese women, squeezed out of the symbolic order, reinitiated the careful work of self-narration and aligned themselves with a feminized, sinicized, Third World imaginary. However, except for the rare film—Dai devotes an entire chapter to "Human, Demon, Emotion"—female subjects in the cinematic moment Dai explores presently suffer invisibilization at the hands of the male-dominated mainstream culture. And moreover, just as Dai leaves the regnant male subject twisted between patriarchal speech and speechlessness, she also introduces the sign of the Hua Mulan or woman warrior to demonstrate what she argues is the double bind of Chinese women. When female figures present themselves in the social symbolic, they silence themselves as women. The paradox of the contemporary Chinese woman, therefore, is simply that she twists between the fate of the conventional or "essentialized" woman, who is nonetheless bereft of the traditional supports provided in the patriarchal old order, and the masculinized, female, even phallicized object of desire in the eye of a (re)masculinized, reactionary culture.

When the problem is feminism, Dai's oeuvre raises two central questions. First, *City of Mirrors* subtly reinscribes at another location—Beijing, 1995—a transnationalized, psychoanalytic narrative of gendered, historical subject-formation that is substantially distinct from early-twentieth-century, European Freudianism, though obviously related to it.[42] Dai returns to periodically reterritorialize Lacano-Freudian narrative theories of subject formation. She reroutes conventional critical focus in Beijing toward the local cultural codes that privilege homosociality. That is, instead of foregrounding the oedipal desires of a son for father's woman, Dai replaces Oedipus with the homoerotic narrative of the subject of the warrior-brother, Zhong Kui, who returns from the dead to marry off his sister as he has sworn he would. Like the brother whose primary attachment is to his sister, the sister, whose primary erotic attachment is to brother, father, male cousin and son, is not herself immediately inclined erotically outside the patriline at all. She has no erotic feeling for her brothers' fictive brothers even though her brother will eventually find her a husband from among them. Dai's work, in other words, is preoccupied with such saturated analytics as the "orphaned sons," the "carnival of the sons," Hua Mulan, and Zhong Kui. By saturated I mean that when these analytic objects are narrativized in a reterritorialized location, their psychoanalytic accounts of subjectivity are substantially transformed and, most interestingly, are irreducibly congruent with the theoretical operation that Dai is describing and putting into play.

But that is actually not my primary concern right now. Rather than remark on the ways Dai reterritorializes Lacano-Freudian theory *as a cultural specificity*, I want to revisit by way of summary the implications of the basic logic of presence and absence in her theoretical feminism. Probably the most important work that feminism does in Dai Jinhua's writing is put into play a riddle of ideological immediacy or immanency. There are no essential subjects in Dai's analytic work on film or literary representation. There are only ideological and historical formations (Confucian ideology, historical events, and ruptures like the May Fourth patricide) and subjects presencing themselves or latent, absent, recuperated into the representational and desiring order of an Other. This holds true in her discussions of the current relation of First and Third Worlds, West and China, male and female. The verb "*chengxian*" which in location can mean anything from "to surface" or "to visibilize," or "to predicate," is the primary rhetorical operation through which her descriptions of the human, cultural landscape unfold. And as she has shifted into analysis of the immediate social-cultural formations confronting the critic of urban popular culture, Dai has retained this useful tool of in/visibilization to grasp how advertising images and commercial, consumer semiotics operate, predicating the urban, gendered, specialized consumer.

Underwriting this view, that the dynamic of presencing and absencing is a key to grasping gendered subordinations and strategies of liberation, is Dai's presumption that the dialectic is also at work in history itself. In a very recent, unpublished interview, she notes that her vision of 1980s film culture came into focus when she realized that when she or others repudiate the past, repudiate history that includes the horrifying events of modernity (including the forced modernization by the Cultural Revolution, so thoroughly anathema to some intellectuals that they dismiss it as the ten ahistoric or "lost" years), they lay themselves open to the obliviousness of invisibility. They fail to see how they, we, are historically inscribed. Her feminist critique of the masculinist films of the 1980s rested on several insights, she said: That the Fifth Generation filmmakers were actually engaged in a process of renarrativizing history. And that this project of theirs had two points: to bring into visibility important subjects like sexuality that had been long submerged in political taboo, and to recanonize the cultural heritage to bring it into synch with the present.[43]

I have one final point here and that is an odd use of the cliché of women's loyalty to the nation. In her critique of the cinematic tradition of the "Fifth Generation," Dai focuses on the event of 1987 in which the masculinist cinema auteurs who had provisionally bridged the abyss opened during the national, historical castration of imperialism, in the end sell out to the West. Using films like Judou, she argues that in their haste to open outward, the auteurs began to code film narratives for eastern eyes and for western eyes, splitting narrativity into two different interpretive modalities. Finally, these liminal figures in recent cinema history slipped the traces altogether to develop a film language that abandoned the historic tasks set within the nation-state itself, while glamorizing the Orient in and for the gaze of the West. What is striking in Dai's analysis is the way that she genders this work of cultural production. The gaze of the West out onto the geo-space of the world under globalization is a mobile gaze; indeed, can be internalized in a gesture of self-colonization. But fearful of the threat of re-castration, male subjects are more vulnerable. The slow, painful emergence of "women" as a subject, on the other hand, may have commenced with the patricide of the May Fourth, but it must proceed in relation to a national feminine tradition. The historical "emergence" of women into social subjectivity, and women's literature and theory into cultural centrality, is inextricably anchored in the national language, however heterogeneous and colonialized, as it is anchored in the manically transforming national socius. It is the disloyalty of sons which pulls the national cultural tradition toward a preoccupation with the gaze of the West. Dai, in other words, inverts the more common cliché which associates national integrity and female disloyalty; it is the loyalty (and dependency) of women that guarantees the continuity of the national cultural tradition and the male literatus/auteur who seeks phallic integrity in the gaze of the Other.

Tani E. Barlow

Joan Scott and the Feminist West Beside Itself

The subject of feminism was not constant; the terms of her representation shifted, and in those shifts we find not only women's history, but also histories of philosophy, psychology, and politics.

Joan Scott[44]

See, meet, face—be face to face.
Incidence of generations if in large masses. Music in boiling point. Walls of wattles, straw, and mud. A laundering stone and stones for the floor. Gently gently level the ground. This is the leveling of the ground.

Myung Mi Kim, "Exordium"[45]

So far I have sought, in the style of Spivakian political deconstruction, to keep a running epistemological or *non*-reductive argument alive as a means of ongoing political criticism in the context of a larger, overarching, horizon which I mentioned in the beginning of this essay as global, late capital, and its agendas.[46] Arriving at the logic of paradox I enter a problem zone, of course, because *Only Paradoxes to Offer* is a history of *French* feminism, that great repository of all-purpose theory that Joan Scott and Li Xiaojiang and Dai Jinhua and I—like most contemporary theoretical feminists—all lay varying claim to, a body of theoretical insight that threads its way through our work read as a globalized body. (One could, I suppose, join Dai Jinhua, who invokes the metaphor of the "halo" of an oil painting, leaching out beneath an overlayer of pigment: sign of a persistent trace. But that would be a patently compensatory move.) The temptation is to fixate on the originary force of French enlightened feminism and its priorities or provenances. What happens, however, if I place "French feminism" into abeyance for a moment or suspend the question of its provenances?

What emerges forcefully is the "West beside itself." That is to say, a logic of paradox suggests that in a foundationally heterogeneous historical field, any construction called the West will be dubious, since it must form around a disavowal of hierarchical difference—gender, sex, race, class—the usual distinctions. There can never be, Joan Scott suggests, a "West" that stabilizes as such. The task of feminist historians must be to call attention to the construction of "West," since feminism is homologous with the "West," given the paradoxical (and false) assumption in French feminism that the nation extends universal citizenship and given the special status of enlightened feminist philosophy in the history of emancipatory political philosophy. These disputable claims of universality in revolutionary and republican political thought, Joan Scott argues, rest on a sleight of hand that gendered citizenship is exclusively male, leaving females as non-citizens and non-subjects. The claim of universality in "Western feminism" also rests on a sleight of hand, which genders feminism as exclusively Western! Thus "Western feminism" qualifies difference—Third World feminism, Chinese feminism and so on—as either derivative specificity, or unspeakable extrinsicity. Scott's ability to situate ~~French~~ feminist history in the problematic of political claims on ~~French~~ citizenship can be read as a warning that the geo-metaphorical entity simply called "the West" in much scholarship cannot be trusted to cohere, and even less so in what has recently become a sort of court of last resort in feminist scholarship, something often referenced as "the historical."

The result (and the reason that Scott's work appears with the others I have discussed here) is that the logic of paradox affords a means of refusing the stability of the West, of keeping open the question of what constitutes West even as a qualifier of feminism. How does this work? As the capstone of her long preoccupation with questions of equality and difference in feminism, Scott suggests that by feminism in the context of France what is really meant is a tradition of thinking that attaches itself in multiple ways to the trajectory of liberal political theory in Europe in relation to the problem of who gets included by law as a full or voting citizen of the nation, and that this continuous critique takes various shapes over a two-hundred-year history. Paradoxical feminist critics Olympe de Gouges, Jeanne Deroin, Hubertine Auclert, Madeleine Pelletier, and Simone de Beauvoir, Scott argues, beginning in the French Revolution and consequently in each subsequent major political-epistemic era, demonstrated how indecidability haunts the foundational notions of enlightened political theory. This is particularly the case with the abstraction called "individual"; and thus for Scott the major tradition is liberal feminism and its major loophole, a mistaken association of subjectivity and masculinity.

The historical account (the book's subtitle is *French Feminists and the Rights of Man*), while emphasizing the *limitations* of discourses of feminism, also raises three basic problematics. First, it suggests that ~~French~~ feminism is a troublesome lacuna in the discourse of the liberal individual, since the "self" of liberalism is by definition masculine and rests its coherency on the "other" of woman. But, Scott adds, that being the case, feminist agency is a matter of bringing up the contradiction of the split subject of the nation (embedded symptomatically within political and theoretical representation), or perhaps better said, the gendered particularity of the putative universal subject of the nation, into his full clarity in the light of day. What Scott is calling "paradox," the double bind or paradoxical logic *of* feminism, will always circulate around the figure of the feminist whose task it is to "embody, enact, and expose" (16) the insupportable contrariness of the feminist project tout court. Second, Scott stresses the centrality *in* feminism of the matter of legal citizenship. The appropriate framework for writing the history of ~~French~~ feminism is membership in the nation. The strategic initiatives that feminist agents undertake are both epistemic interventions, then, and strategies for ensuring political representation and always in the framework of the nation. Third, the tradition of ~~French~~ feminism (and one can only read this as a metonym) is the "redes[cription of] the concepts (woman, the feminine, the individual, rights and duties) that made their [the feminists'] difference incompatible with equality" (84). In this what Scott means is that feminists do not just "offer" paradoxes, they enact them. In each surge in the feminist struggle for suffrage, for instance, in each different historical context and when confronting each epistemic order, what characterizes the feminist is that s/he *reiterates, repeats,* recycles familiar conditions of inequality, perhaps irrationalizing herself, but also revealing the naturalized order to be foundationally unjust.

That we have placed into suspension the question of origination for the moment is to note that the West beside itself is a West that cannot accommodate much at all. It—this "West"—seems in the end, and for feminism, to be a spectral screen against which the priorities of the privileged are projected and harnessed to the task of insuring a hierarchical stacking of powers. The epistemic privilege of this "West" rests on very shaky grounds. (Surely the dominant position of this "West" lies elsewhere, in political economy.) In fact, a "Western feminism" turns out to be completely paradoxical, since it is founded on the impossible task of embracing difference while claiming equality. But more than that formidable logical double bind, "Western feminism"—even in the cramped confines of a single nation, France—turns out to be a tradition knit up largely out of repetition, reinscription, anointing, and reappropriation, one feminist to the next. When the synechdochic figure of "Western feminism" is in turn recognized, as here, to be another form of national feminism (from ~~French~~ to French feminism) then historically the tradition is quite simply a line of the self-chosen. And here it is wise to return to an exposed place in the narrative of the paradoxes of the unstable critique that is liberal French feminism. And that is to Algeria.

"With the 'subject' of feminism," Gayatri Spivak wrote some time ago, "comes an 'historical moment.' *No doubt any historical moment is a space of dispersion, an open frame of relationships that can be specified only indefinitely.*"[47] And so if I were to follow out the historical fact that Hubertine Auclert rested her case for female suffrage on an endorsement of France's colonialist civilizing mission in Algeria, I might find that the case for women's citizenship per se nestling uncomfortably in the space occupied by the colonial specters of French modernity. And if I were to follow out the implications of Simone de Beauvoir's Tunisian fantasies, to what degree would I find a line connecting Auclert, to Beauvoir, to that entire line of enlightened feminist tradition that comes to rest on a vision of a "gloomy cave—kingdom of immanence, womb, and tomb" of the primitive Arab woman and her antecedent the "Jews of Biblical times"?[48] Certainly this might lead outward into that historical space of "dispersion" and its "open frame of relationships that can be specified" forever. Even when the historical question posed is simply "What events and archives play signifieds in theoretical work?" (and I am thinking via Joan Scott of concrete women like Auclert's servile Algerian Moslems and Beauvoir's oafish Tunisians)? Perhaps, it would lead to the work of Billie Melman, whose *Women's Orients: English Women and the Middle East, 1718-1918* establishes in great empirical detail what the grounding of enlightened feminism looks like when the accounts of the adventurers and evangelicals who gave the Orient to theorists such as Auclert and Beauvoir are considered. What did the women who made it possible for Auclert and Beauvoir to encounter the Orient as already fabricated, already familiar, do to shape a foundationally dispersed historical space?[49]

Conclusions

History will be written about the forces that are situating "China" (that vast network of administrative, academic, ethnic, nationalized neighborhoods inside the governing apparatus of the PRC state machine) in feminist studies. Will these histories consider the complex relation of gendered logics in relation to geopolitical others that I have tackled in this essay? Will institutionalized Chinese feminism transport itself onto the transnational stage by "reading its differences from Western feminism," as Lin Chun has argued? That is not for me to say. Surely any attempt to do so will need to consider Dai Jinhua's remark that the place for historians to start is the present, the space of the "here and now." And that means sharing with my Chinese counterparts in the *mise en abyme* that has so troubled this analysis.[50]

Still there are conclusions to be drawn, nonetheless. First, the critique of the subjects "women/woman" has run its course, but it has not dislodged the discursive logics holding the machinery of predication in place. No amount of comparative or "international" feminism can—in and of itself—dislodge that matrix. Global, Victorian, scientific, sexuality and its problematics of gendered citizenship are transparent now, due in great part to the work of historians like Joan Scott. Displacement is another matter, particularly for those in the semi-, de- and colonial sectors of the history world. For instance, Li Xiaojiang's work is utterly ensconced in a familiar matrix of heteronormativity. What would happen if rather than replicating the heterosexual matrix she thought along the hymen, as Derrida calls it, in "The Double Session," not of "confusion," here, but rather of "theory/history"? What if she were to substitute for the deracinated logic of universal and particular (or even difference and equality) an erotics of penetration, a logic of the hymen? Or to take another example, the logic of the cultural-diffusion models, exemplified in this paper in Chatterjee's ambivalent questions about derivative discourses, rests on certain fixations with copies. The resources available specifically to feminisms in the logics of Irigarayan mimicry and the sex which is never one might help to vitiate that reflex. Or the question of liberal logic that I raised in relation to Chatterjee, set against the ghostly presence of that old trickster Joseph Levenson: methodological liberalism is the default position in most "cross-cultural" studies of gendered subjects in China studies. The nexus formed of tradition and modernity, China and the West leave feminist scholarship searching for the body of the other woman, the voice of the other woman, the ear of the other.[51]

Globalization of theory, like globalization of capital, is a patent reality in our times. A second conclusion that can be drawn from the argument I have made here is that while different feminisms surface at various sites, it is possible to read these theoretical initiatives not simply as superstructural signs or mere signifiers of an underlying economic substructure, but rather in historical terms as singularities embedded in empirical archives. The persistent critique, then, is useful because it holds in abeyance a common default position, which is that the subject of feminisms is "women" and that these "women" are simply the same, but *culturally* (or, for those who do not consider history carefully, *historically*) different. The deficiencies of globalized multiculturalism on the U.S. model have been addressed by many.[52]

Third, I have suggested an alternative to the habitual relation of theory and case, ~~western~~ feminism and Chinese archive. I have argued, following out that strand of Scott's argument, regarding the problematic of citizenship for "Western" feminism, in order to highlight the problem I have noticed confronts Li Xiaojiang. The presumption of universality, the presumption that universality can be tacitly shared, lock Li, like the ~~French~~ feminists Scott reads, in the double bind Scott calls "paradox." I have implied, moreover, that in her deterritorialization of theory and in her chronic, persistent efforts at surfacing a subject "women," Dai Jinhua has actually pointed a way out of Li's dilemma. Dai's effort at establishing a decolonizing, situated feminism is exemplary in the sense that it takes seriously the problems of how to write gender history that is irreducible to another register, and how to recode or reformulate theoretical feminism for use in other times and spaces. This is not an argument to application. That is, I am not concluding that turnabout is fair play and that a history of Chinese women should call on Dai Jinhua's theory of Chinese feminism! Quite the contrary. For me the problem is neither redress nor translation nor initiatives in feminist studies that can substitute true theory for the disabused. Reading historically and historiographically, as I have done here, demonstrates in a prudent and practical fashion that the object is to disarm and displace globalizing moves. Feminist history can, by virtue of its *in*stabilizing force, trouble the macrological notion of translation, which so often neglects the political economy of the translators. Disarmament (in the careful specifications that historians are bound in disciplinary terms to patiently provide) is the historian's special contribution. And there, I think, is where I am sanguine that displacement may in the end be possible.

June 1998

Endnotes
1—Theresa Hak Kyung Cha, *Dictee*, (Berkeley: Third Woman Press) 118. Unless noted otherwise all translations in the paper are my own.
2—For now I adopt Spivak's definition of the transnational world. "That it is impossible for the new and developing states, the newly decolonizing or the old decolonizing nations, to escape the orthodox constraints of a 'neo-liberal' world economic system which, in the name of Development, and now 'sustainable development', removes all barriers between itself and fragile national economies, so that any possibility of building for social redistribution is severely demented." Gayatri Chakravorty Spivak, "Diasporas Old and New: Women in the Transnational World," *Textual Practice* 10:2 (1996), 245.

As always, I owe Donald M. Lowe the most. Jing Wang, Kyeong-Hee Choi, and Venkat Rao indulged my need to talk before I wrote the draft. Joan Scott contributed suggestions for revision. Claudia Pozzana, Alessandro Russo, and Priscilla Wald provided encouraging feedback, and Jon Solomon copy-edited an earlier version, alerting me to several foolish errors. I wrote this essay for the panel "Spectres of the West in Asian Studies" (Association of Asian Studies meeting, 1998) which Naoki Sakai organized, and I delivered the draft once again at the workshop that Sakai, the *Traces* editorial group, and Huang Ping and Wang Hui of the Beijing branch Chinese Academy of Social Sciences organized, entitled "Spectres of the West and the Politics of Translation" (Beijing, 1999). I wish to thank all the participants but particularly Yukiko Hanawa, for her encouragement and support throughout.

3—Gayatri Chakravorty Spivak, "Diasporas Old and New," 262.

4—See Deborah Rosenfelt, "Think globally, teach locally," *Women's Review of Books*, XV. 5 (February, 1998): 28-29. Information regarding the globalization of Women Studies appears here, as does a report on attempts to "gender" area studies. A decade-old Ford Foundation-financed investment in local PRC Women Studies institutions is beginning to overlap with efforts Ford initiated in 1995 to flexibalize and internationalize interdisciplinary curriculum in the US via the "Women's Studies, Area and International Studies Curriculum Integration Project." Actually, Rosenfelt has even suggested that "China" is a metonym for something bearing the title "emerging global feminism." Why? Because the Beijing Fourth United Nations World Conference on Women in 1995 apparently has finally signified to US-located scholars that "dimensions of globalization— economic, cultural and political—*affect all women's lives*."

Rosenfelt does not mention "A Cultural History of Women and Work in twentieth Century China," a Luce Foundation grant to faculty at the University of California, Santa Cruz, empowering its holders to "gender China" in US scholarship and Chinese scholars in metropolitan theory in the U.S. Also see Joan Kaufman, "Ford Support for Gender and Development in China," a paper prepared for the conference, "Gender, Women's Agency and Development in China at the Threshold of the New Century," Boston (March, 1999).

5—Below are just a sampling. Ping-chun Hsiung at the University of Toronto has organized a Canada-China Linkage Project on Women and Minorities dealing with educational transformation. (See their report entitled "Development of Female College Students and Their Education," January 4, 1998). Sharon K. Hom and Xin Chunying, ed., *YingHan funü yu falü cihui shiyi* (English-Chinese Lexicon of Women and Law) (Paris, Beijing: United Nations Educational, Scientific and Cultural Organization and China Translation and Publishing Corporation, 1995) is the collective project of the Chinese Society of Women's Studies, a group of activist, liberal feminist expatriot PRC scholars, who have been granted several Ford Foundation awards. Members of the CSWS also publish individually. See Bao Xiaolan, ed., *Xifang nüx-*

ing juyi yanjiu pingjie (Introduction to Western Feminist Scholarship) (Beijing: Sanlian shudian, 1995); and Wang Zheng, *Nüxing de chuqi: dangdai Meiguo de nüquan yundong* (The Uprise [sic] of Women: The contemporary feminism movement in the United States) (Beijing: Dangdai Zhongguo chubanshe, 1995). Inside the PRC see Zhongguo funü yanjiusuo (Institute for research on Chinese women), ed., *Shijie funü yanjiu gailan* (An overview of global women's studies) (Beijing: Zhongguo funü chubanshe, 1995) which does a similar service in translating and abstracting "Western feminism" as such and making it available to compatriots with the PRC.

6—Indexing the ways that so-called Chinese and other local/national forms of "international feminism" are indebted to US-based donor agencies, United Nations sites, the Clinton doctrine of a gendered geopolitical imaginary, etc. are worthy projects for another time. See Nöel Sturgeon, *Ecofeminist Natures* (Routledge, 1997) for good discussion of the discourses of internationalism in United Nations feminism and Jacqueline Berman, "Engendering Transition: Sovereignty, Sexual Difference, and International Relations in Post-Communist Poland," chapter 5, University of Arizona dissertation, 1998, analysis of the record of the Ford Foundation.

7—A conversation with Kyeong-

Hee Choi helped me to phrase my point in this way.

8—In even entertaining this old marriage of Asia and the West, I am engaging what Diane Elam calls a classic suffragette gesture of disruptive enchainment. She means a situation in which one knowingly links dissimilar entities—the West and Asian studies—across the abyss of their decomposing difference. See Diane Elam, *Feminism and Deconstruction: Ms. en Abîme* (New York and London: Routledge, 1994), 13.

9—Understanding Asian Studies as any study that seeks a stable representation of "Asia" either within the region specified (Asian studies of "Asia") or outside it (Asia area studies outside "Asia").

10—I wish to thank Jing Wang for encouraging this direction in my thinking.

11—Walter Lew, *Excerpts From Dikte: For Dictee,* (New York/ Seoul: Yeul Eum Publishing Co, 1982), 12.

12—Mary G. Dietz, "Introduction: Debating Simone de Beauvoir," in *Signs* 18:1, (Autumn 1992): 76. Li Xiaojiang cites the first edition of the Parshley English translation.

13—Li Xiaojiang, *Xing gou,* (Beijing: Sanlian shudian, 1989). For further elaboration of Li Xiaojiang's work and significance see Tani E. Barlow, "Woman at the Close of the Maoist Era in the Polemics of Li Xiaojiang and her Associates," Lisa Lowe and David Lloyd, ed., *Worlds Aligned: The Politics of Culture in the Shadow of Capital* (Durham: Duke University Press, 1997).

[Since my own essay went into production Li Xiaojiang has written an account of her own on the topic of de Beauvoir's *Second Sex*. In its, she mentions her initial responses to the aphorism that "women are not born they are made" and compares it to her present belief that women are indeed both born and made. See Li Xiaojiang, "Shiji mo kan 'Di er xing'" (Looking at *The Second Sex* at the Century's End) *Dushu* (Reading), (12:1999): 98-103. Thanks to Wang Hui for sending me an early copy of the essay.]

14—*Ibid.,* The objective of the tract is precisely to argue that universality in the logic of sex is not, in fact, similarity but difference, difference rooted in the Nature from which every human community wrests its Humanity. Rather than obscure the truth that natural sexual difference is the ground of universality, it is better to trace how male and female emerged historically. In this counter-discourse (*luoji beilun*) not only are the histories of Woman and Man not synchronous, the colonization of Woman by Man and the imposition universally of the male-centered standard has led to the deindividualization (*feirengehua*) of Women as a historical sex. Citing Beauvoir, Li Xiaojiang argues that the "process of humanization of Nature is also a process of the masculinization of women" (9).

15—*Ibid.,* Li says: "the nature of the evolution of the two sexes is *dis*synchronous and that is the first principle of the foundation of the history of Human civilization. And it is only because this historical datum has been overlooked that we can then speak of an artificial (*renweide*) logical counter discourse. Logical rationales are not purely objective and do not spring purely out of logical speculation, but rather are submerged in the collective unconscious as the end product of the movement of History" (7).

16—*Ibid,* 95.

17—*Ibid.,* Another reading of this book would begin with its drive to repredicate the subjects "man," "Mankind," "humans," "Humanity," "woman/women," and so on. Li's overwhelming task is to situate sexuality and sexual reproduction at the base of her teleologies. See for instance the stipulation that humans are concrete entities (as opposed to the Humanity of idealist historians) with three characteristics: that we are (1) biological entities with (2) sexual drives produced in (3) social relationships (52).

18—Their stunning insistence on the primacy of gendered difference over all other codes and grids of difference certainly leads them to similar repudiations of what each decrees to be pseudoliberation and the inauthenticity of women's gestures. This sacrifices all other conceivable intersections of difference to the Big One of sex. See *The Second Sex*, 77-78, for the parable of the polygamous oriental "idol" and his harem of wives in various states of decay for a sense of how race plays out Beauvoir's thesis concerning the "submergence" of the feminine in the patriarchal social form. The parable's tone of colonial contempt is vivid and excruciating.

This maneuver of reading the "copy" to demonstrate the deficiencies of the "original" is an important reason why Benjamin I. Schwartz's *Yan Fu and the Search for Wealth and Power* (Cambridge: Harvard University Press, 1964) is still an icon in U.S. Chinese studies.

19—Diane Elam, *Feminism and Deconstruction: Ms. en Abîme*.

20—Lin Chun, "Finding a Language: Feminism and Women's Movements in Contemporary China," in Joan Scott, Cora Kaplan, Debra Keates, ed., *Transitions/Environments/Translations: Feminism in International Politics* (New York and London: Routledge Press, 1997).

21—Fedwa Malti-Doublas, "Writing Nawal El Saadawi," in Diane Elam and Robyn Wiegman, ed., *Feminism Beside Itself* (New York, London: Routledge, 1995), 283-296, writes about an experience I have encountered because of my interest in Li Xiaojiang. Malti-Douglas suggests that the reason for the allegations is the fact that El Saadawi is a cause celebre among non-Arab feminists in the United States, like Alice Walker. Some of the Chinese expatriot reception of Li Xiaojiang and her alleged essentialism stems from Li's well known disdain for China born scholars working abroad. But it may also be traced to the way that some U.S. mainstream feminists have taken Li Xiaojiang up as the sole representative of feminism in the People's Republic. In both cases—El Saadawi and Li Xiaojiang—the charges of monstrosity seem related to international notoriety, the simplicity of each womans antipatriarchal textual politics and the claim each lays to representing a national womanhood.

22—Xiong Yumei, Liu Xiaocong and Qu Wen, ed., *Zhongguo funü lilun yanjiu shinian*, (Women's Theoretic Studies in China From 1981-1990), (Beijing: Zhongguo funü chubanshe, 1991), 1. See also Quanguo Fulian funü yanjiusuo zhuban (National Women's Association, Women's Research Center, ed., *'Funü yanjiu zai Zhongguo quanti yantaohui lunwenji*, (Collection of Theses on 'Women's Studies in China'), (Beijing/Huairuo: Quanfunlian funü yanjiu suo chuban, 1995) for further writing of this kind. In the latter collection Jin Yihong argues that the 1980s constituted a "predisciplinary" moment in the development of gender studies, the 1990s a more mature disciplined praxis. (See "Characteristics of China's Women's Studies and Analysis of Factors Affecting Their Social Effects" and "Zhongguo funüxue yanjiu tedian ji yingxiang qi shehui tiaoyung de yinsi fenxi" 1-5. This periodization is consistent with the positions expressed in the longer essays collected in the earlier compendium.

23—The role of de Beauvoir's work particularly remains to be traced through the careers of the founders. Du Fangqin, a foundational figure and a historian, has acknowledged the book's great impact. See Du Fanqin, "A Review of the Last Ten Years: China's Women's Studies Exchanging Experience with Foreign Countries," (*Shinian huiyin: Zhongguo funü yanjiu de duiwai jiaoliu*), in Zhang Yanxia, ed., 69-72.

24—For Tan Shen's review of the inroads that women's studies sociologists are actually able to eke out in Chinese university departments, see "Status of Women's Studies in the World of Sociology" (*Funü yanjiu zai shehui xuejia de diwei*), Quanguo Fulian funü yanjiusuo zhuban, "Theses," 36-38. For Chen Ping see, "A Starting Point for Research into the Chinese Female Population," (*Zhongguo nüxing renkou yanjiu de qibu*) in Xiong Yumei, Liu Xiaocong and Qu Wen, ed., *Funü lilun yanjiu*, 21-51.

25—Many of Li Xiaojiang's associates are focused primarily on ways of strategizing inroads into the disciplines of sociology, anthropology, and psychology. They seem consequently not so enthusiastic about Li's institutional formula of founding a sub-discipline of Marxist women's studies separate from reestablished disciplinary nexes.

26—There are several kinds of writing on disciplinary transformation in the volume I am highlighting, essays that talk about the indebtedness of Chinese women's studies to US (less frequently to Japanese) templates, essays that presume that scientific social sciences transcend national distinctions, and those on aesthetics and ethics which imply that the tradition of communist scholarship is sufficient grounding in and of itself. This latter disciplinization, of ethics, situates itself in the "tradition" of premodernity. It presumes that Western feminism has nothing to say to scholars working to derail the syncretic remains of the Confucian heritage. The confrontation between Li Xiaojiang and expatriot Chinese women graduate students at Harvard in 1992, the 1996 meeting of Women's Studies advocates over a controversial paper jointly authored by Liu Bohong (Chair of the Women Studies Research Center of the ACWA), Lin Chun (Professor of Politics at School of Oriental and African Studies), and Jin Yihong (Institute of Philosophy, Jiangsu Academy of Social Sciences) over the influence of Western women's studies in the growth of the movement in China are two of the better known events. At bottom is the problematic ghost of what in Li Xiaojiang and her associates call "Western feminism."

27—See Ann Ferguson, "Two Women's Studies Conferences in China: Report by an American Feminist Philosopher," *Asian Journal of Women Studies*, 3:1:161-184 for an example of the habitual way a U.S-situated scholar figures "western feminism and the Chinese case." An instance where placement in a special journal issue seems to put the native scholar in the position of a native informant is *Boundary 2*, 24.3 (fall, 1997). Dorothy Ko's *Teachers of the Inner Chambers: Women and Culture in Seventeenth-Century China* (Stanford: Stanford University Press, 1994) suggests the strengths and the weaknesses of empirical studies that apply theory to case study.

28—My point of reference is the "West" in feminism. My position is consistent with a particular stream in transnational feminist scholarship that includes Dai Jinhua, Gayatri Chakravorty Spivak, Aiwha Ong, Inderpal Grewal and Caren Kaplan, Yukiko Hanawa, Naifei Ding and Patricia Seiber, Norma Alarcon, Minoo Moallem and many others who hold that transnationalized forms of feminist thinking offer flexible articulation with political economy, always in association with irreducible difference, since feminist critique is mere ideology unless it is demonstrably historical and patently contingent.

29—Joseph R. Levenson, *Confucian China and its Modern Fate: A Trilogy* (Berkeley: University of California Press, 1968), xvii.

30—For the beginning of a critique of this historiographic tendency see the *Bulletin of Concerned Asian Scholars*, "Symposium on *Rescuing History From the Nation*," 29.4 (1997): 54-69. John Fitzgerald intimates in his contribution that while Prasenjit Duara disavows Levenson's psychologization, Duara ends up recuperating its opposite (*lack* of affect around colonialization) in ways that the evidence does not support.

31—Partha Chatterjee, *The Nation and Its Fragments: Colonial and Postcolonial Histories* (Princeton: Princeton University Press, 1993).

32—See Dai Jinhua, et al, "Chat on the modernity question at the heart of cultural studies," (*Mantan wenhua yanjiu zong de xiadaixing wenti*), *Zhongshan wenxue shuang yuekan* (Zhongshan University Bimonthly Literary Review), 1996:5, 5.23.1996.

33—Myung Mi Kim, "Exordium," *positions: east asia cultural critiques* 4.3(1996): 417.

34—Meng Yue and Dai Jinhua, *Fu chu lishi dibiao: Xiandai funü wenxue yanjiu* (Henan renmin chubanshe, 1989) and reprinted as *Fuch'u li-shih ti-piao: Chung-kuo hsien-tai nühsing wenh-süeh yenchiu* (Women on the horizon of history: research on Chinese modern women's literature) (Taipei: Shih-pao wen-hua, 1993).

35—Dai is the recipient, with Jing Wang, of a Luce Foundation grant to study contemporary Chinese popular culture.

36—Dai Jinhua, *Breaking out of the City of Mirrors: Women, Cinema, Literature,* (*Jingchen tuwei: nüxing, dianying, wenxue*) (Beijing: Harvard Yanjing Press, 1995), 174.

37—This is a departure from the Lacanian-inspired, literary exegesis of a narrative of history that she had developed with Meng Yue. In the earlier book the historical narrative recapitulated the mythic stories of orthodox psychoanalysis—the primal horde, the Name of the Father, the castration of sons and rape of the mother, the castration of the Chinese father in the Western imperialist takeover, and so on. In Dai's shift from literature to film analysis this move toward space/time is obvious and pronounced.

38—Dai, "Chat on the modernity question," 174. Here she is rewriting the ideological imaginary of US-sponsored notions of the "public sphere." In conversation with Li Tuo, He Li, and Song Weijie, Dai is noted as putting into play the analytic notion of "common space" or *gongyong kongjian*. Li attributes the introjection of spatial imagination to Dai and suggests that critics use her insight to elucidate the constructive force of advertising. All discussants seem eager to retain Dai's spatial imperative while discarding the Habermasian historical mythology.

39—"Cultural Criticism that Faces up to the Challenge," (*Mianxiang tiaozhan de wenhua piping*), *Beijing Wenxue* (Beijing literature), 1996:7: 25-6.

40—See Dai Jinhua, "Redemption and Consumption: Depicting Culture in the 1990s," Edward Gunn, trans., *positions* 4.1 (Spring, 1996).

41—See Dai Jinhua, "Those who know, banter: reading Wang Xiaobo" (*Zhizhe xixue: yuedu Wang Xiaobo*) (unpublished). In this manuscript commemorating Wang Xiaobo, Dai writes of the constitutional heterogeneity of contemporary Chinese as a colonial artifact and then, again, as marked by state-sponsored translation projects during the importation of Marxism and supporting European theoretical works in the 1950s. See especially page 14.

42—See an interesting inversion of this argument in Jay Geller, "*Judenzopf/Chinesenzopf*: Of Jews and Queues," *positions*, 2.3 (1994).

43—"Dianying shi de wenhua he fansi ji qita: Dai Jinhua nüshi fangtan" (Culture and spiritual reflexiveness in movie history, and so on: an interview with Ms. Dai Jinhua), unpublished, 9.29.97.

44—Joan Scott, *Only Paradox to Offer: French Feminists and the Rights of Man* (Harvard: Harvard University Press, 1996), 14.

45—Myung Mi Kim, "Exordium," 419.

46—See Barlow, "green blade in the act of being grazed': late capital, flexible bodies, critical intelligibility," *differences* 10.3 (Fall, 1998).

47—Gayatri Spivak, "Finding Feminist Readings: Dante—Yeats," in Spivak, *In Other Worlds: Essays in Cultural Politics* (New York and London: Routledge, 1987), 17, emphasis added.

48—*The Second Sex*, 77-78. I cite in full:

I recall seeing in a primitive village of Tunisia a subterranean cavern in which four women were squatting: the old one-eyed and toothless wife, her face horribly devastated, was cooking dough on a small brazier in the midst of an acrid smoke; two wives somewhat younger, but almost as disfigured, were lulling children in their arms—one was giving suck; seated before a loom, a young idol magnificently decked out in silk, gold, and silver was knotting threads of wool. As I left this gloomy cave—kingdom of immanence, womb, and tomb—in the corridor leading upward toward the light of day I passed the male, dressed in white, well groomed, smiling, sunny. He was returning from the marketplace, where he had discussed world affairs with other men; he would pass some hours in this retreat of his at the heart of the vast universe to which he belonged, from which he was not separated. For the withered old women, for the young wife doomed to the same rapid decay, there was no universe other than the smoky cave, whence they emerged only at night, silent and veiled. The Jews of Biblical times had much the same customs as the Arabs. The patriarchs were polygamous, and they could put away their wives almost at will. . . .

49—Billie Melman, *Women's Orients: English Women and the Middle East, 1718-1918 (Sexuality, Religion and Work)* (Ann Arbor: University of Michigan Press, 1995).

50—An interesting item in such a history of the immediate might be the Shanghai meeting titled "China-US Conference on the Women's Question." The 1990 meeting produced a conference volume edited by the China Women's Press (Zhongguo funü chubanshe) entitled *ZhongMei fünu wenti yantao hui lunwenji* (Conference volume on the conference on Sino-US women's question) (Beijing, 1991) full of essays that reiterate United Nations dicta on globalization at the same time as it is apparently funded and certainly largely attended by representatives of US multinational corporations (e.g., Motorola, Chase Manhattan Bank, etc)! It leads to the fascinating spectacle of state-sponsored Chinese Women's Federation officers swapping views on policy and investment in research projects with corporate spokeswomen from major TNCs.

For instance, among the flood of publications surrounding the 1995 UN meeting is a bilingual volume entitled *The Chalice and the Blade in Chinese Culture: Gender Relations and Social Models* published by the Chinese Partnership Research Group and edited by Min Jiayin. Carefully fetishizing the fact that the Chinese edition of the book is titled *Yanggang hu yinruo de bianqin* or literally "variations of Yang-gang and Yinrou" (or even more literally "variations of yang hard and yin pliable") a title that according to the lead author "mystifyingly" resists translation, Min nonetheless is clear that the study is "a comparative study made under the influence" of Dr. Riane Eisler. Most particularly obvious in both Eisler's work as well as the companion Chinese version is the status and the centrality of the "West."

51—I am thinking here of the profound ambivalence—she knows that she cannot, but she still retains a focus on the body of the other so that its voice can speak to her through the historical archive—that saturates Gail Hershatter's admirable social history of semi-colonial prostitution, *Dangerous Pleasures: Prostitution and Modernity in Twentieth Century Shanghai* (Berkeley: University of California Press, 1997).

52—See Yukiko Hanawa, "inciting sites of political intervention: queer 'n' asian," in *positions* 4.3 (1996). Also see Inderpal Grewal and Karen Caplan, ed., "Introduction," in *Scattered Hegemonies* (Minneapolis: Minnesota University Press, 1994).

INTERLUDES

A Letter from Jacques Derrida

Dear Friends,

There is, of course, *pirate* and *pirate*.

But what separates the one from the other? Is it still a border? Is it the border of a concept, country, Nation-state, language, or legislation? It is in view of this question that I would like to risk, if not justify, this strange distinction. Between pirate and counter-pirate, how is one to decide? How is one to recognize the trace, to determine the wake left by a "good" piracy? A piracy that is "just" although illegal, if not illegitimate?

But first, please forgive me for not having offered to you the promised text on the anticipated date. I would not wish to evade to your invitation, nor especially to be absent, and to appear to "desert," at the very beginning of an adventure that I see as necessary, even urgent, and to the courage and lucidity of which I wish to pay my respects, in admiration, with gratitude. I hope in the future to participate as best I can, but I do not wish to wait to tell you, in a few words, why Traces seems to offer a site, and is today already opening this site, for a space of resistance and affirmation, for an affirmative resistance, for a dissidence and perhaps for an underground movement of the yes. In brief for an entirely other experience of counter-piracy.

Resistance, first of all, to new forms of homogenizing hegemonies, of homo-hegemonization. This resistance can and must take the form—new, certainly, and global this time—of what was called in the

Jacques DERRIDA

translated by
Thomas LAMARRE

Interludes

United States in Thoreau's time, "civil disobedience": the non-respect for "positive" norms, for the legislations and constitutions in force. But such a transgression, sometimes passive, always makes reference to a superior law, to something that resembles the universality of a categorical imperative. From this point of view, and even if you act quite politely and discretely, with good manners, the necessity of a certain piracy will be thrust upon you—of a being outside the law that rather insolently opposes the law, making war—declared or not—on the organized, "legal," and supposedly legitimate piracy of the powers that be in every sovereign country and in the global field of so-called globalization. And in a certain state of international law as well. There is no doubt that we need a counter-piracy, today more than ever. This is what I call the dissidence of "yes," affirmative resistance: piracy against piracy. Most important is not to confuse them, but is this possible? Are there safe, already available criteria for that? I am not sure. In truth, I am convinced that there must not be any, that there must be not any. One must invent them at every instant, at one's own risk. That's what piracy is, the "good" piracy worthy of the name.

I believe I see this desire of yours advancing onto the high seas—or boarding the supersonics that navigate the Web—by way of the concept, practices, and politics of translation that you are taking on. Trace has always meant crossing, translation, transference, passage, transit—passage of the limit toward and from the other, ventured in the night, on the ocean, sometimes in airs as well, through fidelity to the irredentist irreducibility of the other. While sustaining an unconditional respect for the singularity of languages, the irreducible multiplicity of idioms, memories, "cultures" of which these languages are the thinking body, it is a question of opening up unprecedented itineraries among them. Outside the law, unprecedented and above all interdicted, these openings should not reconstitute, in new forms, cultural-colonial dominations, the figures of a disguised sovereignty, simulacra of universal language. We know very well that, today, under the pretext of what is called globalization, a confused and deliberately mystifying concept, all markets (properly economic, financial, but also techno-scientific, academic, media, etc.) are organizing new powers, new hegemonies, that authorize their authority under the flag of alleged transparency and immediate communicability. A certain Anglo-American imposes itself irresistibly as the esperanto of this Old New World wherein not a single powerful State need renounce a sovereignty of theological origin[1] (theologico-political, in truth, essentially European-Christian and inherited by democracies from the monarchy of divine right), at the very moment when weak States are called upon to sacrifice theirs. What to do? How?

It seems to me that one only has recourse to a double injunction: to contest international law, sometimes pirating it, but in the name of its perfectibility; to deconstruct (isn't deconstruction a sort of counter-piracy?) the concept of sovereignty but without forgetting that, in certain cases, the sovereignty of the State can resist concentrations of trans-state capitalistic powers; to transgress the global authority of a single language (Anglo-American) but without forgetting that it can serve "good" piracy, the just counter-piracy; to combat the media empires while extorting from them all kinds of "secondary benefits" (circulation of new models, propagation of critical speech, auto-critique of the media by media professionals and other "counter-pirates"), without also forgetting that all the pirates and counter-pirates on the Web and Internet are not in the service of just causes. There too, one must invent rules, entrust oneself to the unprecedented, know how to fly by night, in order to discern between piracies and piracies, and indeed between more than one counter-piracy. Etc.

There it is, you asked me for or prescribed for me a page. And I'm trying to get away with two or three others as contraband.

With warmest wishes and all my solidarity,

Jacques Derrida

Endnotes

1—If I may add a note here at the bottom of the page and an economic reference to the concept of *globalization* that I proposed in "Faith and Knowledge," to which text I will indulge myself a reference here, I would draw your attention to this simple index: when hundreds of thousands of young Catholics from around the world were recently reunited in Rome, they greeted the Pope by wishing a long life to "J.P.II," in a more or less correct anglo-american pronunciation: "Jay Pee two," "Jeepeetoo."

As I tried to show in "Faith and Knowledge," the *globalization* of the very concept of religion, its universal inscription in law, politics, diplomacy, technoscience, passes through Anglo-American. Irresistibly. It is imperative to take note of this fact and use it as a point of departure.

There Are No Encounters in Theory

Christopher Fynsk

I must begin directly by acknowledging that in the list of terms offered for self-presentation for this valuable issue of *Traces,* I cannot recognize myself. The nature of this awkwardness will form the substance of this brief communication.

My distance from the words offered for this exercise does not stem from a chance inadequacy—as though by some poor luck the chosen terms failed to key my particular concerns. No, even if "the human" or "the inhuman" (my current work could be located somewhere there between) were to appear on this list, I would feel the same awkwardness before this summons to classify my potential relation to the journal under a rubric or theme. This is not the protest of a beautiful theoretical soul (as though it were impossible for me to reduce the wealth or range of my interests to a set of contemporary motifs). I speak rather from an inability to find the grounds of engagement in theoretical terminology, a failure before (and in) the concept. Or perhaps it is more of a refusal, this sense of fatigue, this inability to be "keyed" by a set of theoretical markers. Perhaps it is a form of resistance.

In any case, I know that the problem is theory. I am "interested" in forms of praxis that resist translation into common conceptual terms (however "edgy," however rigorous they might be). I am interested in writing that brings to language an exigency to which it has had to testify, be this exigency as simple as the infancy to which Jean-

François Lyotard addressed some of his last works. Writing that responds to the event and that seeks the an-archic grounds of community cannot but resist theory, even if it is obliged to borrow its paths.

I will be told, perhaps, that once again I take things too seriously, that the list of keywords are like the tokens in a game. Wouldn't this exercise provide an invaluable lesson in the pragmatics of our multilingual endeavour? And if it proves possible to so *key* a conversation, wouldn't it offer a revealing demonstration of the technical (even serial) character of our institutional functions and the translatability of theoretical discourse? Who knows, perhaps it could even produce a differend. The implications for our understanding of our global site in this journal, in any case, could be far reaching, even subversive.

But I will confess that if *Traces* is to have any meaning for me whatsoever, it must speak to more than academic protocols (even their parody or their subversion), and it must speak in something other than the language of theory. For *Traces* should be a site of encounter, and there are no encounters in theory.

COMMUNICATION

There is no word as multitudinous in its meanings, as difficult to comprehend, and as important as communication. This is because communication has to do with the interconnectedness between human beings. To use Hegel's terms, humans are inter-subjective beings. Communication is the very thing that expresses the duality between human individuality and collectivity.

Language is the most important medium making this communication possible. In his early Jena Manuscripts, Hegel speaks of language as the medium of the "*Geist*" (Spirit). Language is no mere tool. It is indeed the medium of the "Spirit." This idea of Hegel's lives on in the tradition of German humanism beginning with Herder. Even before Hegel, Fichte made language (the German language) an important axis of the "internal frontier" (*innere Grenze*) in his Message to the German People. In present-day Japan, there have been repeated incidents in which language has become the cause of mistrust. I am referring here to a recent statement by the Prime Minister Mori, and other senior Japanese politicians, in which they used terms evocative of Japan's wartime state ideology. These are indicative of a weakening of the medium of the "Spirit" itself. This suggests that we are witnessing what could be called a breakdown in communication. How might one explain this pathological state of affairs? In my view, it is the result of a hidden form of violence an attempt to eliminate all "lack of clarity," purifying communication so that it becomes as "transparent" as possible. One can see this in the pursuit of "Japanese-style communi-

KANG Sangjung

cation," "Japanese-style thought," "Japanese-style community," and "Japanese-style non-verbal intuitive communication." The basis for the pathology could well be found in the emphasis placed on the transparency and ease of comprehension supposedly possessed by these forms of discourse prefixed by the expression "Japanese-style." "My transparent self"—these words of the juvenile responsible for the extraordinary and unprecedented child murders in Kobe are still fresh in our minds. They may have been a desperate defense by a youth seeking an "evasion of clarity." Japanese society is now pervaded by the violent attempt to do away even with that, thus seeking to attain total "transparency" of communication. Surely, this means in effect the death of communication. It seems that the pathological condition can only become worse.

Toward the "Dictatorship of the Proletariat"

Kojin KARATANI

translated by Sabu KOHSO

Concerning the concept of "dictatorship of the proletariat," today's Marxists seem to be uncertain, being silent as they are. In the late 19th century when the German Social Democratic Party (SPD) gained power in Parliament, Engels gave up on the idea of the realization of the "dictatorship of the proletariat." Later Lenin revived it as a strategic goal, and his communism resulted in the dictatorship of a party, the dictatorship of a bureaucratic system. Thus Marxists' voices came to be muted. It is time to reconsider this concept anew. In principle, the "dictatorship of the proletariat" is a counter concept to "dictatorship of the bourgeoisie." The latter signifies a representative (parliamentary) democracy: the democratic parliament, that was historically constituted by overthrowing the absolutist monarchy, was equal to a dictatorship of the bourgeoisie. If so, the dictatorship of the proletariat in Marx's sense cannot be any retrogression to before the dictatorship of the bourgeoisie, such as the feudal system or an absolutist domination.

Marx himself saw a concrete image of a proletariat's dictatorship in the Paris Commune. This was, in a sense, a participatory democracy, to be achieved not only in the dimension of political election but also at the actual site of the relation of production. It was both a legislative organ and an administrative organ. It had a system that not only elected but also removed judicial officers as well as administrative bureaucrats.

The real difficulty, however, was in maintaining such a system. One idea was to make both election and recall by secret ballot. But it was finally impossible to prevent bureaucratization, namely, the entrenchment of representatives, entirely by this means. As Max Weber said in his *Politik als Beruf* (1919), the bureaucratic system is inevitable and necessary in those societies where the division of labor is developed; and it cannot be discarded simple-mindedly. According to Marx, in communist society the division of labor is supposed to disappear; but, in the transitional period preceding it, the bureaucratic system as a division of labor is indispensable. For instance, the Soviets in the Russian Revolution were similar to the Paris Commune, a huge social experimentation. It eventually came to be dominated by one party (the Bolsheviks) and the bureaucratic system. Why? It will not suffice to point out the failure and betrayal of the Bolshevik leaders. In the turmoil after the war was lost, it was inevitable. The Paris Commune lasted only two months; it was crushed by government troops supported by the Prussian army. But even if it had lasted longer, it would have resulted in a similar system as Soviet Russia.

The evil of the bureaucratic system lies in its centralization of power. Here it is necessary to invent a technique to avoid that evil, instead of simply swerving away from the bureaucratic system. The only way it can be avoided, I believe, is to introduce a pure contingency into the electoral system. In the concrete, it is to introduce a lottery. Among the multiple candidates chosen by a secret voting, the representative is finally elected by lottery. The idea is to introduce contingency into the topos where power is always concentrated; entrenchment of power in administrative positions can be avoided by a sudden attack of contingency. If universal suffrage by secret ballot, namely, parliamentary democracy, is the dictatorship of the bourgeoisie, the introduction of a lottery should be deemed the dictatorship of the proletariat.

In passing, people believe that the modern representative parliament is a derivative of Athenian direct democracy, but that a direct democracy is possible only in a small community like Athens, while in the contemporary nation-states only a representative system can work. Finally, however, whether direct or indirect is not the real issue. The democracy in ancient Greece and the one under the modern representative system are two different things. The modern system of representative assembly began under the absolutist state and was "universalized" thereafter. That is to say that the representative system was not inherent in a democratic system. As Montesquieu pointed out, the essence of Athenian democracy existed not in the representative system but in the lottery system it employed to choose public officials. He said: " . . . the suffrage by lot is natural to democracy, as that by choice is to aristocracy" (*Spirit of Law*, translated by T. Nugent, New York: Hafner, 1966). In the Athenian assembly, secret voting was invented as a means of removing leaders who tended to be dictators.

Interludes

Even in direct democracies, the appearance of dictators could not be totally prevented. The secret vote, rare as it might have been, was actually used at critical conjunctures. If the technical origin of the bourgeoisie's dictatorship is from Athenian democracy, the technical origin of the proletariat's dictatorship might also be traced back to the Greek political invention—the lottery.

Nevertheless, not everything can be determined by lottery. Even in Athens, lottery was not used everywhere (i.e., in military). And today, lottery is commonly used only in choosing unpopular posts. Considering these examples, what is preferable to us would be to choose the most crucial post by lottery: first choosing three candidates by secret vote and then finally electing one by lottery. Because the last and most crucial stage is determined by contingency, factional disputes or conflicts over successors would not make sense. As a result, a relatively superior, if not the best, representative would take up the post. Furthermore, the one who is chosen could not parade his/her superiority and power, while those who are not have no reason to refuse collaboration. This kind of political technique would be functional and would go beyond the cliché, "all the power will fall."

We should not assume that the human nature of willing to power will ever disappear; that the difference of individual abilities will ever disappear. We rather think that these natures cause evil sheerly because of the institutions or the lack of understanding in them. The evils of power could be avoided by introducing a contingency (by way of lottery) in the magnetic power center. This is not in the least what is to be realized in the future; it can be fully realized at present in various institutions (corporations and government offices). Many people are troubled by bureaucratic monopolization and fixation, even more than the issues of wage and labor time.

And especially, organization for the counter-act against state and capitalism must introduce within itself the device of introducing contingency in the magnetic power center. Yet, on the other hand, various civil acts that have begun to negate power-centralist hierarchical organization remain scattered and are yet to be gathered for a collective intervention for the counter-act. If and only if we introduce the political technique above we will not have to fear centralization.

III

TRANSLATION AND MODERNITY

THE POLITICS OF TRANSLATION AND ACCOUNTABILITY: A HONG KONG STORY

The Episode

"Why in a rush?"
"Why not?"

This crisp exchange may not be alarming to an innocent ear. Yet, in the real-life situation where this occurred, in a department board meeting in a university in Hong Kong, as the retort came from the chairperson in response to a board-member's query as to the rationale of rushing an election that had not been announced as an agenda item, the exchange may well crystallize the authority often resorted to in the face of a challenge to the legitimacy of the exercise of its power. The crude manner in which power is exercised in the assertion of authority within a tertiary institution that professes commitment to liberal-arts education is revealing of the conditions in the institutional setting of universities in Hong Kong. The situation is all the more telling when the department in question is a translation department. The situation foregrounds the question of accountability to others and to oneself, which is the primary concern of translation. It thus highlights the question of the politics of translation.

LAU **Kin-chi**,
HUI **Po-keung**,
CHAN **Shun-hing**

The Politics of Translation and Accountability

In dispute was the grading of final-year translation projects in a first degree programme in translation. The chairperson rushed the election of an assessment panel that would have the final say over all project grades, that is, a panel authorized to overrule grades given by individual supervisors. In this way, the chairperson as well as the majority of the teaching staff in the department argued, "quality" could be assured and "fairness" in the assessment of students' ability could be guaranteed. However, setting up such a system of second assessment in such a way was not designed to serve the democratic purpose of answering student demands for an explication and reconsideration of the first assessment, but rather as a selective check on supervisors considered too "generous" in offering "undeserving" grades to students.[1]

This uninspiring episode of the assertion of authority might have been experienced by those involved as sailing in a stormy sea; but for those outside the storm, it is a rerun, though with a different cast and performed differently, of an old script of the colonial project: the master, a legislator as well as a judge, undertakes to guard a "tradition" by determining what counts as deviations, how deviations are to be punished, and how to ensure that following generations are like him.

Certainly, the rerun is also a re-enacting, a modulation in time. The episode is a modernized version with the cherished quality of tradition taken to be quantitatively representable in an objective assessment. It seems never to have crossed the minds of these "modern old guards" that a translation programme can be one that tries to make sense of itself, that is, to engage itself with a study of translation rather than consumed by the desire to preserve itself and guard its authority. They can only see the task of a translation programme as providing training for students to become professional translators. In fact, it is a peculiar feature of Hong Kong's tertiary institutions that many in them seem to share a similar cast of mind. Among the eight universities in Hong Kong, seven have translation programmes for undergraduate students, programmes that, as stated in their handbooks, aim to train secondary school graduates into professional translators within three years.[2]

The confinement, in the conception of a university programme held by many tertiary educators, within horizons that cannot see further than aiming to produce professionals betrays their understanding with respect to the question of education in general and university education in particular, and, in this case, their specific understanding of translation and the factors immediately related to translation. The insistence on "quality" (i.e., quantity) control and second assessment that deters teachers from relating to students as persons, whose entire learning process (rather than the product of the process alone) should be the primary concern, reveals not only the intellectual poverty of the "modern old guards" but also their inability to hold themselves accountable to others and to themselves by way of "the trace of the other in the self."[3] The state of being unaccountable reflects a state of the closure of mind, of a reluctance to risk making oneself accountable and transforming oneself.

Many in tertiary institutions do not need to be told stories of how power is abused. It is not the interest of this paper to elaborate events in particular institutions in Hong Kong, something which would require detailed accounts to do justice to the different parties involved.[4] Yet, epistemologically, it is important to understand not that such manoeuvrings are the play of the politics of power, but the conditions that make possible such unaccountability in a tertiary institution.

We here offer some details surrounding this particular dispute, and try to make sense of the underlying differences in order to broach the issues of the effects of education in general in Hong Kong, as seen in these "modern old guards" with respect to questions of translation and translation teaching. In this context, the discussion of the politics of translation is not merely a recognition of forces beyond the confines of the narrowly defined field of translation operating in the knowledge/power network, but also an intervention into the current state of affairs.

Assessment and Standardization

The department's guidelines for students doing translation projects summarize some fundamental beliefs of the "modern old guards" regarding why students should adhere to standardized language. It reads:

> You may choose to deviate from the dominant norms in exceptional circumstances. In that case it will be to [in][5] your interest to explain these circumstances and justify your strategies in a preface, and even to produce an alternative version to demonstrate that your choice of strategies is not a result of, say, a poor command of Standard Modern Chinese or an inability to comprehend the source text.
>
> An important aim of the course is to train you as professional translators. You should therefore try your best to produce a work that is publishable in the real world. This means that you must be realistic in making decisions with regard to the goals of translation, the possible venue of publication, and the identity [characteristics] of your target readers... that it is advisable for you to conform with the linguistic, literary and translational norms dominant in professional and academic circles, and that, in most cases, Standard Modern Chinese and a high degree of fidelity to the source text are expected.

The guidelines refer to "dominant norms," "Standard Modern Chinese," "conform[ing] with the linguistic, literary and translational norms dominant in professional and academic circles," and "a high degree of fidelity to the source text," in such a manner that the authority of these norms or the meaning of these terms appears to be beyond doubt. It amounts to saying that the norms are there, so students should make an effort to conform. There is no need to explain what these norms are, how such norms have come about, how they have come to be accepted or contested, and, finally, whether "conforming" is justifiable or problematic in specific cases.

The reference to "linguistic, literary and translational norms dominant in professional and academic circles" makes it appear as if it is already widely accepted what the norms are, hence they need only be mentioned and no elaboration is necessary. Scrutinizing this closely, one cannot but be amazed to find nothing other than abstract objectivism (in Volosinov's words) in this sweeping reference to "norms"; and this kind of irresponsible instruction given to students as "guidelines" is not unfamiliar in statements made by academics taking on the pretence of learnedness and the air of authority and certainty.

First of all, there are immense differences between the ways that professional and academic circles operate. The latter, commonly referred to as the ivory tower, can be insulated from what happens in the "real world." The teacher of an interpreting course may never have been a full-time practising interpreter and still teach (or claim to teach) students "professional" simultaneous interpreting. A course on legal translation may stand on its own without the students ever being taught any concept of law. A course on the "professional" translation of texts on contemporary China may still be drilling students on translating context-free sentences. Yet the claims of academic "professionalism" do not come under interrogation, and the institutional practice of having examination papers approved by an external examiner already serves the purpose of validation.

What can "linguistic, literary and translational norms dominant in academic circles" possibly mean? Linguistic norms dominant in academic circles? Literary norms dominant in academic circles? Translational norms dominant in academic circles? In real-life terms, it boils down to nothing other than what is presented or represented by individual teachers. Put bluntly, the statement instructs students to conform to the positions, tastes and methodology of their individual teachers (or the second assessors), since there is no way students can figure out what these abstract "dominant norms" might be, and because grading by their teachers (or the second assessors) is often the only criterion whereby students come to know, and often only subsequently, if they have "conformed" to the "dominant norms in academic circles."

Furthermore, what can "linguistic, literary and translational norms dominant in professional circles" possibly mean? The diversity of so-called professional circles is conveniently swept under the carpet in this formulation. Translation covers such a wide range of "professional" areas that, unless one is specific about the field, purpose, target audience, and particular context of a particular translation, there is no prescription one can give about what sort of "dominant norms" to conform to. Translating a fax-machine manual, a legal deed, a TV advertisement, or the subtitles of a movie, are tasks which differ immensely. The assumption that "in most cases, Standard Modern Chinese and a high degree of fidelity to the source text are expected" can indeed be very wrong in "professional" translation in Hong Kong. One translation graduate with a first-class honours degree who worked for Cable TV was admonished for not being "colloquial" enough in her translations of news and movie subtitling, and her supervisor complained about the remoteness of academic training from the real world. The professions related to translation and interpreting which graduates take up include newspaper editors, newspaper translators, reporters, and police and court interpreters. In most cases in these jobs, "mixed Chinese" (with a lot of Westernized Chinese and colloquial Cantonese) rather than "pure Standard Modern Chinese" is required. In the case of police and court interpreting, slang and foul language is persistently present in the every-day-life speech of witnesses and defendants. Very often, the interpreter chooses not to follow "a high degree of fidelity to the source text," and skips the foul language while interpreting. One graduate working as court interpreter came back with a story of how she was compelled to interpret a particular foul word that the defendant claimed had triggered off a fight. It would indeed be intriguing to find the "Standard Modern Chinese," or, in this particular case, the "Standard Modern English" equivalent for the curse word that the judge needed to know in order to determine if the defendant could justify his act of rage.[6]

In matters where the "modern old guards" seem to be making an effort to make themselves relevant to the business world, an other which they recognize as being worthy of their attention, their claims of practicality and professionalism are nevertheless nothing more than wishful thinking at best and at worst, deceptive devices to mislead students into submitting to their unfounded authority. With regard to those things which they consider to be within their own sphere, that is, the translation department and the translation programme, they certainly can do more than wish, provided as they are with an environment in which to act out their wishful thinking.

It is no surprise that the following episode took place, and in fact was what induced the issuing of the guidelines on translation projects. The department had a tradition of second assessment of selected translation projects, but before the rushed election in question, the practice was to allow negotiation between the student's supervising teacher and the second assessor, though even here the arbitrariness was also blatant. In this example, a supervisor gave a B+ to an English-to-Chinese translation project. The second assessor graded it D-, a barely passing grade. When challenged by the supervisor, the second assessor explained that the student in question had used Cantonese, not standard Putonghua, for a few terms such as "grandmother," "tomato" and "knee." The supervisor argued against judging a translation simply on its use of so-called "non-standard" vocabulary, contending that "standard" English was not used in the source text, Joyce Carol Oates's Christmas Night, a text narrated from the viewpoint of a small kid, with broken sentences and the so-called vulgar language of the lower classes. The supervisor further argued that the student had managed very well in capturing the rhetoricity of the source text, and that the choice of diction was based on the student's intimacy with the words. The final, negotiated grade was C, which is another instance of the arbitrariness of the "objective" grading procedure.

After this episode, the Department drew up the guidelines quoted earlier in this paper. Power operates, as indicated in the guidelines, in such a way that only certain groups (in this case students who have a potential of deviating from the dominant norms or standard usage) are required to explain their choices, whereas groups in dominant positions (those who choose to conform to so-called Standard Modern Chinese) can simply ride the waves.[7]

The episode of downgrading from B+ to D- illuminates the violence in the imposition of an abstract standard, a constant, as an instrument of control on students and teachers alike, lest any deviation upset the status quo. Dennis Carlson's words, as quoted by Marcia Moraes, are applicable here:

Since their first years in school, students are told emphatically that they have to write correctly; they have to read correctly; and they have to talk correctly. One question emerges from this context that seems particularly relevant: What does it mean to know and to be able to communicate "correctly" in a language? The meaning of correctly in schools has represented and continues to serve as a form of domination in which the standards of language are inextricably linked to the power of dominant groups... From this hegemonic process, especially in bilingual education, students are situated in a process of standardized memorization of vocabulary and grammatical correctness that does not draw upon their cultural background, their lived experiences, and their ethno-linguistic diversity. It follows, therefore, that language becomes reduced to a set of cognitive skills to be acquired in the absence of the students' social identity that delineates their ethnicity, their gender, and their class.[8]

The refusal to recognize that languages are multiple, that there are different languages for different social groups and classes, for specific communities, for different generations, and different languages for different occasions,[9] is a denial of the lived experiences of specific groups or persons. In the "from B+ to D-" episode, the D- was meted out through a deliberate dismissal of the concrete experience of the student as reader and translator, as well as the concrete experience of the narrator in the fiction, as staged by the translator in her translation. The concrete and the particular, charged with dynamic differences, constitute a threat to the "purity" of the standard and therefore must be repressed.

Translation Programmes in Hong Kong

The dispute over assessment and standardization between, for the sake of convenience, the majority and the minority in the department was constituted by and constitutive of differences with regard to what translation is, and how a first-degree programme in translation should operate. At the conceptual stage and in the initial years of the operation of this translation programme which was established in 1991, when most majority and minority members had not yet been recruited to the department, the translation programme placed its emphasis on educating students with an understanding of cross-cultural issues and competence in bilingual skills, who will be capable, on graduation, to manage on-the-job training as translators/interpreters in specific fields, or take up "generalist" jobs as journalists, teachers or administrative executives. Apart from language courses in English and Chinese, and courses on practices in code-switching, a substantial part of the programme were courses on literary, cultural, social and translation studies, including comparative literature, international relations, contemporary China and Hong Kong studies, and translation theories.

Over the years, new staff members were recruited, and differences over what the programme should encompass and how courses should be delivered surfaced and intensified, up to the point when the numeric majority sought to overhaul the existing programme. Taking advantage of the switch to a credit-based system, the majority introduced substantial changes. Whereas in the old system, the cultural and social-studies components accounted for 24 out of the minimum 66 (36%) required credits, in the new programme, they account for only 6 out of 54 (11%) required credits. Almost 90% of the required credits now go to courses defined as practical translation, interpreting, and linguistics courses. The changes were imposed through crude violence. With only a show of hands, existing courses were deleted, amidst protests by the minority over the violation of academic autonomy and the exercise of majority coercion.

The majority for its part defended the change by insisting that what defines a translation programme is precisely those so-called translation, interpreting and linguistics courses. Furthermore, they believe that these courses, being "practical," can help develop students' language proficiency, regarded as the most important factor in turning students into "professional translators." Here are some extracts that present the majority's views:

> If students do not get enough translation practice, the programme would lack credibility. [Three] clearly identifiable areas of student concern could be identified from [a] survey:
> 1. there was not enough translation practice in the current programme;
> 2. there was not enough interpreting;
> 3. there was not enough practice in speaking English.
>
> This is a question of "quality control" of graduates. Interpreting acts to strengthen one's translation skills. Students often don't have the time to devote sufficient time to these courses because of pressures from other courses.
>
> Interpreting helped students improve their language skills... Translation Theory... did not have much practical use for students, so had been made a free elective.[10]

Thus, while making more interpreting courses compulsory, courses like "Translation Theory" or the "History of Translation" are made optional. But in this apparently practical turn, instead of giving due attention to the inter-cultural and interdisciplinary nature of the practice of translation, the increased vocational orientation paradoxically results in what practical translation intends to avoid: consigning oneself to the impractical and the irrelevant.

Let us for a moment take a "pragmatic" approach by looking at the correlation between training and employment, and see how deceptive the claims of "practical" vocational training may be. According to the Graduate Employment Survey conducted by this university, the figures for its 1993, 1995 and 1997 translation programme graduates being employed as translators or interpreters were, respectively, 56%, 22% and 4%, whereas those employed as personnel/administrative/management executives were, respectively, 0%, 20% and 25% (the 1993 graduates were diploma programme graduates). The employment survey of translation graduates of other universities shows similar trends. A polytechnic-school-turned-university had over half its diploma graduates for both 1993 and 1994 employed as translators and interpreters; yet in 1995, when it graduated both diploma and degree programme students, less than one-third took up jobs as translators and interpreters. For another university which graduated its first two batches of about 50 translation degree holders in 1994 and 1995, less than 5% of the graduates worked in translation and interpreting.

The figures show that a smaller and smaller percentage of graduates of translation programmes (especially degree programmes) are actually employed in the field of specialized study that they are trained for. The figures may be interpreted in different ways. Contextualized in the specific sociopolitical situation of Hong Kong of the early nineties, the introduction of a large number of degree programmes was part of a sudden rapid expansion of tertiary education in the run-up to the 1997 transfer of sovereignty. For the seven government-funded tertiary institutions, their first-year intake of first-degree students increased from a total of 7,417 in 1989-90, to 12,090 in 1992-93, to 15,070 in 1995-96. This means that within six years, the intake more than doubled. The percentage of the relevant age group (ages 17 to 20) provided with first-year, first-degree places increased from 8.8% in 1989-90, to 15% in 1992-93, to 17.8% in 1995-96. Research postgraduates also increased from 729 in 1989-90, to 1,943 in 1992-93, and to 2,953 in 1995-96, a fourfold increase.[11] Whether this is read as the conspiracy of the colonial government to produce more people educated in the British colonial heritage, or as a response to an expanding demand for an educated labour force in the age of globalization, the expansion may be seen as offering more opportunities for further study for high-school graduates. Yet this also poses a problem: though the degree programmes may profess to train specialists or professionals in specific fields, a large number of graduates are not employed in their own or even in related fields, and this trend seems to be aggravating.

Thus, in this particular social context, even for pragmatic reasons, a translation programme that focuses primarily on technical skills training is neither sound nor relevant. But there are more important, structural reasons that a translation programme, if it is to be a sensible one, cannot be conceived reductively and abstractly in terms of the learning of technical skills, and this question will be dealt with later on in this paper.

Before going into that, it must be mentioned that such simplistic and complacent assertion about translation and the teaching of translation may well be one of the effects of education in general in Hong Kong on both teachers and students. The massive increase in university enrolments means that the education system can no longer avoid confronting the effects of its own working by rejecting as failures those who are made in it and in fact reflect the very truth of the system itself. That is, the bilingual education system of Hong Kong has consistently failed to deliver what it promises while it has all along been very successful in preventing the majority of students from benefiting from it. This means that universities have now to admit a great number of students who are still far from having a reasonable command of reading and writing skills in both languages, English and Chinese.

Obviously, it would be almost impossible to turn a student with a poor command of English into a professional fluent in spoken and written English in three years, regardless of what curriculum is offered, not to mention enabling students to learn through researching, posing questions that direct a research, and questioning the questions they tend to pose, i.e., to learn to learn as what university education should consist of. It is indeed unimaginable that a degree programme in translation does not bother about theoretical as well as historical questions of translation, despite the fact that translation practice in Hong Kong was obviously the "child of [British] imperialism."[12] The presumptuous pragmatism and impatient instrumentalism may be another of the "Hong Kong characteristics." The design and delivery of translation programmes, the emphasis in examination on assessing students against an abstract measure to assure quality control, and the naive understanding of both translation and language all raise important questions concerning the state of Hong Kong's education in general, the conception of education and university, the question of the study of translation and language, and, last but not least, the question of the intellectuals.

Education in Hong Kong

The common practice of stressing professional training within Hong Kong's tertiary institutions may give one the impression that they are yielding to pressure from business and professional circles. However, the complicity between the commercial world and academia is more complicated than it appears. In fact, agreement between the two is very much confined within the verbal horizon, as the recent controversy over the urge to revamp Hong Kong's education system as a whole reveals.

In September 1999, the Education Commission set up by the government to study how to reform Hong Kong's education system published a report. Addressing the question of the success of the education system in serving the business sector, Professor Cheng Kai-ming, a commission member and Hong Kong University's pro-vice-chancellor, had the following comments:[13]

> We have the money, our infrastructure is good and our students are not bad. Then how come when they graduate, they can't compete and do their jobs competently?... Surely the elite the system has tried to produce has not made the grade... The knowledge and skills this elite possesses may be relevant this year but outdated the next... Many of our most adept students and professionals pick up their skills on their own in spite of, not because of, their education.

As for the reason the education system has fallen into such a sordid state, the Commission confirms the conclusion reached long ago by many, that is, that the system has itself to blame in contributing to its own demise. Simply put, the legacy of Hong Kong's education system is that of a colonial education which depended on an examination-based system for the production of the ruling elite of the colonial government. Thus Cheng Kai-ming said in the reform proposal:

> The examination is the heart and soul of the current system. Without examinations, teachers won't know what to

teach, students what to study and school principals how to be principals.

To cope with the demands of examinations, both teachers and students are forced to adopt rote-based learning, as the sole aim of studying becomes practically geared to passing examinations. Cheng Kai-ming described succinctly the sordid state of learning in these words:

> The present system confines studies to a structured examination syllabus. That which is not in the syllabus is not taught, and that which is not taught is not studied.

In fact, this legacy developed over a time when intellectual learning and critical thought were negative factors in seeking success even for the elite. It may be of interest to quote the Burney Report of 1935, a time when university education was limited to a very small, elite minority:

> The schools are also criticized for being too examination oriented, for giving students insufficient knowledge of Chinese, and for providing insufficient ability in English so that students need special help when they enter Hong Kong University and are unable to cope with the demands of spoken English in the business world....[14]

Alarms about the education system have been sounded time and again over the years, with similar observations about the detrimental effects of an examination-based system. The expansion of tertiary education in the early nineties was championed as a breakthrough in Hong Kong's education. However, the results appear to be far from satisfactory. In view of the pressure coming from drastic and rapid change in the world, with life more and more extensively and intensively organized on the basis of fast-growing knowledges and technologies, the Education Commission, in the last few months of the twentieth century, put forward the slogan "Learning for Life" as the aim of the educational reform, despite the fact that this slogan has been promulgated by the UNESCO for many years.

Another high-level figure also testified to the outdatedness of the legacy in showing his support of the proposal. Professor Chung Yueping, dean of the education faculty at the Chinese University of Hong Kong, said tellingly, "Our employers are no longer looking for cheap labourers who are obedient. They expect staff to have creativity, team-working ability and a tolerance of different ideas."[15] In a similar vein, a survey of the views of 194 employers showed that the qualities in the younger generation where employers would most like to see an improvement are a sense of responsibility (84.5%), interpersonal communication skills (42.8%), mastery over work-related skills (40.7%), and ability for independent thinking (36.1%). Language competence (30.9%) and writing ability (19.6%) ranked only fifth and seventh.[16]

The above criticisms of Hong Kong's education come from people with influence on policies and decisions that affect Hong Kong society differentially. These are people that the "modern old guards" would like to identify with, for they preside from their positions of authority over the maintenance of standards and norms without which "quality control" would become impossible. The message from the educational reform proposal is clear: the tradition the "modern old guards" seek to guard and thereby (wittingly or unwittingly) reproduce through the assertion of their authority is the tradition of an elitist, examination-based system that demands rote-based learning from students, and, further, that is already an obsolete system judging from its failure to produce professionals meant for various sectors of society.

Standard Languages in Hong Kong

In promoting the reproduction of a system in which they reside among the small number of "successes," as against the majority of students failed by the system, the "modern old guards" stress the importance of examination and assessment methods that judge a student by the finished product rather than attending to the learning process. In this, the standardized use of language is a key factor. The argument for acquiring language proficiency through the mastering of the standard language in fact is a translation of the training for success in examinations into the training to be a professional translator, with learning a standard language taking the place of learning model answers. As a model answer is supposed to stand on its own, a standard language is also supposed to be context-free. This partly explains how it is possible for the "modern old guards" to think that language proficiency can be learned by way of model examples, that is, as a universal capability. However, in maintaining such a position of authority, they not only slide into the indefensible position of abstract objectivism through the disavowal of their own experience of language, they also seem to be oblivious of the growing recognition of the untenability of such a stance within the educational sector.

In Hong Kong, after the change of sovereignty in 1997, the educational policy of "two languages and three tongues" (the former being English and Chinese and the latter English, Putonghua and Cantonese) was implemented through an educational reform instigated in 1998-99 in which mother-tongue teaching was generally promoted in secondary schools. In a go, amidst protests from teachers and parents, over 300 schools (a fivefold increase from the previous 70 or so schools) adopted Chinese as the medium of instruction. The 114 schools granted the permission to continue with English as the medium of instruction came to be regarded as providing a better quality education. After a year, support from school principals for the government Chinese language policy reportedly dropped from 85% to 65%.[17]

The official recognition of Cantonese as a "tongue" to be used as the medium of instruction is in reality not so much a drastic turn. Before the reform, although English was officially the medium of instruction, most classes were actually conducted in Cantonese. A survey showed that even in the University of Hong Kong, which is supposed to use English as the medium of instruction, half of classes in some courses were conducted in Cantonese.[18] Thus, the belated educational reform may be read as a formal recognition of the actual pattern of language-use in Hong Kong.[19]

While some may hasten to claim that a process of de-colonization is rolling along, judging from the implementation and timing of the new education language policy, it may still be too early to determine if this is more a gesture than the beginning of a profound transformation. If one traces the history of Chinese-language education in Hong Kong's colonial history, one may be astonished to find that the British were not always antagonistic to the idea of Chinese-language education. Alastair Pennycook documents the changes in policies of the colonial government with regard to English and Chinese education in the late nineteenth and early twentieth century, and sees the debates and policies within the ruling bloc as responses to the events of this tumultuous period, such as the 1911 revolution in China, the 1917 revolution in Russia, or the 1925-27 massive strike and boycott of British goods in Hong Kong.[20] For example, faced with the 1925-27 strike, the British stressed careful monitoring of vernacular education along with intervention in the Chinese school curriculum:

> In such a system great stress should be laid on the ethics of Confucianism which is, in China, probably the best antidote to the pernicious doctrines of Bolshevism, and is certainly the most powerful conservative course, and the greatest influence for good.... Money spent on the development of the conservative ideas of the Chinese race in the minds of the young will be money well spent, and also constitutes social insurance of the best kind.[21]

This impulse led to the establishment of the Chinese Department at the University of Hong Kong and a new government-run Chinese secondary school. About half a century later, in 1974, Chinese was made an official language, while English of course remains dominant in the government, economics and the judiciary. Hence, it cannot be simplistically deduced that the introduction of Chinese language is necessarily a major step in de-colonization. It must also be noted that so-called Standard Modern Chinese (based on spoken Putonghua) mostly represents the assertion of national unity and sovereignty, and control from the centre. While Cantonese is recognized as an important medium of instruction, students using Cantonese in written form are penalized (remember the case of the student using Cantonese terms for "grandmother," "tomato" and "knee" and almost receiving a failing grade with the second assessor).

The crux of the problem thus lies not in which language is recognized, but in the insistence on upholding standard languages and the disavowal and denial of historical contingencies embedded in the standardization and normalization of the languages. bell hooks sees language as a site of struggle and standard English as the "oppressor's language";[22] Pennycook traces "Standard English" as largely a product of nineteenth-century British colonial expansion, specifically the adoption of mass, standard education and language teaching in order to effectively control workers, to reduce the potential for labour unrest, as well as to increase the acceptability of British goods in the colonies. He notes that the written form of Standard English originates from selectively chosen literary canons and that the spoken form derives from the dialect of the southern public school in Britain during the Victorian period. How this "Standard English" developed from the language of a specific group to acquire its "standard" status is by and large a historical contingency which reveals both the inequality of and contention for power among different groups.[23]

Similarly, Standard Modern Chinese is also based on a specific local dialect (one close to the Beijing dialect) and is likewise a product of historical construction. So Yiucheong traces the tortuous paths that vernacular Chinese has taken in the past century and the ways the so-called Standard Modern Chinese normalizes the incorporation of Europeanized syntax and diction and other hybrid elements in the contending discourses of the building of a national identity, the quest for modernization, and the promotion of class struggle and revolution.[24] His genealogy of the absorption (and disavowal) of Europeanized diction and syntax in the standardization of Modern Chinese offers an interesting glimpse into the larger question of the confrontations (and effects of confrontations) of China with global forces of domination in the past century.

A de-colonization project involves the countering of the subjectivization function of language by scrutinizing how the notion of language has been de-historicized and thus turned ahistorical and objective, and how standard languages remain hegemonic with institutional backing. Take again translation for illustration. Just as in studying for an examination in a subject, that subject is taken to be already unproblematically given, training to become a translator similarly presupposes translation as self-evidently an act of bringing what is said in one language, the source language, unquestioningly taken to be a "standard language," into another language, the target language which must also be a "standard language" as required by the profession (read here: examination). Deviation from the "standard target language" must be accounted for. The emphasis on "accountability" in translating and safeguarding the "credibility" of the translation programme quoted earlier can now be understood as requirements stipulated within a system now deemed to be obsolete by the professional world. In other words, the wishful thinking, the stipulation of abstract norms and standards premised on a notion of language described by Volosinov as abstract objectivism that "does not correspond to any real moment in the historical process of becoming… [that] exists only with respect to the subjective consciousness of individuals belonging to some particular community governed by norms,"[25] can only be possible under the umbrella of an institutional setting which is not accountable in the first place.

The Politics of Translation

> "Why in a rush?"
> "Why not?"

The retort is exemplary in revealing that the institution of a system, rule or course of action is founded on a situated decision that cannot be accounted for within the system or by the rule instituted.

To the question "Why in a rush?" which, as a question, asks the respondent to be accountable, that is, to offer an account, an answer, an explication of the reasons, the response is a refusal of accountability: "Why not?" The retort, if taken literally, is to shovel accountability back to the person who asks the question; it may be a step taken with the will to continue a dialogic relation. Yet in the situation under consideration, this retort cannot be taken in its innocent, logical sense—e.g., "what would be the reasons for delaying?"—and can be read only as a rhetorical move to cut short a dialogic relation, a refusal to account for the decision to rush the election, the procedures of which were already underway. The refusal thus poses itself as so fully justified that no more words are needed for an explanation. As such it is a disavowal of the ethico-political nature of any decision to institute something new, for the decision cannot pretend to be made on objective and disinterested scientific ground. Neither can it appeal to any self-evident, transcendental principle. It is this condition that reveals that decisions are made in a world charged with relations of power fraught with dynamics of domination, under specific circumstances, and from a certain position embedded in a system of values and practices.

"Why not?" is a refusal in this case for it is posed as a rhetorical question directed at an Other.[26] But "Why not?" may also be posed reflexively, in which case it will carry the rhetorical force of opening the issue for consideration again, in the recognition that no definite answer, whether a yes or a no, can fully account for itself on its own to all parties involved. Any decision made must be the outcome of a process of negotiation, that is, be ethico-politically made.

However, the decision made in a specific situation is also an ethico-political decision made possible with the termination of the process of negotiation, and is thus haunted by what it represses in the first place, and hence must be made again and again, each time confronted by the return of the repressed. To deny the ethico-political nature of the decision by presenting it as justifiable in terms of objective, neutral and even universal norms and values is to disavow the Other repressed in, yet constitutive of, the decision. Such denial and disavowal, concealed by the representation of knowledge and truth as objective and rational in terms of an understanding of necessary conditions, is at the same time a denial and disavowal of one's complicity with the dominant power. As Foucault's analysis of power shows, "intellectuals, as bearers of the speaking positions allowed within the social regime of truth, are themselves agents and beneficiaries of this system of power."[27] It is the task of intellectuals to engage with this system of power even in the midst of one's complicity with it, not so as to facilitate its maintenance and expansion, but in ways that contribute to forces working for its transformation. It is in this spirit that we have taken up the episode cited in the beginning for examination, both as teachers and as translators, as an intervention into the state of teaching and understanding translation in Hong Kong. The intervention is, following Foucault, based on "the recognition that discourse is implicated in the general regime of power in society,"[28] and that discursive practice is one of the fields effective in the constitution of the configuration of culture, knowledge and power through the assigning of subject positions in the institution of a network of power relations that enables the perpetuation of the prevailing dominant power bloc.

Non-discursive practices, such as training for examination, constitute the other field in the precipitation of a self enabling the formation of seemingly self-reproducing patterns of relations in the configuration of culture, knowledge and power. In short, the institution of a new programme can simply be the product of the articulation of habitual ways of relating to others and getting things done with a particular discourse or a body of discursive elements strategically appropriated from various discourses. The condition for the naturalization of such articulation is that the subject positions assigned to the enunciating subject (the person producing utterances in a specific context) do not allow the space for a practice of the self in which the normal course of action or train of thought is allowed to be disrupted or deviated from. Yet it is only in such disruption and deviation that the other can figure forth in the demand for accountability.

As we have tried to show, the dominant practice in the translation department is a reluctance to account for themselves. In fact, they cannot do so even if they try, for they are speaking from positions guaranteed by an education system that is not even accountable to the professional world it claims to be mainly serving. What they have in fact been doing is a translation of training for examination into training to be a translator. For the facilitation of such a translation, they appropriate an instrumental notion of translation and a convenient and abstract notion of language as standard, leaving no room for the accountability of any assigned subject position. Its claim to being professional, scientific and objective amounts to a dismissive refusal to engage with the relations among culture, knowledge and power.

Borrowing from Henry Giroux's discussion of the contribution of cultural studies to the critical reflection on education, as teachers we must first reject "the assumption that teachers are simply transmitters of existing configurations of knowledge."[29] We must do this in order to disrupt the above unchallenged understanding of translation among mainstream educators and the majority of students, both having run the gauntlet of the elitist examination-based education system and having been scarred in different ways and degrees by it.

The belated acknowledgement by the Education Commission, in its proposals for educational reform, of the destructive practices in the education system is at least a sign of the opening up to change. However, the slogan "Learning for Life" championed by the Commission is still premised on the notion of conformism, that is, it assumes that new situations call for new forms of conformism. Rather than simply confining ourselves to equipping students to better conform to new demands, we believe that teachers, as intellectuals situated within the system of power which elicits their complicity, can go one step further. In the words of Joe Murphy, by giving

> students sensibility to understand economic, political and historical forces so they're not just victims of these forces but can act on them with effect. Giving [students, especially the poor] this power is a threatening idea to many. But it is essential to the health of a democratic society.[30]

If a standard language cannot be as "pure" and innocent as it pretends to be; if language is a multiplicity charged with contesting and even dominating relations of power; if language is not a mere tool of representation, but rather the site where relations of domination and resistance play themselves out; and furthermore, if language is not governed by logic as the identity politics of a standard must presuppose, the implications for translation are disturbing. For then translation is not free of the politics of representation, and in translating, one participates in a process charged with struggles precipitated in history. The materiality or life of language is perceptively described by Bakhtin as follows:

> [A]ll words have the "taste" of a profession, a genre, a tendency, a party, a particular work, a particular person, a generation, an age group, the day and

hour. Each word tastes of the context and contexts in which it has lived its socially charged life.[31]

Furthermore,

[A]t any given moment of its historical existence, language is heteroglot from top to bottom: it represents the co-existence of socio-ideological contradictions between the present and the past, between differing epochs of the past, between different socio-ideological groups in the present, between tendencies, schools, circles and so forth... Each of these "languages" of heteroglossia required a methodology very different from the others... All languages of heteroglossia, whatever the principle underlying them and making each unique, are specific points of view on the world, forms for conceptualizing the world in words, specific world views, each characterized by its own objects, meanings and values.[32]

If it is the life of language to be multiple (or heteroglot in Bakhtin's term), the maintaining of an abstract standard language must suppress this awareness by representing the standard language as preexisting, and always there, as if without a history, in the dictionary and canonized works, for an investigation into the history of a standard language would very soon reveal the arbitrariness of the authority of the standard language, that is, it does not have the legitimacy it claims to have.

The simplistic manner in which the "modern old guards" adhere to the assertion of *the* standard language, with the amazing fact that they even fail to put forward a more workable and defendable notion of standard languages which correspond to the complexity of the contemporary professional world, betrays the fact that the notion of the standard language is serving a different function than aiming to correspond to the actual functioning of the world. Rather than serving to guarantee quality in the production of would-be-professionals, it simply functions as the barely disguised device for the imposition of brute authority.

Standard language and control work for one another. In fact, it is the structure of a desire to control the Other in the constitutive relation between the self and the Other that accounts for the naïve assertion of the normative authority of *the* standard language. The desire to control is basically an expansionist structure and can only maintain itself by constructing more rules and mechanisms of control. In the case we are discussing, the "modern old guards" even go to the extreme of subjecting themselves to the control of the administration whose business is to control.

In resorting to more regulation by administrative and managerial rules, the "modern old guards" are in fact inventing more rules with which to bind both students and themselves. They constantly quote rules and regulations to justify their deeds, while new rules and regulations are being drawn up ad hoc to cover complex situations. Deadlines for student submission of papers or projects are strictly adhered to, with different penalties for different degrees of lateness of submission clearly delineated. There has even been discussion of which hour of the day the deadline should fall on. A near-hysterical control over examination marks is carried out. Imagine an academic with a calculator in hand, in an examiners' board meeting, instructing the teacher of each course to bring down the percentage of students with a B+ or above to within 10% of the total number of students -- only to find out afterwards that a wrong table had been used as reference, that up to 20% of students could have received an A- or above in individual courses according to the university's guidelines. Yet the grossly unjust penalization of students, which caused over 90% of students to graduate with a second-class lower-division honours or below (while the university's guidelines call for 20-30% of students to graduate with second-class upper-division honours or higher), need not be accounted for or redressed.

Whether wittingly or unwittingly, the "modern old guards" are seeking to control administratively through their brute imposition of authority the marking of students, a practice to which they were being subjected when they were students and which produced them as the successful ones. Academically, they seek to control through the imposition of the brute authority of *the* standard language which a student can only learn piecemeal when they are told that they have deviated from a norm. Thus, they are enabled by a system, or rather sub-system, of control, that is itself neither willing nor capable of risking responsibility, to perpetuate that system. The price of such "success" is that they become mediocre-elite-in-power with a closed mind that can see no further than self-preservation through controlling and subduing the Other. By means of invoking words such as "fairness," "objective assessment," "standard," "professional quality," "linguistic proficiency or competence," and the like, they disavow their implication in a system of power, in our case, a system operating with crude techniques of control, and hence the question of politics in general of institutions and the question of the politics of translation in particular.

As we are also part of the teaching machine, we are also in complicity with the system of power in our participation in the role of assessor and examiner, not to mention the game of truth for the preparation of students for surviving in the competitive professional world. Thus it is our task as intellectuals to engage the system of power in critique as an intervention into our complicity. The interrogation of the institutional setting necessarily constitutes for us part of the politics of translation which, in our case, comprises the politics of teaching translation.

As we have been arguing, the "modern old guards" as teachers of translation maintain their authority partly by means of the invocation of an imaginary standard language that only exists performatively, i.e., through the act of interdiction inflicted on students for their supposed deviation from a "norm," irrespective of the question of representation. However, if langauge is a dynamic field, rather than a passive instrumental medium, in which domination and resistance are inextricably woven together, the question of representation and its politics must be taken seriously in the teaching and doing of translation.

In our Hong Kong story, we have been trying to sketch, in quite a preliminary way, the context that is suffocating for any conscientious dialogue about translation and the teaching of translation, not to mention the active engagement in taking the question of the politics of translation seriously.

Instead of leaving us dispirited, this situation makes us feel all the more obliged to attempt to open up a space for more constructive discussion and collaborative intervention. In fact, what we have outlined so far can be regarded as suggested directions for more substantive and extensive researches, such as the effects of schooling experience we can read in various sectors of the professional world and the government with regard to their ways of relating to things and to one another, both conceptually and practically. Another area of research would be the various disruptive responses resisting or deviating from specific relations of domination. Here, in view of the dominant practice around us, we think it appropriate to begin the discussion of the politics of translation by pointing to a sensitivity of language that is soaked in the dynamics of life. For doing that we think Gilles Deleuze's and Gayatri Spivak's discussion of rhetoricity and the minor use of a major language can be very helpful.

Rhetoricity: minor use and resistance

In Daniel Smith's reading of Deleuze, the standard as an ideal constant determines a relation of domination between the majority and the minority, designations which do not reflect quantitative differentiations, but rather a relational differentiation of power. Thus the model made up of designations such as "white, Western, male, adult, reasonable, heterosexual, residing in cities speaking a standard language…" represents the norm, and "any determination that deviates from this axiomatic model, by definition and regardless of number, will be considered minoritarian."[33] While "the majority is in fact an abstract standard that constitutes the analytic fact of 'Nobody,'"

> [a] minority by definition has no model; *it is itself a becoming or a process*, in constant variation, and the power of a minority is not measured by its ability to enter and make itself felt within the majority system. Minorities have the potential of promoting compositions (connections, convergences, divergences) that do not pass by way of the

capitalist economy any more than they do the state formation.³⁴

The standard is the rule of the majority represented in the rule of law. A minority of course has to struggle to be written into the constitution, but that is not where its power lies. The standard, the majority, the norm, the representative and the typical are what are normally represented; and publishing institutions, the media, academia, state institutions and business circles play crucial roles in their circulation. Thus the first question in the politics of translation should be, in Spivak's words, "What is it that you are making accessible? The accessible level is the level of abstraction where the individual is already formed, where one can speak individual rights."³⁵ In other words, the making accessible of a text through translation already involves entering into the sphere of the majority where, for the translator, the publishing institutions or the relevant body that commissions the translation are the immediate force of seduction determining one's complicity with the majority. For example, for a market-oriented economy, being readable and consumable is of course a crucial consideration guiding translation practice. Similarly, large official bodies, from national governments to international political bodies, large corporations including publishing, and specialized bodies such as universities and chemical and engineering firms, are often confined to working within the boundaries defined by a certain rule or model. These are forces of seduction for staying on the "safe" side, that is, to go along with the majority. In view of this, Spivak stresses that:

> I remain interested in writers who are against the current, against the mainstream. I remain convinced that the interesting literary text might be precisely the text where you do not learn what the majority view of majority cultural representation of self-representation of a nation state might be.³⁶

What Spivak points to here is not simply an unproblematic identification with the position of the minority, for majority and minority are relational terms, making the relation between the two a tricky one.

First of all the minority always relates to the majority as belonging together in sharing a major language as a condition of daily existence. Thus the point is not to exclude oneself from the major language, but, as bell hooks says, to use the oppressor's language, not simply for the purpose of survival, but also as the medium for various minority groups to build solidarity in their struggles against oppression. In other words, a major language always contains in itself the relation between the majority and the minority. As Spivak says, "Cultures... have a dominant sphere in its traffic with language and contingency."³⁷ This contingency is a line of flight where a minor use of the major language is possible: "Only the possibility of setting up a minor practice of major language from within allows one to define popular literature, marginal literature, and so on."[38] Together, contingency and the minor use of the major language constitute the specificities of the language, which are all lost in the standardized language.

Accountability in the practice of translation does not allow one to content oneself with the prevailing standard use of a language, for the acquisition of language is a formative process of individuals in the fashioning of social identities and the securing of specific forms of authority to which the individual is subjected. On the one hand, power cannot circulate without the institutionalization of "standards," standards which constitute the structure one cannot but inhabit. On the other hand, the institutionalization of "standards" is historically embedded in a process of the assertion of authority and its contestation. Historical research, that is, research into the history of the language and the history of the author's moment, as well as the history of the language the translator employs in the translation, can enable a glimpse into the relation of forces in the determination of what is said and the way it is said, allowing one to go beyond the assumption of an intending subject using language (conveniently understood as a standard language) as a tool. In other words, if language is not composed of ready-made standards, but rather is engaged in a process of becoming, as Bakhtin and Deleuze teach us, then language cannot be exhausted by the meaning. Whatever "standard" and "meaning" we ascribe to language, they are not only slippery, but very often also in tension with one another, with the "standard" often turning out to be empty, not meaning anything, while the "meaning" often overflows any formulaic expression.

Following from this, accountability in translation cannot be understood in terms of correct standard usage and the adequate transfer of content. Accountability demands not only taking note of the negotiation involved in the dialectic between the imposition of authority and the corresponding resistance in the constitution of the self/Other relation. It also requires taking note of the contingencies in the process of becoming, contingencies that cannot be understood in terms of purposeful and rational maneuvers. This calls for a different relation to the language of the text than merely learning the language quickly or merely being able to conduct a conversation in it.

Spivak, in her discussion of the politics of translation in the context of the feminist movement, points to the danger of inserting the Eurocentric concern with individual rights and "a species of neocolonialist construction of the non-Western scene" in the translation of a third world woman's text when an intimate relation to that third-world language is lacking, and translation is taken to be transferring content. For Spivak, without making any effort for oneself to be intensely involved in the other language, so that one may sometimes even prefer to talk about intimate things or discuss complicated issues in that language, without questioning oneself the way one is representing the other, one would be committing dubious politics even if one thinks that one is honouring the other's right by representing her or him through translation.[39]

The instrumental approach to language in translation has the political implication of attempting to control the other and of remaining inscribed within the discursive practice in the construction of colonial relations between the self and the Other. In fact, one cannot control the other if one cannot control the self; hence the instrumental approach to language works for both the source language and the target language. In contrast, in order to give up control of the language which seeks to render otherness, the incomprehensible, manageable in terms of the meaningful and the communicable, one must go beyond logic and court the language by "hanging out," earning the right to be intimate with it. That is, rather than relating to language as a formal structure that necessarily presupposes language to be an instrument for the representation of logical relations in an ideal world, language is seen as an everyday life practice in which rhetorical force has priority over logic. The rhetorical use of language not only points to the specificity of the historical, social and cultural context without attention to which the rhetorical force would be lost, it also points to the limits of language, the possibility of absolute contingency.

From the point of view of logic, meaning is stable and definite: an identity. From the point of view of rhetoric, meaning is only the effect of rhetorical force in a specific context. For rhetoric to be effective it cannot have meaning as identity. Its life is in the production of effects in linguistic performance rather than the transfer of meaning. Thus, contradictions and juxtapositions of apparently unrelated items not admissible to logic can have rhetorical force in specific situations. On the one hand, language must be more or less stable and definite ("iterable" in Derrida's words), for it to be in circulation among people addressing one another. On the other hand, we have rhetoric, which makes itself felt in the disruption of the "logical systematicity" of language. As Derrida and Wittgenstein teach us, though it is, even if minimally, a condition of language's performativity, logic can only be the effects of language's rhetorical nature. Discursively speaking, the tension between the force of control of logic and the disruption of this force constitutes the life of language:

> The jagged relationship between rhetoric and logic, condition and effect of knowing, is a relationship by which a world is made for the agent, so that the agent can act in an ethical way, a political way, a day-to-day way; so that the agent can be alive, in a human way, in the world.[40]

Thus, rather than seeking to instrumentally control the text to be translated, the practice of translation is first of all a reading, a close and intimate reading that is attentive to the disruption harboured in the text. At the same time, it is also an engagement with one's present, translating the disruptive force into a destabilising potential against the domination of the standard. Certainly, no fast-food approach to language can enable one to familiarize oneself with a language to such an extent. However, even this degree of familiarization is still on the level of the meaningful effects of the becoming of language. For Spivak, the politics of translation in relation to the other requires us to go further; for the level of the meaningful effects remains within the efforts to contain the simple possibility that something might not be meaningful, that is, it remains within the discursivity of language, where individual identities are constituted. The rhetorical force cannot be autogenous: "Rhetoric must work in the silence between and around words in order to see what works and how much."[41] The silence, the magma of life or being, or "the subindividual force-fields of being,"[42] is the field where absolute contingency rules over the production of the effects of identities. The silence as magma is concretely material, specific and multiple. It is the difference naming the limits of language, which is very much active, working together with logic and rhetoric, in the production of the text.

Spivak calls logic, rhetoric and silence the three-tiered notion of the performativity of language. For a translation to be responsible, that is, responsive even to silence, to the other as absolute alterity, the translator must be able to court the language so intimately that translation is realized as the most intimate act of reading. For it is in such a relation of surrendering to the text, the other, that one can earn the right to surrender one's identity and the stake of the claim to identity in controlling the other. It is only by being attentive to "the three-part staging of (agency in) language,"[43] that we can take note of the minor use of a major language in the negotiation with the authority of the standard. And as Spivak also says, the dominant group's "way of handling the three-part ontology of language has to be learned as well—if the subordinate ways of rusing with rhetoric are to be disclosed."[44]

This nuanced attention to language, rather than parroting empty words that both confirm and conceal relations of domination, is a recognition that translation is an intellectual activity within a context structured by domination and hegemonic practices. It is also a critique of, borrowing Paul Bové's words,

> the intellectual and pedagogical inertia and irresponsibility of those very common professorial figures who not only fearfully mock serious intellectual practice as "theory" but retire into the semiemployment of their "teaching," "scholarship," and above all "administration," safely away from hard work, the public-intellectual sphere, and the intransigent political and cultural issues facing our society.[45]

Against the pretension to innocence of parroting that barely conceals its crude imposition of authority, being attentive to language is also a response to the increasingly urgent task confronting intellectuals today. Borrowing again from Bové, this is the recognition that we are living "in an age that increasingly exercises both hegemony and domination in and through sign-based structures,"[46] that is,

> In an information-based society that relies increasingly on the manipulation of symbols, signs, and testing data to control and exploit political and economic opportunities—often to the detriment of less powerfully placed people at home and abroad.[47]

Thus, it is all the more important for translation to be seen as a multiple attentive reading by intellectuals who would confront themselves in committing to painstakingly mapping out the resistance of minor uses in the process of uncovering the dominant's ways of deploying language and by so doing effecting a disarming of its framing power.

Endnotes

1—The department's guidelines of 1999 say, "You should also note that your work might be subject to second assessment. The practice of last year was that all projects graded B or above by the supervisor were assigned a second assessor."

2—Traditional elite universities such as the University of Hong Kong, which introduced a bachelor's degree in translation in 1974, emphasized literary studies in a curriculum including minimal technical translation. "Practical translation," meaning translation in practice, was mostly limited to literary translation and appreciation of translations of classical texts. The polytechnics and colleges offered diploma programmes in translation, with emphasis on the translation of government, media and business documents. With their upgrading into universities in the early nineties, more undergraduate degree programmes in translation have been introduced. This, however, coincided with a trend toward vocational courses in university curricula. It may be interesting to note that the generation of government translators (those with the title of Chinese Language Officers under the colonial government, and even after the 1997 transition; Chinese having been made an official language in 1974) and police and court interpreters recruited before the late seventies were mostly secondary school graduates, with neither university education nor any formal training in translation and interpreting.

3—Gayatri Chakravorty Spivak, *Outside in the Teaching Machine* (New York and London: Routledge Press, 1993), 179.

4—Specific accounts of other similar episodes of procedural violence or suppression of difference are not quoted here, but these likewise constitute the material forces enabling the crude settling of intellectual differences.

5—The words in parenthesis are revisions added to the guidelines when they were reissued in 1999-2000.

6—It is tempting here to cite one other episode, also a story recounted by a fresh graduate working as a court interpreter. In a case in which a woman was charged with illegal hawking, on hearing the woman describe her background and how she had suffered the harassment of the hawker-control squad, the graduate could not stop sobbing and hence could not perform her duties as an interpreter. Could this be read as a "high degree of fidelity to the source text" in that she had already faithfully performed her interpreting for the hawker woman?

7—A related episode also illustrates the dominant group's evasion of any responsibility to explain their actions. To exert further control over the grades, there was the rushed "election" of the assessment panel with final say. Soon afterwards, the same supervisor awarded another student's project a B, a grade which the assessment panel lowered to a B-. When the supervisor appealed, the panel responded by further downgrading the project to C+. No explanation was given to the supervisor, nor was his opinion about the student's performance or his grading criteria ever sought. When the supervisor asked for an explanation from the panel convenor, the latter said he was not responsible and recommended that the complainant write to the department head, which the supervisor did. Despite repeated enquiries, there was never any written or verbal response, and he was not given an opportunity to argue the case. In yet another instance, despite the university's rule that students' appeals on examinations results receive the subject teacher's signature on the appeal form, the translation department decided to uphold the same grades in several appeal cases, without consulting the subject teachers concerned or even requesting their signatures. Such changes in procedures had never been formally adopted at any department board meeting, nor had staff or students been notified of a procedural change.

8—Marcia Moraes *Bilingual Education: A Dialogue with the Bakhtin Circle* (Albany: State University of New York Press, 1996), 8-9.

9—Simon Dentith *Bakhtinian Thought: An Introductory Reader* (New York and London: Routledge, 1995), 35.

10—These views were presented in different occasions and meetings.

11—University Grants Committee Secretariat *University Grants Committee of Hong Kong: Facts and Figures,* 1998, 2. The figures for 1998-99 are: 14,488 first-year intake of first-degree students, which was 18.6% of the relevant age group; research postgraduates were 3,607.

12—Tejaswini Niranjana *Siting Translation: History, Post-structuralism, and the Colonial Context* (Berkeley: University of California Press, 1992), 72.

13—Alex Lo "Exam-based school system 'fails everyone'," *South China Morning Post* (Hong Kong), 23 September 1999, 6.

14—Alastair Pennycook, *English and the Discourses of Colonialism* (London: Routledge, 1998), 125.

15—Cynthia Wan "Reforms to widen pupils' learning," *South China Morning Post* (Hong Kong), 23 September 1999, 6.

16—This survey was conducted by the YWCA in May 1999, and reported in *Apple Daily* (Hong Kong), 21 May 1999.

17—Wong Honghung "Principals' support for mother-tongue teaching dropped," *Sing Tao Daily* (Hong Kong), 5 June 1999, 12.

18—"Acceding to students, lecturers teach with a mix of Chinese and English," *Ming Pao* (Hong Kong), 5 May 1999, 7.

19—According to the 1996 census, 88.7% of the population spoke Cantonese, 1.1% Putonghua, and 3.1% English. Dialects such as Fukien (1.9%), Hakka (1.2%) or Chiuchow (1.1%) were spoken as much as, if not more than, Putonghua. A survey conducted in the early nineties of the tongues spoken among over 300 middle-management personnel in industrial and commercial firms indicated that Cantonese was used for daily communication, with about 30% speaking English frequently and 5.3% speaking Putonghua frequently. The use of English and Putonghua in external relations was higher, but still reached only 39.3% and 21.7% respectively. Daniel W. C. So, "One Country, Two Cultures and Three Languages: Sociolinguistic Conditions and Language Education in Hong Kong," (1997), 10.

20—Alastair Pennycook *English and the Discourses of Colonialism* (New York: Routledge, 1998), 95-128.

21—R.H. Kotewall, quoted in ibid., 123.

22—bell hooks, "'this is the oppressor's language/yet I need it to talk to you': Language, a place of struggle," in *Between Languages and Cultures: Translation and Cross Cultural Texts*, eds. Anuradha Dingwaney and Carol Maier (Pittsburgh: University of Pittsburg Press, 1995), 295.

23—Alastair Pennycook *The Cultural Politics of English as an International Language* (New York: Longman, 1994), 107-144.

24—Yiu-cheong So, "Review and Critique of the Controversies over Europeanization of Vernacular Chinese" (in Chinese), M.Phil. diss., Lingnan University, Hong Kong, 1997, 16.

25—V. N. Volosinov, *Marxism and the Philosophy of Language* (Cambridge, MA: Harvard University Press, 1973, 66.

26—When Other is used with capital O, it refers to the self/Other relation in which identity is constituted discursively in the discrimination of the self against an Other. For other with a small o, two things are designated at the same time: one is relation to another person in general in which the question of identity is not of immediate concern, the other is the absolute alterity that cannot be contained by any articulation of identity.

27—P. Patton, "Michel Foucault: The Ethics of an Intellectual," in *Michel Foucault: Critical Assessments*, ed. Barry Smart, vol. 3, (NewYork: Routledge, 1994) 162-169. (First published in *Thesis Eleven*, 10-11: 71-80, 1984-1985.)

28—Ibid.

29—Henry Giroux, "Is There a Place for Cultural Studies in Colleges of Eduction?," eds. Giroux, Lankshear, McLaren, and Peters (New York: Routledge, 1996), 46.

30—The words of Joe Murphy, former CUNY chancellor, quoted in ibid., 47-48.

31—Mikhail Bakhtin, *The Dialogic Imagination*, tr. Caryl Emerson (Minneapolis: University of Minnesota Press, 1981), 293.

32—Ibid., 291-292.

33—Daniel Smith, "Introduction; 'A Life of Pure Immanence': Deleuze's 'Critique et Clinique' Project" in Gilles Deleuze, *Essays Critical and Clinical*, tr. Daniel Smith and Michael A. Greco (London and New York: Verso, 1998), xlii.

34—Ibid., xliii.

35—Gayatri Chakravorty Spivak, *Outside in the Teaching Machine* (New York: Routledge, 1993), 191.

36—Ibid., 189.

37—Ibid., 187.

38—Gilles Deleuze and Félix Guattari, *Kafka: Toward a Minor Literature*, tr. Dana Polan, *Theory and History of Literature*, vol. 30, (Minneapolis: University of Minnesota Press, 1986), 18.

39—Spivak *Outside in the Teaching Machine*, 191.

40—Ibid., 181.

41—Ibid.

42—Ibid., 179.

43—Ibid.,183.

44—Ibid.,186-7.

45—Paul Bové *In the Wake of Theory* (Hanover: Wesleyan University Press, 1992), 25.

46—Ibid., 26.

47—Ibid., 29.

THE POLITICS OF TRANSLATION: MODES OF ORGANIZATION IN THE CHINESE TRANSLATION MOVEMENT OF THE 1980s[1]

WANG Xiaoming

translated by Kenneth DEAN

I.

In mainland China, the 1980s[2] deserve to be called another golden age of written translation, following that of the late Qing and early Republican period. Especially in its cultural aspect, one can speak of this period as having started a translation movement of great scope. According to statistics, from 1978 to 1987, in the field of social-science[3] translations alone, more than 5000 were done,[4] probably ten times the amount translated in the preceding thirty years. And the situation in other fields, for example that of literary translations, was similar.

But to say that the 1980s were a golden age of written translation is not only based on the quantity of translations, but rather because the translations of this period occupy an extremely prominent position in the cultural transformations of the entire society. From the end of the 1970s, more and more Chinese people realized that Chinese society had fallen into an awful condition. Not only was it far, far behind Western developed countries, it also clearly lagged behind Japan, Hong Kong, and even Taiwan. Because of this, it was felt that the entire society had to undergo a major reform, in order to avoid the risk of exclusion from "global citizenship," in the midst of the major historical tendency towards globalization. This is also to say that the '80s were a period during which the people of the People's Republic of China once again reacted to and reflected on current social conditions in China, and on the basis of these conditions once again determined to pursue development. In this process, those translated works that came primarily from the Western humanities and social sciences, including literary works, formed precisely at this moment the basic framework through which Chinese people once again reacted to and reflected on reality. These translations became important factors inspiring and guiding their reactions and reflections. In this sense one could even go so far as to say that, with a clear view of the '80s translation movement, one would also grasp a key "trace" which would allow one to understand the cultural transformation of China's "new age."

In comparison to the situation of the almost thirty years from 1950 through to the end of the "Great Cultural Revolution," or even in comparison to the situation of the first half of the twentieth century, the translation movement of the 1980s manifested its own exceptionally vivid characteristics.[5] I plan here to enter the discussion from a very broad sense of "social-science"[6] translation, in order to analyze one of its aspects, that is, its mode of organizing translation, a mode novel in the context of the preceding thirty years.

The 1980s social-science translation scene was extremely grand. The numbers of translators increased sharply, and any publishing house with the least bit of life to it was eager to accept and publish this kind of work. In the mid-'80s, the number of publishing houses exceeded 400, having increased threefold from the 1976 level.[7] One can imagine the grandness of the scene. If one observes somewhat more closely, however, one sees that among all this activity, those translation projects which formed organized series functioned to guide and form a model for the flourishing of the entire translation movement. Translation projects of this kind resulted in a set of translations, that is, a translation series. And it is precisely the formation, realization, and completion of these translation projects that clearly reveals a new form of organization of translation, unlike anything seen in the preceding thirty years. In the following, I will take three of the best-known sets of translations series as examples, describing and analyzing four aspects in particular. These three sets are the *Aesthetics Translation [monograph] Series* edited by Li Zehou, the *Walking towards the Future Series* edited by Jin Guantao, and the *Culture: China and the World Series* edited by Gan Yang.[8]

First of all, there emerged a group of quite particular organizers of translation activity. In the thirty years prior to the '80s, translation and its publication, along with other forms of writing and publishing, remained consistently under the strict control of the state through the publishing houses, which always set the topics and then invited a suitable translator to do the translation. Another aspect of control was the fact that, due to the contacts and arrangements made by each publishing house, a group of professional translators gradually emerged.[9] Together with another group composed primarily of professors in university foreign-language departments, they made up the "world of translators" that surrounded the publishing houses. But in the '80s, circumstances were indeed different, and a new group of humanistic scholars, with no affiliation to this realm of translators and who had never received commissions from the publishing houses, emerged to establish translation projects and to organize and lead these projects through to their realization. To take the editors of the aforementioned three translations series as examples, none had done formal translation work. Li Zehou was an aesthetician; Jin Guantao a philosopher-historian with extremely broad academic interests; and Gan Yang a scholar who specialized in studying contemporary Western philosophy. Prior to planning the *Culture: China and the World Series* (and like Li and Jin) Gan was not known as a translator. These men not only were not the aforementioned professional translators, they were also all quite young. They belonged to what was currently known as the "small-number generation" (referring to the fact that, up until the mid-70s, the PRC's cultural sphere was controlled by men in their sixties, seventies, or even older). In 1980 Li Zehou was fifty, and the man who assisted him in managing the work on the entire *Aesthetics Translation* series was most likely the managing editor Sheng Shouyao, who was Li's M.A. student and barely over thirty at the time.

Neither Jin Guantao nor Liu Qingfeng, the managing editor who assisted him, were yet forty. Gan Yang, the youngest of all, was not even thirty in 1985. Of the other two series editors, Su Guoxun was just over thirty, and Liu Xiaofeng was only twenty-six. As for the two editorial committees of the *Walking toward the Future* and the *Culture: China and the World* series, of the seventy-odd members, there was scarcely one over forty-five at the time. Clearly one could say that the two most outstanding characteristics of this new group of translation activity organizers were that they were young and not members of the "translation realm."

Moreover, these organizers clearly had a new understanding of the meaning of translation, which they brought to the organization of translation activity. In the thirty years preceding the 1980s, translations of social-science texts in mainland China basically were taken as tools that would serve official political purposes and support official Communist ideology. Only a very few translations could to a certain extent break free of these restrictions, and thus make a contribution in the sense of adding to the accumulation of culture. And during the "Cultural Revolution" even these series were all completely stopped, as the entirety of translation activity was absorbed into the orbit of official ideological propaganda. Given this background, the motivation for this new group of translation organizers appears especially striking. In the general preface to the *Aesthetics Translation Series*, Li Zehou states,

Currently we must organize our strengths in order to translate Western works of aesthetics as rapidly as possible. I am convinced that this will have great significance for the improvement of the condition of our research in aesthetics. Such valuable translation work is far more useful than valueless essay writing.[10]

Even though he was speaking of the "conditions" of aesthetic research, you certainly can feel his concern for the entire cultural condition; Li clearly was attributing an extremely broad significance to what would seem to be translations of quite specialized aesthetic works.

At the beginning of the 1980s, Chinese intellectuals had started moving away from years of reflection on tragedies of the sort of the Cultural Revolution, turning towards a new road opened up in the field of philosophy (the current phrase was "worldview"). Due to the particular cultural conditions of that time, literature played a prominent role in this transformation of the spirit of society. These philosophical openings and worldviews first were raised in the theoretical debates in literature and aesthetics. Due to this, we can take Li Zehou's term "aesthetics" virtually as a pronoun, that is, as standing in for the names of what he was in fact speaking of—not only "aesthetics," but also "thought," "worldview" and even all of "philosophy."

Throughout, Li Zehou maintained at least some degree of reserve, but such things were expressed even more clearly in the *Walking toward the Future* series. In the opening sections of "Offered Phrases," the author does not talk of translation, nor of written works, but of the unusual moment of historical change,

> Our age is abnormal. The scientific technological revolution is rapidly and profoundly changing the social life and mode of existence of the human species. People feel strongly that we must seriously and earnestly confront a richly embattled and constantly transforming future.

It was precisely at this historical juncture that the Chinese nationality began another true revival within its own ancient history.[11] It was, precisely, based in this understanding of their serious historical mission that the authors of "Offered Phrases" used Marx's words as their forerunner, to reveal the meaning of their organization of this series:

> Marx has a phrase which states, 'When the lightning of thought strikes this untouched garden of people, the German people will be liberated and become human.' Today, the lightning that illumines our people's thought is a combination of Marxism, a scientific spirit, and the excellence of our people's traditions, as well as the innovations this [combination] has begun.

At the conclusion to "Offered Phrases" the authors maintain an even less concealed sense of solemnity, quoting Bacon's words to express their own motivations: "Don't look at it as an idea, but as a cause, and believe that what we are doing is not establishing a basis for one school or theory, but is for all men's happiness and dignity." It could not have been put more clearly. They not only looked on the editing of this series as an act of academic work, but they also saw it as pushing the entire process of social transformation, as a flash of lightning that would "liberate" society. In a private conversation at that time, Jin Guantao clearly expressed the group's wish to set in motion a movement, similar to the May Fourth movement, in the Chinese intellectual realm.[12]

In the same way, by the middle of the Eighties, when the tide of the "liberation of thought" had swelled into a magnificent spectacle, the organizers of the *Culture: China and the World* series began to expand their understanding of translation activity, viewing it from a different perspective. They practically always held that contemporary Chinese people needed to establish their own thought and philosophy, and that this process requires a systematic construction.[13] The first step was to comprehensively introduce contemporary Western thought. The second step was to deeply critique this philosophic thought. Only then could the third step—the establishment by Chinese scholars of a framework of thought and a philosophic discourse that would not be inferior to those of other peoples—be effected. This aim was quite clearly expressed in the "General Preface" to the *Western Academic Collection*:

Liang Qichao once said, 'If today China wants to strengthen itself, then it should take the translation of books as its first mission.' This statement is still not out of date today. But we deeply believe that with the daily deepening of the understanding of the progress of world academic culture by Chinese scholars, it should not be too long from now that [we see] the great creative expansion of contemporary Chinese academic culture.[14]

It was in this context of a conception of the reconstruction of the entirety of contemporary Chinese philosophic thought that Gan Yang and others gave their interpretation of the meaning of the translation work that they had planned. It was to be the foundation of the revival of contemporary Chinese people's thought and philosophy, the secure foundation of a new house of philosophy. Similarly, it would not only have a concrete disciplinary or academic meaning, but, even more importantly, it would involve the reconstruction of the entire culture and spirit of Chinese society.

Looking back on this today, the meaning attributed to translation activity by these organizers, from Li Zehou to Gan Yang, clearly carries the mark of the 1980s. They neither took as their point of departure the needs of official ideology, nor, as in the '90s, the need for the construction of professionalism or academic disciplines. Rather, they started off from the premise of the need for the transformation of the thought and culture of the society as a whole, from their sense of their own social and historical mission as intellectuals, and so threw themselves into the work of organizing these large-scale translation activities. To them this was not merely technical work, nor mere academic work, rather it was intellectual labor, the work of enlightenment of the spirit. Given their understanding of the meaning of translation, you can easily think back seventy or eighty years, to Liang Qichao and Yan Fu, and the slightly later "New Youth" understandings of translation. One might also recall the motives of the Zhou brothers (Lu Xun and his brother Zhou Zuoren) in their translation of *Collection of Tales from Beyond the Realm*. Certainly, those early twentieth-century enlighteners of thought and social revolutionaries, thinkers whose attitude towards translation was that of the "theft of fire," had a deep influence (perhaps an unconscious influence) on this group of 1980s organizers of translation projects.

Furthermore, this movement represented the establishment of an independent, translation-led mechanism. Precisely because they clearly thought of themselves as "smugglers" of the fire of the spirit, the first task the 1980s organizers of translation wanted to accomplish was to break away from the translation publication system organized around the State publishing houses. They had to take the guiding control over translation into their own hands. That is to say that, from the selection of topics to the choice of translators and the review of the draft translations, all these decisions had to be their own, direct responsibility, and not be decided by the publishing houses. In this respect, the *Aesthetics Translation Series* was exceptional. Li Zehou relied on the reputation he had already established in the field of aesthetics and the support of those colleagues who had participated in the National Aesthetics conference he organized in 1980,[15] along with the support of the Chinese Academy of Social Sciences,[16] to establish a successful chief editorial responsibility system that lived up to the name. He and his assistants (the most important of whom were his M.A. students) selected the original works and their translators, while the publishing house took responsibility for the copy-editing and textual editing. And because this monograph series was distributed between four publishing houses (the Chinese Academy of Social Science Press in Beijing, the Chinese Literary Association Press, the Guangming Newspaper Press, and the Liaoning People's Press in Shenyang), no single press could on its own bring extra pressure to bear on the chief editors. Looking at it in retrospect today, it was precisely this strategy of working the four publishing houses that secured the "chief editorial responsibility" necessary to carry out their project from start to finish.

But things were not quite the same when Jin Guantao and Liu Qingfeng planned the *Walking towards the Future* monograph series. Jin and Liu were not satisfied with simply establishing the "principle" of editorial responsibility. Instead, they established a editorial "collective"[17] that was independent of the publishing houses; this was the "Walking towards the Future Editorial Committee" established in 1982 with Bao Zunxin as the first chief editor. The committee included twentyfour members, all of whom were naturally soulmates. Under this committee, they established another committee with Jin Guantao as the managing director. It goes without saying that under the social system of the 1980s any group that tried to gather together simply as individuals would have no way to stand up to the official publishing houses. Therefore, after several twists and turns, Jin Guantao and others finally saw to it that the editorial committee was absorbed into the Youth Research Institute of the Chinese Academy of Social Sciences, an affiliation which made them a subsidiary, second-tier organization of the Institute. In this way, the editorial committee was finally able to obtain official recognition and legal status that allowed it to act independently of the publishing houses and to take complete control of the entire process of bringing out the series, from selection to final editing. The committee had their own bank account and was authorized to employ assistants. Thus their control over every aspect of the series was of course greater than Li Zehou's. At first Jin Guantao et al. approached the Hunan People's Press to discuss the publication of the series, but this press was unwilling to relinquish the power of final review. So they contacted the Sichuan People's Press making the power of final review their first condition. Precisely because they controlled the entire power of allocation, the series' editorial committee was able to establish what for that time was a very thorough and structured system of three levels of editorial review.[18] An editorial collective that was independent of the publishing houses, and a complete system of editorial review—both features indicate that a new, translation-led mechanism had been created. This was a pioneering undertaking in the history of publishing in the People's Republic of China.

After this, the planners of the *Culture: China and the World* series also used this method, also establishing an editorial committee independent of the publishing houses and an institutional affiliation with a state research unit.[19] They too established a managing editor and chief editor under an editorial committee with complete responsibility for the entire editing process, including the selection of texts and translators. They also had to break off dealings with one publishing house (the Workers' Press) over the issue of final editorial review, before switching to another. By the late '80s and early '90s, many translation (as well as non-translation) series were employing this kind of independent editorial committee to carry out publication projects of varying sizes. This continually widening path of new modes of planning and organizing publications was first opened up by these organizers of the translation series.

Finally, the function of these editorial committees grew ever greater. Originally established in order to translate and edit these series, the committees found their functions growing almost daily, due to the great influence these monograph series exerted. For example, the editorial committee of the *Walk-*

ing towards the Future series had originally only planned to publish two collections, the first a set of translations, and the second a series of original works by Chinese scholars. And their greatest interest was actually in the latter. But from the summer of 1987 on, they began planning a whole series of activities that went beyond the publication of the monograph series. First, there was the publishing of a magazine, which came out about the time of the third installment of the *Walking* series (in August of 1986, the magazine, also entitled *Walking towards the Future*, was published in Chengdu).[20] Second, the committee organized large-scale academic conferences, held in the winter of 1987 in Chengdu and the spring of 1989 in Beijing. The series editorial committee organized two international conferences in collaboration with the Chinese University of Hong Kong and the Chinese Cultural Institute.[21] Third, they planned to establish an independent publishing house in Beijing, and they also considered initiating simultaneous publication projects in Beijing, Hong Kong and Taiwan. Fourth, they organized the "Twenty-first Century Research Institute," raising some funding for the project and even making contact with a governmental unit that would grant them official affiliation. Fifth, the committee organized and participated in non-literary artistic activities. They organized a "Walking towards the Future" art exhibit in Chengdu in November 1987, and planned to organize an even larger comprehensive arts festival. At the same time, the series editorial committee invested in filmmaking, and had a major role in the planning and filming of the documentary *River's Lament*.

Likewise, the editorial committee of the *Culture: China and the World* series were not satisfied with translation work alone. In accord with their concept of "Three Steps" toward the reconstruction of Chinese contemporary philosophy,[22] at the same time that they planned the translation series, they also organized another series of studies that would explicate these classical Western works. The members of the editorial committee naturally made up most of the writers of these studies.[23] In addition to publishing books, and just as Jin Guantao and his group had done, they also published a magazine with the same name as the series. This actually was an independent journal produced by the same people, with writings of the editorial committee members making up the majority of each issue. In addition, Gan Yang and the others planned a widely noted contemporary art exhibit in Beijing in February 1989.[24] Although not all of these varied plans and actions would come to fruition, together they clearly reveal the comprehensive nature of the ideas of the series organizers in their push for socio-cultural change. Among Chinese intellectuals of the '80s, those who, like Gan Yang, sought step-by-step cultural transformation—and saw in translation the first such step—were very common. (In fact this way of thinking has continued ever since the new intellectuals of the late Qing first believed that China was inferior to the West in everything from politics to culture). And since they understood their translation work in this way, at the moment that they believed that the cultural transformation of Chinese society had taken a turn towards a deeper development, it was natural that they would want to take the second step, the third and then the fourth step. Those organizations that they originally established in order to publish translations would also naturally give rise to many new functions. To these people, translation work was only one strenuous part of the entire cultural transformation. They thus found nothing untoward in taking on many tasks that had nothing to do with the professional scope of these great editorial committees.

From these four aspects, we can clearly see how a mode of organized translation activity that had not been seen in the thirty years prior to this time could step-by-step take form, develop and then expand into other activities. In my opinion, the rapid expansion of the social and cultural function of these editorial committees was precisely the political nature of this new mode of organization of translation, and it manifested itself very evidently.[25]

II.

This special mode of translation-organization must inevitably have an influence on the translation activity itself and the results of this activity. I will discuss several aspects of this below.

First let us look at the selection of topics for translation. The individuals involved throughout the entire translation project shared certain special characteristics, whether one considers their estimation of the condition of culture and contemporary social thought, or the meanings they attributed to their own translation duties as a result of these views. Or, take into consideration their background knowledge, interest in academics, the scope of their academic activity, as well as the scope of those people they could contact and organize, etc.—all these aspects left their mark on their selection of works for translation. Take the *Aesthetics Translation* series as an example. Li Zehou clearly states in his general preface that he wanted to "make up lessons," that is, to correct the past situation in which, due to culture being largely sealed off, no works exhibiting non-orthodox Marxist aesthetics were allowed into China. "As long as it has reference value, it should all be taken in." Due to the influence of his and his chief assistants' intellectual background, the selection of works for the *Aesthetics* series naturally inclined towards Euro-American, non-Marxist theories. Out of the fifty works in the series, only six were Marxist, and these included the works of Lukács, which had always been considered "revisionist" in China. The series included a total of seven works from the Soviet Union and Eastern Europe. All the rest were written by Western scholars, while the works of contemporary U.S. scholars made up one third or seventeen of the titles. Interestingly, there was not a single work from the Frankfurt School.

The other two series showed similar tendencies. Of the twenty-four works in the *Walking towards the Future* series, half were of American origin, and only three were non-Western. Since Jin Guantao and Liu Qingfeng at that time emphasized science and philosophy of science, and because a good number of the members of the editorial committee were themselves scientists, the translations in the series clearly leaned towards science and philosophy of science.[26] As for *Culture: China and the World*, the vast majority of its editorial committee was made up of graduate students specializing in Western philosophy, so they simply used "modern Western academic collection" as the main name for their translation series. The selection of texts in this collection came primarily from philosophy, sociology and anthropology, the three subjects which most interested Gan Yang and his group at the time. In general, because all the groups agreed that, in the transformations of the social thought and culture of the '80s, the import of Western modern theory had an essential and important role to play, and because the members' background knowledge and academic interests were mutually implicated in their understandings, we see a high degree of similarity in the selection of texts—and a strong inclination towards modern Western theory—in all three of these series.

Secondly, let us consider the selection of translators. As mentioned above, in the preceding thirty years China had already developed a substantial "realm of translators," and moreover, the most important of these translators specialized in literature and humanist theory. But an examination of the translators working in these series, demonstrates that, like the directors of these collections, the translators did not come from the "realm of translators." Of the over one hundred translators of works in these three series, with the exception of a very few (such as Miao Lingzhu and Wu Yuetian), all were young people unknown to the official publishing houses. The majority were recent, or even not yet matriculated, graduate students, and some were even undergraduates. At least one third were "part-time," since they all were doing their own research, working in their respective fields of specialized study. Translation was an occasional occupation for them.[27] For example, none of the translators of the *Walking toward the Future* series was studying in a foreign-language department, and all were "part-timers." This situation clearly had much to do with the scholarship and pattern of activity of the directors of these projects. Not translators themselves, they naturally lacked contacts within the translation realm. They were also very young, you might say too young, and so as they went looking for the number of people needed to take on these projects, they were bound to motivate people of their own generation. The result was that, as these series gradually came out, a whole new group of translators grew up. From this point of view one can certainly say the unique organizational mode of these three series, as it was adopted by many subsequent translation series, certainly greatly transformed the structure of the Chinese translation realm. A large group of nonprofessional translators, most very young, and in some cases not terribly proficient in foreign languages, entered into the activity of translation (and not only social-scientific translation). It goes without saying that this had very extensive effects.

Also important were decisions regarding basic translation tactics. The question, How should one translate foreign works? has been debated since the late Qing. Generally speaking, as Chinese translators' level of foreign-language proficiency gradually improved, and as the Chinese people's knowledge of foreign lands deepened, along with the gradual, systematic organization of translation activities after the 1950s, the demands with regard to translation within the Chinese translation realm became more and more fastidious and strict. The publication of a large number of retranslations in the literary realm was a result of this tendency. Under these circumstances, after having engaged in extremely careful, conscientious and usually very lengthy polishing, and to then bring out something that could be called a definitive translation naturally became the heart's desire of the majority of translators—indeed, this gradually coalesced into a unquestioned "public law" of the realm of translators. However, the organizers of the translation activity that we are introducing here were consumed by a desire to transform Chinese social thought and cultural conditions, and so flung themselves into translation work, perceiving a need for their products to be brought out quickly in order to place the translations in the hands of readers as speedily as possible. Thus it was extremely difficult for them to respect the aforementioned "public law" of the translation realm. In his general preface to the *Aesthetics Translation* series, Li Zehou proclaimed

> With regards the so-called "aesthetics craze," at a time when people are in grave need of books, the idea of spending ten years to polish a sword, and slowly to bring out one or two perfect definitive versions is not as good as to relax and selectively translate and to bring out more books within a few years time.

Li put it very clearly: the speed of translation is most important. This does not mean that the directors encouraged irresponsible translation. However, when it came to the ideal of the definitive version conflicting with the timetable for the completion of the translation project, then it was necessary to put these traditional kinds of aspirations to one side. I assume that this demand for speed was one reason why Li Zehou and the others were more willing to invite nonprofessional translators, for such translators would not likely feel constrained by the "public law" of the search for the definitive version.

In fact, some translators in these series

took the translation of many volumes. Teng Shouyao is one example. Independently or with the aid of others, he translated five books. Even more common were collective translations. Almost half of the books in these series were translated jointly by from two to several translators. Take for example the following statement: "In this volume, chapters 1, 7, 8, 9, 10, 11, and 12 and appendices A and B and the index of personal names were translated by Su Xiaoli. Chapters 2, 3, 4, 5, and 6 were translated by Zeng Yi and Li Jiexiu."[28] This is a typical working model commonly used by the translators of the *Aesthetics Translation* series. Due to this, sometimes even expectations regarding the status of the original edition of the work had to be lowered. In the translators' afterword to *A Critique of Taste*, we read the following explanation, "The preface and first and second chapters of this volume, along with "A brief introduction to semiotics" were translated by Wang Keping from the English version. Chapter three and the appendix were translated by Tian Shigang based on an Italian version."[29]

In the same way, the directors of the *Walking towards the Future* series also held the opinion like Li Zehou that they "dared to act first." This series used a thin and long format, and each volume's total word count is only a third of those in the *Aesthetics Translation* series. Nonetheless the phenomenon of collective translation is still very common. Of twenty-four volumes, only six were translated by a single translator. Jin Guantao, etc., even used the phrase "editorial (committee) translation" which has seldom been used since the 1930s. Five out of the six volumes in the first two subsets of the series use this expression. In the process of translating and editing Max Weber's *The Protestant Ethic and the Spirit of Capitalism,* the editorial committee simply did away with the book's footnotes.[30] As many similar examples demonstrate, Jin Guantao, etc. were of the opinion that there was no need to hold fast to the customary search for perfection which characterized the translators' realm. In order as rapidly as possible to have these translations enter into the battlefield of the transformation of social thought, these thinkers were ready to adapt all kinds of flexible translation tactics.

In comparison, the editorial committee of the *Culture: China and the World* series seems to have been more circumspect. In the "Collection of Western Academic Works" collective translations gradually declined.[31] Indeed, each volume had one person responsible for cross-checking, and most volumes were personally copy-edited by the three chief editors. Gan Yang edited over 3,000,000 words, while Liu Xiaofeng edited almost 2,000,000 words. And they edited very conscientiously. It can be said that of the three series, Gan Yang, et al. had the highest expectations with regard to quality of translation. But rather than attributing this to a consideration of the search for definitive translations, it relates instead to the editorial committee's estimation of the basic conditions of contemporary sociocultural transformations. By this time it was already the middle of the 1980s, and the atmosphere of tension that had led the pioneers to feel that they had no time for second thoughts seemed to be dissipating; and what then seemed more important was the respectable establishment of secure foundations for the great edifice of new thought and philosophy. Since these young people had taken on the task of planning out the entire path of the future development of Chinese thought, they naturally emphasized in particular the quality of the fiery thought that they were bringing in from the West. Their demands regarding the quality of the translations also had to do with this view. With this in mind, Li Zehou or Jin Guantao's "dare to stand up and speak back," and, in contrast, Gan Yang's "one should translate well," each confirms a particular perspective. The calculation these men made of the entire cultural condition had a decisive influence on the translation tactics they adopted.

Finally, closely connected to the selection of translation tactics is the matter of the hypothetical reader. For even if one shares an understanding of translation as the vital path towards the enlightenment of thought, how does one determine the scope of the readership of the translations—how do fellow enlighteners calculate the object of enlightenment? This question becomes crucially important. One can see from the general preface to the *Aesthetics Translation* series that the circle of readers that Li Zehou has in mind is not an audience of specialists but instead the broad masses of youth, the so-called "amateurs" of literature and aesthetics. This hypothesis is even more clearly stated in the editorial directions of the *Walking Towards the Future* series. With an eye to the "future," Jin Guantao, etc. in this series clearly make "youth" their most important readership. Their design of the covers (which use black and white abstract art), the limited size of the volumes (each volume in principle not exceeding 120,000 words), and in the transformations of titles (the editorial committee clearly chose titles which were clear and would excite interest, such as "The Modernization of Man," "The Creation of Mankind," and "Why Did Japan 'succeed'?"), etc., etc., the desire was to meet the needs of young readers. As for the editorial committee of the *Culture: China and World* series, they created a separate series entitled the "New Knowledge Collection" with smaller and thinner volumes, distinct from the "Western Academic Collection." The new series had far more volumes than the first collection, in order to attract a non-specialist readership which would became an important audience for the committee's communicative effort.

Clearly, the people in these editorial committees were a group of young scholars who were sensitive to and understood the particularly spiritual thirst of their own generation. Accordingly, their hypotheses and their choices with regard to their readership were extremely timely. They believed that young people were the group in society that would be most willing to accept Western thought, and the sales figures for these publications confirm their judgment. The very first sets of the *Aesthetics Translation* series reached 30,000 to 40,000 in their first printing. The first thousand-print run of the first set of *Walking toward the Future* series sold out within four hours. It was repeatedly reprinted after that, and the first set of 12 volumes have had an average print run of over 200,000, with some over 300,000. As for the *Culture: China and the World* series, not only are many volumes in the "Western Academic collection" still being reprinted, the print run of the "New Knowledge Collection" greatly exceeds the former set.

III.

If we were to place the mode of organization of translation described above in a larger time frame, one of course could not say that it was an entirely new phenomenon. Even within the history of translating in the modern period, starting with the large-scale translation projects of the missionaries, through the translations and publications of first Yan Fu's and then Lu Xun's generations, all the way to the translation series that introduced Marxism in the late Twenties to the mid-Thirties, all provide instances of the kind of translation organization described above. But from another perspective, from the founding of the People's Republic of China until the 1980s, this kind of translation organization was indeed a completely new phenomenon. From this perspective one cannot help feeling sadness at the tragic nature of the history of Twentieth-Century Chinese society and culture. But what I want to emphasize here is the profound influence that this mode of translation organization has had on the entire translation movement of the 1980s. The three series discussed here were pulling at the bit, so to speak, racing to set the trends in translation throughout the entire decade. In their reliance on a principle of selecting avant-garde works, and in their objective, record sales figures, they have become a model which has attracted many imitators. Ever since these series' appearance, one could say that most of the influential translation activities have taken the form of published monograph series. Furthermore, most of the directors of these projects have directly modeled their methods on those of Li Zehou to Gan Yang. Finally, precisely because these series had such an enormous influence,[32] throughout the '80s "social science" and literary translation maintained a central position within translation activities as a whole.[33]

It goes without saying that these developments have had a decisive effect on the rebuilding of the Chinese translation realm; on the destruction and reestablishment of "public law" in this realm; on a new generation of readers of translations and the development of their reading tastes; and on the renovation of the entire mechanism of translation and publication.[34] And due to the broad distribution of these series, today there are very few among those people aged 30 to 50, and who take an interest in society, politics, and culture, who have not read these translations. They have had an enormous influence on Chinese social thought and culture in the '80s and the '90s. Many of the particular developments in the fields of thought, in academics and in the wider culture of contemporary China have to varying degrees had their origins in these influential translations. These translations loom over and cast their reflections on the ways in which the realm of Chinese thought leans towards Western thought (and away from non-Western resources) and on tendencies for change within contemporary written language usage—especially theoretical language usage—not to mention their influence on concrete instances of trends and substitutions in literary, artistic, humanistic and social-scientific theory. Thus one cannot underestimate the impact of the mode of translation organization I have described here on Chinese social and cultural change.

The last issue I would like to raise is the question of why it was (or, how was it possible) that this mode of translation organization could arise in the '80s? Because of a lack of space, I can here only briefly sketch a few explanations. First of all, there was of course the influence of the atmosphere of political change throughout the nation. After the end of the so-called Cultural Revolution, the third National Congress of the Eleventh Plenary of the Chinese Communist Party emphasized "the liberation of thought." A few relatively open-minded members of the CCP were working with the intelligentsia to spread a "movement to liberate thought." The powers favoring reform of the popular sector continuously responded to this call. By the end of the '80s the currents of reform had been turned back several times but were nevertheless reaching their peak. Without this historic background, the efforts of Li Zehou and others would never have succeeded; nor would they even have been able to come up with projects of this kind. The gradual disintegration of the Cultural Revolution-style official ideology and the appearance within the government of an element of open-minded officials, combined with the propaganda that this created, led to the slight loosening of the publication system. Only by placing events in the context of these wider developments, developments that played a key role in the successful working of the new mode of translation organization, can this success be understood. Had it not been for the support of the Chinese Academy of Social Sciences and one or two publishing houses, Li Zehou's project would have remained just one project. And the fact that *Walking toward the Future* and *Culture: China and the World* were able achieve the qualifications that allowed them to "perch" within national institutions was only possible due to the support of a small group of open-minded officials.

Also important was the provocation of the great spiritual thirst and the quest for knowledge felt by the entire society. Beginning in the 1950s, the government had intentionally pushed a policy of a sealing off of

The Politics of Translation

culture, pursuing this policy with great force and great success. After the beginning of the "Great Cultural Revolution" the policy was in fact reinforced, leaving virtually nothing untouched, and causing the entire nation to be suffocated, both on a spiritual level and on the level of knowledge. But precisely at that point, the Cultural Revolution ended, society slowly but surely began opening up, and bits and pieces of news from outside the country began making their way in. At the moment when this long period of confinement had begun to open up, the spiritual thirst and hunger of the entire society built up into an enormous need, drawing upon the cultural realm to supply it. Encountering this moment, Li Zehou and others seized the opportunity moving with sensitivity and timeliness. In my opinion, this historical occasion had an extremely important effect both in guiding and supporting the creation and success of the "new" mode of translation organization.

The third cause I would like to discuss is the emergence in the 1980s of a new kind of "young intellectual clan" (I can't think of a more appropriate term, and this is in fact what they were called). Relatively speaking, the members of the editorial committees of *Walking towards the Future* and *Culture: China and the World* more closely display the characteristics of such a "clan": aged between 25 and 40, clever, with different lengths of time spent in rural labor or in factories; having received (or still receiving) a college education (usually in the humanities); disenchanted with the hypocrisy of the official ideology, thirsting for a new spiritual life, and filled with a passionate "idealism"; instilled with a traditional desire to rule the world and save the nation; having some familiarity wtih foreign language, but not too much; and with a definite understanding of events outside of China, but not enough to speak in systematic terms or in any kind of depth—this very special kind of young person was the product of the tortuous twists and turns of Chinese history between the 1950s and the 1970s. He or she was historically unique, not seen before this and probably not to be seen again. Certain of their characteristics differed from those of their predecessors, and others are gradually disappearing in the succeeding generation. I personally feel that many of the cultural, economic, and political phenomena of the "New Age" are connected to this "clan" of people. Among this clan are a few who later became renowned cultural figures (such as the directors of the translation series projects), but the vast majority have undergone all kinds of twists and turns, leading to the dissipation of their thought, their careers, and their life ideals. But during the '80s this "clan" of people were the force that pushed forward the transformation of the thought and culture of the entire society. Of course, my discussion of the new mode of translation organization, and the great rise and ebb of the tide of translation in the '80s, is all intimately linked to this "clan." The directors of these three translation series all belong to this "clan," as do most of the translators of the books in these series. Probably the majority of the first readers of these books also belonged to this class of person, and in turn went on to influence others to whom they were close. Of course, it is not my purpose to research the history and social function of this "clan,"[35] and such an endevor probably exceeds the usual limits of "translation research." I only wish to point out that the existence of this "clan," from the point of view of social structure, is the most intrinsic cause of the creation and ultimate accomplishment of the new mode of translation organization.

Endnotes

1—This article is based on a research report presented to the Chinese University of Hong Kong Translation Research Centre, where I was a guest researcher. It is the result of a research project entitled "The Warp and the Weft of the Chinese Translation." I would like to specially thank the organizer of that research project, Professor Kong Huiyi. In the process of writing this paper I received the help and inspiration of several colleagues and friends, especially the following: Liu Xiaofeng, Liu Qingfeng, Jin Guantao, Lin Jianfa, Li Zhaozhong, Qian Honglin, and Wu Bin. I would like to express my deep thanks to all of them.
2—For the purposes of this paper, the "'80s" refers to the time period from the end of the '70s until the June 4, 1989 affair.
3—Here "social science" is used in a very broad sense, which would include the human sciences.
4—See Chen Jiuren ed., *A comprehensive list of Chinese academic translations 1978-1987, social science segment* (Changchun: Jilin Educational Press, Changchun 1994): 1.
5—For example, in tending clearly towards the West in the contents of translations.
6—Including "social science" and "human sciences." From here onwards in this paper, the

term social science has this broader meaning.

7—Cheng Fong-ching and Jin Guantao, *From youthful Manuscripts to River Elegy: The Chinese Popular Cultural Movement and Political Transformation 1979-1989* (Hong Kong: The Chinese University Press, 1997),181.

8—Planning for the *Aesthetics Translation* Series began in 1980, with the first books published in 1982. A total of over fifty volumes were published (see Appendix 1). *Walking towards the Future* was planned in 1982, with publication beginning in 1984, ultimately in five series with seventy four titles. Of these seventy four only twenty four were actually translations, while an additional ten titles, called "edited works," contain large amounts of translation (see Appendix 2). The *Culture: China and the World* series was planned in 1985; publishing continued from 1986 to 1995, during which time a total of eighty four volumes were produced (see Appendix 3).

9—This category includes people who for various reasons were stripped of their writing positions and transformed into translators, such as Zhou Zuoren and Lu Yuan.

10—This general preface reappears at the front of every volume of the *Aesthetics Translation* series.

11—"Offered Phrases" forms the first page of text of every volume in the *Walking towards the Future* series.

12—See note 7.

13—This is based on notes from an interview with Liu Xiaofeng held on Feb. 19, 1998.

14—Prior to 1990 this preface was published at the head of every volume of the "Western Academic Collection."

15—Li Zehou first announced his thoughts about the *Aesthetics Translation* series at this conference.

16—Li Zehou's general preface starts with a quote from this conference's overview ("The overview of the First National Conference on Aesthetics held in July, 1980 states. . . ") in order to show not only the origins of the project but also to indicate the support of the entire field of aesthetics.

17—Of course, this has another cause. Since these young people did not have the same representation as Li Zehou's, they would have been even more dependent on some organization for support, before they could stand up to the pressures from the publishing houses.

18—Since the members of the editorial committee were scattered all over the country, they also published a monthly "Work Report" to let people know how work was progressing.

19—This time they sought affiliation with the Sanlian (United) press, which itself had only recently achieved independence from the People's Press.

20—According to Jin Guantao's presentation to the the Workshop on The Warp and the Weft of the Chinese Translation Movement of the Chinese University of Hong Kong Translation Research Centre on March 6, 1998, the idea for the magazine preceded that for the translation series.

21—See note 8.

22—Refer to earlier discussion on p. 273.

23—This series was later published by the Shanghai People's Press under the title "Humanities Series."

24—They were also working on a number of other projects, including some that had no chance of success at that time. To tell the truth, many of the afore-mentioned projects of Jin Guantao and his group were not able to take shape.

25—This aspect can be clarified by raising an extreme example: In April and May of 1989, Gan Yang used the name of the *Culture: China and the World* editorial committee to assist the political work he was doing with student leaders at the time. He clearly did not concieve of the committee as simply a cultural organization. Of course, this activity of his met with opposition from many members of the editorial committee.

26—On this point, see also note 4, 118-119.

27—The three volumes of selected translations by Chinese scholars included in the "Western Academic Collection" are a somewhat different case. Many are selected from the translations of distinguished translators.

28—"Walking towards expressionist aesthetics", translator's preface. Translated by Su Shaoli et al. (Beijing: Guangming Ribao chubansho, 1990), 9.

29—Ibid., 279.

30—This primarily had to do with considerations of the length of the texts.

31—This was even more evident later.

32—Of course, behind these kinds of influence, there were extremely complex social and political elements involved, which cannot be discussed in detail here.

33—After the beginning of the 1990s, translations of leisure materials with an eye for profit gradually took over the center of translation activity.

34—Before the 1980s, in Beijing and Shanghai only a very few publishing houses were allowed to publish social-scientific translations. Nowadays, more than a hundred times as many can publish this kind of material.

35—It is my impression that this "clan" no longer exists as an entity today.

Appendix:*

Table of Contents of Aesthetics Translation Series

Table of Contents of Walking toward the Future Series

Table of Contents of Culture: China and the World Series

* Editors' note: The list included in this article of the published monographs of Chinese translations only refers to the titles that are available in Chinese with the translated titles and transliterated authors' names. In the Chinese publishing industry it is not an established routine to include in the translation the title of the original and the author's name in the original language. The translators and editors have done their best to find the originals in their original languages, but the task was extremely difficult. Consequently the list is not complete. We owe much to Ken Dean of McGill University and the author, Wang Xiaoming for their laborious search for originals. In addition, we were fortunate at the last minute to be assisted by Dongming Zhang of Cornell University in further compiling the titles in English and other languages. The editors of this volume express their gratitude for their valuable assistance.

The Politics of Translation

A: 美学译文丛书
AESTHETICS TRANSLATION SERIES

书名 TITLE	著者 AUTHOR	译者 TRANSLATOR	出版时间 PUBLISHING TIME	初版印数 THE NUMBER OF COPIES
1) 美感：美学大纲 THE SENSE OF BEAUTY	(美) 桑塔耶纳 SANTAYANA, GEORGE	缪灵珠 MIAO, LING-ZHU	1982	55,000
2) 艺术问题 PROBLEMS OF ARTS	(美) 朗格 LANGER, SUSANNE	滕守尧、朱疆源 TENG, SHOU-YAO & ZHU, JIANG-YUAN	1983	50,000
3) 作为表现的科学和一般语言学的美学的历史 AESTHETICS AS THE SCIENCE OF EXPRESSION AND GENERAL LINGUISTICS	(意) 克罗齐 CROCE, BENEDETTO	王天清 WANG, TIAN-QING	1984	35,000
4) 美学与哲学 AESTHETICS AND PHILOSOPHY	(法) 杜夫海纳 DUFRENNE, MIKEL	孙非 SUN, FEI	1985	30,000
5) 艺术原理 THE PRINCIPLES OF ART	(英) 科林伍德 COLLINGWOOD, G	王至元、陈华中 WANG ZHI-YUAN & CHEN HUA-ZHONG	1985	38,000
6) 艺术哲学 PHILOSOPHY OF ART	(美) 奥尔德里奇 ALDRICH, VIRGIL	程孟辉 CHENG, MENG-HUI	1986	38,000
7) 情感与形式 FEELING AND FORM: A THEORY OF ART	(美) 朗格 LANGER, SUSANNE	刘大基 等 LIU, DA-JI & OTHERS	1986	40,000
8) 审美特性 INVESTIGATIONS OF THE CHARACTERISTICS OF BEAUTY	卢卡奇 LUKACS, GEORG	徐恒醇 XU, HENG-CHUN	1986	?
9) 论艺术的精神 CONCERNING THE SPIRITUAL IN ART	(俄) 康定斯基 KANDINSKY, WASILY	查立 ZHA, LI	1987	44,000
10) 美学与艺术原理 AESTHETICS AND THEORY OF ART	(德) 德索 DESSIOR, MAX	兰金仁 LIAN, JIN-REN	1987	22,000
11) 艺术与视知觉：视觉艺术心理学 ART AND VISUAL PERCEPTION; A	(美) 阿恩海姆 ARNHEIM, RUDOLF	滕守尧、朱疆源 TENG, SHOU-YAO & ZHU, JIANG-YUAN	1987	30,000

1

PSYCHOLOGY OF THE CREATIVE EYE			
12) 电影作为语言 LE LANGAGE CINEMATOGRAPHIQUE	(法) 马尔丹　吴岳添、赵家鹤 MARTIN, MARCEL	1988　5,000	WU, YUE-TIAN & ZHAO, JIA-HE
13) 中世纪美学 HISTORY OF AESTHETICS	(波) 塔塔科维兹　褚大维 等 TARTARKEIWICZ, WADYSAW	1991　2,400	CHU, DA-WEI ETC。
14) 眼与心 EYE AND MIND	(法) 梅洛-庞蒂　刘韵涵 MERLEAU-PONTY, MAURICE	1992　5,000	LIU, YUN-HAN
15) 艺术史原理 PRINCIPLES OF ART HISTORY; THE PROBLEM OF THE DEVELOPMENT OF STYLE IN LATER ART	(瑞士) 乌尔富林　梁再宏 WOLFFLIN, HEINRICH	?　?	LIANG, ZAI-HONG
16) 艺术即体验 ART AS EXPERIENCE	(美) 杜威　邢培明 DEWEY, JOHN	?　?	XING, PEI-MING
17) 创造力 CREATIVITY; THE MAGIC SYNTHESIS	(美) 阿瑞提　钱岗南 ARIETI, SILVANO	?　?	QIAN, GANG-NAN

------ THE ABOVE-LISTED BOOKS ARE PUBLISHED BY THE CHINESE ACADEMY OF SOCIAL SCIENCE PRESS

18) 艺术 ART	(英) 贝尔　周金环、马钟元 BELL, CLIVE	1984　21,000	ZHOU, JIN-HUAN & MA, ZHONG-YUAN
19) 走向科学的美学 SCIENTIFIC METHOD IN AESTHETICS	(美) 门罗　石天曙、滕守尧 MUNRO, THOMAS	1984　10,000	SHI, TIAN-SHU & TENG, SHOU-YAO
20) 美育书简 ON THE AESTHETIC EDUCATION OF MAN	(德) 席勒　徐恒醇 SCHILLER, FRIEDRICH	1984　35,500	XU, HENG-CHUN

------ THE ABOVE-LISTED BOOKS ARE PUBLISHED BY THE PUBLISHING HOUSE OF THE CHINESE ASSOCIATION OF LITERATURE AND ARTS

21) 视觉思维：审美直觉心理学 VISUAL THINKING	(美) 阿恩海姆　滕守尧 ARNHEIM, RUDOLF	1986　?	TENG, SHOU-YAO
22) 想象心理学 IMAGINATION; A METAPHYSICAL CRITIQUE	(法) 萨特　褚大维 SARTRE, JEAN PAUL	1988　360,000	CHU, DA-WEI

23)艺术哲学新论 PHILOSOPHY OF ART	(美)杜卡斯　王科平 DUCASSE, CURT JOHN	1988　8,000 WANG, KE-PING	
24)艺术与人的发展 THE ART AND HUMAN DEVELOPMENT	(美)加登纳　兰金仁 GARDNER, HOWARD	1988　10,500 LAN, JIN-REN	
25)趣味批判 CRITIQUE OF TASTE	(意)沃尔佩　王柯平、田时纲 VOLPE, GALVANO DELLA	1990　5,200 WANG, KE-PING & TIAN, SHI-GANG	
26)走向表现主义的美学 THE THEORY OF BEAUTY	(英)卡里特　苏晓离 等 ?	1990　4,900 SU, XIAO-LI AND AND OTHERS	
27)艺术极其对象 ART AND ITS SUBJECTS	(美)阿恩海姆　傅志强、钱岗南 ARNHEIM, RUDOLF	1990　4,300 FU, ZHI-QIANG & QIAN, GANG-NAN	
28)艺术语言 LANGUAGES OF ART: AN APPROACH TO A THEORY OF SYMBOLS	(美)古德曼　褚大维 GOODMAN, NELSON	1990　7,000 CHU, DA-WEI	
29)智能的结构 FRAMES OF MIND	(美)加登纳　兰金仁 GARDNER, HOWARD	1990　? LAN, JIN-REN	

------ THE ABOVE-LISTED BOOKS ARE PUBLISHED BY THE GUANG-MING DAILY PUBLISHING HOUSE

30)批评的循环—文史哲解释学 THE CRITICAL CIRCLE	(美)霍埃　兰金仁 HOY, DAVID C	1987　30,500 LAN, JIN-REN	
31)视觉艺术的含义 MEANING IN THE VISUAL ARTS	(美)潘诺夫斯基 傅志强 PANOFSKY	1987　36,000 FU, ZHI-QIANG	
32)美学新解—现代艺术哲学 PHILOSOPHY OF ART	(美)布洛克　滕守尧 BLOOKER, GENE	1987　40,000 TENG, SHOU-YAO	
33)符号学美学 ELEMENTS OF SEMIOLOGY	(法)巴特　董学文、王葵 BARTHES, ROLAND	1987　37,000 DONG, XUE-WEN & WANG, KUI	
34)接受美学与接受理论 TOWARD AN AESTHETICS OF RECEPTION & RECEPTION THEORY; A CRITICAL INTRODUCTION	(德)尧斯，(美)霍拉勃　周宁、金元浦 JAUSS, HANS P HOLUB, ROBERT C	1987　33,500 ZHOU, NING JIN, YUAN-PU	
35)艺术的真谛 THE MEANING OF ART	(英)里德　王柯平 READ, HERBERT	1987　44,000 WANG, KE-PING	

36) 艺术风格学 PRINCIPLES OF ART THEORY: THE PROBLEMS OF THE DEVELOPMENT OF STYLE	(瑞士) 沃尔夫林 WOLFFLIN, HEINRICH	潘耀昌、杨思梁 PAN, YAO-CHANG YANG, SI-LIANG	1987	39,200
37) 抽象与移情 ABSTRAKTION UND EINFUHLUNG	(德) 沃林格 WORRINGER, WILHELM	王才勇 WANG, CAI-YONG	1987	35,000
38) 创造的秘密 CREATIVITY; THE MAGIC SYNTHESIS	(美) 阿瑞提 ARIETI, SILVANO	钱岗南 QIAN, GANG-NAN	1987	38,300
39) 真理与方法 TRUTH AND METHOD	(德) 加达默尔 GADAMER, H。G。	王才勇 WANG, CAI-YONG	1987	35,500

------ THE ABOVE LISTED BOOKS ARE PUBLISHED BY THE LIAO-NING PEOPLE 'S PRESS

B：走向未来丛书
WALKING TOWARDS THE FUTURE SERIES

书名 TITLE	著者 AUTHOR	译者 TRANSLATOR	出版时间 PUBLISHING TIME	初版印数 THE NUMBER OF COPIES
1) 增长的极限 THE LIMITS OF GROWTH: A REPORT FOR THE CLUB OF ROME 'S PROJECT ON THE PREDICAMENT OF MANKIND	罗马俱乐部 THE CLUB OF ROME	李宝恒 LI, BAO-HENG	1984	12,700
2) GER — 一条永恒的金线 GODEL, ESCHER, BACH: AN ETERNAL GOLDEN BAND	(美) 霍夫斯塔特 HOFSTADTER, DOUGLAS R	乐秀成 编译 LE, XIU-CHENG, ED.	1984	16,500
3) 现代物理学与东方神秘主义 THE DAO OF PHYSICS: AN EXPLANATION OF THE PARALLELS BETWEEN MODERN PHYSICS AND EASTERN THOUGHT	卡普拉 CAPRA, FRITJOF	潘耕 编译 PAN, GENG, ED。	1984	13,400
4) 人的现代化 BECOMING MODERN: INDIVIDUALCHANGE IN SIX DEVELOPING COUNTRIES	(美) 英格尔斯 等 INKELES, ALEX & SMITH, DAVID	殷陆君 编译 DUAN, LU-JUN, ED。	1985	82,000
5) 没有极限的增长 THE ULTIMATE RESOURCE	(美) 西蒙 SIMON, JULIAN	黄江南 等 编译 HUANG, JIANG-NAN, ETC。	1985	63,500
6) 新的综合 SOCIOBIOLOGY: THE NEW SYNTHESIS	(美) 威尔逊 WILSON, EDMOND	李昆峰 编译 LI, KUN-FENG, ETC。	1985	62,400
7) 定量社会学 CONCEPTS AND MODELS OF A QUANTITATIVE SOCIOLOGY	(德) 韦德里希 WEIDLICH, W。G。HAAG	郭治安 等 编译 GUO, ZHI'AN, ETC。	1986	33,000
8) 系统思想 SYSTEM CONCEPTS	(美) 迈尔斯 MILES, ROBERT	编 杨志信、葛明浩 YANG, ZHI-XIN & GE, MING-HAO	1986	40,000
9) 日本为什么成功 WHY JAPAN HAS SUCCEEDED	(日) 森岛通夫 MORISHIMA, MICHIO	胡国成 HU, GUO-CHENG	1986	50,000
10) 佛罗依德著作选 SELECTED WORKS OF	(奥) 佛罗依德 RICKMAN, J。	贺明明 HE, MING-MING	1986	55,000

5

SIGMUND FREUD

11) 十七世纪英国的科学、技术与社会 SCIENCE, TECHNOLOGY, AND SOCIETY IN SEVENTEENTH CENTURY ENGLAND	(美) 默顿 MERTON, ROBERT	范岱年 等 FAN, DAI-NIAN, ETC。	1986 25,000
12) 梁启超与中国近代思想 LIANG CHI-CH'AO AND THE MIND OF MODERN CHINA	(美) 勒文森 LEVENSON, JOSEPH	刘伟 等 LIU, WEI, ETC。	1986 24,000
13) 新教伦理与资本主义精神 THE PROTESTANT ETHIC AND THE SPIRIT OF CAPITALISM	(德) 韦伯 WEBER, MAX	黄晓京、彭强 HUANG, XIAO-JING & PENG QIANG	1986 ?
14) 增长、短缺 与效率 GROWTH, SHORTAGE, AND EFFICIENCY	(匈) 科尔内 RNAI, JANOS	崔之元、彭强 CUI, ZHI-YUAN & PENG, QIANG	1986 38,000
15) 计量历史学 QUANTITATIVE METHODS IN HISTORICAL STUDIES	(苏) 科瓦尔琴科 主编 KOVALCHENKO, I. D., ET. AL。	闻一、萧吟 WEN, YI & XIAO, YIN	1987 42,000
16) 哲学的还原 PHILOSOPHY AND LINGUISTIC ANALYSIS	(?) 查尔斯沃斯 CHARLESWORTH, MAXWELL	田晓春 TIAN, XIAO-CHUN	1987 103,000
17) 社会研究方法 THE PRACTICE OF SOCIAL RESEARCH	(美) 巴比 BABBIE, EARL	白桦 等 编译 BAI, HUA, ETC。	1987 103,000
18) 社会选择与个人价值 SOCIAL CHOICE AND INDIVIDUAL VALUE	(美) 阿罗 ARROW, KENNETH	陈志武、崔之元 CHEN, ZHI-WU & CUI, ZHI-YUAN	1987 110,000
19) 对科学的傲慢与偏见 THE TWO CULTURES: SCIENCE AND GOVERNMENT	(英) 斯诺 SNOW, C. P。	陈恒六、刘兵 CHEN, HENG-LIU LIU, BING	1987 108,000
20) 马克斯 韦伯 MAX WEBER	(英) 帕金 PAVKIN, FRANK	刘东、谢维和 LIU, DONG & XIE, WEI-HE	1987 96,000
21) 现代化的动力 DYNAMICS OF MODERNIZATION	(美) 布莱克 BLACK, CYRIL	段晓光 DUAN, XIAO-GUANG	1988 32,000
22) 科学家在社会中的角色 THE SCIENTIST'S ROLE IN SOCIETY	(以色列) 本--戴维 BEN-DAVID, JOSEPH	赵佳苓 ZHAO, JIA-QIN佳	1988 32,000

6

23) 平等与效率　　　　　　　　(美) 奥肯　　　　　　王忠民、黄清　　1988　32,000
EQUALITY AND EFFICIENCY: OKUN, ARTHUR, M。　　　　　　　　　WANG, ZHONG-MIN
THE BIG TRADEOFF　　　　　　　　　　　　　　　　　　　　　　& HUANG, QING

24) 维特根斯坦哲学导论　　　　(荷兰) 范坡伊森　　刘东、谢维和　　1988　32,000
LUDWIG WITTGENSTEIN:　　(DUTCH) PEURSON, C。A。VON　　LIU, DONG
AN INTRODUCTION TO HIS　　　　　　　　　　　　　　　　　XIE, WEI-HE
PHILOSOPHY

Wang Xiaoming

C：文化：中国与世界丛书
CULTURE: CHINA AND THE WORLD SERIES

书名 TITLE	著者 AUTHOR	译者 TRANSLATOR	出版时间 PUBLISHING TIME	初版印数 THE NUMBER OF COPIES
1) 悲剧的诞生 THE BIRTH OF TRAGEDY	(德) 尼采 NIETZCHE, FREDERICH	周国平 ZHOU, GUO-PING	1986	5,000
2) 存在与虚无 BEING AND OTHINGNESS	(法) 萨特 SARTRE, JEAN PAUL	陈宣良 等 CHEN, XUANLIANG, ETC．	1987	3,700
3) 存在与时间 BEING AND TIME	(德) 海德格尔 HEIDEGGER, MARTIN	陈嘉映、王庆节 CHEN, JIA-YING & WANG, YING-JIE	1987	5,000
4) 结构主义与符号学 STRUCTURALISM AND SEMIOTICS: SELECTED READINGS		李幼蒸 编 LI, YOU-ZHENG, ED．	1987	5,000
5) 科学知识进化论 TRUTH, RATIONALITY, AND THE GROWTH OF SCIENTIFIC KNOWLEDGE	(英) 波普尔 POPPER, KARL	纪树立 JI, SHU-LI	1987	1,500
6) 新教伦理与资本主义精神 THE PROTESTANT ETHIC AND THE SPIRIT OF CAPITALISM	(德) 韦伯 WEBER, MAX	于晓 等 YU, XIAO, ETC．	1988	10,000
7) 哲学与自然之境 PHILOSOPHY AND THE MIRROR OF NATURE	(美) 罗蒂 RORTY, RICHARD	李幼蒸 LI, YOU-ZHENG	1988	1,500
8) 文化模式 PATTERNS OF CULTURE	(美) 本尼狄克特 BENEDICT, RUTH	王㸚 等 WANG, FU, ETC．	1988	16,000
9) 语言哲学名著选读：英美部分 SELECTED READINGS IN LINGUISTIC PHILOSOPHY (ENGLAND & U．S．)		涂纪亮 TU, JI-LIANG	1988	2,000
10) 语言与神话 LANGUAGE AND MYTH	(德) 卡西尔 CASSIRER, ERNST	于晓 等 YU, XIAO, ETC．	1988	2,000
11) 批评的批评 CRITIQUE DE LA CRITIQUE	(法) 托多洛夫 TODOROV, TZVETAN	王东亮、王晨阳 WANG, DONG-LIANG & WANG, CHEN-YANG	1988	1,000
12) 为自己的人	(美) 佛罗姆	孙依依	1988	15,000

	MAN FOR HIMSELF: AN INQUIRY IN TO THE PSYCHOLOGY OF ETHICS	FROMM, ERICH	SUN, YI-YI
13) 符号学原理 ELEMENTS OF SEMIOLOGY	(法) 巴特 BARTHES, ROLAND	李幼蒸	1988 7,000 LI, YOU-ZHENG
14) 接受美学译文集 AN ANTHOLOGY OF RECEPTION AESTHETICS		刘小枫 编	1989 3,500 LIU, XIAO-FENG, ED。
15) 资本主义文化矛盾 THE CULTURAL CONTRADICTIONS OF CAPITALISM	(美) 贝尔 BELL, DANIEL	赵一凡 等	1989 5,000 ZHAO, YI-FAN, ETC。
16) 摩西与一神教 MOSES AND MONOTHEISM	(奥) 佛洛依德 FREUD, SIGMUND	李展开	1989 6,500 LI, ZHAN-KAI
17) 发达资本主义时代的抒情诗人 CHARLES BAUDELAIRE: A LYRIC POET IN THE ERA OF HIGH CAPITALISM	(德) 本雅明 BENJAMIN, WALTER	张旭东、魏文生	1989 3,500 ZHANG, XU-DONG & WANG, WEN-SHENG
18) 生物学与认识 BIOLOGY AND KNOWLEDGE: AN ESSAY ON THE RELATIONS BETWEEN ORGANIC REGULATIONS AND COGNITIVE PROCESSES	(瑞士) 皮亚杰 PIAGET, JEAN	尚新建 等	1989 30,000 SHANG, XIN-JIAN, ETC。
19) 影响的焦虑 THE ANXIETY OF INFLUENCE	(美) 布鲁姆 BLOOM, HAROLD	徐文博	1989 3,000 XU, WEN-BO
20) 占有还是生存:一个新社会精神基础 TO HAVE OR TO BE?	(美) 佛罗姆 FROMM, ERICH	关山	1989 7,000 GUAN, SHAN
21) 俄国形式主义文论选 SELECTED READINGS IN RUSSIAN FORMALISM		方珊 等	1989 2,500 FANG, SHAN, ETC。
22) 变化社会中的政治秩序 POLITICAL ORDER AND CHANGING SOCIETIES	(美) 亨廷顿 HUNGTINTON, SAMUEL	王冠华	1989 10,000 WANG, GUAN-HUA
23) 审美之维 THE AESTHETIC DIMENSION: TOWARD A CRITIQUE OF MARXIST AESTHETICS	(美) 马尔库塞 MARCUSE, HERBERT	李小兵	1989 3,000 LI, XIAO-BING
24) 时间与传统 TIME AND TRADITIONS:	(加拿大) 欣格尔 TRIGGER, BRUCE G。	蒋祖棣、刘英	1992 2,500 JIANG, ZU-DI &

ESSAYS IN ARCHAEOLOGICAL INTERPRETATION		LIU, YING	
25) 分析心理学的理论与实践 ANALYTICAL PSYCHOLOGY: ITS THEORY AND PRACTICE	(瑞士:) 容格 成穷、王作虹 JUNG, C. G.	1992 4,000 CHENG, QIONG & WANG, ZUO-HONG	
26) 科学与社会秩序 SCIENCE AND THE SOCIAL ORDER	(美) 巴伯 顾昕 等 BARBER, BERNARD	1992 3,000 GU, YU, ETC.	
27) 艺术与诗中的创造性直觉 CREATIVE INTUITION IN ART AND POETRY	(法) 马利坦 刘有元、罗选民 MARITAIN, JACQUES	1992 3,500 LIU, YOU-YUAN & LUO, XUAN-MIN	
28) 论道德的谱系 GENEAOLOGY OF MORALS	(德) 尼采 周红 NIETZCHE, FREDRICH	1992 7,000 ZHOU, HONG	
29) 小说的兴起：笛福、理查逊 菲尔丁研究 THE RISE OF THE NOVEL	(英) 瓦特 高原、董红钧 WATT, IAN	1992 2,000 GAO, YUAN & DONG, HONG-JUN	
30) 哲学研究 PHILOSOPHICAL INVESTIGATIONS	(英) 维特根斯坦 汤潮、范光棣 WITTGENSTEIN, LUDWIG	1992 5,100 TANG, CHAO & FAN, GUANG-DI	
31) 心理学与文学 PSYCHOLOGY AND LITERATURE	(瑞士) 容格 冯川、苏克 JUNG, C. G.	1992 2,500 FENG, CHUAN & SU, KE	
32) 词语 *words*	(法) 萨特 李培厌 SARTRE, JEAN-PAUL	1989 6,000 LI, PEI-YAN	

D：新知文库
NEW KNOWLEDGE SERIES

书名 TITLE	著者 AUTHOR	译者 TRANSLATOR	出版时间 PUBLISHING TIME	初版印数 THE NUMBER OF COPIES
1) 佛罗依德的使命 SIGMUND FREUD'S MISSION; AN ANALYSIS OF HIS PERSONALITY AND INFLUENCE	(美) 佛罗姆 FROMM, ERICH	尚新建 SHANG, XIN-JIAN	1986	70,000
2) 劳伦斯 LAWRENCE	(英) 克默德 KERMODE, FRANK	胡缨 HU, YING	1986	15,000
3) 我与你 ICH UND DU	(德) 布伯 BUBER, NARDIN	陈维纲 CHEN, WEI-GANG	1987	40,000
4) 存在哲学 PHILOSOPHIES OF EXISTENCE	(法) 华尔 WAHL, JEAN	翁绍军 WENG, SHAO-JUN	1987	31,000
5) 经济体制－资源是怎样分配的 ECONOMIC SYSTEM: HOW RESOURCES ARE ALLOWED	(瑞典) 艾登姆 等 EDIDEM, ROLF & VIOTI, STAFFAN	王逸舟 WANG, YI-ZHOU	1987	30,000
6) 西西佛的神话 THE MYTH OF SISYPHUS	(法) 加缪 CAMUS, ALBERT	杜小真 DU, XIAO-ZHEN	1987	20,000
7) 容格心理学入门 A PRIMER OF JUNGIAN PSYCHOLOGY	(美) 霍尔 等 ?	冯川 FENG, CHUAN	1987	100,000
8) 伦理学 ETHICS	(美) 佛兰克纳 FRANKENA, W. K.	关键 GUAN, JIAN	1987	35,000
9) 科学与谬误 SCIENCE AND UNREASON	(美) 拉纳德 等 RADNER, DASIE & RADNER, MICHAEL	安保明、张松林 AN, BAO-MING & ZHANG, SONG-LIN	1987	20,000
10) 瓦格纳 WAGNER	(德) 麦耶尔 MAYER, HANS	赵勇、孟兆刚 ZHAO, YONG & MENG, ZHAO-GANG	1987	10,000
11) 科学是一种文化过程 SCIENCE AS A CULTURAL PROCESS	(美) 李克特 RICHTER, MAURICE N.	顾昕、张小天 GU, XIN & ZHANG, XIAO-TIAN	1987	35,000
12) 欧洲小说的演化 EVOLUTION OF EUROPEAN NOVELS	(英) 吉列斯比 GILLESPIE, GERALD	胡宗峦、冯国志 HU, ZONG-LUAN & FENG, GUO-ZHI	1987	15,000

13) 思维的训练 TEACHING THINKING	(英) 德波诺 DE BONO, EDWARD	何道宽、许力生 HE, DAO-KUAN & XU, LI-SHENG	1987 40,000
14) 自然科学的哲学 PHILOSOPHY OF NATURAL SCIENCE	(美) 亨普尔 HEMPEL, CARL G。	张华夏 等 ZHANG, HUA-XIA, ETC。	1987 9,000
15) 生活的科学 THE SCIENCE OF LIVING	(美) 阿德勒 ADLER, ALFRED	苏光、周晓琪 SU, GUANG & ZHOU, XIAO-QI	1987 45,000
16) 法律哲学 PHILOSOPHY OF LAW	(美) 戈尔丁 GOLDING, MARTIN P。	齐海滨 QI, HAI-BIN	1987 15,000
17) 雅斯贝尔斯 KARL JOSPERS	(德) 萨尼尔 SANER, HANS	张继武、倪梁康 ZHANG, JI-WU & NI, LIANG-KANG	1988 4,500
18) 成长心理学 GROWTH PSYCHOLOGY	(美) 舒尔兹 SCHULTZ, DUANE	李文邗 LI, WEN-HAN	1988 50,000
19) 历史哲学 PHILOSOPHY OF HISTORY	(美) 德雷 DRAY, WILLIAMS H。	王凫、尚新建 WANG, FU & SHANG, XIN-JIAN	1988 15,000
20) 自然科学的形而上学基础 METAPHYSISCHE ANFANG SGRUNDE DER	(德) 康德 KANT, I。	邓晓芒 DENG, XIAO-MANG	1988 10,000
21) 认识萨特 CONNAITRE SARTRE	(法) 加涅宾 CAGNEBIN, LAUVENT	顾家琛 GU, JIA-CHEN	1988 20,000
22) 艺术判断 KUNSTUVTEIL	(德) 博格似特 BOGERST, CLAUS	刁承俊、蒋芒 DIAO, CHEN-JUN & JIANG, MANG	1988 15,000
23) 跨文化传通 UNDERSTANDING INTERCULTURAL COMMUNICATION	(美) 萨姆瓦 等 SAMOVAR, LAWY A。, PORER, R。E。& JAIN, NEMI C。	陈南 等 CHEN, NAN	1988 10,000
24) 马克斯 韦伯 MAX WEBER	(德) 菲根 FUGEN, HANS N。	王榕芳 WANG, RONG-FANG	1988 10,000
25) 里尔克 RAINER MARIA IN SELBSTZEUGNISSEN UND BILDDOKUMENTEN	(德) 霍尔特胡森 HOLTHUSEN, HANS EGON	魏育青 WEI, YU-QING	1988 10,000
26) 教育哲学 PHILOSOPHY OF EDUCATION	(美) 麦克莱伦 MCLELLAN, JAMES E。	宋少云、陈平 SONG, SHAO-YUN & CHEN, PING	1988 12,000

27) 知识论 THEORY OF KNOWLEDGE	(美) 齐硕姆 CHISHOLM, RODERICK M.	邹惟远、邹晓蕾	1988 85,000 ZOU, WEI-YUAN & ZOU, XIAO-LEI
28) 语言哲学 PHILOSOPHY OF LANGUAGE	(美) 阿尔斯顿 ALSTON, WILLIAM	牟博、刘鸿辉	1988 12,000 MOU, BO & LIU, HONG-HUI
29) 浪漫主义与现实主义 ROMANCE AND REALISM	(美) 考德威尔 CAUDEWELL, CHRISTOPHER	薛鸿时	1988 10,000 XUE, HONG-SHI
30) 超现实主义 LE SURREALISME	(法) 杜布莱西斯 DUPLESSIS, YVONNE	龙高放	? ? LONG, GAO-FANG
31) 罗兰 巴特尔 ROLAND BARTHES	(美) 卡勒尔 CULLER, JONATHAN	方谦、李幼蒸	1989 4,000 FANG, QIAN & LI, YOU-ZHENG
32) 文学结构主义 STRUCTURALISM IN LITERATURE: AN INTRODUCTION	(美) 休斯 SCHOIES, ROBERT	刘豫	1989 5,000 LIU, YU
33) 社会科学哲学 PHILOSOPHY OF SOCIAL SCIENCE	(美) 鲁德纳 RUDNER, RICHARD S.	曲跃后、林金城	1989 5,000 QU, YUE-HOU & LIN, JIN-CHENG
34) 叙事虚构作品 NARRATIVE FICTION: CONTEMPORARY POETICS	(以色列) 里蒙—凯南 RIMMON-KENAN, SHLOMITH	姚锦清	1989 3,000 YAO, JIN-QING
35) 表现主义 EXPRESSIONISMUS	(奥地利) 巴尔 BAHR, HEMANN	徐菲	1989 3,000 XU, FEI
36) 基督的人生观 FACING LIFE WITH CHRIST	(英) 里德 REID, JAMES	蒋厌	1989 12,000 JIANG, YAN
37) 数学哲学 PHILOSOPHY OF MATHEMATICS	(美) 巴克尔 BARKER, STEPHEN	韩光焘	1989 5,000 HAN, GUANG-TAO
38) 心的哲学 PHILOSOPHY OF MIND	(美) 沙佛尔 SHAFER, JEROME A.	陈少鸣	1989 10,100 CHEN, SHAO-MING
39) 比较法律文化 COMPARATIVE LEGAL CULTURES	(美) 埃尔曼 EHRMANN, HENRY W.	贺卫方	1990 5,000 HE, WEI-FANG

THE TOTAL NUMBER OF TITLES IN THE ORIGINAL LISTS IS 158。
THE TOTAL NUMBER OF TITLES IN THIS LIST IS 134。

MODERNITY IN SUSPENSE: THE LOGIC OF FETISHISM IN KOREAN CINEMA

Kim Soyoung

The International Monetary Fund (IMF) stalks South Korea as I write. The problem, as always it seems, is foreign debt and unemployment. The president of the IMF speaks, from an interview room, words full of reason and reasonableness, telling the national television audience about lay offs. Yet an image—or rather, a series of them—disturbs the rationality of his address: the oversized American dollars that are papered over the walls of the room. The U.S. dollar speaks a language of magic as well as reason. And although it is the gold charms which Korean citizens sell to bail out the country that apparently play out the traditional role of fetish, the very size and number of the American dollars also recalls the role of fetish, demanding a kind of passionate submission to them. This is what the shifts in exchange rate also seem to have done: confronted with the stability of the American currency's value, South Korea can only adopt an attitude of passionate submission. The highly touted role announced for South Korea, as a new and active member of the OECD (Organization for Economic Cooperation and Development), is ultimately only a passive one—finally not globalizing but globalized.

In the imaginary of South Koreans, the triumph of finance capital over industrial capital (signalled by the IMF) is understood against the familiar backdrop of imperialism and colonialism. It is even expected that the most "advanced" mode—as announced by the global order—should triumph. As finance capital appears to triumph, the recurrent image is that of the late nineteenth century, when imperialist forces took control of the Chosun Dynasty that reigned on the Korean peninsula. Despite its anachronistic nature, this image comes to mind because, in the national imaginary, it marks the advent of modernity. It demarcates the division between the premodern (Chosun) and the modern (Korea). Yet it is not easy to speak of modernity together with the Korean nation in this way. This nation is always understood as something seized or rigged, and of course divided, by the forces of modernity, of modern imperialism. The Korean nation is seen as somehow in tension with modernity—Western modernity—and as a consequence, modernity continues to be imagined as an unattainable yet somehow desirable state that always exists elsewhere. So it is that the spectacle of the IMF with its monstrous dollars can so easily displace the scene of human suffering in South Korea.

Confronted with this unprecedented crisis in all its complexity, I confess that I do not have a conceptual framework for dealing with the present situation. Yet the question of modernity recurs, and I feel compelled to work through it. I work with the cinema of South Korea, particularly that of the postcolonial period (elsewhere understood as the end of the Asia-Pacific or of the Second World War). In this context, I am interested in films that deal strategically with the forces of colonialism and modernization. I am especially interested in films with something like ghosts or ghostly qualities, films in which modernity appears not so much as a terrible threat but as a source of enchantment and puzzlement, a kind of siren's song that beckons us into uncharted seas. In such films the logic of the fetish comes to the fore, as a kind of passionate submission that disturbs many of the familiar oppositions that suspend Korea between the premodern and the modern, thus suggesting new ways of thinking about Korean cinema and Korean modernity—or, I would venture to say, cinema in Korea and modernity in Korea.

I use the idea of the fetish as a way to link some rather disparate observations. It serves as a tentative point of departure for drawing connections between the binary divisions set up by capitalism and colonialism as well as in cinematic narratives of a Korean modernity haunted by premodern specters. It is significant that the idea of the fetish emerges in a colonial context: specifically, exchanges between Europeans and West Africans, in which Africans surrendered their gold in order to obtain trivial objects from the West. Thus the colonized, apparently unaware of modern value, were cast in the role of fetishists. Yet Marx reminds us that capital too has the qualities of a fetish, and there are magical tales about capitalism, tales that continue to divide that West from the rest and the modern from their others.

If we adopt the position constructed for the other of the West (the one who is allegedly entranced by the West's trivial but strangely compelling commodities), however, then we find a different story. For the colonized, the advent of modern capitalism is supposed to be in the form of magic, witchcraft and general malediction—which magic apparently affords no resistance or relief. This story of the colonized is one that we seldom hear and at the same time hear too much of—the tale of colony people's impassioned and tortured submission to the West. If something rings false about this story, it is the supposition that the colonized remain in a state of purity with respect to the fetish, in a sort of one-way relationship, a generalized Experience of the Colonized. In fact, composite modes abound. The layers attached to the translation of the term fetish into Korean attest, in a facetious way, to such complexity. There are *chumul*, *mulshin*, and *oyonmul*. *Chumul*, which designates shamanistic objects, conjures up an aura of the premodern. Yet it is already a mediated premodernity: the term first appeared under Japanese colonial rule in Korea, with the introduction of anthropology. *Mulshin* is the term closest to "commodity"; it could be used in the context of something like Lukácsian reification, for instance. Finally, *oyonmul* came with the translation of psychoanalysis into Korean, with the works of Freud and Lacan, to designate the object of desire or love objects.

The existence of such complexity in translation inspires me to say, at the outset, that fetishism always involves something other than a simple binary division such as that given in our common stories about the West and the rest. There is more to modernity than a neat bifurcation of cultures and experiences. The logic of the fetish, with its layers of cultural specificity, affords a way to explore this complexity and to challenge the inevitability of modern binarisms, such as modern versus premodern or modern versus traditional.[1]

Early Cinema and Korea

In *Fetishism and Curiosity*, Laura Mulvey links the cinematic illusion to the logic of the fetish. "The cinematic illusion," she writes, "has continued to flourish on pleasure in belief, or rather, on the human mind's ability and desire to 'know' and to 'suspend disbelief' simultaneously. From this perspective, the cinema accuses the rational world, once again, of a credulity that belongs to the origin of the term 'fetishism.'"[2] Her stance elucidates some of the exchanges that accompany the introduction of cinema into Korea—exchanges that combine belief and disbelief, and which suggest a fetishistic desire for truth and for fantasy.

Burton Holmes, an American traveller who penned volumes based on his voyages, visited Korea in 1899. He brought with him a small portable machine for the projection of moving pictures, which captured the fancy of the city of Seoul.[3] Needless to say, that cinema came so quickly to Korea reminds us that the invention and dissemination of cinema was coeval with the peak of imperialism. In the mad scramble for the globe, the imperial powers—Japan, Russia, Germany and the United States—forced Korea (or rather, Chosun) to open its ports to them.

Holmes's apparatus caught the interest of the imperial family, and the young prince was apparently so delighted with it that he wished to keep it. After a few days, however, he returned the borrowed device to Holmes and his company, along with a box of gifts containing precious green silks and fans. When Holmes and company accepted an invitation to the royal palace, their guide and translator, Park Kiho, worried that the prince intended to take the apparatus. Holmes, however, wrapped it and presented it to the prince, and in return his company received a wealth of silks as well as two scroll paintings and silver. And another surprise awaited them: a court dance performed by royal courtesans, a performance that impressed the world traveller as much as moving pictures had impressed the royal family. In this early exchange, in which a court performance crosses paths with the cinematic apparatus, is there not an anticipation of a general pattern of exchanges and interactions between traditional and modern modes? A pattern of exchange in which both the traditional and modern are drawn into the realm of commodities? It comes as no surprise, then, that the era of silent films in Korea came to be characterized by the omnipresence of courtesans, as both performers and spectators.[4] Courtesans became professional actors because respectable women refused to appear in movies. And in one of the earliest Korean films, "The Story of Chunhyang" (*Chunhyangchon*, 1923), the renowned courtesan Hanryong played the lead.[5] One had only to close the cycle of exchanges that occurred between Holmes and the royal family to arrive at moving pictures with courtesan performers.

Such a closing of the cycle of exchanges was precipitated by the prior fusion of commodities and films. In the 1890s for instance, the English-American Tobacco Company and the English-American Electric Company began to show films in order to promote their respective products, tobacco and the streetcar. Ten box labels from Old Gold tobacco or twenty from Drumhead tobacco afforded one admission to a screening. Thus began the double enchantment or double bind of spectator as consumer. And thus began colonial modernity in Korea: modern in its modes of exchange yet with colonizing modes of production. But then, one might say that all modernity is colonial in this sense of its modes of production—it is only a matter of degree.

Because Japan annexed Korea to its empire in 1910 and ruled until 1945, early, silent cinema in Korea were subject to Japanese colonialism, at once dependent on the Japanese empire and in some respects resistant to it. As Japanese policy in Korea shifted from military occupation and exploitation to the so-called "Cultural Policy" of the late teens and twenties, cinema in Korea became associated with the wave of prosperity and began to lend its services directly to money matters. One film from this period, "Wolha's Pledge" (*Wolhai Maengsae*, 1923), was basically a propaganda film produced by the Postal Service Department to encourage saving. The heroine of the film, Wolha, pays her husband's gambling debts out of her savings account, and the film concludes with her determination to save more money for future crises. This presentation of wifely virtues—saving to pay gambling debts—may strike us as odd now, even for a propaganda film, yet we should recall that this was a time of transition, and in its eccentric way this film expresses the vacillation between different value systems.

Robert J. Foster discusses a similar situation in his account of how the Australian Reserve Bank developed a program to encourage the natives of New Guinea to put their money in Australian banks, a strategy calculated to generate capital to finance territorial development. With commissioned films and pamphlets designed to produce a fetishization of money, the bank enforced a certain paradigm for the modern individual. "Money's fetishization," writes Foster, "facilitates projecting the image of a progressive, self-disciplined individual—an image that returns us to the sort of moral education implied in the Reserve Bank's program."[6]

In these examples, we see a rapid and uncanny convergence of spectator, consumer, and the saving account—the emergence of a certain kind of modern identity for which cinematic experience provides a locus. Moreover, these examples serve as a reminder that modern identity always implies a process like colonization, with the emergence of new kinds of economic unevenness around figures like wives and natives. This highlights the idea that modern forms of unevenness—and colonial relations themselves—are never entirely outside the nation; and as they divide the nation, they also give it cohesiveness. Thus the residual, so-called premodern forces of society are not necessarily forms of resistance; they may even be part of modernity itself.

It is not surprising then that, with the advent of locally produced films in Korea, spectators and filmmakers participated in modes of representation that hovered between the all-too-familiar and the novel. Something like "kino-drama," which suggests novelty, becomes in Korean, *yonswaekuk* or "linked drama." This is to say, it was a hybrid form, combining the screening of a short film with the theatrical performance of a *shinpa* drama. Shinpa or "the new school" of theatre derived from the Japanese *shinpa* theatre which had itself emerged in the late nineteenth century, in response to European theatre, as a movement against the supposedly outmoded traditional kabuki theatre, aiming to present contemporary dramas in a westernized or modern style—an instance which again serves as a reminder of the intersection of modern hybridity and colonial unevenness.

Kino-drama brought with it stories like that of "The Revenge of Justice" (*Uirichok*

Kuto, 1919), in which the eldest son fights his stepmother to restore order in the family, that is, stories of the most traditional kind in a novel medium. In this way, kino-drama adjusted the expectations of spectators familiar with theatrical performance with the mechanically reproduced images of cinema. Its effect was not unlike that of the nickelodeon as discussed by Miriam Hansen, as "an accidental effect of overlapping types of public sphere, of 'non-synchronous' layers of cultural organization. This non-synchrony seems to characterize both the cinema's parasitic relationship to existing cultural traditions, and within the emerging institution, the uneven development of modes of production, distribution, and exhibition."[7] Her description is an apt one for the effect of kino-drama in Korea, although the "parasitic relationship" might wrongly suggest that the uneven relationship goes in one direction, that only the new media feed on the "host" of traditional media. On the contrary, the unevenness brings with it a kind of commensualism, in which benefits are mutually accrued despite the asymmetry of the relationship. In Korea, the non-synchrony layers that accompany cinema clearly implicate the colonial relationship between Japan and Korea, within the interplay of shinpa and shinpa. Which might lead one to ask whether the nickelodeon is not implicated in colonial unevenness as well.

With the first full-length feature film, "Frontier of the Nation" (*Kukgyong*, 1923), with the proliferation of local productions and movie theatres, kino-drama began gradually to give way to new forms of cinematic expression and reception. Yet spectators still treated the medium as a source of wonder, and one often reads in histories of national cinema that audiences continued to find the cinematic machinery more interesting than the moving images themselves. Projectionists encouraged spectators to believe that there was a miniature world inside the projector and if the film broke, they recited a magical incantation over the projector, "Suri suri masuri" or "Abracadabra." But then, the histories of early cinema in Japan often insist on the "primitive" character of spectators, emphasizing their fascination with the machinery, avoiding the fact that similar relations existed within Europe and North America. It is as if histories of non-Western national cinema inevitably strive to re-enchant the arrival of Western, by positing non-Western natives whose credulity leads them to fetishize rather than to master technology. One need only recall, however, Mulvey's take on the fetish—that it involves a desire for belief, or a suspension of disbelief—to ask who is the fetishist in this scenario.

William Pietz argues that fetish is a word coined in response to an unprecedented situation, in which there are relations between "cultures so radically different as to be mutually incomprehensible."[8] It is true that the arrival of cinema in Korea presented a form of non-synchrony, one far more radical than existed in Europe or North America, and, as a result, it is arguable that Koreans tended to fetishize the cinematic apparatus more than did Westerners. Thus cinema could serve to cover over the gaps in the industrial infrastructure of an "underdeveloped" society. Still, in this respect, the Korean difference is not in kind but in degree—in the magnitude of intensity on the new global continuum. And as cinema "magically" interpellated spectators into industrial culture, those intellectuals who resisted it also turned to cinema, to effect decolonization predicated upon faith in Marxism, nationalism, and the Enlightenment. One kind of fetish (the "traditional" *chumul*) encountered another kind (the modern commodity fetish *mulshin*) constructing a modern field of contestation between colonizing and decolonizing forces, a field that became visible in early cinema and has continued into postcolonial cinema in Korea. It has been argued that the post-colonial period in South Korea has never achieved a true decolonization.[9] Of course, this can be explained in terms of continuity between the colonial and postcolonial periods. Yet another question arises, of whether the nation, usually the rallying point for decolonization, is not also the site for the return of the West. This is the spectre that haunts cinema in Korea, as national cinema.

Freeze!

In the final scene of many South Korean films, it is the freeze-frame that draws the narrative to a close. Images unwind, and then, Freeze! This is such a standard form of cinematic address that it has become natural for local spectators; and as such, it seems to present, quite directly, a cinematic articulation of a general structure of feeling.[10] It is hard not to interpret the ubiquity of the freeze-frame in terms of a sense of entrapment, immobility, and eternal suspension, which is the experience of spectators who live with the history of colonization, partition, and an intensive concentration of industrial capitalist development. It seems plausible that the freeze-frame somehow renders this experience with all its violence and suspense. Then too, it recalls Walter Benjamin's account of the crystallized image, or the dialectical image at a standstill—a moment in which the past awaits the flash. "Thinking," he writes, "involves not only the flow of thoughts but their arrest as well. Where thinking suddenly stops in a configuration pregnant with tensions, it gives that configuration a shock, by which it crystallizes into a monad."[11]

Indeed the frozen surface of the image betrays a tension reminiscent of the "petrified unrest" that Benjamin detects in a series of dialectical images. This petrified unrest offers the possibility for allegory, for a violent wresting of the image from its everyday fluidity, which would serve to prevent new structures of experience from being monumentalized under outmoded aesthetics. In this respect, the unresolved crises in Korean cinema are not so much impasses as possibilities that open into a future, not a denial of modernity but an attempt to crack it open. Is the ubiquitous freeze-frame not a petrified yet restive desire for a new society? Or is it simply an expression of nostalgia, or of a fear of entrapment, an atavistic attachment to an outmoded past?

"The Man with Three Coffins" (*Nakune Nun Kil Esoto Swijji Annunda*, 1987) is a road movie, popular in Korea, which ends with a freeze-frame. In it, national partition hinders the mobility of protagonists, making it impossible for them to reach their destination across the DMZ (demilitarized zone). In his account of road movies, Kyung Hyun Kim calls attention to how the female body becomes a nodal point in this film, serving as the locus for fantasizing the past.[12] The old man in "The Man with Three Coffins" gazes on a faded, treasured photo of his wife, which image dissolves into that of the young nurse who attends him. It is rather like Deleuze's account of the fetish, which in distinction from the symbol, he calls "a frozen, arrested, two-dimensional image, a photograph to which one returns repeatedly to exorcise the dangerous consequences of movement, the harmful discoveries that result from exploration; it represents the last point at which it was still possible to believe."[13] And in a general way, it would seem that the freeze-frame has something of the fetish about it, in that it tends to turn the action back toward the past, in effect to live in the past. And yet the apparent blockage is not necessarily a return to an idealized past, nor to the image of a unified and utopian nation.

For instance, in "La Vie en Rose" (*Changmipit Insaeng*, 1993), the adventures of two gangsters end with a freeze-frame that shuts down the film in 1988, the time of the Seoul Olympics, at the moment touted as marking the coming of age of South Korea, or indeed its absorption into the global order. Kyun Hyun Kim notes the overwhelming sense of immobility in this film. The premise of the film's genre—on the road in search of something—remains unfulfilled, and the characters often find themselves caught between the communist North and the capitalist South. The merest indication of transgression of the North-South boundary seems, by some strange logic, to demand the death of the heroes. This leads Kim to argue that movement in the road movie does not simply return to the notion of a pure national identity. The ironic twist that brings the search to its non-conclusion "produces a multiple cultural signification of the nation's history," to quote Kim's turn of phrase. He concludes, "The road movies allow this discursive effect without offering an alternative that seeks to resolve the threatening and ambivalent qualities that are attached with the discourse of the nation."[14]

If we return to the frozen image with this national and historical ambivalence in mind, it is easier to see how such freeze-frames might operate like allegory in the Benjaminian sense. "Whereas in the symbol destruction is idealized and the transfigured face of nature is fleetingly revealed in the light of redemption," Benjamin writes elsewhere, "in allegory, the observer is confronted with the *facies hippocratica* of history as a petrified, primordial landscape."[15] More than a nostalgic return to a tradition or an idealized experience of the nation, the freeze-frame, in a moment that resembles Benjamin's "flash," breaks into allegory and confronts the spectator with a history that opens into the future. Rolf Tiedemann sums up the significance of allegory in a way that illuminates the freeze-frame:

> The gaze, which exorcized images from objects blasted loose from time, is the Gorgon gaze at the "facies hippocratica of history," the "petrified primordial landscape" of myth. . . . But in that mystical moment when Past and Present enter "lightening-like" into a constellation—when the true image of the past "flashes" into the "now of recognizability"—that image becomes a dialectically changing image, as it presents itself from the messianic perspective, or (in materialistic terms) the perspective of the revolution.[16]

It is not in the freeze-frame itself, however, but rather in the unsettling films of Kim Kiyoung that the allegorical possibilities presented in the freeze-frame are actualized.

Kim Kiyoung

Chungmoo Choi, in her discussion of postcolonial South Korea, evokes Antonio Gramsci's notion of an interregnum, an in-between time in which a variety of morbid symptoms come to the surface—and in which one is caught between the already-over and the not-yet-arrived. Interregnum rather appropriately describes the start of the filmmaking career of Kim Kiyoung. Kim Kiyoung began his career with an anti-communist propaganda film, "Box of Death" (*Chukumui Sangcha*, 1955), funded by a film unit set up by the United States military during the Korean War. By that time, American forces occupied the southern half of the newly partitioned Korean peninsula, bringing a kind of neocolonial rule in the wake of the Japanese colonial rule. From that time, throughout the thirty-one films he made before his death in 1998, Kim excelled in the production of morbid and grotesque images. Indeed, in view of the time span of his career and the overabundance of uncanny imagery, it is tempting to characterize him as the "interregnum" filmmaker par excellence.

In his celebrated "Housemaid Trilogy" consisting of "The Housemaid" (*Hanyo*, 1961), "The Woman of Fire" (*Hwayo*, 1971) and "The Insect Woman" (*Chungmo*, 1972), Kim explores the double bind of modernity through the confrontation of two rather stereotyped figures: a lower-class *femme fatale* who works her charms in order to seduce and threaten the authority of a man with bourgeois ambitions and pretensions. The woman from the underclass—typically either a maid or a prostitute—is associated with the irrational, the institutional, and the biological, while the man belongs to an emergent middle class that surrounds itself with Western commodities—as Chris Berry remarks when he calls attention to the prevalence of modern appliances in the Western-style houses in "The Housemaid" and "The Insect Woman."[17] Thus, by seducing her master, the woman disturbs the tidy emergence of the middle class, with the result that there emerges a kind of allegorical confrontation between the traditional and modern, in these figures in a seduction. Yet what would be a romance quickly becomes a source of terror, and Kim's use of the conventions of the horror genre allow him to explore the tensions between the forces of the traditional and the modern.

Where does the horror come from? And how to stop it? As if to tease us with answers to such questions, Kim frequently weaves an investigation into his films (as in "The Insect Woman" and "The Woman of Fire)" offering a thread of rational interrogation, a touch of the thriller. A male figure of authority—a detective, a reporter, a doctor—investigates the double suicides, and the response tends to confirm biological explanations—for instance, the clash between the male instinct for sexual consummation and female instinct for reproduction (overdetermined by the animalistic overtones of his titles). A moral warning ensues, delivered so readily and so archly that it fails to convince. The male authority strives to reduce the complexities and dynamics of these histories to an essentialized discourse on biology, yet his explications fail to resolve the tensions or to heal the wounds that run through the text—wounds which simply will not go away. They haunt these films because they go far beyond the cinematic text, echoing the conflicts born of the period of rapid and intensified modernization.

Women from poor rural areas suffered doubly in the postcolonial "recovery," exploited by the forces of advanced capitalism as well as the patriarchal authority of village life. In Kim Kiyoung's films, such women return as seductresses with uncontrollable powers. They return to haunt the scene of modernization, a scene they have never really left despite attempts to forget or conceal their miserable conditions. Kim's preference for the term *hanyo*—used for "housemaid"—evokes a female figure already obsolete at the time of the films; the hanyo had already given way to the *sikmo*, who tended to the kitchen. Without skills to survive modernization, she cannot even lay claim to enough technical ability to play the role of chef. Instead, she calls on her allegedly biological instincts as a woman, relying on these to assure her social mobility. Men in Kim's films are presented with a range of options, passing the bar exam or marrying a rich girl as in "The Coachman" (*Mabu*, 1961) or "Mr. Park" (*Park Sobang*, 1960), respectively. Women, in contrast, depend solely on their supposedly dangerous instinct for reproduction, evidently as a means to move up in society. Yet, in a manner at once eerie and perfectly appropriate, the menace of these remnants only emerges in contemporary settings, as if the force of the premodern could only be configured and conceptualized within the framework of modernity. With such an obvious conflation of premodern monstrosity and modern commodity, a question arises about the way in which Kim's films use women in order to mobilize the dreaded instinct that, in his view, characterizes the human condition. Where does this leave women? Do they stand in opposition to modernity, at once as relics of the past and as reminders of the evil that lurks in humanity? Or is it merely that they are doubly erased in Kim's films, victims both of modernity and of tradition?

Recently, Paul Willemen has taken up the question of modernization in South Korea and its cinema. He notes a complex blockage, historically and culturally specific to South Korea, remarking that "both the way back to tradition and the way forward to modernity are blocked, as both directions appear to open onto anti-modern, absolutist, and corrupting social organizations."[18] "Killer Butterfly" (*Salinnapirul chotnunypsa*, 1978), an amalgam of science fiction, horror, and thriller, presents three episodes in the life of a history student. In the second of its "historical" explorations, a 2,000-year-old skeleton comes to life, as a beautiful young woman who seduces the history student. The film ostensibly explains these events in scientific terms, but the overall effect is a radical collapse of differentiation between ancient and modern. Regardless of era, women and men are caught in manic cycles of patriarchal oppression and female hysteria. If one adopts linear, scientific criteria for modernity (in the manner of modernization theory), then it is clear that there is nowhere to go—as Willemen suggests, all is corruption; and maybe this is an exercise in anti-modern sentiment. Yet in this film as in others by Kim Kiyoung, the horrific blockage of linear histories challenges us to rethink the terms of modernity.

In "The Housemaid," the forces of modernization prevent the upward mobility of the maid. "The Sunny Trail" (*Yangsando*, 1955), however, presents the story of a peasant girl in the Chosun era, showing the caste system as equally hostile to social mobility. Although the woman has a loyal lover from the same caste, she is forced to marry an aristocrat to save her father, and her beloved kills himself when he hears of it. Death awaits her, too. The mother of her dead lover kills her in order to conduct a wedding ceremony with a dead bride and groom, to assure that their spirits will finally entwine. The women in Kim's modern movies fare somewhat better, although the logic of these films is much the same. The working-class women in the Housemaid Trilogy and in "Carnivore" (*Yuksik Tongmul*, 1984) drag their masters into hell with them. With their nightmarish, gothic confrontations between the working class and the upper-middle class, such movies anticipate the social confrontations that only emerged, and were publicly addressed, some twenty or thirty years later.

To return to the question of the blockage of linear histories in Kim's cinema, I can't help feeling that, among the many reasons, for this are practical issues of distribution and circulation that also inform these texts. For instance, the Korean Motion Picture Promotion Company, set up by the government, has done little to promote Korean films overseas. While the South Korean film industry has produced some 200 films (or more) each year over the past fifty years, the market remains domestic. Alternatively, one might frame an argument about the "Korean cultural constellation" itself, as Paul Willemen does. Surely the problem is overdetermined. In any case, in addressing the question of how films can break into the international art-house circuit, Chris Berry suggests that Kim Kiyoung shows promise. "They satisfy the demand for an *auteur* and are stylistically distinctive, differentiating them from other films already circulating through the art-house and festival circuit."[19] Nevertheless, they have yet to attract international attention. I think, however, that they deserve such attention precisely because they deal with issues so fundamental to cinema and modernity, mobilizing fetishism as a way to stage the blockage of linear progression and a breakthrough into an alternative modernity. Yet to write of films that really have not been shown very much outside South Korea puts me in a strange enunciative position—that of introducing and promoting another unknown cinema, which is always envisioned as a national cinema. As I address questions of modernity and fetishism in cinema, the specter of modernity haunts my words, guides my observations, and projects the modern nation onto an international scene.

Laura Mulvey explains that "both Freud and Marx use the concept of fetishism in an attempt to explain a refusal, or blockage, of the mind, or a phobic inability of the psyche, to understand a symbolic system of value, one within the social and the other within the psychoanalytic sphere."[20] Almost inevitably, as one moves between the psychic and social registers of fetishism in cinema, one arrives at national culture—as I have done, albeit somewhat reluctantly—which in turn leads one to conclude that it is the impossible tensions of Korean culture which are translated into (and from) Kim's movies. Yet this ineluctable turn to national culture and national cinema is complicated by fetishism, with its psychosocial blockages and passionate submission.

If Kim's films prove to be a breakthrough locally and internationally, they might not only provide different ways of reading modernity in South Korea but also strategic ways of addressing it. The popularity of his films with his contemporaries in the 1960s and '70s, as well as with young spectators in the late 1990s, suggests that his approach to unresolved social confrontations has remained relevant for audiences throughout the postcolonial period. Still, Kim's vision is far removed from the concerns of South Korea's postcolonial intellectual filmmakers and critics, who have sought to construct nationalism by way of realism—as is the case with Yu Hyunmok's films such as "Stray Bullet" (*Obaltan*, 1961). As a result, despite (or because of) his popularity at the box office, prior to the mid-1990s, most critics and filmmakers dismissed Kim's work as ahistorical, artificial, and sexually excessive. Ironically, the same qualities are currently attracting attention, locally and internationally. At the Berlin Film Festival, for instance, Erica Gregor likened him to Fassbinder or Sirk.[21] The comparison is apt in a certain respect, for the films cited thus far exhibit a tendency to lavish attention on the erotic possibilities of American commodity culture—to fetishize it, as it were. Yet the logic of fetishization is such that it goes beyond lavish attention, becoming a spectacle of excess, investing things with life, purpose, and authority over the viewer—thus always on the verge of de-fetishizing the same objects.

Kim's films show an aesthetic affinity with the fetishistic scopophilia that Mulvey found to be characteristic of the films of Josef von Sternberg. In the midst of the clutter of objects that swarm onto the scene emerges the figure of the mother, at once cruel and nurturing, shrouded in layers of veils, revealed through netting. Of course, in her classic account of visual pleasure, Mulvey glosses over the link between this fetishism and masochism, yet it is precisely this masochistic possibility that opens the psychological register into economic and social concerns, for the modernizing male submits passionately to the "premodern mother." Thus Kim's films set up a critical oscillation between the modern and premodern, the rational and irrational, the civilized and primitive, the sacred and profane, the scientific and the superstitious, in a series of binarisms demarcated by gender, thus allowing for perverse couplings. Instead of deploying the ubiquitous freeze-frame, which suspends the oscillation between pairs, Kim tends to let the pairs couple and interpenetrate, only to cancel each other out. This is most obviously figured in the eventual death of both the man and woman. Patriarch and mistress both perish in the confrontation, and even the eldest son, the prize of Korea's neo-Confucian patriarchy, dies or proves impotent, illegitimate, or ineffectual. As the binary pairs interpenetrate and collapse, the very ground of modernity surges to the surface. With analytic excess and intense irony, Kim traces the convolutions forced to the surface by the pressures of South Korea's condensed modernization—which traces are themselves an actualization of its modernity.

Imaging Another (Is)land

One of the most perplexing of Kim Kiyoung's films is "Io Island" (*Iodo*, 1977). Like "Killer Butterfly," it has no intertextual connection to his well-known "Housemaid Trilogy" and its spin-offs, which films repeat certain themes that lend themselves well to feminist, auteur, and genre criticism. In contrast, however, "Io Island," defies generic classification, presenting neither melodrama, horror, woman's film, nor science fiction but some combination of these. It might be classified as a "shaman film" along with "Daughter of Fire" (*Im Kwontaek*, 1983), yet it also defies the usual paradigm, in which shamanism is exorcised from modern life. "Io Island" actually avoids modern urban spaces. Iodo or Io Island is an imaginary island, believed to lie somewhere off Cheju Island at the tip of the Korean peninsula. To the imaginary Io Island and Cheju Island, the film version of "Io Island" adds yet another island (one that does not appear in the fictional work by Lee Chungjun on which the film is based). It inserts Parang Island, an archaic island of women. Apparently located between Cheju Island and Io Island, Parangdo comprises a zone of indeterminacy between the real and the imaginary. Parangdo shares certain features with Chejudo, also alleged to be an island of women because there it is the labor of female divers that provides support for the family. In the film, the presentation of Parang Island follows what has become iconic for Cheju Island: women divers and rocky coastlines pounded by waves, and rugged hills swept by winds.

Significantly, tourism activates the story. Unlike Chejudo, Parangdo appears untouched by tourism. Then, with the construction of a luxury hotel on the island, things begin to change, and values to transform—particularly in relation to fantastical images of matriarchal society. One of the male protagonists, Chun Namsuk, protests the luxury hotel, which is to be named "Iodo" after the imaginary island. His woman, Minja, confesses that she herself is Iodo, establishing links between Iodo, Parangdo, and beautiful, mysterious feminine presence, which serves to console and protect men. Legend has it that an image of Iodo appears to comfort the spirits of fishermen lost or drowned at sea; on Iodo these men enjoy a life of peace and plenty. But then, we also learn from the film that Iodo is an invention, one intended to persuade fishermen to risk their lives on perennially stormy seas. Thus the film undermines the mist-shrouded realm of the sacred with suggestions of profane intentions. And so, when we hear Chun's rhapsody on the life of ease made possible for men by female divers on Parangdo, we understand that here, too, other forces are at work.

In a similar ruse, Minja disguises herself as a bar hostess to get what she wants. Chun has decided to live with a widow, Mrs. Park, who is portrayed as barren, because he wishes to avoid fathering children on Parangdo. And so, Minja, disguised as a bar hostess, approaches Chun, begging him to leave Parangdo before the ghost of Iodo seizes him. Only much later, after Chun is dead and claims are made for his corpse, does Minja reveal herself, and then only to stake her claim to his body. Yet her encounter with his corpse complicates matters. Minja's effort to communicate with Chun through the medium of a female shaman turns out to be an attempt to have sex with another man, the publicist for the hotel, who becomes the father of her son. It is as if the film becomes a shamanistic medium.

The film opens in the future, with a meeting between the publicist and Minja (he visits Parangdo to see her and her son). On this, his second, visit to Parangdo, the publicist says that he feels the grief of his first wife, who died childless. A flashback suggests that his impotence is the cause: at a city hospital, his first wife, impressed with the sperm bank, asks him to deposit his seed. Yet it is not the sperm bank that saves day. At the end of the film we learn that it was not science but necromancy that consummated the relationship. A series of prophecies sets the stage—Chun promises Minja that, after his death, a man will come and father her child—and later Minja's seduction via shamanism is the moment of fulfillment.

The film opens with an investigation and a promise of resolution: on his second visit to Parang Island, the publicist is intent on solving the mystery. Then we flash back to the events that took place four years earlier, when Chun accused the publicist of defiling the sacred legend of Iodo by naming the new luxury hotel on Parangdo after it. After Chun threatens to expose him publicly, then disappears, the publicist is charged with his murder. Chun has, in fact, set out to find Iodo. Later, when the publicist returns to Parangdo, the people of the island tell him that the ghost of Iodo has taken Chun, and informs him that Chun's family has been doomed for the preceding five generations. At this point, special effects intervene to present the enigmatic disappearance of Chun's father. Later, of course, Minja uses a shaman to draw Chun's corpse back to Parangdo, then seduces the publicist.

So it is that the film deploys legends, ghosts, spirits, and magical acts to cloak the islands of Iodo and Parangdo in mystery. And yet it relies on modern discourses and institutions to pull it off. Initially, the premodern seems to function as a realm of belief, and the modern as the domain of knowledge. For instance, the film depends on a number of scientific institutions and discourses, from sperm banks and pisciculture (Chun runs an abalone farm) to the disastrous effects of chemicals and the tourist industry on the island environment. Yet as the film progresses, the lines between the two realms at first waver and then vanish. It ends with a puzzle: the publicist gazes, perplexed, on the boy who is believed to be his son yet who remains impossibly distant from him; and ultimately, he fails not only to ascertain the boy's identity but also to discover any reasons for Chun's death and disappearance. Nor is there any explication of Minja's seduction of him. From his perspective all is mystery and speculation, and his voice-overs speak of an island unchanged from time immemorial, weighed down with ancient taboos and inhibitions. The film, however, shows something quite different. It shows that even an island of rock can be whittled away by the forces of historical transformation.

In brief, the film sets up a tension between two different cinematic looks (or regimes). On the one hand, it appears to adopt, rather shamelessly, a kind of tourist perspective on an "underdeveloped" and insular community. It recalls Chungmoo Choi's remarks on the film *Sopyonje*. Choi demonstrates how the logic of tourism mobilizes a nostalgic desire for the past, wherein the past appears to offer a sense of home and security that is threatened by the rootless existence of the industrialized world.[22] On one level, this is what Kim's *Iodo* offers: a spectacular cinemascope view of Parangdo, accompanied by zoom shots that emphasize the smallness of humans in an immense landscape. There is an aura of utopian possession to such panoramic vision as well as the possibility for a nostalgic look at a non-urban Korea. Yet there is little that is consoling about the island landscape (unlike those in *Sopyonje*)—winds scour the land, and waves thunder on the rocks, and even the bodies of the women divers, so open to exploitation in tourist brochures, defy an eroticized look. Rather than linger on these bodies as a source of scopophilic spectacle (as is so common in Cheju postcards), the film offers up images of bodies so exhausted that they seem unable to sustain the burdens of reproduction. Indeed, this becomes a theme of the film, and one character remarks that women divers are not particularly alluring since their bodies are prematurely aged by their harsh labor. In sum, there is a continual tension between the visual regime of tourism and the bleak, even grotesque imagery of an over-labored nature (with special effects as an intermediary between the two regimes).

Part of what is at stake in this visual tension is female subjectivity itself. On one level, the issue seems straightforward. There is a process of self-primitivization in which native men make women into the primitive other of modernity (a scene of nativity, so to speak), which is grounded in the possibilities of a tourist vision. For instance, Chun, a native of Parangdo, returns in order to exploit local women, intending to take as much money from the women divers as possible. In fact, he has already raped and robbed Minja. Yet Chun himself appears as something of a victim and an outsider, and his actions work against any clear-cut polarization or resolution of pairs (such as insider/outsider, native/foreign, or victim/victimizer). Moreover, Minja is endowed with modern subjectivity in specific ways. She is nicknamed "news-crazy" because she is the only one on the island who reads the newspaper. And her obsessive pursuit of Chun disturbs our reading their relationship in terms of the projection of a male fantasy of an ideal woman. The film suggests that Chun's mother has imparted the obsessive mission to Minja, for she tattoos Minja just as her own mother-in-law had tattooed her. Chun's mother sees the tattoo as a token exchanged only between women. Needless to say, it does not really constitute a communal bond between women insofar as it amounts to a joint contract for the birth of sons. Nevertheless, despite its emphasis on the birth of sons, the film does not allow for the fulfillment of the ideals of Confucian patriarchy, particularly of the sort that were so common in the family melodramas of the 1970s, in which the eldest son inevitably assumed the burden of father's uncompleted tasks. Minja's son doesn't even fit into a legitimate lineage. The film makes a mockery of the feminine virtues so treasured in South Korean cinema: the virginity of the heroine and the successful delivery of a male heir. Minja's alleged virginity is subject to constant doubt and ridicule, and the birth of her son on Parangdo does not resolve any of the contradictions implicit in the island of women.

It comes as no surprise then that the pure and untainted rural nature that lies at the heart of the nostalgic journey into the premodern past in films such as *Sopyonje* proves impossible in *Iodo*. The site of the premodern in *Iodo* is that of the emergence of grotesque morbidity, a site of uncontrollable transformation and hybridization. Just as the fetish breaks into multiple translations in Korean—shamanist objects, love objects and commodities—so the film breaks into multiple, conflicting visual regimes, even as it works from their polarization. In this respect, *Iodo* is yet another instance of the blockage that runs through cinematic modernity in Korea, but it moves beyond an inability to imagine traditionalism through modernity, and works with the enunciative difficulty of posing historical transformation and cultural hybridization as an alternative modernity. It is as if Parang Island were a distorted miniature of the modernization of the 1970s, of the nationwide campaign launched by the military government to eradicate remnants of the premodern, a campaign in which traditional styles of residential architecture were banned and village shamans were tracked down. *Iodo* iterates that drive yet generates innumerable fetishes which serve to scramble the direction of such binary tendencies. In that respect, the dark, allegedly satanic work of Kim Kiyoung remains forever untimely, constructing a heterocosm that flashes forward to a reality only plausible for future spectators. Not surprisingly, his audience is still to come.

Acknowledgments

An earlier version of this paper was presented at the "Postcolonial Classics of Korean Cinema" conference at the University of California, Irvine in 1998. I am grateful to Paul Willemen, Meaghan Morris, and Walter Lew for their comments and suggestions. Special thanks to Chris Berry and Thomas Lamarre for their most careful readings of a final draft of the paper, and to all the participants at the Traces workshop on "Spectres of the West" in Beijing in June 1999.

Endnotes

1—*Fetishism As Cultural Discourse*, ed. Emily Apter and William Pietz (Ithaca: Cornell University Press, 1993), also deals with this issue and informs my exploration of the three sites of controversy related to fetishism as a cultural discourse in the West: the historical construction of gendered identities, the social life of capital, and the ideologies lived in visual culture.

2—Laura Mulvey, *Fetishism and Curiosity* (London: BFI, 1996), 7.

3—See Cho Hi-Mun, *Cho chang ki Hankuk oyong hwasa oyon ku* (A Study of Early Korean Film History: The Introduction and Reception of Motion Pictures between 1896-1923), PhD dissertation, Changang University, 1993.

4—See Kim Soyoung, *Cinema: Blue Flower in the Land of Technology* (Seoul: Yolhwatang, 1996), 102-123.

5—On the relationship between Korean cinema and women spectators, see Kim Soyoung, "Questions of Women's Film: *The Maid, Madame Freedom*, and Women," in Chung-moo Choi, ed., *Post-Colonial Classics of Korean Cinema* (Irvine: Korean Film Festival Committee at the University of California, Irvine, 1998), 13-21.

6—Robert J. Foster, "Your Money, Our Money, the Government's Money: Finance and Fetishism in Melanesia," in *Border Fetishism*, ed. Patricia Spyer (New York: Routledge, 1998), 68-69.

7—Miriam Hansen, *Babel and Babylon* (Cambridge: Harvard University Press, 1991), 93.

8—William Pietz, "Fetishism and Materialism: The Limits of Theory in Marx," in *Fetishism as Cultural Discourse*, 138.

9—Chungmoo Choi, "The Discourse of Decolonization and Popular Memory: South Korea," in *Formations of Colonial Modernity*, ed. Tani E. Barlow (Durham: Duke University Press, 1997), 349-372.

10—Paul Willemen, in his lectures in the School of Film and Media at the Korean National University of Arts in 1997, called attention to this form of cinematic address.

11—Walter Benjamin, "Theses on the Philosophy of History," in *Illuminations*, ed. Hannah Arendt (New York: Schoken Books, 1969), 262-263.

12—Kyung Hyun Kim, "Korean Cinema on the Road," in *Postcolonial Classics of Korean Cinema*, 24-25.

13—Gilles Deleuze, *Coldness and Cruelty* (New York: Zone Books, 1989), 31.

14—Kyung Hyun Kim, "Korean Cinema on the Road," 30.

15—Walter Benjamin, *The Origin of German Tragic Drama* (London and New York: Verso, 1985), 166. Special thanks to Walter Lew for bringing this to my attention.

16—Rolf Tiedemann, "Dialectics at a Standstill," in *On Walter Benjamin*, ed. Gary Smith (Cambridge: MIT Press, 1988), 287-288.

17—Chris Berry, "Introducing 'Mr. Monster': Kim Ki-young and the Critical Economy of the Globalized Art-House Cinema," in *Post-Colonial Classics of Korean Cinema*, ed. Chungmoo Choi (Irvine: Korean Film Festival Committee, University of California, 1998), 39-47.

18—Paul Willemen, "Questions of Modernization and Korean Cinema," 5.

19—Berry, "Introducing 'Mr. Monster,'" 46.

20—Mulvey, *Fetishism and Curiosity*, 2.

21—Commentary from the discussion session following the screening of "Carnivore" at the Kim Kiyoung retrospective at the Second Pusan International Film Festival.

22—Chungmoo Choi, "Nationalism and Construction of Gender in Korea," in *Dangerous Women: Gender and Korean Nationalism*, ed. Elaine H. Kim and Chungmoo Choi (New York: Routledge, 1998).

Modernism as Translation

What is, could be, or should be, the status of the most general concepts of a genuinely transnational cultural theory? And what is the relationship of their forms of universality to other, philosophical and empirical, conceptual forms? To what extent does the theoretical prehistory and process of formation of such concepts impinge upon their use in the present? In particular, is there any way in which such concepts can avoid the fate of becoming little more than intellectual markers, or even symbolic enhancers, of global processes of cultural domination and hegemony? Indeed, can or should there be general concepts—concepts of sufficient generality to embrace the full geopolitical range of a genuinely transnational cultural theory—at all? Alternatively, can there be transnational cultural theory without them?

These are live questions, in the sense of being both urgent and unresolved, open questions, which trouble the otherwise implacable progress of the competing yet overlapping problematics which make up the field of cultural theory today: problematics for which the labels "postcolonialism," "postmodernism," "globalization," "critical anthropology," "new ethnography," and even "cultural studies" itself stand in as so many half-empty phrases, marketing thoughts "in progress" as if they were finished products: off-the-shelf items, ready-to-wear, in the new international supermarkets of knowledge. These are in many ways unhappy problematics: the more established, the more unhappy. Yet together they represent a vast and complex field of writing and research which is fundamentally transforming the conceptual land-

Peter OSBORNE

scape of disciplines in the humanities and social sciences—not least, via a recognition of the inextricability of economic and cultural processes and practices.

This paper approaches these questions 1) via a translational model of theoretical generality and 2) through a reconsideration of the logic of the concept of modernism. And it does so from the standpoint of a specific disciplinary interest—I am tempted to say a disciplinarily specific melancholy: the standpoint of "philosophy." Although it should be said that to address these questions from the "standpoint" of philosophy is not necessarily the same thing as addressing them from *within* philosophy. Since "what philosophy is," as they say in the undergraduate primers in Western universities, is one of the things at stake in the discussion. But what might philosophy become?[1]

Contemporary cultural theory is the often swaggering, sometimes awkward, but always anxious, occupant of a conceptual space from which philosophy has largely been banished, although its exile is in part self-imposed: the space of totalization.[2] Pragmatically robust, the more strictly theoretical terms of this occupancy are nonetheless unresolved. The question of the status of the terms of a transnational cultural theory opens onto the question of the status of philosophical concepts in two ways: 1) as a question about the cultural-historical constitution and hence *limits to universality* of all thought and 2) as a question about the productive *transcendence* of thinking beyond both the conditions of its own possibility and the range of its currently empirically justifiable applications. (This is the transcendence of the present towards the future, that is, *finite* transcendence, in the early Heideggerian sense; transcendence towards the being-in-common of a "finite history."[3]) The concept of modernism is paradigmatic in this regard, as a Western cultural form subsequently generalized at a global level in a hotly disputed process suspended between the imperialism of an obliteration of social differences and the productivity of alternative, counter-hegemonic interpretations and conceptions. Either way, the meaning of the concept has undoubtedly been transformed by its extension to "non-Western" contexts, situations, and instances, while nonetheless retaining a certain highly abstract, but still recognizable, shape. Furthermore, modernism is in certain respects directly akin to a traditional philosophical concept in designating the cultural affirmation of a particular phenomenological structure of time. That is to say, it would appear to be a concept belonging to a phenomenological philosophy of history, as well as, at lower levels of abstraction, to empirical-typological histories of cultural forms.

I return to the logic of modernism as a philosophical concept below. First, however, let us consider the translational model of theoretical generality, which underlies the practice of theory construction in much contemporary cultural study. For it is in its function as a medium of translation, I shall argue, that the concept of modernism maintains a certain legitimate universality as a generic concept of a transnational cultural theory.

Peter Osborne

1. A translational model of theoretical generality

It is a theoretical virtue of comparative concepts in cultural theory that they force us to rethink the abstract opposition of "philosophical" to "empirical" concepts and to focus instead on the conceptual semantics and dynamics of the processes of generalization of particular terms. One increasingly common way in which these processes are understood is through the metaphor—or at least, what looks at first sight like a metaphor—of translation. Theoretically, however, translation may be understood in any of a number of different ways. It is the theory of translation underlying the use of the idea of comparative analysis as a process of translation that determines the philosophical meaning of the concepts concerned. Take, for example, the following passage from the prologue to a recent book by James Clifford, *Routes: Travel and Translation in the Late Twentieth Century* (1997), in which he is discussing the status of comparative concepts in cultural theory:

> all broadly meaningful concepts, terms such as "travel," are translations, built from imperfect equivalences. To use comparative concepts in a situated way means to become aware, always belatedly, of limits, sedimented meanings, tendencies to gloss over differences. Comparative concepts—translation terms—are approximations, privileging certain "originals" and made for specific audiences. Thus, the broad meanings that enable projects such as mine [i.e., rethinking spatiality as itinerary—an immanent temporalization of a specific set of spatial relations] necessarily fail as a consequence of whatever range they achieve. This mix of success and failure is a common predicament for those attempting to think globally—globally enough—without aspiring to overview and the final word.[4]

This passage is exemplary in its use of the idea of translation to instill a certain postmodern scepticism into the heart of comparative analysis. On the one hand, it is admirably epistemologically cautious: it associates the empirical specificity of contextual self-consciousness with an awareness of "limits, sedimented meanings, [and] tendencies to gloss over differences." On the other hand, however, it extends and hypostasizes this caution into the "necessary failure" of all "broad meanings." (But failure to do what? And according to what criteria?) What begins as a practically-based concern with context turns into a scepticism about theoretical concepts in general. The concept of translation which was used, to begin with, to open up the field of comparative generality, is turned back upon that field and closes it down. The hinge of this movement is the idea of the "privilege of the original." It is the primacy of the original context, in which the concept is seen to be "made for specific audiences," which for Clifford dictates the "failure" which necessarily accompanies whatever success in translation there may be.

Yet one might very well question the

model of translation underlying this view. For rather than using the idea of translation to extend and thereby *transform* the meaning of theoretical concepts through their application to new contexts, Clifford"s use of the idea of the "privilege of the original" insulates such concepts from the very contexts which would change them. What we have here, in fact, is a traditional anthropological model in which the "other" is assumed to be preconstituted in its otherness prior to the encounter, thereby establishing an a priori limit to the possibility of translation. But is this what cultural alterity and translation are actually like? There are good conceptual grounds for thinking not. For not only is the "otherness of the other" a dialectical *product* of the encounter—that is, something to be inferred from the necessity for translation, rather than the preestablished ground of its inevitable failure[5]—but the meaning of "the original" cannot be supposed to reside wholly "within" the original itself. Given the increased range and intensity of the social exchanges which have made the idea of a transnational cultural theory both necessary and possible, one might do better to consider the alternative model of translation contained in Walter Benjamin's notion of the "translatability" of the original. For Benjamin,

> [t]ranslatability is an essential quality of certain works, which is not to say that it is essential that they be translated; it means rather that a specific significance inherent in the original manifests itself in its translatability.... The life of originals attains in [translations] to its ever-renewed latest and most abundant flowering.[6]

Indeed,

> no translation would be possible if in its ultimate essence it strove for likeness to the original. For in its afterlife—which could not be called that if it were not a transformation and a renewal of something living—the original undergoes a change. Even a word with fixed meaning can undergo a maturing process....[A] translation, instead of resembling the meaning of the original must lovingly and in detail incorporate the original's mode of signification, thus making both the original and the translation recognizable as fragments of a greater language, just as fragments are part of a vessel.

In this way, all significant works of translation extend the boundaries of the language into which they translate.[7]

The relevant questions thus become: What is the "mode of signification" of the original? What "specific significance" is manifest in its translatability? And what changes does it undergo as a consequence of particular translations?

At the time of this essay, in 1923, Benjamin still conceived of this process in only weakly historical terms, as a process of the concealment and revelation of a metaphysical "language of truth":

the tensionless and even silent depository of the ultimate truth which all thought strives for ... the true language ... whose divination and description is the only perfection a philosopher can hope for ... concealed in concentrated fashion in translations.[8]

But, one may reinterpret it in the spirit of Benjamin's own later, more deeply historical conception of *construction,* in order to develop it as a basis for the theorization of the mode of generality of the concepts of a transnational cultural theory. On such a model, the process of translation would be a reflective part of the broader historical process of construction which *produces* the "truth" which the early Benjamin tended to see, in quasi-Platonic terms, as already implicit. After all, what is conceptual determination but a re-presentation as "universality" of the immanent ideality of a historically produced and sedimented, yet necessarily incomplete and hence speculative, generality? There is a dialectic of universal and particular—conceptual determination and empirical particularity—internal to all theoretical concepts as a consequence of their historicity. In this respect, the idea of translation at work in this essay (general concepts as "translation terms" or media of translation) is less a metaphor than the metonymic register of the interpretative dimension of the processes of social intercourse and exchange in general. As Derrida has put it: "With the problem of translation we are dealing with nothing less than the passage to philosophy"—that is, with the question of the possibility of universality in discourse.[9]

So, how does "modernism" function as a translation term? What is its mode of signification? What specific significance is manifest in its translatability? And what changes does it undergo as a consequence of its translation into "non-Western"—for example, Chinese—contexts?

2. Modernism as a philosophical concept

In its broadest sense and most fundamental theoretical determination "modernism" displays the universality of a philosophical concept. This is not to deny that modernism is a historical and hence in part a "sociological" phenomenon—the name for an historically emergent and hence derived form of historical self-consciousness, associated with a specific range of cultural objects and practices, in particular kinds of society—or that it comes in many guises. Rather, in comparing "modernism" to a philosophical concept, I wish simply to draw attention to its transcendental or quasi-categorial status as a temporal form, across and within the particular modes of historical life in which it is found, and to the peculiar quality of universality inherent in the radical abstractness of this form. More specifically, as the name for the *cultural affirmation of a particular temporal logic of negation* ("the new," the temporal logic of the modern), modernism is the cultural condition of possibility of a particular, distinctively future-oriented series of forms of experience of history as temporal form. The questions raised by this for a transnational cultural theory are: How is this temporal logic of negation produced and played out under different, but always related, social and historical conditions, at the level of particular cultural forms? And what kinds of relations does it enter into with whatever might be taken to fall under the increasingly dubious heading of "national cultures"?

I am opting, then, for an expansive definition of "modernism." In its most basic or core "temporal" sense (as seen above), its reference cannot be restricted in advance either to the social domain of the arts, or to some chronologically bounded historical period (that is, one which has already ended), or to any particular geopolitical space (such as "the West"). Rather, modernism is in principle "aesthetic" only in the technical sense of the Transcendental Aesthetic in Kant's *Critique of Pure Reason*, where aesthetic is the name for the "doctrine of sensibility" and transcendental aesthetic is "the science of all principles of *a priori* sensibility"—that is, the pure forms of intuition: space and time.[10] Such a usage is no "looser" than more extensionally restricted definitions, although it is more abstract; no more abstract, though, than the aspect of actuality which it grasps. Such abstractness both registers the actually existing temporal formalism of "the modern" as a structure of time-consciousness, or what Foucault would have called an historical *a priori*, and is the condition for its translatability into an increasing number of different geopolitical contexts. Similarly to labor-power, one might say, the modern is a real abstraction. It is in the distinctive and contradictory features of the mode of abstraction of the modern, and their relations to the concrete multiplicity of its empirical forms, that the specific significance of the translatability of "modernism" resides.

More specifically, as the name for a structure of experience which is both categorial (that is, provides a functional unity of representations) and intuitive (that is, a form of affection), "the modern" is *schematic* in Kants's precise sense of offering "a rule of pure synthesis" or a "transcendental determination of time" which mediates the relation of appearances to categorial forms—"a monogram of pure imagination" in Kant's evocative phrase.[11] As a practical affirmation of the historical schema of "the modern," modern*ism* is thus what we might call *a practical historical schema*. As such, it structures the temporal form of subjectivity, the temporality of the "I," through its mediation of culturally received (intuited) temporal forms with new acts of production. It is for this reason that modernism in its most general sense is associated with a particular configuration of *temporalizations of history* or *historizations of temporality*—as I have argued elsewhere.[12]

As I have said, by emphasizing the philosophical dimension of the concept of modernism, I do not wish to imply that it is

Peter Osborne

independent of history either in its origins or immanently, within itself. Rather, it raises in a particular instance the general question of the relationship of philosophical to historical form. However, in insisting on the quasi-categorial status of modernism, in its most fundamental determination, as a name for the affirmations of a particular form of time-determination, I am attempting to free myself from the restrictions of the dominant empirical-typological conceptions of modernism in literary and art history, which are so often a given of sociological analysis in this area: that is, the conception of modernism as a particular, chronologically defined, period style.[13] Different versions of this conception are still hegemonic in recent writing on the subject, for all its additional theoretical or sociological sophistication.[14] But they miss what is most fundamental about modernism: namely, its character as a temporal dynamic of cultural form. In particular, one might note (1) that the use of chronological periodization is in tension with the radically temporalizing character of the phenomenon in question, and (2) that the restriction to style, in conjunction with some more sociological notion of modernism as a self-conscious cultural movement, fails to come to grips with either the pervasiveness or the contradictory complexity of modernism as a cultural form. Indeed, the translatability of "modernism"—the power of modernism as a medium of transculturation, one might say[15]—indicates the extent to which the concept can be unified, ultimately, only at the level of pure temporal form.

However, the point of criticizing such typological-stylistic analyses is not to sidestep the empirical multiplicity of modernisms as a complex and developing set of concrete historical forms, by retreating to some self-contained realm of philosophical abstraction. Rather, the aim is to establish the terms for rethinking this material from the standpoint of the more fundamental determination of modernism as a temporal-cultural form, and thereby, to acquire a more adequate sense of its specifically *historical* (rather than either merely chronological or abstractly temporal) logic. For if we understand by modernism the cultural affirmation of a particular temporal logic of negation (the new), the meaning of any particular such negation will be determined by the delimitation of the received cultural field upon which, and within which, it acts. The specification of what delimits or gives conceptual unity to the field of a particular practical negation, and the level at which that negation operates, will constitute the varying historical significances of different, historically and geographically specific, "modernisms." These are, if you like, the terms of the translation, which reveal the "specific significance" of modernism, manifest in its translatability—a significance which is most visible in its translation into "non-Western" contexts. For it is at this point that the issue of *difference* enters the picture as the question of the status of the various forms of classification—of conceptual unity and division—which are involved in constituting the various fields of negation which make up the shifting object-domains of modernist culture.

If modernism has the universality of a philosophical concept, then—a concept constructed at the level of a certain phenomenologically absolute (albeit historically conditioned) universality—it nonetheless derives its concrete meaning from the distributive unity of its specific instances, as a particular constellation of fields of negation, at any particular time. Hence its potentially contradictory manifestations in, for example, both radically nationalistic and radically anti-nationalistic, cosmopolitan forms, in different historical and national contexts, or, according to different political projects within the same historical and national context. This is dependent upon whether its field of negation is constituted internally or externally to the idea of "national culture."

3. Modernism and National Culture

Whatever "national culture" may be, there can be no conceptually necessary relationship between it and modernism as a cultural form, specifiable in advance. There are only historically specific conjunctural relations, constructed by the (politically defined) terms of identification of particular fields of negation. In particular, one can make no legitimate inferences from the founding conjunction of specific canonic modernisms with particular national projects to the possibility or impossibility of other forms. Indeed, the "national" character of specific modernisms is often national in a dialectical sense only, as determinate negations of received national-cultural forms: internally oppositional cosmopolitan projections, only later put to hegemonizing nationalistic use. Rather, at base, the concept of modernism offers a general interpretative framework for identifying and examining a specific form of time-determination—a specific temporal logic of negation—across and between different social and cultural fields. This is true, although the distance from traditional cultural forms registered by this radical temporal abstraction does indeed associate it with a particular culture—the culture of capital—which exists unevenly within the cultural formations of capitalist societies. (And paradigmatically, of course, commodity culture is "made in the USA," where the "national" tradition is more inherently capitalistic than elsewhere.) As such, it is of increasing and not decreasing global relevance. This should not, however, be taken to imply that the political content of any particular modernism is in some way compromised by this affinity, in advance, since the social embodiment of a particular modernism's abstract temporal logic—what is being affirmed—might be quite different from that from which that logic evolved, historically.

It is thus mistaken, in my view, to think of "Chinese modernism," for example, in painting and film, as culturally specific variants or exotic indigenous inflections of medium-specific modernisms conceptually defined in formal-stylistic terms by their Western counterparts—as both Alice Yang and Xudong Zhang still tend to do, in different ways, for all their reflectivity about the structure of "othering" constitutive of such Western modernisms.[16] The implications of the translation of "modernism" into the context of China are far more complicated than that. In temporal terms, Soviet-style Socialist Realism is a far more credible candidate for the role of an inaugural modernism in Chinese painting than any extension of the formalism of its traditional visual culture,[17] just as the dynamics of revolutionary-socialist, state-led modernization constitute at least as important a part of its specific modernity as do either market relations or any more nationally specific cultural traits. (Unfortunately, we still lack anything approaching an adequate theorization of socialist modernity as a cultural-historical form.)

This power of generalization has nothing, at base, to do with any generic autonomy of philosophical concepts; although, internationally, concepts like modernism have become generalized cultural resources. Rather, it follows from the global generalization of the various dynamics of social transformation which underlie the time-consciousness of modernism as an affirmative (and often in some sense "alternative") cultural project: namely, the various articulations of *economic*, *social-geographic*, and *interstate* logics which determine the rhythm of "modernity" as a condition of change. The only thing that is distinctive about "modernism" as a cultural form *per se*—prior to its translational specification—is that the modes of identification which it designates involve a rupturally futural sense of the present as an (always, in part, destructive) transition to a new (temporary) order. Such is its abstract universality, as distinct from the *concrete* universality which is the historical product of the development of its increasingly generalized empirical forms. The problem is thus not how to rethink the notion of modernism from the standpoint of national cultures (modernism as national allegory, for example). It is, rather, how the problematic of the modern, concretely applied, can help replace the problematic of "national cultures," with a broader conception of the temporal-cultural dimensions of social relations—social relations through which "the nation" is itself produced as a cultural-ideological effect of various forms of state power.[18]

The changes that the concept of modernism undergoes as a result of its translation into "non-Western" contexts are changes of reference (and hence, in Benjamin's account of translation, enrichments of *sense*) consequent upon its association with a radically extended range of forms of cultural experience of temporal difference or non-synchronicity. These new forms of production of "the modern" fracture its identification with its Euro-American "original," retrospectively transforming that original in turn. Furthermore, if we understand space as "the material support of time-sharing social practices," and "globalization" as the planetary extension of such practices made possible by the new information technologies,[19] it is clear that questions about "non-Western" modernities and modernisms can no longer be separated from questions about a global modernity and globally projected modernisms—not simply because of the enforced generalization of European and American models of development (through colonialism and imperialism), but because of the opening up of more generalized spaces of translation in the "real virtuality" of what Castells calls the "space of flows." Although, as Castells is quick to point out, these new forms of communicational relations exist in contradictory relations to the political dynamics of the more established "space of places."

If the question "What is modern?", which underlies all modernisms, is asked in these circumstances, it will be spatially double-coded as: 1) What is modern, here and now (in this place—city, province, nation, region, continent)? And what is modern now, *tout court* or globally? It is in the increasingly complex exchange between these two questions—an exchange through which the West/non-West relation is currently being radically transformed—that the full scope of modernism as a term of translation manifests itself, as the name for the temporal form through which the political contest between competing futures continues to be played out.

Endnotes
This is a revised version of a paper presented to the Conference 'Spectres of the West and the Politics of Translation' organized by *Traces* and the Chinese Academy of Social Sciences, Beijing, 26-7 June 1999. An earlier version of parts two and three was presented to a panel on 'Modernism and National Culture' at the Mellon Sawyer Seminar on Cities and Nations, at the International Center for Advanced Studies, New York University, in November 1998. I would like to thank Harry Harootunian and Thomas Bender for the opportunity to participate and the other participants in the seminar for their comments and criticisms on that draft.

1—This question, which projects a resolution to the disciplinary crisis of philosophy through a new relation to the positive sciences, within the culture of modernism, is at least as old as Feuerbach's "Necessity for a Reform of Philosophy" (1842). But it retains both its urgency and its force. See Ludwig Feuerbach, "Necessity for a Reform of Philosophy," *The Fiery Brook: Selected Writings of Ludwig Feuerbach*, trans. Zawar Hanfi (Garden City, NY: Anchor Books, 1972), 145-52.

2—For reflections on this substitution, see my "Philosophy and the Role of Intellectuals," in Peter

Peter Osborne

Osborne (ed.) *A Critical Sense: Interviews with Intellectuals*, (London and New York: Routledge, 1996), vii-xxviii, and the title essay in my *Philosophy and Cultural Theory* (London and New York: Routledge, 2000.) The mediating term—an increasingly vanishing mediator—is, of course, Marxism.

3—See Jean-Luc Nancy, "Finite History," in his *The Birth to Presence*, trans. Brian Holmes et al. (Palo Alto, Ca: Stanford University Press, 1993), 143-66.

4—James Clifford, *Routes: Travel and Translation in the Late Twentieth Century* (Cambridge, MA: Harvard University Press, 1997), 11.

5—As Sakai puts it: "the untranslatable, or what can never be appropriated by the economy of the translational communication, cannot exist prior to the enunciation of translation. It is translation that gives birth to the untranslatable." Naoki Sakai, *Translation and Subjectivity: On "Japan" and Cultural Nationalism* (Minneapolis: Minnesota University Press, 1997), 14.

6—Walter Benjamin, "The Task of the Translator," in his *Illuminations*, trans. Harry Zohn (London: Fontana, 1973), 71-2.

7—Ibid., 73, 78, 80.

8—Ibid., 77.

9—Jacques Derrida, *Dissemination*, trans. Barbara Johnson (Chicago: University of Chicago Press, 1981). Cf. Andrew Benjamin, *Translation and the Nature of Philosophy* (London and New York: Routledge, 1989), 1.

10—Immanuel Kant, *Critique of Pure Reason*, trans. Norman Kemp-Smith (London and Basingstoke: Macmillan, 1933), 65-7 (A19-22, B33-36).

11—Ibid., B178-81.

12—Peter Osborne, *The Politics of Time: Modernity and Avant-Garde* (London and New York: Verso, 1995), chs.1 & 5.

13—See for example, Malcolm Bradbury and James McFarlane (eds) *Modernism, 1890-1930* (Harmondsworth: Penguin, 1976); or in the case of art history, the Open University course book by Frascina et al., *Modernity and Modernism: French Painting in the Nineteenth Century* (New Haven and London: Yale University Press, 1993), and its companion volume, Paul Wood et al., *Modernism in Dispute: Art Since the Forties* (New Haven and London: Yale University Press, 1993).

14—See, for example, Astradur Eysteinsson, *The Concept of Modernism* (Ithaca, NY: Cornell University Press, 1990); and Steve Giles (ed.), *Theorizing Modernism: Essays in Critical Theory* (London and New York: Routledge, 1993), respectively.

15—See John Kraniauskas, "Transculturation and the Work of Translation," in this volume.

16—Alice Yang, "Modernism and the Chinese Other in Twentieth Century Art Criticism," in her *Why Asia? Contemporary Asian and Asian American Art* (New York and London: New York University Press, 1998), 129-46; Xudong Zhang, *Chinese Modernism in the Era of Reforms: Cultural Fever, Avant-Garde Fiction and the New Chinese Cinema* (Durham: Duke University Press, 1997). The theoretical frameworks of these two works are very different—T.J.Clark's socialized version of Greenbergian modernism and Jameson's cultural theory, respectively—but the basic tendency is nonetheless the same.

17—I am thinking, in particular, of the history-painting campaign of 1960, in which Socialist realism was introduced into Chinese visual culture as a specific political dictate.

18—For reflection on the use of culture as "a supplement to the state" in "the inculcation of a particular mode of subjectivity," in the inhabitants of a particular territory, "as a prerequisite to participation in the business of the state, even if participation, here, means no more than accepting 'being represented'," see David Lloyd and Paul Thomas, *Culture and the State* (New York and London: Routledge, 1998). The phrases quoted appear on 46-7.

19—Manuel Castells, *The Information Age: Economy, Society and Culture. Volume 1. The Rise of the Network Society* (Oxford: Blackwell, 1996), 411.

INTERLUDES

ECHO MULTINOME

You have asked me to say something on these words in any language. How will I explain this list in my mother tongue?

Translation. Anubâd or Torjoma. I can *anubâd* or *torjoma* this word in a fairly straightforward way. This is an old word.

Resonance. This word too comes into Bengali in a reasonably straightforward way. This is one of the main supporting columns of Sanskrit poetics.

Resonance, or "dhoni."

Having come to this point, your request that I say something specifically on these words is bringing me to a halt. Do I think of these words in my mother tongue. Whether thought is languaged may be disputed, but there can be no doubt that words are.

I think of translation, I think of resonance, and then?

Now I hear that in your so-called multilingual journal there will be East Asian languages, and European languages--surely the translation will be from the English, apart from Japanese, which I hear will be directly from the Bengali?

Take supplementarity. What should I say? To explain precisely what I think about supplementarity in Bengali, how would I translate the word supplementarity properly into Bengali? And then on which word should I opine? The English words, the Bengali word, or the energy of translation? Translating *is my habit*. Supplementarity is a word of Latin origin, to find an equivalent I would have to go to Sanskrit again, to the lexicon of the classical language of Northern India.

Gayatri Chakravorty Spivak

translated by Siddhartha Deb

A massively conservative language, and standing in its agora I cannot think that only the West claims theory. This kind of East-West dualism seems to me irrelevant and inconsequential. Sanskrit is not a matter of the subaltern classes.

Then I have to think of 1967, when I started reading *Grammatology*. That is the moment of arrival of supplementarity upon the threshold of my thought. I have to think about this foreign workplace from a perspective of supplementarity. Does news of the Indian subaltern classes reach there?

Then, let us take multiplicity. If there is a shadow of multiplication when one understands this in English, then we would have to say "gûn" in Bengali. But "gûn" won't be included in the literal translation. If you want me to free associate, I would say that the mystery of the word "gûn" in Bengali comes from Sanskrit. "Gûn" is not only "quality" but also a sketch of different personalities (characters): the personality-type of truth (*shatto*), of passionate action (*rajo*), and of darkness (*tamo*). These are all implicit in the various orthodoxies of Hinduism. And there is no trace of multiplicity here.

Literally multiplicity means "bohu" (many). This word reminds me of my own education in adolescence. Newly-minted post-colonial doctrine: unity in multiplicity. India is a multilingual country but one entity. Hinduism a religion of many gods but one source. Et cetera. Patriotism, nationalism, whose contagion I have been attempting to survive all my life.

Affect. What would affect be? *Ros*? *Ros* and *Dhoni*—affect and resonance—belong to the entire aesthetic theory of Northern India. That we will find a politically correct theory as soon as we escape the grasp of the Western world, I am not Eurocentric enough to think this. Whatever source it may come from, thinking will reveal class distinctions. My humble proposition is this: that history should not be seen in such a reduced perspective, beginning, that is, with western colonialism.

© Gayatri Chakravorty Spivak

১

বহুগুণ প্রতিধ্বনি

আপনারা বলেছেন যে কোনো ভাষায় এই কথাগুলি সম্পর্কে কিছু বলতে।- আমার মাতৃভাষায় এ তালিকা কী করে বোঝাব ?

Translation ॥ অনুবাদ অথবা তর্জমা। এ কথাটিকে আমি সোজাসুজি অনুবাদ অথবা তর্জমা করতে পারিই। পুরনো কথা।

Resonance ॥ এ কথাটিও সোজাসুজি বাংলায় আছে। এবং সংস্কৃত কাব্যতত্ত্বের একটী মূল খুঁটি।

Resonance অর্থ "ধ্বনি।"

এ পর্যন্ত এসে, আপনাদের অনুরোধে, সে বিশেষ করে এই কথাগুলির ওপরেই কিছু বলতে হবে, আমাকে আটকে দিচ্ছে। আমি কী মাতৃভাষায় এ কথাগুলি ভাবি। চিন্তা ভাষিক কী না, এ নিয়ে দ্বন্দ্ব আছে, কিন্তু কথা যে ভাষিক, তাতে ত' সন্দেহ নেই। অনুবাদের কথা ভাবি, ধ্বনির কথা ভাবি, তারপর? এখন আবার শুনছি আপনাদের

২

অশ্রেণিমিত বহুভাষিক পত্রিকায় পূর্ব এশিয়ার ভাষাগুলি থাকবে, আর থাকবে য়ুরোপের ভাষা – ইংরেজীর থেকে অনুবাদ হবে নিশ্চয়, জাপানীতে ছাড়া?

ধরুন, supplementarity.। কী বলব? বাংলায় supplementarity সম্বন্ধে আমি কী মনে করি জানতে এবং জানাতে, যথাযথ ভাবে supplementarity শব্দটি আমি কী ভাবে অনুবাদ করব? আর তারপরে কোন্ শব্দটির সম্বন্ধে মতামত জানাব? ইংরেজী কথাটি, বাংলা কথাটি, না অনুবাদ করবার প্রয়াসটি? তর্জমা করা আমার অভ্যাস। Supplementarity লাতিন শৈলীর কথা, পরিভাষা খুঁজতে আমাকে আবার যেতে হবে সংস্কৃতে, উত্তর ভারতের প্রাচীন ভাষার শব্দকোষে। বিরাট রক্ষণশীল ভাষা, তার প্রাঙ্গনে দাঁড়িয়ে ভাবতে পারি না, সে একরাশ পাশ্চাত্যই তত্ত্বের দাবী করে। এ ধরনের পূর্ব-পাশ্চিম দ্বৈতবাদ আমার কাছে বাতুলতা থেকে, ফলপ্রসূ মনে হয় না। সংস্কৃতভাষা নিম্নবর্গের ব্যাপার নয়। আবার ২২৬৭র কথাও মনে করতে হবে, যখন আমি Grammatology পড়তে শুরু করি। তখন আমার চিন্তার অঙ্গনে supplementarity-র

৩

উদ্বোবিন। এই প্রবাসী কর্মক্ষেত্রের কথা ভাবতে হচ্ছে supplementarity-র পরিপ্রেক্ষিতে। সেখানে কী ভারতীয় নিম্নবর্গের খবর পৌঁছেছে?

তারপরের বস্তু multiplicity । ইংরেজীতে বুঝতে গেলে যদি multiplication-এর ছায়া পড়ে তবে বাংলায় বলতে হবে "গুণ"। আক্ষরিক ভাবে কিন্তু গুণ আসবে না। আপনারা যদি চিন্তাবিলাস চান, তবে বলব বাংলায় "গুণ" কথাটার রহস্য আসছে সংস্কৃত থেকে। গুণ শুধু quality নয়, বিভিন্ন ব্যাঞ্জনবর্ণের অসবর্ণও বটে। যথা সত্ত্বগুণ, রজোগুণ, তমোগুণ। এ ত' হিন্দুধর্মের যত গোঁড়ামির মধ্যে প্রচ্ছন্ন। আর multiplicity-র হদিশ নেই ওখানে।

আক্ষরিক ভাবে "multiplicity" বলতে "বহু"। এ কথাটা আমার কৈশোরের শিক্ষা মনে করিয়ে দেয়। নয়া উত্তরঔপনিবেশিক শিক্ষা: বহুতে এক। ভারতবর্ষ বহুভাষিক দেশ কিন্তু একসত্তা। হিন্দুধর্ম বহুদৈবিক ধর্ম কিন্তু একসূত্র। ইত্যাদি। দেশাত্মবাদ, জাতীয়তাবাদের ছৌয়াচ, সারাজীবন কাটিয়ে উঠতে প্রয়াসী।

৪

Affect. ॥ Affect কী হবে? রস? রস আর ধ্বনি — affect আর resonance — উত্তর ভারতের উচ্চাঙ্গ তত্ত্ব। সাম্রাজ্যের হাত থেকে বেরোলেই যে আমরা বিশুদ্ধ রাজনীতির তত্ত্ব পাব, আমি সে চিন্তা করবার মত প্রতীচ্যকেন্দ্রিক নই। যে উৎস থেকে আসুক না কেন, চিন্তার বর্গবিভেদ দেখা দেবে। আমার বিনীত বক্তব্য এই : ইতিহাসকে যেন অত হ্রস্ব প্রেমিজে, অর্থাৎ পশ্চিমের ঔপনিবেশিকতা থেকে শুরু করে, না দেখা হয়।

© গায়ত্রী চক্রবর্তী স্পিভাক — কলম্বিয়া বিশ্ববিদ্যালয়

TOWARD A TRANSLATION THAT RESISTS "TECHNOLOGIES OF INDIVIDUATION"

SAKIYAMA Masaki

Translated by
J. Victor KOSCHMANN

I hold in my hand the beautiful book entitled *The Story of Colors* (La historia de los colores), put out by the small, Texas publisher, Cinco Puntos. The author of this book—which, if forced to categorize, one would have to call a bilingual edition in Spanish and English—is "Sub-Comandante Marcos," a member of the Zapatista Liberation Army which, since 1994, has continued its unique, tenacious struggle on behalf of the existence and dignity of indigenous peoples in Chiapas, Mexico.

The English translator of the text observes that, "To many, Marcos' language, syntactical structures and punctuation may seem idiosyncratic. It's been noted in several places that his conversational writing is influenced by the Spanish of the indigenous people around him, and their Spanish is, of course, their second language."

From the viewpoint that there must be a "single, correct translation," disallowing any "slippage" between "different languages," this is "mistaken, ruptured" language. That is because from that viewpoint, the "language" that makes this kind of translation possible must be taken to be a transhistorical, closed system from which the indigenous peoples of Chiapas have already been excluded by colonialism and racism.

Such a "single, correct translation" is becoming steadily more powerful. In other words, as expressed in the movement of global capital, it constructs all beings as a single "thing" that can be brought into agreement and thus controlled, and it is precisely the ability to bring about such a "thing" that forms and reproduces this "translation" as hegemonic. In terms used by Antonio Negri, it forms a "controlled, globalized, open unity"; it is none other than the violent subordination brought about by the "technologies of individuation," which dissolve and disperse the previous collective categories of "class" and "people."

Yet, has not the translation ushered in by the struggle in Chiapas discovered a locus of dis-agreement, a point of rupture, within subordination itself? Is that struggle not an attempt by the multitude to resist? And to do so in a manner that utilizes the forces latent in present reality to suggest entirely new possibilities, that is, alternative forms of material expression?

No doubt *Traces* also seeks through its collective labors to discover precisely such possibilities.

MULTIPLICITY

CHUA Beng Huat

All citizens of Singapore born before 1959, started life as 'British subjects', became 'Malaysians' in 1963 and then 'Singaporeans' in 1965. As British-subject, they were classified under a set of elaborate census categories by the different Chinese, Southeast Asian and South Asian languages they spoke; those who were English educated were privileged. In 'Malaysian' years, Bahasa Melayu was made the 'national' language. However, before it was entrenched into school curricula, English was brought back to independent Singapore as the language of education, government and commerce, as the language of advantage in capitalism. Meanwhile, the languages spoken on the island were drastically simplified to three 'official' languages of Mandarin, Malay and Tamil, as administrative devices to generate the Chinese, the Malay and the Indian community, respectively. Thus emerged the ethnic-Singaporean, including Other-Singaporean for those other than Chinese, Malay or Indian. The other displaced languages were relegated as 'dialects' and denied their places in the government controlled mass media. In the late 1980s, it was discovered that 'Singaporeans' were among people who possessed 'Asian values', supposedly distilled from Sino, Indic and Islamic civilizations and supposedly able to bequeath capitalist competitive advantages. The vastness of Asia was absorbed into the smallness of Singapore. As ethnic-Singaporeans and Asians, the citizens now stand. One would have thought that with the rapidity of changes, citizens of Singapore would wear any identity marker lightly and deploy the chameleon-like quality of the concept at will, if not to their own advantages.' Not so. 'What is the Singaporean identity?' is a question ceaselessly deployed ideologically/politically, by those in authority to impose rigid boundaries on others, such as politicians on electorate, parents berating children and by ego as technology of the self and the limits this implied. The discursive and substantive politics of multiple identities, in Singapore as elsewhere, constantly irritate, cause rage and frustration and demand intellectual and political vigilance from public intellectuals.

TRANSLATION

J. Victor Koschmann

While working as translators in Tokyo in the 1970s, I and my colleagues (both Japanese and American) tacitly assumed that in principle anything could be translated so long as one concentrated on meaning rather than words. That is, we believed that a good translation would result only if the meaning of the "original" language (for us, this was always Japanese) were thoroughly understood, and then expressed fluently and naturally in English. Excessive preoccupation with the words and grammatical form of the original would result in a literal translation (*chokuyaku*) that would obscure rather than illuminate the "essence" of the text, which was its meaning. Any difficulty experienced by the translator was to be attributed to misunderstanding of the Japanese, insufficient fluency in English, or the Japanese language's incorrigible quirkiness (sometimes interpreted, indeed, as backwardness). For example, it was generally accepted that the Japanese language was more "emotional" than cognitive, vague and allusive rather than rational; and that a Japanese essay often proceeded elliptically rather than directly from premises to conclusions. It was therefore sometimes necessary to rationalize, that is, to correct the Japanese text. Therefore, underlying the practice of translation was the assumption that Japanese is "particular" alongside the "universality" of English. To provide a good translation was to rationalize the expressive form of the Japanese while successfully demonstrating the "universality" of its "meaning" (i.e., its ultimate commensurability with English).

Part of the mission and, to me, the attractiveness of Traces is its effort to overcome the equation of English (or any language, including German, French, Japanese, etc.) with universality; such an effort parallels the decoupling of "theory" from "the West" and from the imperialism that has seemed intrinsic to it in its Western guise. But is it possible to decouple both language and theory from domination while continuing to theorize, and to strive for a "good" translation that focuses on meaning rather than words? Such is both the promise and the challenge of *Traces*.

MODULARITY

Harry D. Harootunian

The status of modularity has been recently and often dramatically put into question in discussions concerning the prospect for a proper approach to comparative studies. The target of this critique has been Benedict Anderson who in his Imagined Communities implied the replication of a model of modernity through the agency of print capitalism which, unfortunately, is more about print than capitalism, more about communication than the deterritorializing force of capital and labor. Anderson's accusers condemn his conception of 'modularity' for having smothered native imagination and reducing all to consumers of modernity. Yet what is at stake is the conviction of an "alternative modernity" which claims for itself the authority and originality of inner resources of native culture which, miraculously, have remained immune to the corrosions of modular forms devised elsewhere and imposed by the force of capitalism and colonialism. We can only assume what the alternative modernity is an alternative to even though it seems to have more in common with a reified conception of Tradition once confidently embraced by enthusiasts of modernization theory. Despite the effort to evade the iron cage of Western narratives, this attempt to envisage an alternative modernity (and alternative to modernity, perhaps?) succeeds only in recuperating the mythic unity of the West, affirming the relationship of "late developer" to industrial societies promoted by both Marxian and modernizing strategies and upholding the purity of an authentic inner experience whose value (presumably a return to use value) has remained fixed since the stone age in the interest of rescuing imagination. While a proper critique of modularity is very much a necessity for the current intellectual agenda, it cannot rest on spurious claims of difference (identity) that owe more to European romanticism than to recessive native resources that are always, already there, ready to exceed history.

IV

INTERNATIONALISM AND TRACES

ZADANKAI IN BEIJING

**Lau Kin-chi,
Peter Osborne,
Wang Hui,
Naoki Sakai**

Zadankai, baxianzhuo, or roundtable discussion

Naoki Sakai (NS): We have just finished a two-day conference at the Chinese Academy of Social Sciences in Beijing, and some of the papers presented over the last two days will be included in this inaugurual issue of *Traces*. I have asked three people, Lau Kin-chi of Lingnan University in Hong Kong; Peter Osborne of Middlesex University in London; and Wang Hui of the Chinese Academy of Social Sciences to join me in a roundtable discussion with a view to reflecting upon some interesting and constructive debates that arose at the conference and in the project of *Traces* in general. This type of forum is usually called *zadankai* in Japan. I'm sure you have some equivalent forms or genres in academic or popular publications in China and in Europe as well as in North America. The *zadankai* has been widely used in the Japanese publishing industry, particularly in periodicals. The *zadankai* literally means "sitting in a circle and talking together." I don't think we have to follow the format of the Japanese *zadankai* closely. We might as well modify this genre as we wish whenever we find it necessary. [Lau] Kin-chi, Peter [Osborne] and [Wang] Hui all have had experience editing journals, so I'd like to ask you for your opinions about the inclusion of a different or new genre or format in the multilingual journal of cultural theory.

Peter Osborne (PO): In *Radical Philosophy* we use interviews—edited versions of recorded conversations—both to generalize knowledge across disciplines and to address a broader, politically rather than academically, defined readership. The journal is called *Radical Philosophy*, but it's not primarily read by philosophers. The directness and informality of recorded discussions allow readers with different backgrounds much easier access to theoretical materials.

Lau Kin-chi (LK): For *Alternative Discourses*, which is a journal of cultural studies critique in Hong Kong that I'm involved in, we invite people from different backgrounds to roundtable discussions, especially people from so-called academic backgrounds and people from the social movements. Though some discussions might be spontaneous, they could touch on dynamic issues and contesting perspectives. We did that more for the process of dialogue and interaction between scholars and activists. We sometimes ask the participants to edit the transcript so that, in rereading the discussion and rethinking the issues, they might be prompted to rewrite their parts. The output is not an end in itself, but a means to facilitate a process of retrospection and interaction. Furthermore, besides being the occasion for contributing to a specific project not necessarily their own, such meetings can offer a space for the working out or enhancing of affiliations or alliances between the different parties.

Wang Hui (WH): There are the same kind of discussions in *Dushu* and other magazines in China. It's a form for intellectuals to raise questions or open up some topics. In the '80s, there was a series of discussions on the theme of "Chinese Literature in the 20th Century" by three scholars from Peking University in *Dushu*, which became the beginning of the rewriting of modern Chinese literature, of the history of Chinese literature. In 1994 a series of discussions on the "Humanistic Spirit" were published in *Dushu*, which raised a series of debates in different papers, journals and magazines. Some people give a title to these discussions, the "Table of Eight Gods" (*baxianzhuo*), a term from Chinese legend.

LK: It is a square table that can seat eight people, and the eight are referred to as the *baxian*, the eight gods. *Xian* means gods, deities, some sort of folklore immortals. These eight have very distinct and different talents. *Yuanzhuo* is exactly the word for "roundtable." But the roundtable itself was imported from the West, I think, but I am not sure. Most traditional Chinese tables were square, I presume. I wonder when the idea of roundtable discussion started in Asia.

NS: I only know that by the 1920s the genre of *zadankai* was already fairly widely used in the publication of periodicals in Japan.

PO: In Britain, the egalitarian connotation of the "round table" goes back to the legend of King Arthur and the competition between knights for the King's favor. The "knights of the round table" were supposedly equally privileged in their relation to the King. So it's of feudal origin—like so much in British political culture.

LK: For people sitting at the *ba-xian* table, there is also no particular privileging of anyone on whatever side. I would like to elaborate a little more about the eight immortals. All the eight had their own special strengths and weaknesses, and different backgrounds. But they all had to cross to the other side of the sea, each had his or her own resources, and each exhibited his or her own magical strengths for the endeavor. So there was also a certain common concern, a common purpose, a common project for which they mobilized all their different individual strengths.

WH: But the table itself may be a symbol of the sea.

PO: Yes, but do some of them not come back?

(general laughter)

NS: Does the eight-gods table mean there is no front or back, there is no sort of a "chair" position, which means that the table could be rounded and changed?

LK: Actually the idea is also that there is no head or end of the table, it is "round" in that sense, but still there are the four edges. (general laughter)

In fact, the tension between "being round" and "having four edges" can be read as representing the tension between theory and practice. The image of roundness can be seen as representing a horizontal relation which a group of individuals are striving to maintain in their commitment to engage themselves in a process in the constitution of a "center," by taking up positions on the edge. Rather than being dominated by any party, the center is maintained open to the future in the horizontal relationship. The "table" relates to the "requirements" of the body constituted in history, and the four edges the material limitations and possibilities in specific contexts of practices.

NS: Of course this has a lot of resonance with our project, for we are going to publish *Traces* in at least five languages according to the current arrangement, and we might as well think about a sixth and even a seventh one. Although the English language in fact serves as a sort of the common medium, we are committed to creating a forum in which six, instead of eight, six sides in fact, interact without making any language as a predominant one. Nonetheless, we do not want to overlook the fact that there are quite sharp edges, unevennesses among these languages of *Traces*, but that we simply cannot avoid these.

Multilingualism in Hong Kong

NS: I'd like to talk about the situation in Hong Kong, since there was a very interesting presentation by professors Hui Po-Keung and Lau Kin-chi about multilingual education in which, in fact, English is absolutely a minor language. Yet it is supposed to be the standard language for education in Hong Kong. I would just like to know how you deal with the situation of multiple languages?

LK: I think it's fraught with contradictions, because in most schools before 1997, it was pretended that the official medium of instruction was English, from kindergarten to university. However, a recent survey showed that, even at the most elitist university, the University of Hong Kong, for some courses about 50 percent of classes were conducted in the local dialect, Cantonese. With universities imposing both quality control and the language used in classes, still it has to be stated that the reality is that although reading materials and student assignments are in English, everyday class discussions are mostly conducted in Cantonese. Except when, for example, the teacher is non-Cantonese-speaking. We may say this situation is the colonial legacy. What is interesting after 1997 is that there is a need to demonstrate that Hong Kong is now an integral part of China. In the spirit of the assertion of sovereignty, a new policy on the medium of instruction in the secondary and primary schools has been introduced since September 1998. Only about 25 percent of schools are allowed to retain English as the medium of instruction, while others are forced to adopt Cantonese as the spoken medium of instruction and Chinese texts for most courses. This triggered a fierce competition among the schools for the prestigious status of using English as the medium of instruction. And parents took to the street to protest their children losing the opportunity for education in English. This is quite ironical.

WH: There's a story about Hong Kong that professor Leo Lee told me. He was a member of the Research Grants Committee—that's the committee holding all the resources for the university spending. Before '97 when he was a member, they were trying to fight for Chinese to be used for projects on Chinese language, but after '97 it was reversed: from then on they were trying to fight for English to be used.

NS: Let me speak from my own experience. I sometimes go to Taiwan. Of course, Taiwan being the former colony of Japan, some old people still want to speak the Japanese language. I often find it very unsettling or difficult to speak Japanese in Taiwan, and I'd rather speak English because I cannot speak Taiwanese or Mandarin well enough. In spite of the fact that the English language is the dominant and domineering language globally today, the English language works in a different, sometimes conformist, but some times interventionist, way, depending upon the local situation. The political significance of the English language is ambiguous and cannot easily be assessed. I believe this is why we cannot afford either to wholeheartedly embrace or to dismiss the critique of English-language imperialism. It's not as neatly delineated as it may appear. It is not just that, even at the core of English-language hegemony, the relation between English and other so-called minor languages is constantly changing.

WH: It's my experience in Hong Kong. When I go to shopping malls, or administrative offices, if I speak in Mandarin then people's attitude toward me is not so good. But when I change to English they become friendly.

Lau Kin-chi, Peter Osborne, Wang Hui, Naoki Sakai

LK: Yes, that's true. The interweaving of language and power is particularly manifest in the colonial relationship, where the desire for and fear of the Other, wittingly or unwittingly displayed by the colonized, is molded by forces linked to choices between "life" and "death."

In the early '70s one significant social movement, especially starting from among the students, was to fight for the Chinese language as an official language. This was one of the movements of the radicalized youth, after 1968 of course. Parallel to this was the anti-corruption movement and the "Defend the Diaoyutai Islands" campaign. The language movement was one of the landmarks in the process of anti-colonialism. I think maybe the issue after 1997 is that English seems to have been de-linked from the colonial rule of Britain, and is instrumental in maintaining links to the "global" world, so as to guarantee the distinction of the "Hong Kong system" from that of China. This peculiar trajectory of the nationalist movement in Hong Kong requires us to rethink the question of colonization and decolonization and the question of the inseparable relation between language and power in the complex configuration of the so-called global-local relation.

NS: As I remember, two or three years ago, before the return of Hong Kong to China, Hong Kong was often referred to as an exceptionally interesting site of transnationality and hybridity. Some people argued that, in fact, Hong Kong was a special place where you could constantly shift from one nationality to another, and it would never become a nation-state. Was that assessment correct or ...

PO: Overly optimistic?

LK: Maybe people who are not really so involved have a more critical view?

Transnationalism and Internationalism

PO: I think of the term transnational as something which developed in order to describe certain transformations in the international dynamics of capital: an increasing independence of capital from the political logic of its national bases. Its more general uses, in expressions like "transnational cultural theory" or the "transnationality" of individuals, follow in the wake of this primary usage, and are always more speculative. This can make it difficult to think of the term critically, because whatever's transnational is in some sense so in order to keep up with capital—to shadow capital, as it were. Capital is the driving logic of transnationalism. The cultural use of "transnationality" to which Naoki refers still seems to me better served by an older expression like "multinational," derived from the previous phase of capital accumulation: constellations of specific nationalities. Although the idea of the multilingual is also important here, of course. The term transnational points toward the dissolution of a national problematic in some quite fundamental way, whereas culturally and politically, there is a constant re-articulation of the national; especially, through the points of interface and conflict between different national languages.

NS: Well, there are two aspects to the question of transnationality. One that is widely recognized is that, in fact, the emphasis on nationality or nationalism in general is always linked to a reaction to global, transnational movements. Nationalism is a reactionary and reactive response to the imagined dissolution of national distinction. The second is somewhat related to the need to trespass borders and boundaries in order to apprehend how borders, discriminations, and classifications work to constitute nationalities. A border or boundary cannot be apprehended unless one assumes, either in actuality or imagination, the plausibility of seeing it from the other side. I wonder how you view the situation. In order to criticize the movement of capital you always have to make some trespassing moves. In a sense you really have to follow the passage of capital in order to criticize it.

WH: Yes. In this case, we have to make some distinctions between internationalism and transnationalism—

(all speaking at once): Yes, yes...

WH: The term *transnational* is associated with the transnational movements of capital. *Internationalism*, in my view, is a term to be used to describe social movements—a reactive movement to the movement of capital. Internationalism, in those Third-World countries, at first was interwoven with nationalistic movements, but these national liberation movements were not pure nationalistic movements because they always had international dimensions.

They tried to go beyond nationalism, became a kind of internationalism. It means that even in the last century and the first half of this century, internationalism used to be associated with social movements within a national boundary, while the movements contained the connotations of a critique of the transnational movements of capital or colonialism.

PO: I agree. Historically, internationalism is associated with a discourse of solidarity, but it's hard to turn the notion of the transnational in this direction because it has no inherent spatial basis. It describes a peculiar form of movement which is not just de-territorializing and re-territorializing, but treats social space as a contingent, *external* condition of its action. It's hard to think of relations of solidarity in a transnational space because, conceptually at least, transnationalism represents a de-spatialization of social logics.

LK: So what I would like to distinguish is that, when we say transnationalism, we are talking about the movement of capital. But the movement of labor is a different story. The majority of the population remains tied to a location. We have migrant workers, but still the mobility is limited, unlike transnational capital which, by one phone call or by the touch of a key on the computer, crosses almost all national borders.

Lau Kin-chi, Peter Osborne, Wang Hui, Naoki Sakai

WH: In the late 19th century and the early 20th century, some people used the term internationalism to distinguish their movements from anarchism. It is the differentiation of socialism and anarchism.

LK: We also have to see why and how, for example, during the two world wars, workers who were supposed to unite were assembled under the banner of fascism and patriotism. There is a crucial, a qualitative distinction between the flows of capital and of the workers. That's precisely why we need to scrutinize the question of this internationalism. And in this connection, the question of gender, indeed the question of the relation of gender to transnational structures, needs to be raised. Inderpal Grewal and Caren Kaplan have provided some very useful arguments on this question in their introduction to *Scattered Hegemonies*.[1] They point out that today's world is structured by transnational economic links and "cultural asymmetries," and these transnational cultural flows are the material conditions that structure women's lives in diverse locations. Rather than constructing a totalizing hegemonic power, be it the imagined unitary capitalist West or the dominating (Western) male, they put forward the idea of "scattered hegemonies" to denote the "multiple patriarchies" and the international economic hegemonies linked by the mobility of information and capital. These "scattered hegemonies," such as global economic structures, patriarchal nationalisms, "authentic" forms of tradition, local structures of domination and legal-juridical oppression, work on multiple levels in the oppression of women, and the resistances of women therefore take various forms. Feminist practices must be located within these structures of violence and try to map these scattered hegemonies and link diverse local practices, in order to open up a terrain of transnational coalition and cooperation, rather than foreclosing the opening up with the projection of the Western model of universal sisterhood.

NS: It seems to me that our project of *Traces* can be called an international one. In dealing with the peoples and regions in the world, different languages, different social strata and so on, we cannot ignore the legacies of histories. In pursuing international collaboration for our project, therefore, diplomatic politeness alone does not work to relate the heterogeneous members of our collective to one another. It seems that we are, rather, forced to confront the amazing differences and unevennesses that exist among peoples. It's difficult to simply know what those differences are, because they are embodied in all sorts of strata and contexts even within one nation state, not to mention differences between many countries and regions. As (Wang) Hui pointed out, aggressive nationalism may well be a reaction to the moves of transnational capital and colonial maneuverings, but may contain something international in it. But it is also important to keep in mind that transnational capital and colonial domination have operated in the forms of nationalism as was the case with Japanese nationalism in the 1930s or with American nationalism. Imperialists were almost invariably earnest nationalists. Aggressive nationalisms of the colonized arise out of the scars left behind on colonized people by those imperial nations. One has to be very sensitive to psychological injuries left behind by histories, and I'm particularly concerned about the current situation in East Asia. We have to create a constructive engagement among people, beyond a very simplistic notion of formal equality.

Multiplicity in *Traces*

LK: May I ask questions about *Traces?*—because I'm very new to this project. As Raymond Williams said, you cannot understand an intellectual or artistic project without also understanding its formation. Could you talk about the formation of the project of *Traces?*

NS: About three years ago, a few people in North America and East Asia began to talk about the possibility of multilingual journals. At that time it was just a sort of dream. Following that incentive, a few of us actually contacted people in Europe, East Asia and North America and began to talk about *Traces*. Surprisingly enough, we received very positive responses from people like Hui, Peter and Chungmoo Choi, who teaches at the University of California at Irvine, and then a number of people including the editors of an Austrian publishing house, Turia und Kant. Of course, a very positive response came from Sanlian Publishers in China and Iwanami Shoten Publishers in Japan. So, we started to organize the project of publishing an international journal of cultural theory in a few languages, and that's how it started. In that process we started thinking about how we can possibly understand the international transactions, international communications among intellectuals in accordance with the ideas expressed in the prospectus of *Traces*. Then, finally, just the day before yesterday, we have had the first international conference for the journal here in Beijing. Prior to this conference, we organized two last year, and then one early this year, [and] editorial meetings in places like Tokyo, Japan and Ithaca, New York, in the United States. Now our project appears all the more real and concrete.

LK: Since I do not know much about the project, maybe I have the privilege of asking some naive questions? In this idea of a multilingual journal, how do you tackle the question of what is conceived of as a "major" language? A "major" language, such as English, does not necessarily come from the center, that is, England or the United States, but may come from the Philippines, or India, or some parts of Africa. It may be the same for Spanish. Will this project draw on varieties and differentiations embedded in each language, and [acknowledge that] a "major" language may not be associated with the major centers? Yesterday we talked about "the West

Lau Kin-chi, Peter Osborne, Wang Hui, Naoki Sakai

and the Rest," and later on we talked about "China and the West." So what about "the Rest of the Rest"? Indeed, the project needs to start from feasible, realistic resources, and it is not to cover the whole world, a United-Nations-type, so there must be a certain emphasis.

NS: Probably what you have just asked about has something to do with the notion of multiplicity implied in this multilingual journal of cultural theory. As far as *Traces* is concerned, the multiplicity of multilinguality is not conceived in such terms of the numerical plurality that we would be compelled to want to cover as many languages as possible. It is not only because we want to reach a numerically larger population that we want to publish our journal in many different languages. Our journal is not designed to cover as large an area of the world as possible in order to give voices to those who express themselves in minor languages. In this respect, we are fully aware that the relation between major languages and minor languages is crudely political. It cannot be avoided. In this respect we are not trying to understand the multiplicity inherent in the project of *Traces* in terms of representing as many different languages, nationalities and cultures as possible. Our project is not to reproduce a small United Nations in international intellectual dialogue. Rather, as you mentioned as regards the situation in Hong Kong, we would like to address ourselves to those people who speak the foreignness of some language, those people who always live in languages as foreigners, as somebody other than the identity usually defined in terms of the national languages. Different versions of *Traces* are linked to one another through translation. Yet, our apprehension of translation is slightly different. We are not trying to create a transparent transfer of meaning from one language to another: rather we are trying to take advantage of the, so to say, failure which necessarily happens in the process of translation from one language to another. Or let me refer to the example you mentioned. When you think about the English language, it's almost impossible to define the identity of English in terms of nationality or ethnicity today. You would possibly refer to Philippines, Singapore, Ireland or India. But that is precisely the kind of space we would like to create internationally where we would interact among different languages. Internet technology might help us create it, where the articles to be published in *Traces* are translated into other languages. But the point I want to emphasize is that this space is generated in and as the process of translation. Translation here is understood as the place of social action where people from different geographic, linguistic and social loci are made to interact with one another and engage in an endless debate. In this place and space of translation, translation cannot be conceptualized according to the communication model and it, in fact, is endless, as Walter Benjamin once asserted about it. By definition, no translation can ever be adequate to itself or completed. Any translation is open to the future. It is future-oriented. In this specific sense, translation is always a failure which waits to be corrected. And we would really encourage readers to complain about translations, thereby engaging themselves in this place/space of *Traces*. Readers, I hope, will be able to constantly give us different translations of the articles and then point out how we failed to translate. And that way we would like to create endless debate, and we will continue to engage ourselves in the process of creating and recreating different versions of translations.

PO: I take the advantage of defining the journal in terms of relations between languages to be that the geographical boundaries of linguistic relations are different from those of nation-states: there are disjunctions and overlaps. The discussion we were having earlier about nationalism, internationalism and transnationalism was a discussion grounded on relations between nation-states. Whether it is a nationalism of nation-states, an internationalism of solidarity between members of nation-states, or a transnationalism freeing the logic of capital from the constraints of nation-states, it's all focused on nation-states. Language offers an alternative cultural-political geography to that of the nation-state, without leaving it behind completely. It disrupts the logic of nation-states, without moving to a conceptual de-territorialization. In particular, in many cases, relations between languages give you a regional geography: in Latin America, for example, apart from Brazil, which then becomes an interesting exception—a knot in the regional culture. Furthermore, this geography of languages is a result of the histories of various colonialisms—it's a shadow geography of colonialism—because the reason these same languages are spoken in all these different places is that they've been carried by colonial history. So on the one hand, it's disruptive of nationality; but on the other hand, it's tied to the legacy of colonialism.

For me, this is the interesting thing about a linguistic definition of a cultural project: how can we think the relationship between the disruptive logic of the relations between languages and the way these relations tie us back to the past through the logic of colonialism? *Traces* has a specific formation in this regard, deriving from its focus on relations between Euro-America, on the one hand, and East Asia on the other, which is then broken down into linguistic areas, with three languages internal to each. You can't escape the logic of these regional blocs, because the logic of the bloc is the logic of geopolitics. The ironic problem for *Traces* is that its linguistic definition frees it from the logic of nation-states, re-spatializing cultural relations, but the *publishing industries* are still tied to nation-states. So the project itself, in its very beginning, stages the problematic relationship between linguistic and national spaces, in its relation to publishing.

NS: We are still at an earlier stage in this project: we have to spend a lot of time and effort simply to negotiate this problematic relationship. There's another level in addition to what Peter (Osborne) has just mentioned. That is the legacies of European scholarship

Lau Kin-chi, Peter Osborne, Wang Hui, Naoki Sakai

in East Asia. What today sustains common topics among intellectuals from China, Taiwan, Japan, Vietnam or Korea is not only the heritage of the Chinese empire and its successive dynasties, which used to dominate those peripheral countries in East Asia, sometimes as tributaries or sometimes as independent polities, but more importantly the legacies of European scholarship, for instance, the sharing of German philosophical vocabulary or of a certain British Liberalism and Romanticism, even though different configurations can be seen among those topics in each country. And in fact you cannot simply understand the histories of modernization in East Asian countries without reference to European legacies, in addition to the increasing importance of American colonial policies and popular culture in the twentieth century, particularly after the Asia-Pacific War. Against the background of these Euro-American legacies, the international separation of those nation-states—China, Japan, Vietnam and Korea—emerged.

Traces of the Trace

WH: That's why we need many characters, all of which can be translated into "trace." In this sense, the term traces does not necessarily have to be explained in the sense of Derrida's theory. In Chinese, the direct translation of "traces" is "Ji," which has been used in classical Chinese philosophy and modern Chinese archaeology and historiography. As early as the Wei-jin period, Guo Xiang uses the term as a philosophical term to argue that all of the Confucian classics were not essence but only "traces" of ancient sages or emperors, cosmos or history comes from the movements of itself, but not from something outside of it. From here, Guo Xiang created his ontology without essence. In modern China, the thinking of *ji* became a critique of the origin of history in historiography and archaeology, which focused on the issue of *Yu Ji* (Yu, the first emperor's, traces). Xia, Shang and Zhou have long been thought as the earliest dynasties and the origin of China, and Yu was the first emperor of Xia. In the climate of modern nationalism, modern Chinese archaeologists formed a version of ancient Chinese history centered on the Yellow River through the discoveries of Yangshao Culture and Longshan Culture. Their version of Yellow River-centered history was a counter-narrative of Eurocentrism. But since the 1970s, archaeologists have found the Liangzhu Culture in the lower Yangzi River, Dawenkou-Longshan Culture in the lower Yellow River and Hongshan Culture in the Liao River outside of the Zhougyuan area, which has shaken the traditional version of ancient history. There are two things important here. The first: Xia, Shang and Zhou were not the continuous steps of one civilization, but different groups developed in different areas. There were a lot of groups besides them at that time. The second: archaeologists found a lot of "*Yu Ji*" (Yu's traces) not only in the Yellow River area, but also in the Liao River, the Yangzi River and other areas. This means many things: The first, others' traces have been integrated parts of our own culture or history; the second, China is not from one origin, but from a long process of communications, wars and migrations, etc.; the third, if the Yellow River-centered version of ancient history is a counter-narrative to Eurocentrism, the discoveries of *Yu Ji* (Yu's traces) in different areas are the deconstruction of the Yellow River-centered version of ancient history. The idea of "traces" is the key concept of a new version of history, which provides us with a new approach to seeing the formation of a culture.

PO: It predates national consciousness.

NS: I was aware that the term, exactly the same term, was used in some Buddhist theology as well as in a seventeenth-century school of Confucianism. But your example is very suggestive as it implies that the trace of *Traces* can be found almost everywhere.

LK: Then, when you started, how did you select the title *Traces*?

NS: We were interested in interactions and translation among many regions and groups of people in the world. But, above all, we did not want to get caught in the business of deciding who culturally or intellectually owes whom, or whose indebtedness to whom and the whole question of originality and influence. Secondly, and particularly, because we wanted to include Europeanists in East Asia and to show how important it was for intellectuals in Asia, Latin America and Africa to study European and North American scholarship in the formation of their local social realities. In order to do that we really needed to find a different format of understanding the transmission of ideas and the transcultural processes. So the most handy term came from Derridian vocabulary, but the point was, we really wanted to avoid the whole notion of influence and copying, sort of a simplistic notion of imitation, in our attempt to understand how modern knowledge has been produced, not only in Europe and North America but in Asia and elsewhere as well.

LK: There is the problem of theory being from and of the West and empirical data, with Asia as the locality. How does this project aim to react to this kind of distinction? Will there, for example, be "empirical" data from Germany? Or will the localities basically be East Asia?

Theory and its Traces

NS: I do not believe that the validity of theory solely consists in its capacity to subsume many empirical data under conceptual generality. Starting from a specific locale at a particular place, we are able to universalize an experience which cannot hitherto be rendered commensurate in terms of the existing conceptual schemes. In other words, we should be able to find universality in our local experience by respecting its singularity. Since

Lau Kin-chi, Peter Osborne, Wang Hui, Naoki Sakai

our experience at stake here is basically of an antagonistic nature, the singularity of the experience, to which theory is a response, cannot be divorced from the problematic of social change. As long as each of us is engaged in an experience of social change and conflict, I do not see why theory ought to be somewhat monopolized by the so-called West.

But, at the same time, there are institutional and historical constraints which any project of publication cannot overlook. Because we happened to start with the contingent connections between East Asia—mainly three countries, China, Korea and Japan or, if you include Taiwan, four countries with a sizable reading audience for publications of our kind—and the North Atlantic, we selected those three or four countries. We are also very much concerned with societies in Southeast and South Asia. Of course, we feel obliged to explore the possibilities in other places such as Latin America and Africa, but it will be very difficult to sustain the publication of a periodical where readers are few. In order to carry out the translation and manufacturing, we have to find a market that is large enough.

LK: As an example, what would be the target readers of a German edition of *Traces*?

NS: People in various disciplines, I would say. For instance, cultural studies is gaining some popularity among the younger generations of scholars in German-speaking countries. I hope that *Traces* will appeal to them.

PO: German intellectual culture has been far less transformed by the development of cultural studies than most other places; in part, I suppose, because of the way that it is dominated by philosophy, and the specific character of German philosophy. One has the feeling that Heidegger, for example, connects to cultural studies in Japan, in China, in America, but not in Germany. *Traces* will be much more of an avant-garde for cultural studies in Germany than elsewhere, where it is an established and lively field.

LK: So, for example, for the readers of the German edition, would they be seeing Heidegger as theory in relation to, for example, the different localities in East Asia? Or will the localities also be German-speaking places? I think this is a problematic that we need to address.

PO: I see the danger, but to what extent should we continue to define a theory by its point of origin, once it has achieved a certain breadth of dissemination and development? To do that is always to trace its meaning back to its source. You turn the "Japanese" Heidegger into "essentially German" Heidegger as read in Japan, as opposed to "essentially German" Heidegger as read in China, for example. This leads you to ask which is closest to the original; rather than "what work are Heidegger's concepts doing in this or that context of appropriation?" "What work is it doing on them?" and "What does this interaction tell us about the context of appropriation, about Heidegger, and about Heidegger's context, etc.?" Your question becomes a challenge: the challenge to find and to produce work in which theory is used in such a way that it becomes more than a reference back to its origin, more than reflex of national location. It's a serious challenge.

NS: I would just like to mention that we had to spend a long time talking about the practical side of the situation. We have faced and will constantly face the problem of the lack of people who can translate from East Asian languages into German. There are so few people who read East Asian languages, and very little modern work produced in East Asia has been translated into German. So the German publishers until recently only translated so-called typically exotic materials like old Confucian and Buddhist classical texts into German and so on. In comparison with the number of people who study German texts in East Asia, very few people study the contemporary and modern intellectual activities ongoing in East Asia. So, in a sense, we are trying to create a different flow of information. And I do not think that it is merely because of the ideological arrangement that the West supposedly monopolizes theory and that the non-West is regarded as the sources of raw data. There are other institutional frameworks within which any theoretical work produced in East Asia is, almost always, automatically shut out from, for instance, European and North American audiences. I am not saying, however, that theoretical knowledge cannot move and spread irrespective of or despite this Eurocentric configuration. But, generally speaking, this has been the state of affairs in global intellectual exchange. So there has been little encouragement for the intellectuals in East Asia to be engaged in theoretical production or critical work today. So I hope *Traces* will somewhat open up the possible passages through which intellectuals from many parts of the world, Western Europe, North America, East, Southeast and South Asia, Australia and so forth, can engage in theoretical debates and conversations. I'm not saying that the East Asian intellectuals have to create theoretical knowledge which is marked with the cultural uniqueness of East Asia and export it to Europe and North America. That is exactly what we want to avoid. What we seek is engagement and debate involving people from many regions at the same time.

Theory and Marxism

PO: If one thinks of the space of international theory today, one thinks of cultural theory, and the exportation and situational appropriation of certain things American (albeit with fairly heavy labor inputs from France). However, if one thinks back to thirty years or so ago, there was another space in international theory: Marxism. International Marxism was a common theoretical discourse which developed through the relationship between its various national forms. (This raises the whole question of Maoism as an international form,

Lau Kin-chi, Peter Osborne, Wang Hui, Naoki Sakai

for example). Furthermore, in a certain sense, Marxism made today's (resolutely non- or post-Marxist) international cultural theory possible. The international history of Marxist theory is a condition for the possibility of the *Traces* project, for example—albeit an increasingly invisible one. I'd be interested to know about the place of discourses of Marxism in Chinese theory today. Is there still the hope that they might mediate the rapidly translated culture of Western theory? Or is the perception of Marxism so tied to inherited domestic political forms—as it was in Eastern Europe—that people just want to be free of it?

WH: There is a long tradition of Marxism in China. In my view, in the first half of the 20th century, the turning point of Chinese Marxism is the year 1930. Before that year, there were a lot of discussions on Marxism, but it was only one of the issues in cultural debates at that time. After 1930, the situation changed because different political schools—no matter whether or not they were Marxists—began to use the terms of Marxism in their interpretation of Chinese history. We could divide scholars involved in debates on Chinese history into four groups: the Kuomintang group, the Communist group, the Trotsky school and the liberal group. Why did so many different people suddenly begin using Marxist terms? The point is that all of them had to deal with the issues of history at that time—they all felt it necessary to have a historical narrative for their political agendas. There were two factors stimulating the debate and the popularization of Marxist terms. The first: after the failure of the Northern expedition in 1927, intellectuals began to reflect on why the revolution failed so rapidly, and the reflection itself resulted in divergences among intellectuals who got involved in the social movements. The second: the early 1930s was a relatively peaceful period, when urban industrialization developed following the increase of international and national investments and the rural economy collapsed because of importing a lot of silk and agricultural products from foreign countries. Both factors forced people to answer the question: What's the nature of Chinese society—a feudal society, a capitalist society, or a semifeudal and semicolonial society? Against this background, people adopted Marxist terms to describe their version of Chinese history and the nature of Chinese society.

The background against which Marxism is reviving in contemporary China is similar to the 1930s. One of the issues discussed by some intellectuals is globalization and the activities of transnational capital. But it is not the only reason for the revival of the interests in Marx. Let me develop this a little more. Though the main theories for economic reform and the new enlightenment in the '80s came from Marxist economics and Marxist humanism, and the creative tensions between "real Marxism" and orthodox Marxism, the people, especially of my generation, rejected using Marxism for political reasons after the Cultural Revolution. But in the '90s, there is a reviviscence of Marxism among younger generations. The turning point is the 1989 social movement in Beijing, which is the starting point of the process of collapse of the socialist system of Eastern European States and has the label of "the end of the Cold War." The dominant interpretation of 1989 is the end of history, the failure of socialism and the victory of new liberalism. My observation is totally different: the social movement for democracy in 1989 contained the connotation of going against new capitalism. We could divide the process of Chinese reform into two steps. The first is from 1978 to 1985, when the reform focused on the transformation of land system in rural areas and the price system of agricultural products, and it changed the unequal relationship between the rural and the urban, which was formed in the process of industrialization guided by the state plan. Thus, the achievements of the reform in the rural areas should be viewed as the victory of establishment of a relatively equal relationship between the rural population and the urban population.

The second step is from 1985 to the '90s, when the reform focused on the transformation of the urban economic system—especially the system of state-ownership and the price system—which was the period of creating a market system systematically. The main labels of this phase were the establishments of "special economic zones," the formation of "double price systems," and the "privatization" of state-owned properties which had any democratic institution of supervising. The slogans like "combating official speculations and profiteering" and "against corruption" in the 1989 social movement revealed the strong feeling against privileges and the making of an unequal market system. Under such social conditions, the purpose of the social movement in 1989 was not only a pure political one, but a comprehensive set of requirements for democracy. Here is the key for understanding the significance of the social movement in 1989: the state which the movement resisted was not an old-fashioned socialist state, but a state in the transition to a new market system; the violence against the student movement and the social movement did not come from a state which took the planned economy as its social base, but rather a state which was pushing the campaign for reforming the planning system and building a new market system. The state that suppressed the social movement for democracy was the same state that launched the economic reform. The fact, which has long been neglected consciously and unconsciously, means that it is impossible to create a market society without state violence. The so-called spontaneous order of the market system (especially its price system) is a result of violence; it is a construction under the state's plan. The fact itself explains where the corruption and social injustice come from. Without the violent suppression of the 1989 social movement, there would not be the establishment of the so-called market price system. It is against this background, I think, that the dynamics for the social mobilization in 1989 came from the requirements for social equality, a value people were so familiar with in their thinking of socialism. Here the socialism is not of the socialist state that took the planned economy and the centralization of state power as the basic approaches to modernization, but the principle of and requirements for a democratic society. So, in my view, the reviviscence of Marxism is not the simple result of importing Western theory, but rooted in the great transformation of Chinese society and the global system. At the same time, the reusing of Marxist terms cannot be interpreted as a simple reviving of old Marxism, but a new trend in a new context. Actually, the younger generation of intellectuals is using Marx's terms and theory together with different theories—postmodernism, social democracy and even liberalism.

LK: I think it's very interesting how there's this revived interest in Marxism.

PO: You think there's a revival?

LK: There is a revival of interest. My graduate student has chosen a topic on the translation in China of Marxist terms in the first half of the 20th century. I was interested in why an urban youth from Hong Kong from a middle-class family should be interested in this topic and wanted to look for alternative interpretations of Marxist theory or Marxist terms. I feel that, perhaps, Marxism had been seen either as an utopian ideology, or part of the propaganda of the state machine. However, with the grim realities, violences and crises in China, where the problems are being seen as consequental of the implementation of capitalism under the rule of the Communist bureaucracy, there is a need to access theoretical resources for explication or critique. Hence Marxism is returned to in the endeavor for social change and revolution, albeit in varying ways in different sites.

I am interested in how *Traces* aspires to facilitate the flow of ideas. The term "social change" has figured so many times in the past two days, and I feel that somehow there is something that is shared in this group of people that met here, though what is shared is not very explicitly articulated. Would you want to make it explicit here or not?

(General laughter)

The New Interest in Marxism

PO: From my brief experience of intellectuals in Eastern Europe since '89—in four very different countries: Slovenia, Ukraine, Czechoslovakia and Poland—it's clear that the term Marxism remains so semantically linked to a political ideology of state socialism that it is almost impossible to disengage it and re-articulate it to the idea of Marxism as a critical analysis of capitalism. For example, if you approach the analysis of commodity-form through Volume One of *Capital*, you will meet with great resistance. But if you come at it through a cultural theory of reification, and the experience of marketization, and avoid a certain theoretical language, they [intellectuals in these four countries] recognize it immediately, completely; but you remain stuck at the phenomenological level. It's a political problem. There seem to be three things at play here, with gaps between them: there's first the political history of Marxism as international communism and it's various, complicated internal relations; second, there's the theoretical history of Marxism as a critical analysis of capitalism; and third, the problematic of social change, more broadly. The tragedy of Western Marxism—and the revival of Marxist theory in Europe in the 1960s and '70s—was that it could forge no alternative political articulation of its critical analysis of capitalism to movements of social change, other than through groups formed by an earlier history of communism. But with the demise of the historical remnants of those forces, and the sea change in the ideological climate which has accompanied it, the difficulty has been exacerbated rather than eased. The question of how you articulate critical-analytical discourses with movements of social change remains unanswered.

NS: Peter, you talked about a certain internationality of Marxism in the 1960s and '70s. Under the name of Maoism the ideas from China spread to many places in the world irrespective of the "West and the Rest" configuration. They were much less orientalized. But I am also thinking about the 1920s and 1930s when the intellectual concerns with Marxist problematics in fact created an international space of intellectual debates beyond national borders. In this regard, I do not think it was a sheer accident that the word "theory" was frequently associated with Marxism. In connection to Peter's question, I would like to ask you, Hui, why you mentioned this particular date—you said you can even pin down the year 1930—a year which involves a lot of things in the context of Japanese Marxism as well. In that year, to my knowledge, the international space of Marxism, in which Chinese, Japanese, American, European and other Asian intellectuals had actively participated, began to collapse.

PO: Can you explain what you mean by Japanese Marxism here?

NS: In the 1920s Marxism very rapidly became dominant in Japanese academia. This is the period when Marxism was adopted as academic method as well as a political agenda by many academics and intellectuals in fields such as philosophy, history, literary studies, not to mention economics and sociology. Many of them made deliberate efforts to understand Japanese history and social formation in terms of the specific features of Japanese capitalism. This is highlighted by what is generally referred to as "the Debates on Japanese Capitalism" (*Nihon-shihonshugi Ronso*).[2] As the young elites were attracted to Marxism, the Japanese State and conservatives were alerted and began to apply many anti-socialist measures, particularly in education. Until the 1970s, however, the legacies of Marxism were clearly visible in Japanese higher education. For instance, economics departments at the top universities were predominantly Marxist, and many of the elite governmental bureaucrats and business leaders in the 1960s and 70s were Marxist-educated despite their conservative political orientation. Deprived of its international and political commitment, Japanese Marxism became a science concerned with the most rational management of capitalism. I find it very hard to understand what is referred to as the Japanese "economic miracle" of the 1950s and '60s without taking into account certain contributions of Japanese Marxism.

1930 is precisely the year when Marxism in Japan, and by implication the international space of theoretical debate, began to retreat. There had been a rich communication between Chinese intellectuals and Japanese Marxists in the 1920s, but around that time that alliance was beginning to be severed, and Marxism was gradually divided into two different directions, the exclusively scientific analysis of capitalism on the one hand, and the political movement on the other. Eventually the political movement was suppressed until after the war. So I am surprised that you could pin down that year. I'd been wondering why I could actually pin down exactly the same year in Japan.

WH: I have some reasons for this. In 1924, Guo Muoro translated a Japanese Marxist book entitled *Social Organization and Social Revolution* into Chinese.[3]

In 1927 a group of left intellectuals came back from Japan to China, and, in the next year, they launched the discussion on "revolutionary literature," which was the first time in China to have such a Marxist intellectual movement on such a scale. At the same time, in 1927, just after the failure of the Northern Expedition, Guo Muoro, Mao Dun and some other intellectuals who were involved in the Northern Expedition were exiled to Japan. The discussion on the social history of China and the nature of Chinese society was sparked by Guo Muoro's book entitled *A Study of the Ancient Society of China,* which was published in 1929 or 1930 and was written during his exile in Japan. The time of the debate on the social history of China and the nature of Chinese society coincided with the economic crisis in the 1930s. It is clear that the left-wing intellectuals who insisted that China was a semifeudal and semi-capitalist society were trying to put their analysis on Chinese history against the new background of global capitalism. The main sources for them, I believe, was Lenin's theory of imperialism, which highlighted the international dimension of the struggle of the working class within a nation-state.

PO: Is there a parallel debate now about the nature of Chinese society?

WH: Yes, there is. In 1997, I published a long article entitled "Contemporary Chinese Thought and the Question of Modernity" in *Tianya* magazine,[4] which caused a series of debates that have been labeled as a debate between "new lefts" and "liberals." The questions here are how to evaluate the achievements and failures of Chinese socialism, how to understand the new enlightenment in the 1980s, and how to evaluate the process of marketization and how to understand the process of globalization. The key point is the relationships between economy and politics, the state and the market.

Marketization is never a process of pure economic changes, but it is a process of political arrangements, and thus inequality, injustice and corruption are not only an economic question but also the results of political arrangements. "New liberals" believe that the force of the market itself is a deconstructive force to the socialist state, and they identify themselves as a continuity of the new enlightenment, which was considered by them to be an anti-feudalistic movement. Critical intellectuals argue that the marketization itself is a result of the reform policy of the state, and it cannot be simply thought of as a process outside the state power and the purpose of Mao's state was not feudalization but modernization.[5] Thus, the reflection on Mao's socialism should be a reflection on modernity itself.

Another thing is that your question is actually about an alternative. For in your question you referred to Marxism as a state ideology. Marxism in China was not only a state ideology, but a modernization ideology. But following the process of reform, a new market ideology has formed though the state still, on the surface, insists on socialism. The situation itself is the best testimony of how the marketization relies on the state. In this case, it has become possible to make a distinction between Marxism or socialism as a state or modernization ideology and Marxism or socialism as critical theory in the context of globalization.

As the global situation surrounding socialism has changed, it has become possible to talk about a distinction between kinds of Marxism and socialism, a distinction between critical theory and the liberal celebration of globalization/modernization. When China now is so deeply involved in the globalization process, we might find some fragments of socialism in China, in order to assert a critical potentiality of socialism once again. This is to say that fragments of this kind became sort of an inspiration for alternatives in the present situation. In the past there was partial socialism, the state socialism. As I said about the 1989 social movements, their socialism took a form opposed to the state socialism. In a sense, critical thoughts come from the process of the great transformation of the socialist state, and they are critical because they do not adhere to socialism as a totality of the state, but [to] fragments of socialism. I do not think that this critical thrust comes from Taiwan and Hong Kong, because it's so intimately connected to the socialist history. Because a lot of things have been accumulated in the last forty years, only after the collapse of state socialism did you find out that these legacies can be seen as critical resources. Socialism became a kind of source of criticism. It's not only a theory but some fragmented remnants of the socialist history which people actually lived. So when people ask me what the alternatives are today, I say that some alternatives are here; it's not merely a theory; it's not our imagination; it's here as an historical experience, historical practice,

Lau Kin-chi, Peter Osborne, Wang Hui, Naoki Sakai

but not as the totality but as fragments. These are becoming critical sources for the new totality of global capitalism.

LK: These fragments are not theories or ideas per se. The history of the Chinese revolution is not just that of the Chinese Communist Party as presented in the history books. The peasants, the workers, they were and are part of the experience of struggle in resistance. I think there is a need for us to distinguish between what is theorized and what is practiced. I very much agree with what you just said, that from these fragments, there are alternatives, which are not something abstract, as the truth out there, but [something that] is there in daily experiences.

WH: Yes, that kind of experience became extremely important for us, because of the critical tradition in Marxism in Europe. It is that they tried to create a space between the capitalist West and the socialist East. And at that time they had to identify the West and the East in that sense as totalities, and so then they have to create some kind of critical theory. That kind of theory always emphasized the cultural as a subject. So when we talk, only after the collapse of traditional socialism, we find some new possibilities to establish a new space, based upon those historical precedents. Those fragments became possibilities for our theory: it's not only the cultures they are in or not only some others, but it's socialism, socialist tradition, part of the socialism, the tradition of socialism in our own history, our own experience.

In China some intellectuals are asking the question, "are there any possibilities for us to find a new way of going beyond the Western Marxism, which will be based on our own experiences?" This is a counternarrative to Eurocentrism, a counternarrative to the Eurocentric description of 1989.

So, in that sense, we could find something, maybe, going beyond the so-called Western Marxism.

PO: Western Marxism seems to have dissolved into a much more generic form of cultural theory.

Cultural Theory and Internationalism

NS: Well, the word "culture" is not exclusively for ethnic, national, racial or civilizational identities. The notion of culture can be transformed into something much less particularistic which is capable of universalizing historical experience while respecting the singularity of the locale. This is why, I believe, a new cultural theory, to which *Traces* is devoted, is in demand.

It's surprising that, in the 1930s, a similar thing was going on in the name of Marxism across regions and nations, in spite of the Soviet Union's nationalistic and imperialist efforts to manipulate the Comintern. It is also surprising we have not been aware of that amazing contemporaneity and simultaneous development in intellectual fields that was taking place in many parts of the world. I just wonder what has prevented us from recognizing it?

WH: But for me, when I read some Japanese documents on Chinese history and Japanese history, especially those of historians working on Chinese history in Japan after 1930, I realize that actually a lot of Chinese historiography of the period was formed in those debates. I found that some historians, Japanese historians, were talking about— there was a lot of discussion about the Beiwei dynasty. That's sixth-century China. A lot of discussion about autonomy, so-called economic autonomy in this sixth-century dynasty. They formed a debate on the nature of Chinese history in the ancient empires, that's where the so-called "Chinese history" came from.

It's interesting that most of Japanese scholarship on Chinese history focused on the nature of Chinese society after the transition from Tang to Sung. They thought that the Sung Dynasty was already a nation-state. Their narrative of Chinese history is already based on the model of nationalism or the nation-state.

NS: Nation-states, yes. But, ironically, as I retrospectively read the Japanese historical studies of the 1930s and 1940s, I feel that even Marxist historians worked somewhat covertly to establish the most "scientific" form of the national history which, out of the methodological and epistemic necessities, posited a substance called "the Japanese nation" or its premodern ethnic unity prior to the formation of Japan as a nation-state.[6]

WH: The critique of that model mainly came from Marxist historiography. Is it true? So that model is more liberal in some sense.

NS: Yes, in some sense. In the late nineteenth century the Japanese state established the scheme of the national history as a measure to institute the modern nation-state, of the history generally called *kôkokushikan*, based on the fictive continuity of imperial genealogy. Compared with this imperial historiography, Marxist historiography was certainly more liberal.

WH: And some others focus on autonomy, if not economy, on autonomous economy. It's deeply influenced by Marxism. That's at the base, as I read it, among the Japanese historians in the field of Chinese history from the 1930s to the 1940s. Which is different from the politics that is based on the figure of the emperor or the dynasty, so those historians were talking about the nation's economic autonomy during that period. The discussion of Chinese history by Japanese scholars was deeply influenced by the discussion on the nature of Chinese society.

We knew something about how Chinese intellectuals made responses to the issues discussed by Japanese intellectuals, but we did not know much about how Japanese intellectuals responded to the discussions in China in the 1930s and '40s. Last year, however, I found among some Japanese studies on Chinese history that they were responding to the discussions on the nature of Chinese society and the social history of China in the 1930s. For example, in 1947, Utsunomiya Seikichi

Lau Kin-chi, Peter Osborne, Wang Hui, Naoki Sakai

published *The Areas of Medieval Eastern History*[7] to argue against Naito Konan's narrow focus on the Han and non-Han relation in China and against his indifference to "the deep development in content." He turned to the study of economic history in the so-called medieval history of China. Naito's arguments were very influential in the 1930s, and some scholars of Kyoto University at that time took his arguments as their propositions. My impression is that the critiques of Naito and the Kyoto school were responding to Guo Muoro and other Chinese Marxist historians' discussions. Here, Marx's view of history played a role in the interactions between Japanese intellectuals and Chinese intellectuals.

NS: I think it's probably connected to the internationalist nature of Marxist scholarship at that time. It has something to do with developments in the historical scholarship in Japan as well, because in the late '20s you can probably find the first, initial development of Marxian study of Japanese society of the Tokugawa period.[8] It's not Sung, but it's in fact related to what you mentioned. It's a recognition that economy had become a sort of autonomous domain of inquiry, as you argued with regard to China in your recent publication in Japanese.[9] It was an attempt to write Japanese history as an economic history.

Basically until the mid-nineteenth century, economy never constituted an autonomous domain of academic inquiry. The combination of Chinese characters, *keizai* or *jingji*, which signifies economy in Japanese today, did not refer to the social formation based upon the circulation of money before the mid-nineteenth century, although many had already written about the management of money and money's social effects in the seventeenth and eighteenth centuries. In the late nineteenth and early twentieth centuries, the domain of economy emerged, perhaps for the first time, as an independent field of academic discipline. Until then you cannot find any sort of systematic study of Tokugawa Japan on the basis of economic phenomena. Neither can you find the notion of economy as an autonomous domain of human activities.

Multiple Modernities and the Project of *Traces*

NS: I wonder if those Japanese historians were also interested in the comparative studies of Chinese and Japanese capitalisms, if they were concerned with how to prove the historical advance of Japanese capitalism over the Chinese version.

The initial interest of Marxist history was in how to analyze the contemporary Japanese society, namely contemporary Japanese capitalism, in terms of historical transition. Both Chinese and Japanese historians tried to explain the idea of revolution in terms of transition from a feudalistic society to a bourgeois society, and, in that sense, just as you mentioned, the relation between the feudal past and modern present was always assumed to be of a chronological order, and more specifically, of a modernizationalist order. I believe that Peter has called into question that understanding of historical development.[10]

PO: What's interesting for me about the project of *Traces* is the way that it complicates the problematic of modernity; not only by the need to conceptualize the specificities of non-Western modernities, but also by the idea that there are different relations between different non-Western modernities, and different relations between these non-Western modernities and various Western ones. The theoretical field is so much more complex and rich here than the classical sociological paradigm allows.

The concept of modernity is still mainly used to encode the transition from feudalism to capitalism, culturally, as a movement from tradition to modernity, as forms of the experience of historical change. This was the founding distinction of bourgeois sociology. "Modernity" has become conceptually fixed—reified—as the signifier of an experience of historical change associated with the development of capitalism in the West. The traditional/modern distinction, mapped onto the West/non-West distinction, is now applied internally to the non-West, so that *its* modernity is associated with "Western" capitalism, too. But this reified understanding of modernity in terms of a particular social content is a barrier to grasping the complexities and specificities of experiences of historical change.

To break it up, we need to do two things: first, to provide a more fundamental conceptual analysis of "the modern," and related terms, as a structure of historical time-consciousness with a variety of social sources; second, to distinguish qualitatively different forms of modernity, in terms of their different articulations of this basic temporal logic, within both Western and non-Western contexts. Fascism, for example, represents an alternative (and distinctive) type of modernity to liberal capitalism, in my analysis. Then there is the specific quality of modernity associated with revolutionary state-led modernization programs—international communism as a distinctive form of modernity or structure of historical time-consciousness. There are the colonial and postcolonial modernities instantiated by the processes of colonial government and national independence, etc., with their own temporal-historical logic. We need a much broader typology of modernities, articulated at the level of temporal-historical form.

In the case of China today, for example, we need to examine the competing dynamics of modernity associated with state-led modernization, with the new market-relations, and with the legacy of colonial relations. It is not only the market which is "modern." "Chinese modernity" is an internally differentiated and tense conflictual field. Calling this "postmodernity," in order to differentiate it from an earlier "Western modernity" doesn't really help, since, in my view, the problematic of postmodernism functions to *maintain*, rather than to challenge, the conventional understanding of the traditional/modern distinction, by updating it with the category of the postmodern. The idea of a "Chinese postmoder-

Lau Kin-chi, Peter Osborne, Wang Hui, Naoki Sakai

nity" just fills this in with a particular empirical content. Rethinking the *concept* of modernity in relation to non-Western contexts is a much more fruitful path to follow, since it will react back upon and undermine the classical sociological problematic.

NS: I wonder if you foresee some kind of concrete consequences of this kind of project, concrete consequences where it is glaringly obvious why the assumption of Western theory and non-Western empirical data is misleading? Can you foresee some political consequences that you would like to bring about?

LK: From the discussions and the papers presented in the past two days, I have a feeling that you have very good people for this project, and that the project itself is very interesting, with a lot of potential, because it's not just to produce a journal, it's to facilitate an exchange of experiences. With it is a critical-ness, a self-criticalness, which helps us with new resources, to see what we can do, where we stand, and what the problematics are. At the same time, because everyone has his or her own agenda, networks and commitments, the question then is why this project should be prioritized with regard to others, and how it adds value to our existing work. There could be many different priorities and concerns which might just tear the project apart. In addition, there is the question of how this project relates to similar projects. I see that some people in this conference or on the editorial board are also working on the project of Inter-Asia Cultural Studies. How the two projects have different emphases and still complement each other will be a question of concern and interest. As for this project [*Traces*], I can also see that there may be huge problems to deal with, such as the issue of the monopoly of copyright, or of translation. Still, I must congratulate you for the enthusiasm in embarking on this huge project. I also feel that among the participants, there is in general a good feeling that we are interacting with very interesting people and generating exciting ideas.

I believe this is a relation of openness that is conducive to the working out of a terrain for collaboration and cooperation among different individuals and different groups. It is true that we must be attentive to specific histories, the specificities of people, but this is not to give in to a relativism that is ironically based on the assertion of originary identities. Returning to the transnational-feminist practices briefly discussed before, scattered hegemonies need to be acknowledged as marking specific histories. Hence, in trying to work out the specific histories against the appropriation of dominant forms of History, the traces of the Other in the self must also be traced. Just as transnational feminist practices are concerned about the politics of relations between the self and the other, knowing that asymmetrical relationships are irreducible and are currently structured by the flow of capital and information—with modern science, modern technology and modern warfare being among the crucial forces affecting the flow—*Traces* may also be understood as the acknowledgement of complex, multiply constituted identities as effects of the expansion of the histories of imperialism and colonialism in various forms. This is how I see the project of *Traces* as linked to the projects I am engaged in.

PO: One advantage of such a broad and ambitious project like *Traces*, in which one comes into contact with people one wouldn't otherwise meet, from a variety of different cultural and intellectual backgrounds, for me, is that it helps refocus one's intellectual work on new problems by disengaging it from purely professional academic logics. In Britain the connection between intellectual work done in the academy and broader streams of cultural and political thought has become increasingly problematic. If universities used to be places where intellectuals earned their livings by teaching, but in which they could think from the standpoint of their own cultural and political projects, this is no longer so easily the case. Intellectual agendas are increasingly overdetermined by professional, academic, disciplinary ones. A broad, international, multidisciplinary, multilingual project like that of *Traces* forces one to think beyond that. It can shock one back to the real problems.

NS: This is one of the reasons behind our decision to make *Traces* what one might call a general intellectual journal, to distinguish it from other academic journals which are disciplinary based.

WH: And actually, last time, when we met in Tokyo in October 1998, we suggested that we could have 20 or 30 percent of the space of each issue devoted to some local contributions, which would not necessarily be translated into other languages or published in other languages. Some parts of the journal could be edited by the local editors and then focus on something—actually that kind of discussion could be a linkage between intellectual levels, our discussion and some local issues. In that case, there will be slight differences among different versions of *Traces*. That space could be used to make the linkage between inside and outside.

NS: We really have to try to create a different space, away from the typical, professional sort of academic journals that are prevalent in the United States. Hence, we might try to pursue a slightly different concept of consensus among the members of the collectives. The issue of the locale that cannot be easily appropriated into the general space of transnationality is very significant, in this respect. And because our collectivities are numerically large, it is virtually impossible to have any assembly where everybody can meet. Instead we would like to have a different sense of agreement.

Yes, as Hui mentioned, at the preliminary editorial meeting in October 1998, those suggestions concerning the local conditions of publication came from the Korean and mainland Chinese publishers and from *Traces* editorial members from mainland China and Korea. We agreed that the Chinese and Korean versions of *Traces* will have contributions in addition to the core set of articles which are translated and published in all the languages of the journal.

Of course, decision-making procedure

Lau Kin-chi, Peter Osborne, Wang Hui, Naoki Sakai

and some basic principles have to be agreed upon, but to some extent agreement should imply that, in a sense, as you mentioned, we agree to continue to debate. That was what I implied by translation. It's not the perfect matching but the discrepancies among ourselves that should be a sort of motif behind this project, so that we continue to argue among ourselves and readers, and that way we constantly face our practical problems and obstacles; but nonetheless, if we can manage in one way or another to conceive of the connections differently and of a different notion of agreement, then we might be able to continue to do this.

On the other hand, I think, understandably we share a lot, but in terms of customs in publications and academic practices and activism and so forth, we constantly encounter misunderstandings among ourselves. Inevitably we will have continual problems about our communication. So my idea is basically that we would rather feed on miscommunication and misunderstanding—and then keep on going. Otherwise I don't think we would be able to accomplish much. I hope that *Traces* will give rise to an international space of intellectual debates which will continue to disclose misunderstanding and miscommunication among us, heterogeneity in us as a collectivity.

LK: That's a good start, to assume misunderstanding in taking off on a collective project. (general laughter)

28 June 1999 in Beijing

Endnotes

1—Inderpal Grewal and Caren Kaplan, eds., *Scattered Hegemonies: Postmodernity and Transnational Feminist Practices* (Minneapolis and London: University of Minnesota Press, 1994).

2—Two major schools of Marxist thought engaged in a series of debates in the 1920s were respectively called the Lecture School and the Labor-Agrarian School. For an analysis of Japanese capitalism, see Noro Eitarô, *Nihonshihonshugi hattatsushi* [The history of the development of Japanese capitalism] (Tokyo: Tettô Shoin, 1930. Reprint Tokyo: Iwanami Shoten, 1983) and Yamada Moritarô, *Nihonshihonshugi bunseki* [The analysis of Japanese capitalism] (Tokyo: Iwanami Shoten, 1934. Reprint 1977).

3—Kawakai Hajime, *Shakai soshiki to shakai kakumei ni kansuru kôsatsu* [Speculations on social formation and social revolution] (Tokyo: Kôbundô, 1923).

4—Wang Hui, "Contemporary Chinese Thought and the Question of Modernity," *Tianya*, no. 5, 1997.

5—Gan Yang, "A Critique of Chinese Conservatism in the 1990s," *Social Text*, 55. Zhang Shuguang, "Geren Quanli he Guojia Quanli," Gonggong Luncong, no. 1, 1995. As for the new enlightenment's understanding of socialist state, see Tin Guantao and Liu Qingfen, *Xingsheng yu*

Weiji (Changsha: Hunan People's Publishers, 1984).

6—See Isomae Junichi's critique of Ishimoda in Isomae Junichi, "Kigi shinwa no meta historie" [The meta-history of the Japanese ancient mythology] (Tokyo: Yoshikawa Kôbunkan, 1998).

7—Utsunomiya Seikichi, "The Areas of Medial Eastern History," *Tôkô*, no. 2, May 1947.

8—For major publications about the historical analysis of Japanese capitalism, see Hattori Shisô, "Meijiishin-shi" [History of the Meiji Restoration], in *Marukusu Shugi Kôza* [Lecture Series, Marxism] (Tokyo: Ueno Shoten, 1928); and Hani Gorô, "Seisan Meiji-ishin-shi" [Summary history of the Meiji Restoration] in *Shinkô kagaku no hata no motoni* (Under the flag of new science) 1928).

9—"Marukusu karamita Gulobarizumu" [Globalism from the viewpoint of Marx] dialogue with Kôjin Karatani, in *Sekai*, no. 660 (April 1999) : 183–200.

10—Peter Osborne, *The Politics of Time* (London: Verso, 1995), forthcoming in a Chinese translation from Commercial Press, Beijing; the first chapter is forthcoming in Japanese translation in *Shisô*, Iwanami Shoten Publishers, Tokyo.

INTERLUDES

TRACES OF A B C D...

MULTIPLICITY

We must begin with ***multiplicity*** or ***multiplicities***. It is a name for decisive divides, watersheds. If one thinks of the *contemporary* as a relationship that is ontologically constituting itself in the present in the very critique of all the forms of transcendence, ***multiplicity*** or ***multiplicities*** is the operator of philosophy *insofar as* this philosophy is of this contemporaneity. From Bergson, up to Foucault, Deleuze or Badiou, the contemporary announces philosophy as an ontology of multiplicities (the concept is the primary of all the multiples) and as a pragmatics of singularities (singularity as the destruction in performance of the categorical opposition of One and Many: every singularity is *virtually collective*). It is because of ***multiplicity*** or ***multiplicities*** that Spinoza is projected into the primary position among the contemporary: his Ethic is an ethics of multiplicities that is brought to the power of the Action-Thought. Inversely, Phenomenology and Analytic Philosophy will never be contemporary: Phenomenology being a thought of Incarnation (the Incarnation of the One : the *Un*-carnation), and Analytic Philosophy being a logic of Class (logic is the classification of many). What defines, in contrast, the affirmative range of ***multiplicity*** in its radical excess to the religious in thought (hermeneutics) and to the Stalinism of thought (the police of utterances) is to explore the real conditions of a "superior materialism" in the Age of the Virtual. In its regime of cultural ***multiplicity*** or ***multiplicities, Traces*** could well be an expression of their constructions and a construction of their expressions.

Éric ALLIEZ

Translated by
Naoki SAKAI

Interludes

COMMUNICATION
The most *commercial* notion needed in order to say what happens (or does not happen) by the **circulation** of **affects, affinities, resonance, defacement**.....

CONVERSATION
A word, obviously too much of "craze". With the exceptions of **transcendance, transparence** and **transfer**, replace it with all the words with "trans": **translation, transformation, transversality,** etc. Let us begin with **transpiration**: nothing better than a small conversation in order to make oneself perspire. Continue with **transsubstantiation**: conversation in reverse, wine **transformed** into water. Then one should put oneself in the state of *trance* (*trans(e)* in French) for good.

FLESH
Something nice to give to the **pirates**. The flesh is too soft to mount, on the plain of expression, a contemporary thought which is heavy enough to resist postmodern enzymes. **Flesh** is the **restance** of moribund Christianity; it is Christianity's last reflexivity. One is to become a Body-without-Flesh as a surface for inscribing the identity: Expression = Construction.

Vienna, 21 June 2000

THE NIGHT IN THE END

最后是夜晚
　　　　　车前子

■手
肩■
眼■
左■
腹部
■甲
指甲
头■
■部
左手
左眼
左轮枪
■臂
■胸
胸■

CHE Qianzi

translated by
Yunte HUANG

Interludes

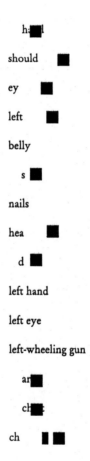

*Author's note: This poem, inspired by an African taboo stick entitled "The Ghost," is an investigation of the relationship between linguistic violence and social violence. Translator's note: "Left-wheeling gun" is a literal translation of "revolver" in Chinese.

Traces Publishers:

Chinese:
Sanlien Shudian
SDX Joint Publishing Company
Meishuguang Dongjie 22
HaoBeijing 100010
P.R China
Tel: +010.64002713
Fax: +010.64002729

Japanese:
Iwanami Shoten Publishers
2-5-5 Hitotsubashi
Chiyoda-ku, Tokyo
Japan
Tel: +81.3.5210.4000
Fax: +82.3.5210.4039

Korean:
Moonhwa Kwahaksa
#704 Namdo Bldg.
198-16 Kwanhun-dong
Chongro-ku, Seoul
Korea
Tel: +82.2.335.0461
Fax: +82.2.335.1239
E-mail: <transics@chollian.net>

Traces Editorial Office:
388 Rockefeller Hall
Cornell University
Ithaca, NY 14853-2502
USA
Fax: +1-607-255-1345
E-mail: <traces@cornell.edu>